POETRY

OF THE TRANSITION
1850-1914

EDITED BY
THOMAS MARC PARROTT, 1866-19/60, ed.
AND WILLARD THORP, 1899-

Granger Index Reprint Series

BOOKS FOR LIBRARIES PRESS
FREEPORT, NEW YORK

52305

First Published 1932
Reprinted 1972

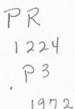

Library of Congress Cataloging in Publication Data

Parrott, Thomas Marc, 1866-1960, ed.
    Poetry of the transition, 1850-1914, ed. by Thomas Marc
Parrott and Willard Thorp. Freeport, N.Y., Books for Libraries Press
[1972] xli, 622 p. 22 cm.
(Granger index reprint series)
    Reprint of the 1932 ed.
    Bibliography: p. 599-604.
    1. English poetry—19th century. 2. English
poetry—20th century. I. Thorp, Willard, 1899-
joint ed. II. Title.
PR1224.P3 1972   821'.008   72-5594
ISBN 0-8369-6384-9

FOREWORD

There is a reason for this anthology. It has its own peculiar aim, method, and limitations. It is not an *omnium gatherum* of English verse, not even of nineteenth-century verse. Its purpose, more fully elaborated in the Introduction, is to trace the development of a new strain in English poetry from the middle of the last century to the outbreak of the World War. This new strain reflects in poetry the changing thought of an age that saw changes in all the phases of man's life on earth, an age, too, that directly underlies our own. It breaks with the Victorian convention; it discards didacticism and sentimentality; it strives for greater freedom in form, and more direct utterance of thought; it is marked by deeper intimacy of self-revelation and by keener susceptibility to nature, tending at times even towards a mystical interpretation of the world.

In accordance with this aim no poets of what may be called the older school have been admitted; the Spasmodics, the followers and imitators of Tennyson, Browning, and Arnold are not represented here. And since in every collection of this sort a *terminus ad quem* must be fixed, no poet is included who had not definitely established his claims to the title before the World War. This is not to deny the claim of living poets: on the contrary, Kipling, Masefield, Noyes, to name no others, find a place here. But the outbreak of the World War marks definitely the end of an era and the time has not yet come — it is perhaps far distant — when a final verdict may be pronounced upon those poets whose work reflects the catastrophe of the War and the chaotic years that follow.

One further limitation may be noted. This anthology is primarily intended for the use of schools and colleges, and no poet has been included from whose work it was, in the judgment of the editors, impossible to gather a sufficient number of poems to furnish material for at least one conference or recitation. Many men are poets in their youth; many poets live on in anthologies by one or two poems, and many of these are true and lovely poems, but long experience in teaching has shown that little is to be gained by a class discussion of isolated specimens.

On the other hand, it may be said with some degree of assurance that no poem has been included to fill a page or round out the proper number to be printed under one heading. So far as the judgment of the editors goes — and in the compilation of an anthology the right of private judgment is supreme — there is no single poem included which has not in itself absolute poetic merit. Here are no nonsense poems or popular songs, no poems that have a merely historic or incidental interest. The one aim has been to cull a true anthology of modern English poetry. Whether that aim has been successful must be left to the judgment of others.

CONTENTS

✢ CONTENTS ✢

✣ CONTENTS ✣

xiii

❖ CONTENTS ❖

❖ CONTENTS ❖

❖ CONTENTS ❖

❖ CONTENTS ❖

xvii

✣ CONTENTS ✣

✣ CONTENTS ✣

INTRODUCTION

I

The biologists have so thoroughly taught us to consider ourselves organisms preoccupied with getting ourselves born, nourished, matured, and propagated that we unconsciously transfer the analogy to our thinking about history and the arts. We talk of poetry as if it waxed and waned, as if it were, indeed, a continuous life-force which manifests itself in particular poems, and is subject to hereditary influences and capable of transmitting acquired characters. Actually there is no such thing as *poetry*. There are only poems — *The Hound of Heaven* and *Hertha*. If you would take the savour of a rose (or feel the ridiculous warts on a gourd) you have no need to examine the soil from which it grows. If you persist in doing so, you may, without wishing it, become a horticulturist and lose your gusto for the fragrance of the rose. The reader who has injudiciously begun this introduction must turn at once to the poems, unless he has some justifiable interest in the ideas which influenced poetic inspiration between 1860 and 1914 and the new forms and moulds into which the individual poetic inspirations flowed.

A curiosity about these matters is meet and right for a student of the history of ideas; our bounden duty if we wish to have an intelligent reason why particular kinds of poetic roses and gourds were raised during these years. There has never been a time when the poets themselves were so acutely aware of the circumstances controlling the kind of poetry they might write (and still be understood by their contemporaries) and so concerned with technical problems. England enjoyed, for a season, the kind of literary warfare thought to be the peculiar habit of the French nation. We can surely be excused for evincing as much interest in literary biology as the poets themselves.

The predominant trait of the poetry of the years of transition from Victorian reticence and respectability to the chaos of the War is its individualism. And yet all the divergences and differences which make the period so entertaining and comparatively so great are referable to a common centre — the disintegration of the English Protestantism in sway over men's minds since the sixteenth century and the confident advance of biological and physical science. Since poets are especially sensitive to the intellectual and emotional temper of their day, the task was left to them of humanizing the violent and deranging theories of the more cold-blooded natural philosophers who cared nothing at all for the spiritual indigestion they had caused. An account of English poetry for these years is inevitably resolved into a description of how the poets transmuted or evaded the unparalleled spiritual alterations which mark their time in history.

It is difficult to convince any one born since 1900 that the Victorian loss of religious faith was a more serious mishap than the mislaying of a tippet. Actually the bottom had dropped out of everything, and sensitive men who were at all aware of what had happened, realized with horror that they were suspended over a deep black hole. When a thoughtful young man in 1870 saw the predicament he was in, his parents became, during his struggle for freedom and escape, total strangers to him. To this inconvenience was added the unpleasant discovery that his new freedom had effected no real emancipation, but rather proved to be an enslavement to a new faith which no one, not even the leaders who taught its necessity, could define.

The 'old time religion' had subsumed all human thought and activity. Science had been legitimated in the seventeenth century only because the laws which it promulgated could be reconciled with revealed theology. A man was good because God wished him to be good, or, in the eighteenth-century view, because He had designed the realization of man's own innate goodness as the end of man. For eighteen hundred years the sanctions of art had likewise been religious, though this is not to say that all painters and poets were mystics whose delight was to hymn the glory of God. It means that the artists felt insensibly that there was a design behind the visible, material world. Ultimately the fragments of reality which floated so various and beautiful before their eyes, the sounds of the birds and the moving waters which touched their ears, would be merged in a universal whose beneficence could be trusted beyond all the suffering and degradation incident to life.

Slowly but unmistakably the whole aspect of the world changed. The landscape grew black and a sinister gloom crept over loved and familiar objects. For the scientist whose confidence expanded with each successive vindication of his ' method,' the shadows were a challenge to the strength of his flashlight. To the poet the world was a desert covered with darkness.

None of the Victorians saw more clearly than Matthew Arnold what the new order would mean for his kind. He courageously put the old world of dead faith behind him, though his apprehension of what the new world, now powerfully a-borning, would be like, forced from him a whimper in the dark. But he lifted a finger and directed the seekers along a path called Culture. At least one might trust the best that had been thought and said in the world. There was comfort here, the comfort of a persuasive minority and the distinction of erring — if it should come to that — with Plato and Goethe. Perhaps the high seriousness of one's aim would offset the painful eventuality that one had been honestly mistaken all along. Man must look to the sifted wisdom of mankind if he would save himself, for the alternative to Anarchy is Culture.

Arnold's permission to make man the measure of all things was responsible for a new renaissance. The poets set about learning what it means to be a human animal. They explored sensation and in the course of their explorations made public announcement of some sensations which men and women in the previous era had acknowledged shamefacedly only to themselves. This new enthusiasm for all things which could delight man Walter Pater summarized in *Marius the Epicurean:*

> Flavian could see that his first business was to be forcibly impressed, the next to make visible to others that which was visibly apparent, delightful, of lively interest to himself to the exclusion of all that was but middling, tame, or only half true even to him.

Pater stands in the spiritual succession from Arnold, though Arnold's laying on of hands, had he been invited to the installation, would have been more violent than benignant. He preached with seductive eloquence that man's highest pursuit is to burn always with the hard, gemlike flame of his moments of ecstasy. Let him seek, not the fruit of experience, its culled wisdom, but experience itself. There will be no time remaining in this brief life to 'make theories about the things we see and touch.' Poetry for two decades after the publication of Pater's *Renaissance* conforms to the demand there put forward, that we should realize the 'splendour of our experience and its awful brevity.'

Pater by insisting that we should exhaust the possibilities of each moment stood as a powerful propagandist for the Pre-Raphaelites. Their work was a record of perfect moments. Moreover it was doubly significant because they expressed these 'passionate attitudes' by the help of the two media of verse and paint. In this quest for the complete measure of man they have twice as much to tell us as other poets, since by virtue of double vision they have seen twice as much.

Rossetti's two disciples, Morris and Swinburne, had no occasion to be uneasy about the philosophical implications of their poetry. The experience of the moment sufficed for both. Morris was busy over his dye vats and looms. In poetry he was content to be an idle singer and further ornament a world made more habitable by the labour of his hands. Swinburne, the last of the poet-liberals of the century, was engaged in a final battle with the old but still potent dragons of tyranny and superstition. His 'religion of humanity' was more of a rhapsody over the emancipation of thought and feeling than a serious prophecy for the new age.

The newer generation of poets, whom Mr. Arthur Symons has importuned us for many years to call Decadents, collected on the limb that Pater grew for them and with each successive volume of verse sawed a little deeper into their safety. The fate of this 'tragic generation,' who took Rossetti for their god and Pater for the Law and the Prophets, is a sad one. They found that to live perfectly required the continuous discovery of new moods. Life became a ritual, and a Cult of Beauty came into being which demanded of the catechumen that the concern of each moment be entered into with devotional intensity. Thus Wilde describes the rapture of discovering and imitating the old French artificial forms in terms appropriate to a religious enthusiasm: 'It was during my undergraduate days at Oxford; days of lyrical ardours and of studious sonnet-writing; days when one loved the exquisite intricacy and musical repetitions of the ballade and the villanelle with its linked and long-drawn echoes and its curious completeness; days when one solemnly sought to discover the proper temper in which a triolet should be written.'

The Decadents were obsessed with the notion that they were leading momentous lives, as a result of their major discovery that ' art is art because it is not nature.' This sense of their importance flavours delightfully the pages of their voluminous memoirs. It has obliged Mr. Symons to retell the story of his life a dozen times with charming variations. It may account for Lionel Johnson's megalomania, oddly manifested in those imagined conversations with Gladstone and Newman which he repeated so circumstantially that even his friends did not doubt their genuineness. But when the exquisite moments had been emptied and one grew weary of astonishing one's self and one's admirers, the only thing left to do was to produce sensations for the astonished middle classes; and though no English Nerval ever led a lobster on a chain down Piccadilly, the *Yellow Book* and the *Savoy* outraged British propriety sufficiently to discredit ideas which were innocently enough put forward in the first instance.

What killed the cult quite as much as the robustiousness of Kipling and Henley was the sense of comedy that possessed and mastered some of the idolators. Wilde refused to take anything seriously, even his own seriousness about Pater — he once called the *Renaissance* the very flower of decadence and claimed to carry it with him as a *viaticum* on every journey. Beardsley's mocking at the rose-laden life he drew in fragile, sinister outline, effaced the memory of woman ' romantic and mysterious, the priestess of her shrine ' which had been the chief symbol of the cult since Rossetti painted the Sybilla Palmifera and replaced it, so Mr. Yeats observes, ' with a kind of beauty that eliminated every outline that suggested meditation or even satisfied passion.' In the next decade Swinburne and not Dowson or Symons survived to be the model of fledgling poets at the universities. The school vanished in sterility, but it lasted long enough to produce the perfect lyrics of Dowson, the early Irish symbolism of Yeats, the best of Symons' impressionistic studies of music hall and café, the most

rococo poem in English (Wilde's *Sphinx*) and enough bio-
graphical mysteries to keep the literary historians busy for
years.

For all our talk about the yellow '90's the phenomenon of
those years is not Decadence but Kipling. Within a fortnight
of his discovery by the *Academy* in its review of *Departmental
Ditties* he was notorious. The loud bang accompanying the
return of poetry to the people alarmed the Decadents. One
of their number, Mr. Le Gallienne, rang their knelling bell in
his criticism of Kipling: 'We are in the thick of one of the
most cynically impudent triumphs of the Philistines the world
has seen. All that should be meant by civilisation is a mock.
The once kindly fields of literature are beneath the heels
of a set of literary rough-riders. . . . All the hard-won gains of
nineteenth-century philosophers are thrown to the winds. . . .
Everywhere the brute and the bully . . . and for the ape and
tiger a glorious resurrection!' The bitter pill had to be taken
down. Philistinism was in; Culture was out. The road which
Arnold had advised and along which Pater had been so illumi-
nating and charming a guide ended in an exotic marsh. To all
but the Decadents a firmer highway seemed to have come into
view.

Now that the shouting has died away, we may ask what
Kipling had stumbled into that might be of permanent use
to poetry and society. It would be stiff-necked to deny the
excitement, the humour, and the novelty of his verse. Even at
this date, when we have been over-fed with realism, we can
muster as much enthusiasm for these qualities as any one
who first read him in 1890. But Mr. Le Gallienne was to a
degree in the right of it: for the young Kipling, at least, much
that civilization has meant was a mock. The great virtue is
action; the most desirable possession is power.

Kipling put into words what people at the end of the cen-
tury ardently longed to have said. The Church had failed them
and Culture only propounded more questions and evaded its
own responsibility to answer them. But man, the ordinary
man, by himself had conquered the sea and would soon sub-
due Nature's only remaining stronghold, the air. Henley, who
found Kipling the twin of one side of his nature, feverishly
thrilled by an automobile ride, evokes a poem on speed which
rises to a ritualistic chant at the end:

xxvi

So in the Eye of the Lord,
Under the Feet of the Lord,
Goodness and grace
In the Hand of the Lord,
Speed!

Kipling's God is busy tightening the bolts and making every-
thing shipshape like his own M'Andrew. He is made in the
image of the Dynamo. At the moment when in a thousand
churches of the new vitalist dispensation the Philistines were
being urged to 'get in tune with the infinite' because God is
not Love but Power, the emancipated were reading Nietzsche
and both groups were exulting in Kipling.

In time, we may believe, Kipling's imperialism, though not
his pictures of the men who built the Empire with the mortar
of their blood, will seem as dusty as his worship of the ma-
chine. But we should not forget that he counselled England
to sober up after her drunkenness on the 'sight of power.'
He did not urge that the White Man's Burden should have
any of the Black Man's Gold tucked away under the straps.
We cannot, however, disregard the fact that his ethic, other-
wise, seems to be that of his soldiers who risk more than other
men and care least for what they are risking. Henley sought
to justify, in his *Song of the Sword*, this thinly-veiled bar-
barism by a lyrical Malthusianism:

I am the Sword . . .
Sifting the nations,
The slag from the metal,
The waste and the weak
From the fit and the strong;
Fighting the brute,
The abysmal Fecundity . . .

We are not likely to forget the importance of the fact that
Kipling persuaded the clerk and the labourer, and for that
matter a good many university men, to trust poetry to be
entertaining and comprehensible. Men, red-blooded and two-
fisted and hard-hitting, sang *Mandalay* as lustily as they sang
and marched to *Over There* during the War. Masefield (whose
appointment to the Laureateship is a tacit tribute to Kipling)
properly evaluates the service of Kipling's influence: 'What-

xxvii

ever their faults and shortcomings these poets have been a school of life instead of artifice. However harshly the next school may treat them, that school must be a little livelier for their efforts.' But the counsel to be ruthless is no better guide in a perplexed age than Pater's injunction on his followers to capture the splendour of experience. When the hand grows weak and can no longer hold the sword, the phantoms of materialism and determinism recommence their processioning.

Their ghostly walk began as early as 1860, an inevitable consequence of Darwin's evolutionary hypothesis and the mechanistic theories of the physicists. It was immediately responsible for a revival of the philosophy of Naturalism. In its simplest form this explanation of the existential world implies that Nature considers man just another of her creatures and ignores his claim to be akin to the angels. Our strongest animal impulses are most fundamental to life's continuance and are therefore most to be trusted. Such doctrine may premise the conclusion that good is certain to come of this yielding to the basic instincts since the life-force of which they are born promotes an evolution to higher forms. Two obstacles prevented faith in such a notion in 1870: the horrible fact that primal Nature, the ' Nature red in tooth and claw ' from which Tennyson recoiled, is cruel, prodigal, and indifferent, and the theory, exploded in this century by the new quantum physics, that the universe is analogous to an automatic machine. Thus men sadly concluded that we move of necessity, not of our own volition, and to ends which, being those of a Nature indifferent or downright malevolent,' are not comforting to consider. In ways which vary with their temperamental organizations several of the more courageous poets, in particular Thomson, Davidson, Hardy, Meredith, Bridges, and Housman, sought to circumvent the Victorian compromise by boldly embracing the dispiriting conclusions of the new science.

None of this group sank deeper into the slough than James Thomson. His melancholia, physical in origin and augmented by the pitiful circumstances of his life, was fortified by the idea that Necessity governs all our days. With him the notion that God is definitely malignant and implacable soon gives place to the doctrine, which anticipates a favourite belief of Hardy, that the ' will of the world grinds out death and life and good and ill, without purpose or mind or heart.' Eager
xxviii

to follow his hero Shelley to a faith in humanity, he was balked by his inability to see anything perfectible in man.

One disciple of the new materialism, John Davidson (1857–1909) drew from it the exact reverse of any counsel of despair. Having inherited in abundance the side of the Scotch nature which fulfills itself in apocalyptic prophecy and exhortation, he rejected all the easy solutions and consolations of traditional philosophy and applied himself to working out a poetical interpretation of materialism. Davidson ridiculed Victorian poetry because it viewed the world imitatively and lacked a strong, imperious imagination of its own. The new learning compelled, he believed, a complete revision of ethical values based on the evident fact, now demonstrable, that the soul is no more than the sum of the powers of the body and the body is one with the forces of the universe. Matter has formed nothing more wonderful than man and through man matter becomes vocal. The poet, it will be seen at once, exercises a most vital function:

> I dare not die, must not die: I am the sight
> And hearing of the infinite; in me
> Matter fulfills itself; before me none
> Beheld or heard, imagined, thought or felt;
> And though I make the mystery known to men,
> It may be none hereafter shall achieve
> The perfect purpose of eternity.

Davidson was as belligerent in his hatred of creeds as Swinburne. His rejection of orthodoxy carried him to a kind of Blakean Satanism: ' No one in a passion of any kind feels sinful; no man gloriously drunk feels sinful; no deep-set ambition ever accuses itself of sin. . . .' Like Swinburne (in *Hertha*) he challenged men to penetrate the mysteries of the life-force but not to cringe in adoration before it. ' Worship, culture, is the letter that kills; exhausted air, it kills by asphyxiation. Knowledge is always virgin soil and the air of the mountains.'

One can imagine that the critics handled Davidson with tongs. He was safer at a distance and might be silenced if sufficiently praised for his ballads and *Fleet Street Eclogues*. His *Testaments* (five in number), which he hoped would change the course of poetry, they left to fizzle themselves out and be forgotten. They are historic documents as well as poetry for in them we find the most complete and jubilant expression of nineteenth-century materialism.[1]

Mr. Housman, like the silver swan, has sung his first and last and sung no more. Though it would be ludicrous to call him a Naturalist or anything so categorical, his songs are as inexorable in their insistence on man's brief end and the ailing of high heaven and of earth as anything Thomson or Hardy wrote. None of the poets who reflect the pessimism of the closing century has achieved such general favour. There must be a whole congress of men who could repeat the *Shropshire Lad* and *Last Poems* by heart. The strong native rhythms, familiar in our ears from a thousand ballads and hymns, make his verses stick in the mind. His sentiment is in a form most accessible to those men who, though they are not aware that they are adherents of a particular school of philosophy, really possess the stoic temper. Hardy's Naturalism has too many ' parts ' and too easily gets out of order if an accessory idea falls to the ground. Thomson rails overmuch. Housman indulges in no dogma, asks no questions of his fate, and does not complain aloud. He accepts what little respite from evil is offered by ale and companionship, and is ready to lie down and pull the sod over him.

Hardy, Meredith, and Bridges were intellectually equipped to understand the new science and each was ready to hear the whole truth and to take the consequences. They held in common the view that our falling to earth is no different, to the will of the universe, from the decay of the oak leaf. Each recognized that man has developed consciousness further than his animal brothers. At this point the three poets diverge. Hardy, looking on the conflict between the pitiful emotions, desires, and ambitions which consciousness brings to life and the indifference of the Immanent Will, could see, in the main, only a tragic waste. Meredith envisaged the high points of civilization as those moments in history when human consciousness achieves the greatness of which it is capable, that perfect tempering in the individual and in a people of all the elements of flesh and spirit. For Bridges consciousness is the

[1] In spite of his importance in literary history and his absolute excellence, no poetry of Davidson has been included in this anthology. It would be impossible to represent him adequately except by his longer poems.

perfect flower of our animal nature, capable at its best of producing great ethical beauty, as the aim of the plant is to flower. Beauty's gift to man is joy.

One is tempted to extract a homily from the careers of these three poets. They shouldered the whole responsibility of living in an age of transition; they fought to discover any possible human values in the spiritual chaos of the new order. Their art prospered and the zest of the battle seemed to give them long life. Each was called in turn ' the last of the Victorians,' but their only Victorian trait was an indomitable desire to create for themselves, since it could no longer be had by the act of faith, a harmonious world. Hardy and Bridges lived so far into our time that they were able to minister to the broken post-war generation of poets who had lost even the most fundamental urge of the artist, the impulse to creation.

The poets who most successfully rode out the storms whipped up by Naturalism were mured within the Catholic faith. The Church of Rome is experienced in crises of this sort. That many of the poets in this period should be Roman Catholics is remarkable certainly, but entirely explicable. Patmore, Alice Meynell, Hopkins, Johnson, and Dowson submitted themselves to find authority, a permanent peace and fulfillment. Francis Thompson, alone, was born to the faith and showed what a difference that makes, as Patmore admitted: ' He is of all men I have known most naturally a Catholic. My Catholicism was acquired, his inherent.' Dowson and Johnson in their long quest for cultural satisfactions, like Beardsley and Wilde who were also converts, found the Church at the end of the road, holding within her sanctuary what in western Europe had most continuously ennobled and illuminated life. For Alice Meynell the renunciation was as complete as the assurance which followed: ' I received the Church so that whatever she could unfold with time she would unfold it there where I enclosed her, in my heart.'

A practical reason why the poetry of this group found its way to favour with such ease can be discovered in the renewed prestige of the Church which under the Cardinalates of Wiseman, Newman, and Manning regained a portion of the power in English life that it had lost at the time of the Reformation. Wilfrid Meynell, a Catholic, directed a distinguished literary journal, *Merry England,* whose pages were of course freely opened to Catholic poets. He could give Francis Thompson help of a substantial kind when his genius was, almost literally, deposited on Meynell's doorstep. It would be absurd to make too much of any fortunate conspiring of circumstances in the reputations of these poets. Their memory is fresh to-day because of the quality of their poetry, to which their religion is incidental — except in the case of Thompson, where it is ' wel nigh alle and some.'

The poets of the '90's talked so much about the *fin de siècle* that people began to be convinced that the breezes would veer into a new quarter on the stroke of midnight, December 31, 1899. This feeling that something was ending and something new beginning seems to be a fancy peculiar to this particular end-of-the-century. The romantic poets reckoned time from the Year One of the French Revolution. The literary historians of this century were the first to notice the significant fact that Dryden died in 1700. Yet it is possible to justify this trembling expectancy of the Muse in 1900. When we review the ' state ' of poetry at that moment, we do sense the lull, or better, since that suggests a storm which did not blow up, a freshening breeze at sun-down.

The makers of sensation in the decade just past were busy at new tasks or dead or getting ready to die. Kipling's three volumes of verse, *Barrack Room Ballads, Departmental Ditties,* and *The Seven Seas,* were a part of history and he was opening up new provinces in the short story. Henley published once more (*Hawthorn and Lavender*) before death, which he had for so many years kept furiously at bay, carried him off. Thompson issued no verse after the *New Poems* of 1897. Wilde, devoted to paradox to the end, wrote in 1898 his most famous poem, *The Ballad of Reading Gaol,* which in its professed love of humanity belongs to 1910 rather than 1898, and died with dramatic promptness in 1900. John Davidson's most impassioned work, the five *Testaments* and two of the projected parts of the trilogy of the *Triumph of Mammon* enlivened the first years of the new century for the initiated few who were wise enough to appreciate his significance, but shortly they marked his pitiful farewell to ambition in his last volume: ' The time has come to make an end. There are several reasons. I find my pension is not enough; I have therefore still to turn aside and attempt things for which people will pay. My health also counts. Asthma and other annoyances I have tolerated for years; but I cannot put up with cancer.' He drowned himself within the year.

Critics and readers had not accommodated themselves to the harsh and unsonorous verse of Thomas Hardy. He was obliged to wait nearly twenty years for intelligent appreciation of his greatness as a poet. The immediate future of English poetry seemed in 1900 to rest on the willing hands of William Watson and Stephen Phillips. They were traditionalists, Watson a not inconsiderable poet whose lines have a disconcerting fragrance of Wordsworth and Arnold about them, but who said what he had to say with epigrammatic concision. The critics who praised Phillips, if they have been allowed to survive, ought by now to be thoroughly ashamed of themselves. They should have known how dangerous it is to say of a poet that he is ' not unworthy of mention in the same breath with Dante and Homer.' But Phillips was supposed to be the restorer of poetic drama, and a Messiah had long been awaited in that department. The merit found in these two men suggests that the poetic temper of the new age was not yet perceptible because it was as yet unformed.

New names emerge, none of them widely known until 1912 when the anthology called *Georgian Poetry* announced boldly that ' English poetry is now once again putting on a new strength and beauty.' If one reads the contributions of the seventeen poets who joined in the manifesto, one recognizes immediately that they possess qualities in common which may very well be given a general name like that which they adopted. There is, to be sure, a Georgian poetry, distinct from any poetry that has gone before.

The poem by which Mr. Masefield is represented in that volume, *Biography,* epitomizes the attitude of the members of the group who issued their challenges from the back room of the Poetry Bookshop. Like him they had ' by many waters and on many ways, known golden instants and bright days.' The grey corduroy curtains that turned day into night had been stripped from Lionel Johnson's windows; the poets had decided to live instead of allowing their servants to do it for them, as Villiers de L'Isle Adam, god-father of the Symbolists, had advised. Another Georgian, Mr. John Drinkwater, proclaimed that the modern poet ' seems to be less preoccupied with his attitude towards life and art than with the joy of contemplating and feeling what is good in them.'

This is true. The Georgians waste no time in analyzing their moods or in lamenting the transitoriness of life. They are 'great lovers' and their love is catholic enough to embrace dining-room tea, kingfishers, Lake Leman, hares, and Miss Loo. Their new-found joy had no very great philosophic depth and they are inclined to admit that absolute knowledge is beyond attainment, but a continuity of vivid experience (Pater is ambushed here) is not beyond attainment, 'and such activity of experience is the fulfillment of the highest function of which man is capable.' This might have been said by a member of the Rhymers' Club in 1892, but we can descry on closer scrutiny a fundamental difference from the mood of the '90's. By experience the Georgians mean the little moments of life such as a sensitive, educated man relies on to make his day significant: the benison of material comforts, the gratifying eccentricities of human nature, vicarious living in legend and art, intimations everywhere of the wonder and mysteriousness of life. 'To destroy the lethargy of the spirit,' as Mr. Drinkwater put it, 'is the aim of every rightly disciplined mind.' Alertness and sensitiveness are the stigmata of the Georgian inspiration. The days are too short for Mr. Davies to absorb the full delight he has in nature; Rupert Brooke watches, hour after hour, the happy fish whose 'bliss is older than the sun.' Mr. De la Mare is haunted by the loud-ringing lutes of Arabia; Mr. Sturge Moore cries in *That Land:*

> Oh, would that I might live for ever
> Where those that make me happy dwell!
> Because she other place names never
> Desire doeth excellently well,
> Now, wooing me;
> There ease weds grace;
> There thought is free,
> Born like a smile upon a face,
> Expressed as simply as a child
> Kisseth its playmate, laughing gaily;
> There, there, the courteous, joyous, mild,
> Train life to beauty daily.

✣ INTRODUCTION ✣

One can understand why the successive volumes of *Georgian Poetry* sold with an acceleration which astonished the contributors. Here, for the first time since early Victorian days, was poetry untainted with materialism or aestheticism, well-bred poetry, safe for old and young, exhibiting the un-Victorian charms of intimacy and colloquial diction. The poets did not pretend to have exalted thoughts or an exceptional inspiration. Each could have subscribed to Bridges' modest declaration: ' I did not suppose that the poet's emotions were in any way better then mine, nor mine than another's.' Though the new dress disguised the fact, several occasional traits of this new poetry put roots down into the previous century and were not so novel as some supposed. Thomson's *Sunday up the River* and Davidson's *Fleet Street* are quite as realistic as anything devised by Mr. Gibson or D. H. Lawrence. Mr. Monro's eroticism in *The Virgin* exceeds Swinburne only in that the object of his analysis is not a medieval Cornish lady of romance but your next door neighbour. The same poet's *Impressions* would scarcely have come into being except for Henley's example.

The Georgians' avidity of passionate experience, induced by their feeling that the act of experiencing exercises one's nature ' in the only full and significant way,' was responsible for a fine humanity in their poetry. One of their number holds that the man whose thought is alert and whose spirit is responsive to the beauty and awe of the world, does not tolerate the terrible evil of injustice. This humanitarianism was, moreover, a logical development in the renaissance of man's interest in man. It is not at all strange that the enthusiasm for man's achievements which produced a new eclecticism in the arts and a passion among the historians for the archaeological reconstruction of every detail of previous eras should have yielded also a compassion for mankind itself. The evolution of this logic can be followed in the life of a single individual, William Morris, who turned from an interest in the production of useful and beautiful objects, guided by the taste of the past, to a concern about the social condition of the worker who made them. The exhortations of another Georgian, Sir Ronald Ross, in his *Philosophies,* are inspired by this *Zeitgeist.* He urges upon his generation the duty to investigate, ' to comprehend the forces of nature . . . to enlighten the monstrous misery of our fellows. . . . Lost in many speculations, we leave our house disordered, unkept and dirty.'

Two poets of the group made a conscious about-face when the current of humanitarianism swept against them. Mr. W. W. Gibson's three volumes of dilute Tennysonianism were cast off by him and not reprinted. He secured a reputation for his poetry by writing of the lives of common people which he had with deliberate effort sought to know. Mr. Monro in 1906 issued a collection of the worn coins of poetry, the usual tenuous stanzas about ' golden twilight,' ' dewey-throated melodies ' and ' the withered foliage which through the still air glides.' In 1911 he dedicated his *Before Dawn,* a work of a very different sort, to those who are gazing in delight towards where on the horizon ' there shall be dawn.' Two visions move before him; the first — of an older order — drifts formless out of sight:

> True to no cause, yet swift in all deceit.

The second is the Titan of the dawn — Humanity:

> His visionary eyes looked out afar
> Beyond the transient semblances of death. . . .
> He bent beneath the burden of no load;
> He lingered not within the dawn to muse.

Knowing the eager hopefulness with which these men looked for a better ordering of society and a destruction of institutions which had wracked the world for years without number, we see why the War in 1914 promised them the millennium. After one has found a cause, there is nothing so needful as an overt act which will let one fight for it. The defeatism and the bitter jesting of the poetry of the 1920's would not have been so extreme if hope for humanity had not been so high just before the War broke over Europe.

II

When the forms of any art remain the same over a considerable period, the presumption is that the ideas and moods seeking expression have stagnated. New ideas need new vehicles of expression. Kipling's galloping stanzas in a Pindaric dress would have looked like a tough in a frock coat and a

top-hat. Henley's hospital verses could no more have been
squeezed into heroic couplets than Cardinal Newman could
have said mass effectively in a Wesleyan chapel. We should ex-
pect that the sixty turbulent years here surveyed would be
enlivened by a revolt against conventional verse patterns and
incessant rhythmical experimentation.

The amazing technical skill of Tennyson and Browning
and the complementary completeness of their art set a stand-
ard for the next generation. To be a poet required, if one
would escape invidious comparison, an extraordinary com-
petence. Rossetti and Morris accepted the challenge and
proved that their versatility in two arts by no means implied
mediocrity in either. Of Swinburne it is customary to say that
he was the greatest technician in verse England can claim. To
have written the best hexameters and sapphics in English may
seem very little if you require it to mean only a certain slavish
imitative correctness. But for Swinburne these thousand in-
struments of which he knew the timbre and gamut, are useful
for the myriad orchestral effects which he requires. They are
not museum specimens. His instigation of a vogue of verse in
two-time, possibly the poet's chief cause to be grateful to him,
did not result from any histrionic desire to write impeccable
dactyls. Some deep urge of his nature found a vent in their
impetuous, sweeping march:

Thou hast loosened the necks of thine horses, and goaded
  their flanks with affright,
To the race of a course that we know not, on ways that are
  hid from our sight.
As a wind through the darkness the wheels of their chariot are
  whirled,
And the light of its passage is night on the face of the world.

So thoroughly did Swinburne transmogrify the rhythms which
he found in the Elizabethans, in Baudelaire, in Greek and Old
French literature that we can catch only occasional reminiscent
pulsations. There is no English poet who owes so much to his
literary ancestors and who so entirely effaces his debt.

Poets to whom his verse must be completely alien in mood,
to say nothing of his deliberate imitators, cannot escape his
influence. What Swinburnean lines were throbbing in his head
when Mr. Kipling wrote these verses?

Will you conquer my heart with your beauty; my heart going
out from afar?
Shall I fall to your hand as a victim of crafty and cautious
shikar?

The recent preoccupation with the technique of verse, which
may have reached a climax in the 1920's, began before the
'90's and increased as romanticism and cosmicism yielded to a
thousand fragmentary attitudes. The influences hitherto little
known in English poetry which are responsible for the new
styles make a motley company: Villon, Poe, Whitman, Ver-
laine, Mallarmé, the Parnassians, Baudelaire, army songs and
sea chanties, Irish folksongs, Blake, Crashaw. In a decade
Swinburne, Lang, Gosse, Wilde, Dobson, and Henley pro-
duced more villanelles, rondeaux, and triolets, it is safe to say,
than all the poets of France in the fourteenth century. Poe
gave Dowson his favourite line which is so typical of Dowson
that he might have given it to Poe:

The viol, the violet and the vine.

Poe directs Kipling's pen while he writes:

As I left the Hall at Lumley, rose the vision of a comely
Maid last season worshipped dumbly, watched with fervour
from afar.

Whitman was admired by Swinburne (though he recanted
under Watts-Dunton's brow-beating), J. A. Symonds, Lionel
Johnson, Dowden, and the brothers Rossetti. Swinburne writes
Baudelaire's requiem and Dowson brings Verlaine perfectly
into English. Arthur Symons does a like service for Mallarmé.
Kipling makes English verse waltz:

My name is O'Kelly, I've heard the Revelly
From Birr to Bareilly, from Leeds to Lahore.

Masefield convinces us by his practice of his theory that dance
music can be dignified into art: ' It is full of lights and scents,
the laughter of pretty women and youth's triumph. To the
man or woman who has failed in life the sound of such music
is bitter. It is youth reproaching age. It indicates the anti-
climax.' From the lyric forms most honoured by traditional

use to those habitual to sailors and marching men, the poets of these fifty years ranged for suitable poetic styles.

The work of three men during this period can be called original in the sense that they created new styles which could be imitated and developed. The studies of Robert Bridges in the problem of quantitative metres in English enabled him finally to write a long poem, *The Testament of Beauty,* in unorthodox alexandrines which have none of the formal quality of blank verse and yet are admirably fitted for continuous reading. We shall have to wait to see whether later poets will care to make use of the tool he bequeathed them. The experiments made by his friend Father Hopkins will be, from present signs, influential hereafter. They open up unsuspected possibilities in the imitation of natural rhythms, as the *Windhover* abundantly shows. The contributions of a third, W. E. Henley, have been inadequately acknowledged.

His free verse differs from Arnold's in consequential particulars, though Arnold usually receives the credit for this new form. Both made frequent use of rhyme to bind their lines together and the iambic pulse of English poetry is still felt in it, though less persistently in Henley than in Arnold. For this reason his verse is nearer the 'cadence' of the Imagists. He was, in fact, the first English poet to feel the rhythm of his subject *sui generis* and apart from a traditional form. Francis Thompson apprehended this and penetrated the reason: 'Only a most delicate response to the behests of inspiration can make such verse successful. As some persons have an ininstinctive sense of orientation, by which they know the quarter of the East, so the poet with this gift has a subtle sense of metrical law, and in his most seeming-vagrant metres revolves always (so to speak) round a felt though invisible centre of obedience.' Lines like the following have no reference to stanza or to the blank verse pattern. Their 'centre of obedience' is the movement of the bells.

> St. Margaret's bells,
> Quiring their innocent, old-world canticles,
> Sing in the storied air,
> All rosy-and-golden, as with memories
> Of woods at evensong, and sands and seas
> Disconsolate for that the night is nigh.

Henley is a pioneer also in the choice of subjects for the embodiment of which his new rhythms were a necessary invention. His Impressionism, devoted to hospital sights and London scenes, which in the '90's opposed the mistiness and vibrancy of Yeats's symbolism, anticipates that style of verse which, culminating in the short-lived vogue of Futurism, was in turn driven from the field in 1915 by Imagism.

This last battle of the styles, ending in the triumph of Imagism, though its first excursions fall within the limits of this book, affected the generation of poets since the War. In spite of its considerable fecundating power, Imagism has few notable poems to its credit. How could it have, since Imagism is simply an insistence on a more accurate observing and recording of exterior phenomena; its aim 'precise and definite description' and its essential to prove that 'beauty may be in small dry things'? As a corrective it cured English poetry of romantic diction. Of the two pictures of the gathering night, we much prefer the second, written in the imagistic manner.

(1)   But lo! across the earth still shadows creep;
      While from above, with all-embracing flight,
      Slowly, like some great bird, sweeps in the night.
                                (Monro, *Autumn Sunset*)

(2)   The cold wind blew the brown leaves
      Deeper and deeper into the dusk;
      The peacocks had hushed their cries;
      The moon had turned her gold into silver,
      And between the black lace of two trees
      One star shone clearly.

                                (Flint, *Dusk*)

Imagism was announced with drum and trumpet in America, the band being provided with an effective subsidy from Miss Amy Lowell. In England, as Mr. Herbert Read has said, the attempts to create an imagist poetry, though they have been 'of great value in the introduction of a clearer tone into poetic expression . . . have remained comparatively obscure because they have not been the vehicle of any momentous intelligence.'

Yet the poets of the 1920's could not so deftly have laid bare the spiritual wounds of the war generation if they had not possessed the scalpel of Imagism. And whatever we shall think hereafter of the bitterness of these 'hollow men' and the cactus art growing in their waste land of the imagination, poetry will never again be permitted to float derivative emotions on a flood of rhetoric. They were the first to take seriously to heart the major discovery of the poets of the transition that the heady wines of the new world are too strong for old bottles. Their accelerated quest for styles will not cease to multiply distinctions until our dismembered universe grows together again.

DANTE GABRIEL ROSSETTI
1828–1882

Dante Gabriel Rossetti, the oldest son of an Italian scholar, patriot, and exile and of his wife Frances Mary Polidori, was born in London in 1828. He grew up in a household permeated by Italian culture. The revolutionary atmosphere of the exile's home left little or no impression on the boy, but from his youth he was steeped in the study of Dante and his contemporaries. At an early age he decided to become a painter but was unable or unwilling to conform to the discipline of the conventional art institute. At the age of twenty he joined with two other young painters, John Millais and Holman Hunt, in forming the Pre-Raphaelite Brotherhood, a little group of artists and writers who declared their faith in a return to the simplicity, significance, and truth to nature of the early Italian school of art. The chequered fortunes of the little band, the outrageous abuse heaped upon them in the press, and their generous defence by Ruskin, need not concern us here. Meanwhile Rossetti was writing both prose and verse, apparently with more success than he was painting. He had early begun the practice of translation, especially from the Italian poets dear to his youth. To *The Germ,* a short-lived magazine designed to proclaim the principles of the Pre-Raphaelite Brotherhood, he contributed the first version of his often revised and best known poem, *The Blessed Damozel.*

About the year 1855 Rossetti came in touch with a group of young men in Oxford, William Morris, Burne-Jones, and Swinburne. Abounding in vitality, wildly unconventional, of dominating nature, Rossetti exercised an incalculable influence over a band of youthful enthusiasts rebelling against the materialism tempered by sentimentality of mid-Victorian England. It is significant that both Morris and Swinburne dedicated their first books of verse to Rossetti and that Burne-Jones, his life-long friend, turned from his destined

1

career in the Church to become a painter of dreams and legends.

Before his meeting with the Oxford group Rossetti had fallen in love with a beautiful milliner's assistant whom he snatched from the shop to become his model. He taught her to draw, to paint, and to write, and much of his loveliest work in painting and in poetry owes its inspiration to her beauty. Their marriage was deferred over a period of nearly ten years because of her delicate health and of Rossetti's constant financial embarrassments. Their married life was short and troubled. She was attacked by tuberculosis and, after a bout of illness, died from an over-dose of laudanum taken, during her husband's absence, to quiet neuralgic pain. In a passion of sorrow and remorse Rossetti placed in her coffin the manuscript volume of poems that he had prepared for publication. ' They are yours,' he said, ' and you must take them with you.'

Before his wife's death Rossetti had published a volume of translations from the early Italian poets and some years later, when failing eyesight threatened to close his career as a painter, he turned again to poetry. Urged by his friends he permitted the grave to be opened and the manuscript recovered, and in 1870 published his first original volume, *Poems by Dante Gabriel Rossetti*. It was lavishly praised by his friends and furiously attacked by a Scotch poetaster who summed up all the Victorian prejudices against bodily beauty in his ' Fleshly School of Poetry.' Had Rossetti been his old self, the attack and the bitter controversy that followed would have left him unmoved, but he was already sinking into a decline; bodily illness, over-sensitive nerves and insomnia led to recurring attacks of profound melancholy. To alleviate his suffering he took chloral and his last years were a tragic alternation of feverish activity and collapse bordering on insanity. A late flowering of poetic power produced his second volume, *Ballads and Sonnets,* in 1881. He died a hopeless ruin early in the following year.

Rossetti was by profession a painter rather than a poet; his poems fill only two small volumes, but his influence is not to be measured by the scanty product of his pen. Ruskin called him ' the chief intellectual force in the establishment of the modern Romantic School in England ' and Gosse speaks of him as 'most prompt in suggestion, most regal in giving, most sympathetic in response, of the men that I have known.'

There are two separate and easily distinguishable styles in Rossetti's poetry. One is like that of the Pre-Raphaelite painters, simple, sincere, and picturesque. Indeed much of Rossetti's early, much of his best, work seems to be a translation into verse of his vision as a painter. The blessed damozel with the lilies in her hand and the stars in her hair, the white rose at her breast and the yellow hair flowing down her back, seems to have stepped into the poem from some old Italian painting. Even more significant perhaps are the lines from *The Portrait* where the painter-poet looking on the picture of his dead lady exclaims:

> There she stands
> As in that wood that day: for so
> Was the still movement of the hands
> And such the pure line's gracious flow.

This was, as Pater noted, 'a really new kind of poetic utterance.'

The other style, Rossetti's later manner, is elaborate, gorgeous in colour, sonorous in diction, heavy-weighted, often over-weighted, with thought. For it is altogether wrong to think of Rossetti as a sensuous rather than an intellectual poet. Sensuous he was to a marked degree but he never sank to the sensuality of the thoughtless man. Totally indifferent to all forms of religion and to the religious controversies that raged about him, he early formulated his own faith and became a devout believer in the religion of Beauty:

> That Lady Beauty, in whose praise
> Thy voice and hand shake still.

This divine Beauty, the same sonnet tells us, is revealed to her worshipper by sea or sky or woman. To Rossetti it was in a very special way revealed by woman, woman the mystery whom man can know 'but as a sacred secret.' And as only the lover can learn this secret, Rossetti is in a very special way the poet of love. The lady of Rossetti's love has the beauty which is genius,

> A bodily beauty more acceptable
> Than the wild rose-tree's arch.

And this beauty is divine because interfused with spirit. Spirit and body indeed seem to him at times not two but one; his ideal lady is one

> Whose speech Truth knows not from her thought
> Nor Love her body from her soul.

It has often been remarked that the blessed damozel of his earliest known poem is anything but a disembodied spirit; so much flesh and blood is she that her bosom warms the gold bar of heaven on which she leans to look down to earth. Something of the mystical medieval woman-worship of Dante and his circle enters into this faith of Rossetti, but he has given it an utterance English and his own.

The tragedy of Rossetti's life may be traced to the frustration of his love. Long wooed, briefly possessed, his beloved was taken from him with dreadful suddenness and in a manner to pierce even a less sensitive heart than a poet's with poignant and lasting remorse. Rossetti lived for twenty years after her death, but a great part of those years was wasted in melancholy idleness, in reckless dissipation, in fruitless longing for what might have been. There is no poem in English so packed with bitter self-reproach as Rossetti's *Last Days*. What work he accomplished in those years was at times superb but it was only a fraction of what he might have done under a happier star, and the man who began by being a lively inspiration to all who knew him ended by an insane distrust of his oldest friends.

Yet after all Rossetti's achievement is magnificent and in its kind unmatched in English. Into the dull Victorian age he brought a new sense of beauty, the beauty of religious tradition, the beauty of medieval romance, the beauty above all of love. To the generation of Anthony Trollope and the lovers of the *Angel in the House* he revealed the spiritual significance of earthly passion. Sensuous delight in colour and in form, a mystical perception of the harmony of body and soul, a direct sincerity of speech and a new music of lyric utterance, these were Rossetti's gifts to English poetry.

4

THE BLESSED DAMOZEL

The blessed damozel leaned out
     From the gold bar of Heaven;
Her eyes were deeper than the depth
     Of waters stilled at even;
She had three lilies in her hand,
     And the stars in her hair were seven.

Her robe, ungirt from clasp to hem,
     No wrought flowers did adorn,
But a white rose of Mary's gift,
     For service meetly worn;
Her hair that lay along her back
     Was yellow like ripe corn.

Herseemed she scarce had been a day
     One of God's choristers;
The wonder was not yet quite gone
     From that still look of hers;
Albeit, to them she left, her day
     Had counted as ten years.

(To one it is ten years of years.
     . . . Yet now, and in this place,
Surely she leaned o'er me — her hair
     Fell all about my face. . . .
Nothing: the autumn-fall of leaves.
     The whole year sets apace.)

It was the rampart of God's house
     That she was standing on;
By God built over the sheer depth
     The which is Space begun;
So high, that looking downward thence
     She scarce could see the sun.

It lies in Heaven, across the flood
     Of ether, as a bridge.
Beneath, the tides of day and night
     With flame and darkness ridge
The void, as low as where this earth
     Spins like a fretful midge.

5

Around her, lovers, newly met
  'Mid deathless love's acclaims,
Spoke evermore among themselves
  Their heart-remembered names;
And the souls mounting up to God
  Went by her like thin flames.

And still she bowed herself and stooped
  Out of the circling charm;
Until her bosom must have made
  The bar she leaned on warm,
And the lilies lay as if asleep
  Along her bended arm.

From the fixed place of Heaven she saw
  Time like a pulse shake fierce
Through all the worlds. Her gaze still strove
  Within the gulf to pierce
Its path; and now she spoke as when
  The stars sang in their spheres.

The sun was gone now; the curled moon
  Was like a little feather
Fluttering far down the gulf; and now
  She spoke through the still weather.
Her voice was like the voice the stars
  Had when they sang together.

(Ah, sweet! Even now, in that bird's song,
  Strove not her accents there,
Fain to be harkened? When those bells
  Possessed the mid-day air,
Strove not her steps to reach my side
  Down all the echoing stair?)

' I wish that he were come to me,
  For he will come,' she said.
' Have I not prayed in Heaven? — on earth,
  Lord, Lord, has he not pray'd?
Are not two prayers a perfect strength?
  And shall I feel afraid?

' When round his head the aureole clings,
  And he is clothed in white,
I'll take his hand and go with him
  To the deep wells of light;
As unto a stream we will step down,
  And bathe there in God's sight.

' We two will stand beside that shrine,
  Occult, withheld, untrod,
Whose lamps are stirred continually
  With prayers sent up to God;
And see our old prayers, granted, melt
  Each like a little cloud.

' We two will lie i' the shadow of
  That living mystic tree
Within whose secret growth the Dove
  Is sometimes felt to be,
While every leaf that His plumes touch
  Saith His Name audibly.

' And I myself will teach to him,
  I myself, lying so,
The songs I sing here; which his voice
  Shall pause in, hushed and slow,
And find some knowledge at each pause,
  Or some new thing to know.'

(Alas! We two, we two, thou say'st!
  Yea, one wast thou with me
That once of old. But shall God lift
  To endless unity
The soul whose likeness with thy soul
  Was but its love for thee?)

' We two,' she said, ' will seek the groves
  Where the lady Mary is,
With her five handmaidens, whose names
  Are five sweet symphonies,
Cecily, Gertrude, Magdalen,
  Margaret and Rosalys.

7

' Circlewise sit they, with bound locks
 And foreheads garlanded;
Into the fine cloth white like flame
 Weaving the golden thread,
To fashion the birth-robes for them
 Who are just born, being dead.

' He shall fear, haply, and be dumb;
 Then will I lay my cheek
To his, and tell about our love,
 Not once abashed or weak:
And the dear Mother will approve
 My pride, and let me speak.

' Herself shall bring us, hand in hand,
 To Him round whom all souls
Kneel, the clear-ranged unnumbered heads
 Bowed with their aureoles;
And angels meeting us shall sing
 To their citherns and citoles.

' There will I ask of Christ the Lord
 Thus much for him and me: —
Only to live as once on earth
 With Love, — only to be,
As then awhile, forever now,
 Together, I and he.'

She gazed and listened and then said,
 Less sad of speech than mild, —
' All this is when he comes.' She ceased.
 The light thrilled towards her, fill'd
With angels in strong, level flight.
 Her eyes prayed, and she smil'd.

(I saw her smile.) But soon their path
 Was vague in distant spheres:
And then she cast her arms along
 The golden barriers,
And laid her face between her hands,
 And wept. (I heard her tears.)

8

MY SISTER'S SLEEP

She fell asleep on Christmas Eve:
  At length the long-ungranted shade
  Of weary eyelids overweigh'd
The pain naught else might yet relieve.

Our mother, who had leaned all day
  Over the bed from chime to chime,
  Then raised herself for the first time,
And as she sat her down, did pray.

Her little work-table was spread
  With work to finish. For the glare,
  Made by her candle, she had care
To work some distance from the bed.

Without, there was a cold moon up,
  Of winter radiance sheer and thin;
  The hollow halo it was in
Was like an icy crystal cup.

Through the small room, with subtle sound
  Of flame, by vents the fireshine drove
  And reddened. In its dim alcove
The mirror shed a clearness round.

I had been sitting up some nights,
  And my tired mind felt weak and blank;
  Like a sharp strengthening wine it drank
The stillness and the broken lights.

Twelve struck. That sound, by dwindling years
  Heard in each hour, crept off; and then
  The ruffled silence spread again,
Like water that a pebble stirs.

Our mother rose from where she sat:
  Her needles, as she laid them down,
  Met lightly, and her silken gown
Settled: no other noise than that.

'Glory unto the Newly Born!'
  So, as said angels, she did say;
  Because we were in Christmas Day,
Though it would still be long till morn.

Just then in the room over us
  There was a pushing back of chairs,
  As some who had sat unawares
So late, now heard the hour, and rose.

With anxious, softly-stepping haste
  Our mother went where Margaret lay,
  Fearing the sounds o'erhead — should they
Have broken her long watched-for rest!

She stooped an instant, calm, and turned;
  But suddenly turned back again;
  And all her features seemed in pain
With woe, and her eyes gazed and yearned.

For my part, I but hid my face,
  And held my breath, and spoke no word:
  There was none spoken; but I heard
The silence for a little space.

Our mother bowed herself and wept:
  And both my arms fell, and I said,
  ' God knows I knew that she was dead.'
And there, all white, my sister slept.

Then kneeling, upon Christmas morn
  A little after twelve o'clock,
  We said, ere the first quarter struck,
' Christ's blessing on the newly born!'

AVE

Mother of the Fair Delight,
  Thou handmaid perfect in God's sight,
Now sitting fourth beside the Three,
Thyself a woman-Trinity, —

Being a daughter born to God,
Mother of Christ from stall to rood,
And wife unto the Holy Ghost: —
Oh when our need is uttermost,
Think that to such as death may strike
Thou once wert sister sisterlike!
Thou headstone of humanity,
Groundstone of the great Mystery,
Fashioned like us, yet more than we!

Mind'st thou not (when June's heavy breath
Warmed the long days in Nazareth,)
That eve thou didst go forth to give
Thy flowers some drink that they might live
One faint night more amid the sands?
Far off the trees were as pale wands
Against the fervid sky: the sea
Sighed further off eternally
As human sorrow sighs in sleep.
Then suddenly the awe grew deep,
As of a day to which all days
Were footsteps in God's secret ways:
Until a folding sense, like prayer,
Which is, as God is, everywhere,
Gathered about thee; and a voice
Spake to thee without any noise,
Being of the silence: — ' Hail,' it said,
' Thou that art highly favourèd;
The Lord is with thee here and now;
Blessed among all women thou.'

Ah! knew'st thou of the end, when first
That Babe was on thy bosom nurs'd? —
Or when He tottered round thy knee
Did thy great sorrow dawn on thee? —
And through His boyhood, year by year
Eating with Him the Passover,
Didst thou discern confusedly
That holier sacrament, when He,
The bitter cup about to quaff,
Should break the bread and eat thereof? —

11

Or came not yet the knowledge, even
Till on some day forecast in Heaven
His feet passed through thy door to press
Upon His Father's business? —
Or still was God's high secret kept?

Nay, but I think the whisper crept
Like growth through childhood. Work and play,
Things common to the course of day,
Awed thee with meanings unfulfill'd;
And all through girlhood, something still'd
Thy senses like the birth of light,
When thou hast trimmed thy lamp at night
Or washed thy garments in the stream;
To whose white bed had come the dream
That He was thine and thou wast His
Who feeds among the field-lilies.
O solemn shadow of the end
In that wise spirit long contain'd!
O awful end! and those unsaid
Long years when It was Finishèd!

Mind'st thou not (when the twilight gone
Left darkness in the house of John,)
Between the naked window-bars
That spacious vigil of the stars? —
For thou, a watcher even as they,
Wouldst rise from where throughout the day
Thou wroughtest raiment for His poor;
And, finding the fixed terms endure
Of day and night which never brought
Sounds of His coming chariot,
Wouldst lift through cloud-waste unexplor'd
Those eyes which said, ' How long, O Lord? '
Then that disciple whom He loved,
Well heeding, haply would be moved
To ask thy blessing in His name;
And that one thought in both, the same
Though silent, then would clasp ye round
To weep together, — tears long bound,

Sick tears of patience, dumb and slow.
Yet, ' Surely I come quickly,' — so
He said, from life and death gone home.
Amen: even so, Lord Jesus, come!

But oh! what human tongue can speak
That day when Michael came to break
From the tir'd spirit, like a veil,
Its covenant with Gabriel
Endured at length unto the end?
What human thought can apprehend
That mystery of motherhood
When thy Beloved at length renew'd
The sweet communion severèd, —
His left hand underneath thine head
And His right hand embracing thee? —
Lo! He was thine, and this is He!

Soul, is it Faith, or Love, or Hope,
That lets me see her standing up
Where the light of the Throne is bright?
Unto the left, unto the right,
The cherubim, succinct, conjoint,
Float inward to a golden point,
And from between the seraphim
The glory issues for a hymn.
O Mary Mother, be not loth
To listen, — thou whom the stars clothe,
Who seëst and mayst not be seen!
Hear us at last, O Mary Queen!
Into our shadow bend thy face,
Bowing thee from the secret place,
O Mary Virgin, full of grace!

THE STAFF AND SCRIP

Who rules these lands? ' the Pilgrim said.
   ' Stranger, Queen Blanchelys.'
' And who has thus harried them? ' he said.
   ' It was Duke Luke did this:
      God's ban be his! '

The Pilgrim said: ' Where is your house?
    I'll rest there, with your will.'
' You've but to climb these blackened boughs
    And you'll see it over the hill,
        For it burns still.'

' Which road, to seek your Queen? ' said he.
    ' Nay, nay, but with some wound
You'll fly back hither, it may be,
    And by your blood i' the ground
        My place be found.'

' Friend, stay in peace. God keep your head,
    And mine, where I will go;
For He is here and there,' he said.
    He passed the hillside, slow,
        And stood below.

The Queen sat idle by her loom;
    She heard the arras stir,
And looked up sadly: through the room
    The sweetness sickened her
        Of musk and myrrh.

Her women, standing two and two,
    In silence combed the fleece.
The Pilgrim said, ' Peace be with you,
    Lady; ' and bent his knees.
        She answered, ' Peace.'

Her eyes were like the wave within;
    Like water-reeds the poise
Of her soft body, dainty thin;
    And like the water's noise
        Her plaintive voice.

For him, the stream had never well'd
    In desert tracts malign
So sweet; nor had he ever felt
    So faint in the sunshine
        Of Palestine.

Right so, he knew that he saw weep
   Each night through every dream
The Queen's own face, confused in sleep
   With visages supreme
     Not known to him.

' Lady,' he said, ' your lands lie burnt
   And waste: to meet your foe
All fear: this I have seen and learnt.
   Say that it shall be so,
     And I will go.'

She gazed at him. ' Your cause is just,
   For I have heard the same,'
He said: ' God's strength shall be my trust.
   Fall it to good or grame,
     'Tis in His name.'

' Sir, you are thanked. My cause is dead.
   Why should you toil to break
A grave, and fall therein? ' she said.
   He did not pause but spake:
     ' For my vow's sake.'

' Can such vows be, Sir — to God's ear,
   Not to God's will? ' ' My vow
Remains: God heard me there as here,'
   He said with reverent brow,
     ' Both then and now.'

They gazed together, he and she,
   The minute while he spoke;
And when he ceased, she suddenly
   Looked round upon her folk
     As though she woke.

' Fight, Sir,' she said; ' my prayers in pain
   Shall be your fellowship.'
He whispered one among her train, —
   ' To-morrow bid her keep
     This staff and scrip.'

She sent him a sharp sword, whose belt
  About his body there
As sweet as her own arms he felt.
  He kissed its blade, all bare,
    Instead of her.

She sent him a green banner wrought
  With one white lily stem,
To bind his lance with when he fought.
  He writ upon the same
    And kissed her name.

She sent him a white shield, whereon
  She bade that he should trace
His will. He blent fair hues that shone,
  And in a golden space
    He kissed her face.

Born of the day that died, that eve
  Now dying sank to rest;
As he, in likewise taking leave,
  Once with a heaving breast
    Looked to the west.

And there the sunset skies unseal'd,
  Like lands he never knew,
Beyond to-morrow's battle-field
  Lay open out of view
    To ride into.

Next day till dark the women pray'd:
  Nor any might know there
How the fight went: the Queen had bade
  That there do come to her
    No messenger.

The Queen is pale, her maidens ail;
  And to the organ-tones
They sing but faintly, who sang well
  The matin-orisons,
    The lauds and nones.

Lo, Father, is thine ear inclin'd,
  And hath thine angel pass'd?
For these thy watchers now are blind
  With vigil, and at last
    Dizzy with fast.

Weak now to them the voice o' the priest
  As any trance affords;
And when each anthem failed and ceas'd,
  It seemed that the last chords
    Still sang the words.

' Oh what is the light that shines so red?
  'Tis long since the sun set; '
Quoth the youngest to the eldest maid:
  ' 'Twas dim but now, and yet
    The light is great.'

Quoth the other: ' 'Tis our sight is dazed
  That we see flame i' the air.'
But the Queen held her brows and gazed,
  And said, ' It is the glare
    Of torches there.'

' Oh what are the sounds that rise and spread?
  All day it was so still; '
Quoth the youngest to the eldest maid:
  ' Unto the furthest hill
    The air they fill.'

Quoth the other: ' 'Tis our sense is blurr'd
  With all the chants gone by.'
But the Queen held her breath and heard,
  And said, ' It is the cry
    Of Victory.'

The first of all the rout was sound,
  The next were dust and flame,
And then the horses shook the ground:
  And in the thick of them
    A still band came.

17

' Oh what do ye bring out of the fight,
 Thus hid beneath these boughs? '
' Thy conquering guest returns to-night,
 And yet shall not carouse,
  Queen, in thy house.'

' Uncover ye his face,' she said.
 ' O changed in little space! '
She cried, ' O pale that was so red!
 O God, O God of grace!
  Cover his face.'

His sword was broken in his hand
 Where he had kissed the blade.
' O soft steel that could not withstand!
 O my hard heart unstayed,
  That prayed and prayed! '

His bloodied banner crossed his mouth
 Where he had kissed her name.
' O east, and west, and north, and south,
 Fair flew my web, for shame,
  To guide Death's aim! '

The tints were shredded from his shield
 Where he had kissed her face.
' Oh, of all gifts that I could yield,
 Death only keeps its place,
  My gift and grace! '

Then stepped a damsel to her side,
 And spoke, and needs must weep:
' For his sake, lady, if he died,
 He prayed of thee to keep
  This staff and scrip.'

That night they hung above her bed,
 Till morning wet with tears.
Year after year above her head
 Her bed his token wears,
  Five years, ten years.

'That night the passion of her grief
  Shook them as there they hung.
Each year the wind that shed the leaf
  Shook them and in its tongue
    A message flung.

And once she woke with a clear mind
  That letters writ to calm
Her soul lay in the scrip; to find
  Only a torpid balm
    And dust of palm.

They shook far off with palace sport
  When joust and dance were rife;
And the hunt shook them from the court;
  For hers, in peace or strife,
    Was a Queen's life.

A Queen's death now: as now they shake
  To gusts in chapel dim, —
Hung where she sleeps, not seen to wake
  (Carved lovely white and slim),
    With them by him.

Stand up to-day, still armed, with her,
  Good knight, before His brow
Who then as now was here and there,
  Who had in mind thy vow
    Then even as now.

The lists are set in Heaven to-day,
  The bright pavilions shine;
Fair hangs thy shield, and none gainsay;
  The trumpets sound in sign
    That she is thine.

Not tithed with days' and years' decease
  He pays thy wage He owed,
But with imperishable peace
  Here in His own abode,
    Thy jealous God.

JENNY

' Vengeance of Jenny's case! Fie on her! Never name her, child! ' — (MRS. QUICKLY.)

Lazy laughing languid Jenny,
   Fond of a kiss and fond of a guinea,
Whose head upon my knee to-night
Rests for a while, as if grown light
With all our dances and the sound
To which the wild tunes spun you round:
Fair Jenny mine, the thoughtless queen
Of kisses which the blush between
Could hardly make much daintier
Whose eyes are as blue skies, whose hair
Is countless gold incomparable:
Fresh flower, scarce touched with signs that tell
Of Love's exuberant hotbed: — Nay,
Poor flower left torn since yesterday
Until to-morrow leave you bare;
Poor handful of bright spring-water
Flung in the whirlpool's shrieking face;
Poor shameful Jenny, full of grace
Thus with your head upon my knee; —
Whose person or whose purse may be
The lodestar of your reverie?

   This room of yours, my Jenny, looks
A change from mine so full of books,
Whose serried ranks hold fast, forsooth,
So many captive hours of youth, —
The hours they thieve from day and night
To make one's cherished work come right,
And leave it wrong for all their theft,
Even as to-night my work was left:
Until I vowed that since my brain
And eyes of dancing seemed so fain,
My feet should have some dancing too: —
And thus it was I met with you.
Well, I suppose 'twas hard to part,
For here I am. And now, sweetheart,
You seem too tired to get to bed.

❖ DANTE GABRIEL ROSSETTI ❖

It was a careless life I led
When rooms like this were scarce so strange
Not so long ago. What breeds the change, —
The many aims or the few years?
Because to-night it all appears
Something I do not know again.

The cloud's not danced out of my brain, —
The cloud that made it turn and swim
While hour by hour the books grew dim.
Why, Jenny, as I watch you there, —
For all your wealth of loosened hair,
Your silk ungirdled and unlac'd
And warm sweets open to the waist,
All golden in the lamplight's gleam, —
You know not what a book you seem,
Half-read by lightning in a dream!
How should you know, my Jenny? Nay,
And I should be ashamed to say: —
Poor beauty, so well worth a kiss!
But while my thought runs on like this
With wasteful whims more than enough,
I wonder what you're thinking of.

If of myself you think at all,
What is the thought? — conjectural
On sorry matters best unsolved? —
Or inly is each grace revolved
To fit me with a lure? — or (sad
To think!) perhaps you're merely glad
That I'm not drunk or ruffianly
And let you rest upon my knee.

For sometimes, were the truth confess'd,
You're thankful for a little rest, —
Glad from the crush to rest within,
From the heart-sickness and the din
Where envy's voice at virtue's pitch
Mocks you because your gown is rich;
And from the pale girl's dumb rebuke,
Whose ill-clad grace and toil-worn look

Proclaim the strength that keeps her weak,
And other nights than yours bespeak;
And from the wise unchildish elf
To schoolmate lesser than himself
Pointing you out, what thing you are: —
Yes, from the daily jeer and jar,
From shame and shame's outbraving too,
Is rest not sometimes sweet to you? —
But most from the hatefulness of man
Who spares not to end what he began,
Whose acts are ill and his speech ill,
Who, having used you at his will,
Thrusts you aside, as when I dine
I serve the dishes and the wine.

Well, handsome Jenny mine, sit up,
I've filled our glasses, let us sup,
And do not let me think of you,
Lest shame of yours suffice for two.
What, still so tired? Well, well then, keep
Your head there, so you do not sleep;
But that the weariness may pass
And leave you merry, take this glass.
Ah! lazy lily hand, more bless'd
If ne'er in rings it had been dress'd
Nor ever by a glove conceal'd!

Behold the lilies of the field,
They toil not neither do they spin;
(So doth the ancient text begin, —
Not of such rest as one of these
Can share.) Another rest and ease
Along each summer-sated path
From its new lord the garden hath,
Than that whose spring in blessings ran
Which praised the bounteous husbandman,
Ere yet, in days of hankering breath,
The lilies sickened unto death.

What, Jenny, are your lilies dead?
Aye, and the snow-white leaves are spread

❖ DANTE GABRIEL ROSSETTI ❖

Like winter on the garden-bed.
But you had roses left in May, —
They were not gone too. Jenny, nay,
But must your roses die, and those
Their purfled buds that should unclose?
Even so; the leaves are curled apart,
Still red as from the broken heart,
And here's the naked stem of thorns.

Nay, nay, mere words. Here nothing warns
As yet of winter. Sickness here
Or want alone could waken fear, —
Nothing but passion wrings a tear.
Except when there may rise unsought
Haply at times a passing thought
Of the old days which seem to be
Much older than any history
That is written in any book;
When she would lie in fields and look
Along the ground through the blown grass,
And wonder where the city was,
Far out of sight, whose broil and bale
They told her then for a child's tale.

Jenny, you know the city now.
A child can tell the tale there, how
Some things which are not yet enroll'd
In market-lists are bought and sold
Even till the early Sunday light,
When Saturday night is market-night
Everywhere, be it dry or wet,
And market-night in the Haymarket.
Our learned London children know,
Poor Jenny, all your pride and woe;
Have seen your lifted silken skirt
Advertise dainties through the dirt;
Have seen your coach-wheels splash rebuke
On virtue; and have learned your look
When, wealth and health slipped past, you stare
Along the streets alone, and there,

Round the long park, across the bridge,
The cold lamps at the pavement's edge
Wind on together and apart,
A fiery serpent for your heart.

Let the thoughts pass, an empty cloud!
Suppose I were to think aloud, —
What if to her all this were said?
Why, as a volume seldom read
Being opened halfway shuts again,
So might the pages of her brain
Be parted at such words, and thence
Close back upon the dusty sense.
For is there hue or shape defin'd
In Jenny's desecrated mind,
Where all contagious currents meet,
A Lethe of the middle street?
Nay, it reflects not any face,
Nor sound is in its sluggish pace,
But as they coil those eddies clot,
And night and day remember not.

Why, Jenny, you're asleep at last! —
Asleep, poor Jenny, hard and fast, —
So young and soft and tired; so fair,
With chin thus nestled in your hair,
Mouth quiet, eyelids almost blue
As if some sky of dreams shone through!

Just as another woman sleeps!
Enough to throw one's thoughts in heaps
Of doubt and horror, — what to say
Or think, — this awful secret sway,
The potter's power over the clay!
Of the same lump (it has been said)
For honour and dishonour made,
Two sister vessels. Here is one.

My cousin Nell is fond of fun,
And fond of dress, and change, and praise,
So mere a woman in her ways:

And if her sweet eyes rich in youth
Are like her lips that tell the truth,
My cousin Nell is fond of love.
And she's the girl I'm proudest of.
Who does not prize her, guard her well?
The love of change, in cousin Nell,
Shall find the best and hold it dear:
The unconquered mirth turn quieter
Not through her own, through others' woe:
The conscious pride of beauty glow
Beside another's pride in her,
One little part of all they share.
For Love himself shall ripen these
In a kind soil to just increase
Through years of fertilizing peace.

Of the same lump (as it is said)
For honour and dishonour made,
Two sister vessels. Here is one.

It makes a goblin of the sun.

So pure, — so fall'n! How dare to think
Of the first common kindred link?
Yet, Jenny, till the world shall burn
It seems that all things take their turn;
And who shall say but this fair tree
May need, in changes that may be,
Your children's children's charity?
Scorned then, no doubt, as you are scorn'd!
Shall no man hold his pride forewarn'd
Till in the end, the Day of Days,
At Judgment, one of his own race,
As frail and lost as you, shall rise, —
His daughter, with his mother's eyes?

How Jenny's clock ticks on the shelf!
Might not the dial scorn itself
That has such hours to register?
Yet as to me, even so to her

Are golden sun and silver moon,
In daily largesse of earth's boon,
Counted for life-coins to one tune.
And if, as blindfold fates are toss'd,
Through some one man this life be lost,
Shall soul not somehow pay for soul?

Fair shines the gilded aureole
In which our highest painters place
Some living woman's simple face.
And the stilled features thus descried
As Jenny's long throat droops aside, —
The shadows where the cheeks are thin,
And pure wide curve from ear to chin, —
With Raffael's, Leonardo's hand
To show them to men's souls might stand,
Whole ages long, the whole world through,
For preachings of what God can do.
What has man done here? How atone,
Great God, for this which man has done?
And for the body and soul which by
Man's pitiless doom must now comply
With lifelong hell, what lullaby
Of sweet forgetful second birth
Remains? All dark. No sign on earth
What measure of God's rest endows
The many mansions of his house.

If but a woman's heart might see
Such erring heart unerringly
For once! But that can never be.

Like a rose shut in a book
In which pure women may not look,
For its base pages claim control
To crush the flower within the soul;
Where through each dead rose-leaf that clings,
Pale as transparent Psyche-wings,
To the vile text, are traced such things
As might make lady's cheek indeed
More than a living rose to read;

So nought save foolish foulness may
Watch with hard eyes the sure decay;
And so the life-blood of this rose,
Puddled with shameful knowledge, flows
Through leaves no chaste hand may unclose:
Yet still it keeps such faded show
Of when 'twas gathered long ago,
That the crushed petals' lovely grain,
The sweetness of the sanguine stain,
Seen of a woman's eyes, must make
Her pitiful heart, so prone to ache,
Love roses better for its sake: —
Only that this can never be: —
Even so unto her sex is she.

Yet, Jenny, looking long at you,
The woman almost fades from view.
A cipher of man's changeless sum
Of lust, past, present, and to come,
Is left. A riddle that one shrinks
To challenge from the scornful sphinx.

Like a toad within a stone
Seated while Time crumbles on;
Which sits there since the earth was curs'd
For Man's transgression at the first;
Which, living through all centuries,
Not once has seen the sun arise;
Whose life, to its cold circle charmed,
The earth's whole summers have not warmed;
Which always — whitherso the stone
Be flung — sits there, deaf, blind, alone; —
Aye, and shall not be driven out
Till that which shuts him round about
Break at the very Master's stroke,
And the dust thereof vanish as smoke,
And the seed of Man vanish as dust: —
Even so within this world is Lust.

Come, come, what use in thoughts like this?
Poor little Jenny, good to kiss, —

You'd not believe by what strange roads
Thought travels, when your beauty goads
A man to-night to think of toads!
Jenny, wake up. . . . Why, there's the dawn!

And there's an early waggon drawn
To market, and some sheep that jog
Bleating before a barking dog;
And the old streets come peering through
Another night that London knew;
And all as ghostlike as the lamps.

So on the wings of day decamps
My last night's frolic. Glooms begin
To shiver off as lights creep in
Past the gauze curtains half drawn-to,
And the lamp's doubled shade grows blue, —
Your lamp, my Jenny, kept alight,
Like a wise virgin's, all one night!
And in the alcove coolly spread
Glimmers with dawn your empty bed;
And yonder your fair face I see
Reflected lying on my knee,
Where teems with first foreshadowings
Your pier-glass scrawled with diamond rings.
And on your bosom all night worn
Yesterday's rose now droops forlorn,
But dies not yet this summer morn.

And now without, as if some word
Had called upon them that they heard
The London sparrows far and nigh
Clamour together suddenly;
And Jenny's cage-bird grown awake
Here in their song his part must take,
Because here too the day doth break.

And somehow in myself the dawn
Among stirred clouds and veils withdrawn
Strikes greyly on her. Let her sleep.
But will it wake her if I heap

These cushions thus beneath her head
Where my knee was? No, — there's your bed,
My Jenny, while you dream. And there
I lay among your golden hair
Perhaps the subject of your dreams,
These golden coins.
                  For still one deems
That Jenny's flattering sleep confers
New magic on the magic purse, —
Grim web, how clogged with shrivelled flies!
Between the threads fine fumes arise
But shape their pictures in the brain.
There roll no streets in glare and rain,
Nor flagrant man-swine whets his tusk;
But delicately sighs in musk
The homage of the dim boudoir;
Or like a palpitating star
Thrilled into song, the opera-night
Breathes faint in the quick pulse of light;
Or at the carriage-window shine
Rich wares for choice; or, free to dine,
Whirls through its hour of health (divine
For her) the concourse of the Park.
And though in the discounted dark
Her functions there and here are one,
Beneath the lamps and in the sun
There reigns at least the acknowledged belle
Apparelled beyond parallel.
Ah Jenny, yes, we know your dreams.

   For even the Paphian Venus seems
A goddess o'er the realms of love,
When silver-shrined in shadowy grove:
Aye, or let offerings nicely plac'd
But hide Priapus to the waist,
And whoso looks on him shall see
An eligible deity.

   Why, Jenny, waking here alone
May help you to remember one,
Though all the memory's long outworn
Of many a double-pillowed morn.

I think I see you when you wake,
And rub your eyes for me, and shake
My gold, in rising, from your hair,
A Danaë for a moment there.

  Jenny, my love rang true! for still
Love at first sight is vague, until
That tinkling makes him audible.

And must I mock you to the last,
Ashamed of my own shame, — aghast
Because some thoughts not born amiss
Rose at a poor fair face like this?
Well, of such thoughts so much I know:
In my life, as in hers, they show,
By a far gleam which I may near,
A dark path I can strive to clear.

Only one kiss. Good-bye, my dear.

THE PORTRAIT

This is her picture as she was:
  It seems a thing to wonder on,
As though mine image in the glass
  Should tarry when myself am gone.
I gaze until she seems to stir, —
Until mine eyes almost aver
  That now, even now, the sweet lips part
  To breathe the words of the sweet heart: —
And yet the earth is over her.

Alas! even such the thin-drawn ray
  That makes the prison-depths more rude, —
The drip of water night and day
  Giving a tongue to solitude.
Yet only this, of love's whole prize,
Remains; save what in mournful guise
  Takes counsel with my soul alone, —
  Save what is secret and unknown,
Below the earth, above the skies.

❖ DANTE GABRIEL ROSSETTI ❖

In painting her I shrined her face
　'Mid mystic trees, where light falls in
Hardly at all; a covert place
　Where you might think to find a din
Of doubtful talk, and a live flame
Wandering, and many a shape whose name
　Not itself knoweth, and old dew,
　And your own footsteps meeting you,
And all things going as they came.

A deep dim wood; and there she stands
　As in that wood that day: for so
Was the still movement of her hands
　And such the pure line's gracious flow.
And passing fair the type must seem,
Unknown the presence and the dream.
　'Tis she: though of herself, alas!
　Less than her shadow on the grass
Or than her image in the stream.

That day we met there, I and she
　One with the other all alone;
And we were blithe; yet memory
　Saddens those hours, as when the moon
Looks upon daylight. And with her
I stooped to drink the spring-water,
　Athirst where other waters sprang:
　And where the echo is, she sang, —
My soul another echo there.

But when that hour my soul won strength
　For words whose silence wastes and kills,
Dull raindrops smote us, and at length
　Thundered the heat within the hills.
That eve I spoke those words again
Beside the pelted window-pane;
　And there she hearkened what I said,
　With under-glances that surveyed
The empty pastures blind with rain.

Next day the memories of these things,
  Like leaves thróugh which a bird has flown,
Still vibrated with Love's warm wings;
  Till I must make them all my own
And paint this picture. So, 'twixt ease
Of talk and sweet long silences,
  She stood among the plants in bloom
  At windows of a summer room,
To feign the shadow of the trees.

And as I wrought, while all above
  And all around was fragrant air,
In the sick burthen of my love
  It seemed each sun-thrilled blossom there
Beat like a heart among the leaves.
O heart that never beats nor heaves,
  In that one darkness lying still,
  What now to thee my love's great will,
Or the fine web the sunshine weaves?

For now doth daylight disavow
  Those days — nought left to see or hear.
Only in solemn whispers now
  At night-time these things reach mine ear;
When the leaf-shadows at a breath
Shrink in the road, and all the heath,
  Forest and water, far and wide,
  In limpid starlight glorified,
Lie like the mystery of death.

Last night at last I could have slept,
  And yet delayed my sleep till dawn,
Still wandering. Then it was I wept:
  For unawares I came upon
Those glades where once she walked with me:
And as I stood there suddenly,
  All wan with traversing the night,
  Upon the desolate verge of light
Yearned loud the iron-bosomed sea.

Even so, where Heaven holds breath and hears
  The beating heart of Love's own breast, —
Where round the secret of all spheres
  All angels lay their wings to rest, —
How shall my soul stand rapt and awed,
When, by the new birth borne abroad
  Throughout the music of the suns,
  It enters in her soul at once
And knows the silence there for God!

Here with her face doth memory sit
  Meanwhile, and wait the day's decline,
Till other eyes shall look from it,
  Eyes of the spirit's Palestine,
Even than the old gaze tenderer:
While hopes and aims long lost with her
  Stand round her image side by side,
  Like tombs of pilgrims that have died
About the Holy Sepulchre.

FIRST LOVE REMEMBERED

Peace in her chamber, wheresoe'er
  It be, a holy place:
  The thought still brings my soul such grace
    As morning meadows wear.

Whether it still be small and light,
  A maid's who dreams alone,
As from her orchard-gate the moon
  Its ceiling showed at night:

Or whether, in a shadow dense
  As nuptial hymns invoke,
Innocent maidenhood awoke
  To married innocence:

There still the thanks unheard await
  The unconscious gift bequeathed:
For there my soul this hour has breathed
  An air inviolate.

SUDDEN LIGHT

I have been here before,
But when or how I cannot tell:
I know the grass beyond the door,
The sweet keen smell,
The sighing sound, the lights around the shore.

You have been mine before, —
How long ago I may not know:
But just when at that swallow's soar
Your neck turned so,
Some veil did fall, — I knew it all of yore.

Then, now, — perchance again! . . .
O round mine eyes your tresses shake!
Shall we not lie as we have lain
Thus for Love's sake,
And sleep, and wake, yet never break the chain?

LOVE–LILY

Between the hands, between the brows,
Between the lips of Love-Lily,
A spirit is born whose birth endows
My blood with fire to burn through me;
Who breathes upon my gazing eyes,
Who laughs and murmurs in mine ear,
At whose least touch my colour flies,
And whom my life grows faint to hear.

Within the voice, within the heart,
Within the mind of Love-Lily,
A spirit is born who lifts apart
His tremulous wings and looks at me;
Who on my mouth his finger lays,
And shows, while whispering lutes confer,
That Eden of Love's watered ways
Whose winds and spirits worship her.

34

Brows, hands, and lips, heart, mind, and voice,
    Kisses and words of Love-Lily, —
Oh! bid me with your joy rejoice
    Till riotous longing rest in me!
Ah! let not hope be still distraught,
    But find in her its gracious goal,
Whose speech Truth knows not from her thought,
    Nor Love her body from her soul.

SISTER HELEN

Why did you melt your waxen man,
                    Sister Helen?
To-day is the third since you began.'
' The time was long, yet the time ran,
                    Little brother.'
            (O Mother, Mary Mother,
Three days to-day, between Hell and Heaven!)

' But if you have done your work aright,
                    Sister Helen,
You'll let me play, for you said I might.'
' Be very still in your play to-night,
                    Little brother.'
            (O Mother, Mary Mother,
Third night, to-night, between Hell and Heaven!)

' You said it must melt ere vesper-bell,
                    Sister Helen;
If now it be molten, all is well.'
' Even so, — nay, peace! you cannot tell,
                    Little brother.'
            (O Mother, Mary Mother,
Oh, what is this, between Hell and Heaven?)

' Oh, the waxen knave was plump to-day,
                    Sister Helen;
How like dead folk he has dropped away! '
' Nay now, of the dead what can you say,
                    Little brother? '
            (O Mother, Mary Mother,
What of the dead, between Hell and Heaven?)

35

' See, see, the sunken pile of wood,
                    Sister Helen,
Shines through the thinned wax red as blood! '
' Nay now, when looked you yet on blood,
                    Little brother? '
          (*O Mother, Mary Mother,*
How pale she is, between Hell and Heaven!)

' Now close your eyes, for they're sick and sore,
                    Sister Helen,
And I'll play without the gallery door.'
' Aye, let me rest, — I'll lie on the floor,
                    Little brother.'
          (*O Mother, Mary Mother,*
What rest to-night, between Hell and Heaven?)

' Here high up in the balcony,
                    Sister Helen,
The moon flies face to face with me.'
' Aye, look and say whatever you see,
                    Little brother.'
          (*O Mother, Mary Mother,*
What sight to-night, between Hell and Heaven?)

' Outside it's merry in the wind's wake,
                    Sister Helen;
In the shaken trees the chill stars shake.'
' Hush, heard you a horse-tread as you spake,
                    Little brother? '
          (*O Mother, Mary Mother,*
What sound to-night, between Hell and Heaven?)

I hear a horse-tread, and I see,
                    Sister Helen,
Three horsemen that ride terribly.'
' Little brother, whence come the three,
                    Little brother? '
          (*O Mother, Mary Mother,*
Whence should they come, between Hell and Heaven?)

'They come by the hill-verge from Boyne Bar,
                    Sister Helen,
And one draws nigh, but two are afar.'
'Look, look, do you know them who they are,
                    Little brother?'
                    (O Mother, Mary Mother,
Who should they be, between Hell and Heaven?)

'Oh, it's Keith of Eastholm rides so fast,
                    Sister Helen,
For I know the white mane on the blast.'
'The hour has come, has come at last,
                    Little brother!'
                    (O Mother, Mary Mother,
Her hour at last, between Hell and Heaven!)

'He has made a sign and called Halloo!
                    Sister Helen,
And he says that he would speak with you.'
'Oh, tell him I fear the frozen dew,
                    Little brother.'
                    (O Mother, Mary Mother,
Why laughs she thus, between Hell and Heaven?)

'The wind is loud, but I hear him cry,
                    Sister Helen,
That Keith of Ewern's like to die.'
'And he and thou, and thou and I,
                    Little brother.'
                    (O Mother, Mary Mother,
And they and we, between Hell and Heaven!)

'Three days ago, on his marriage-morn,
                    Sister Helen,
He sickened, and lies since then forlorn.'
'For bridegroom's side is the bride a thorn,
                    Little brother?'
                    (O Mother, Mary Mother,
Cold bridal cheer, between Hell and Heaven!)

37

' Three days and nights he has lain abed,
                Sister Helen,
And he prays in torment to be dead.'
' The thing may chance, if he have prayed,
                Little brother! '
        (O Mother, Mary Mother,
If he have prayed, between Hell and Heaven!)

' But he has not ceased to cry to-day,
                Sister Helen,
That you should take your curse away.'
' *My* prayer was heard, — he need but pray,
                Little brother! '
        (O Mother, Mary Mother,
Shall God not hear, between Hell and Heaven?)

' But he says, till you take back your ban,
                Sister Helen,
His soul would pass, yet never can.'
' Nay then, shall I slay a living man,
                Little brother? '
        (O Mother, Mary Mother,
A living soul, between Hell and Heaven!)

' But he calls forever on your name,
                Sister Helen,
And says that he melts before a flame.'
' My heart for his pleasure fared the same,
                Little brother.'
        (O Mother, Mary Mother,
Fire at the heart, between Hell and Heaven!)

' Here's Keith of Westholm riding fast,
                Sister Helen,
For I know the white plume on the blast.'
' The hour, the sweet hour I forecast,
                Little brother! '
        (O Mother, Mary Mother,
Is the hour sweet, between Hell and Heaven?)

'He stops to speak, and he stills his horse,
    Sister Helen;
But his words are drowned in the wind's course.'
'Nay hear, nay hear, you must hear perforce,
     Little brother!'
    (O Mother, Mary Mother,
What word now heard, between Hell and Heaven!)

'Oh, he says that Keith of Ewern's cry,
    Sister Helen,
Is ever to see you ere he die.'
'In all that his soul sees, there am I,
     Little brother!'
    (O Mother, Mary Mother,
The soul's one sight, between Hell and Heaven!)

'He sends a ring and a broken coin,
    Sister Helen,
And bids you mind the banks of Boyne.'
'What else he broke will he ever join,
     Little brother?'
    (O Mother, Mary Mother,
No, never joined, between Hell and Heaven!)

'He yields you these and craves full fain,
    Sister Helen,
You pardon him in his mortal pain.'
'What else he took will he give again,
     Little brother?'
    (O Mother, Mary Mother,
Not twice to give, between Hell and Heaven!)

'He calls your name in an agony,
    Sister Helen,
That even dead Love must weep to see.'
'Hate, born of Love, is blind as he,
     Little brother!'
    (O Mother, Mary Mother,
Love turned to hate, between Hell and Heaven!)

' Oh, it's Keith of Keith now that rides fast,
               Sister Helen,
For I know the white hair on the blast.'
' The short short hour will soon be past,
               Little brother! '
        (O Mother, Mary Mother,
Will soon be past, between Hell and Heaven!)

' He looks at me and he tries to speak,
               Sister Helen,
But oh! his voice is sad and weak! '
' What here should the mighty Baron seek,
               Little brother? '
        (O Mother, Mary Mother,
Is this the end, between Hell and Heaven?)

' Oh his son still cries, if you forgive,
               Sister Helen,
The body dies but the soul shall live.'
' Fire shall forgive me as I forgive,
               Little brother! '
        (O Mother, Mary Mother,
As she forgives, between Hell and Heaven!)

' Oh he prays you, as his heart would rive,
               Sister Helen,
To save his dear son's soul alive.'
' Fire cannot slay it, it shall thrive,
               Little brother! '
        (O Mother, Mary Mother,
Alas, alas, between Hell and Heaven!)

' He cries to you, kneeling in the road,
               Sister Helen,
To go with him for the love of God! '
' The way is long to his son's abode,
               Little brother.'
        (O Mother, Mary Mother,
The way is long, between Hell and Heaven!)

❖ DANTE GABRIEL ROSSETTI ❖

‘ A lady’s here, by a dark steed brought,
                Sister Helen,
So darkly clad, I saw her not.’
‘ See her now or never see aught,
                Little brother! ’
          (O Mother, Mary Mother,
What more to see, between Hell and Heaven!)

‘ Her hood falls back, and the moon shines fair,
                Sister Helen,
On the Lady of Ewern’s golden hair.’
‘ Blest hour of my power and her despair,
                Little brother! ’
          (O Mother, Mary Mother,
Hour blest and bann’d, between Hell and Heaven!)

‘ Pale, pale her cheeks, that in pride did glow,
                Sister Helen,
’Neath the bridal-wreath three days ago.’
‘ One morn for pride and three days for woe,
                Little brother! ’
          (O Mother, Mary Mother,
Three days, three nights, between Hell and Heaven!)

‘ Her clasped hands stretch from her bending head,
                Sister Helen;
With the loud wind’s wail her sobs are wed.’
‘ What wedding-strains hath her bridal-bed,
                Little brother? ’
          (O Mother, Mary Mother,
What strain but death’s, between Hell and Heaven!)

‘ She may not speak, she sinks in a swoon,
                Sister Helen, —
She lifts her lips and gasps on the moon.’
‘ Oh! might I but hear her soul’s blithe tune,
                Little brother! ’
          (O Mother, Mary Mother,
Her woe’s dumb cry, between Hell and Heaven!)

41

'They've caught her to Westholm's saddle-bow,
    Sister Helen,
And her moonlit hair gleams white in its flow.'
'Let it turn whiter than winter snow,
    Little brother!'
   (O Mother, Mary Mother,
Woe-withered gold, between Hell and Heaven!)

'O Sister Helen, you heard the bell,
    Sister Helen!
More loud than the vesper-chime it fell.'
'No vesper-chime, but a dying knell,
    Little brother!'
   (O Mother, Mary Mother,
His dying knell, between Hell and Heaven!)

'Alas! but I fear the heavy sound,
    Sister Helen;
Is it in the sky or in the ground?'
'Say, have they turned their horses round,
    Little brother?'
   (O Mother, Mary Mother,
What would she more, between Hell and Heaven?)

'They have raised the old man from his knee,
    Sister Helen,
And they ride in silence hastily.'
'More fast the naked soul doth flee,
    Little brother!'
   (O Mother, Mary Mother,
The naked soul, between Hell and Heaven!)

'Flank to flank are the three steeds gone,
    Sister Helen,
But the lady's dark steed goes alone.'
'And lonely her bridegroom's soul hath flown,
    Little brother.'
   (O Mother, Mary Mother,
The lonely ghost, between Hell and Heaven!)

'Oh, the wind is sad in the iron chill,
>Sister Helen,
And weary sad they look by the hill.'
'But he and I are sadder still,
>Little brother!'
>>(*O Mother, Mary Mother,*
Most sad of all, between Hell and Heaven!)

'See, see, the wax has dropped from its place,
>Sister Helen,
And the flames are winning up apace!'
'Yet here they burn but for a space,
>Little brother!'
>>(*O Mother, Mary Mother,*
Here for a space, between Hell and Heaven!)

'Ah! what white thing at the door has cross'd,
>Sister Helen?
Ah! what is this that sighs in the frost?'
'A soul that's lost as mine is lost,
>·Little brother!'
>>(*O Mother, Mary Mother,*
Lost, lost, all lost, between Hell and Heaven!)

THE WHITE SHIP

Henry I. of England — 25th November 1120

By none but me can the tale be told,
The butcher of Rouen, poor Berold.
>(*Lands are swayed by a King on a throne.*)
'Twas a royal train put forth to sea,
Yet the tale can be told by none but me.
>(*The sea hath no King but God alone.*)

King Henry held it as life's whole gain
That after his death his son should reign.

'Twas so in my youth I heard men say,
And my old age calls it back to-day.

43

King Henry of England's realm was he,
And Henry Duke of Normandy.

The times had changed when on either coast
" Clerkly Harry " was all his boast.

Of ruthless strokes full many an one
He had struck to crown himself and his son;
And his elder brother's eyes were gone.

And when to the chase his court would crowd,
The poor flung ploughshares on his road,
And shrieked: ' Our cry is from King to God! '

But all the chiefs of the English land
Had knelt and kissed the Prince's hand.

And next with his son he sailed to France
To claim the Norman allegiance:

And every baron in Normandy
Had taken the oath of fealty.

'Twas sworn and sealed, and the day had come
When the King and the Prince might journey home:

For Christmas cheer is to home hearts dear,
And Christmas now was drawing near.

Stout Fitz-Stephen came to the King, —
A pilot famous in seafaring;

And he held to the King, in all men's sight,
A mark of gold for his tribute's right.

' Liege Lord! my father guided the ship
From whose boat your father's foot did slip
When he caught the English soil in his grip,

' And cried: " By this clasp I claim command
O'er every rood of English land! "

44

' He was borne to the realm you rule o'er now
In that ship with the archer carved at her prow:

' And thither I'll bear, an it be my due,
Your father's son and his grandson too.

' The famed White Ship is mine in the bay;
From Harfleur's harbour she sails to-day,

' With masts fair-pennoned as Norman spears
And with fifty well-tried mariners.'

Quoth the King: ' My ships are chosen each one,
But I'll not say nay to Stephen's son.

' My son and daughter and fellowship
Shall cross the water in the White Ship.'

The King set sail with the eve's south wind,
And soon he left that coast behind.

The Prince and all his, a princely show,
Remained in the good White Ship to go.

With noble knights and with ladies fair,
With courtiers and sailors gathered there,
Three hundred living souls we were:

And I Berold was the meanest hind
In all that train to the Prince assign'd.

The Prince was a lawless shameless youth;
From his father's loins he sprang without ruth:

Eighteen years till then he had seen,
And the devil's dues in him were eighteen.

And now he cried: ' Bring wine from below;
Let the sailors revel ere yet they row:

' Our speed shall o'ertake my father's flight
Though we sail from the harbour at midnight.'

The rowers made good cheer without check;
The lords and ladies obeyed his beck;
The night was light, and they danced on the deck.

But at midnight's stroke they cleared the bay,
And the White Ship furrowed the waterway.

The sails were set, and the oars kept tune
To the double flight of the ship and the moon:

Swifter and swifter the White Ship sped
Till she flew as the spirit flies from the dead:

As white as a lily glimmered she
Like a ship's fair ghost upon the sea.

And the Prince cried, ' Friends, 'tis the hour to sing!
Is a songbird's course so swift on the wing?'

And under the winter stars' still throng,
From brown throats, white throats, merry and strong,
The knights and the ladies raised a song.

A song, — nay, a shriek that rent the sky,
That leaped o'er the deep! — the grievous cry
Of three hundred living that now must die.

An instant shriek that sprang to the shock
As the ship's keel felt the sunken rock.

'Tis said that afar — a shrill strange sigh —
The King's ships heard it and knew not why.

Pale Fitz-Stephen stood by the helm
'Mid all those folk that the waves must whelm.

A great King's heir for the waves to whelm,
And the helpless pilot pale at the helm!

The ship was eager and sucked athirst,
By the stealthy stab of the sharp reef pierced:

And like the moil round a sinking cup,
The waters against her crowded up.

A moment the pilot's senses spin, —
The next he snatched the Prince 'mid the din,
Cut the boat loose, and the youth leaped in.

A few friends leaped with him, standing near.
'Row! the sea's smooth and the night is clear!'

'What! none to be saved but these and I?'
'Row, row as you'd live! All here must die!'

Out of the churn of the choking ship,
Which the gulf grapples and the waves strip,
They struck with the strained oars' flash and dip.

'Twas then o'er the splitting bulwarks' brim
The Prince's sister screamed to him.

He gazed aloft, still rowing apace,
And through the whirled surf he knew her face.

To the toppling decks clave one and all
As a fly cleaves to a chamber-wall.

I Berold was clinging anear;
I prayed for myself and quaked with fear,
But I saw his eyes as he looked at her.

He knew her face and he heard her cry,
And he said, ' Put back! she must not die!'

And back with the current's force they reel
Like a leaf that's drawn to a water-wheel.

'Neath the ship's travail they scarce might float,
But he rose and stood in the rocking boat.

Low the poor ship leaned on the tide:
O'er the naked keel as she best might slide,
The sister toiled to the brother's side.

47

He reached an oar to her from below,
And stiffened his arms to clutch her so.

But now from the ship some spied the boat,
And ' Saved! ' was the cry from many a throat.

And down to the boat they leaped and fell:
It turned as a bucket turns in a well,
And nothing was there but the surge and swell.

The Prince that was and the King to come,
There in an instant gone to his doom,

Despite of all England's bended knee
And maugre the Norman fealty!

He was a Prince of lust and pride;
He showed no grace till the hour he died.

When he should be King, he oft would vow,
He'd yoke the peasant to his own plough.
O'er him the ships score their furrows now.

God only knows where his soul did wake,
But I saw him die for his sister's sake.

By none but me can the tale be told,
The butcher of Rouen, poor Berold.
    (*Lands are swayed by a King on a throne.*)
'Twas a royal train put forth to sea,
Yet the tale can be told by none but me.
    (*The sea hath no King but God alone.*)

And now the end came o'er the water's womb
Like the last great Day that's yet to come.

With prayers in vain and curses in vain,
The White Ship sundered on the mid-main:

And what were men and what was a ship
Were toys and splinters in the sea's grip.

❖ DANTE GABRIEL ROSSETTI ❖

I Berold was down in the sea;
And passing strange though the thing may be,
Of dreams then known I remember me.

Blithe is the shout on Harfleur's strand
When morning lights the sails to land:

And blithe is Honfleur's echoing gloam
When mothers call the children home:

And high do the bells of Rouen beat
When the Body of Christ goes down the street.

These things and the like were heard and shown
In a moment's trance 'neath the sea alone;

And when I rose, 'twas the sea did seem,
And not these things, to be all a dream.

The ship was gone and the crowd was gone,
And the deep shuddered and the moon shone,

And in a strait grasp my arms did span
The mainyard rent from the mast where it ran;
And on it with me was another man.

Where lands were none 'neath the dim sea-sky,
We told our names, that man and I.

'O I am Godefroy de l'Aigle hight,
And son I am to a belted knight.'

'And I am Berold the butcher's son
Who slays the beasts in Rouen town.'

Then cried we upon God's name, as we
Did drift on the bitter winter sea.

But lo! a third man rose o'er the wave,
And we said, 'Thank God! us three may He save!'

He clutched to the yard with panting stare,
And we looked and knew Fitz-Stephen there.

He clung, and ' What of the Prince? ' quoth he.
' Lost, lost! ' we cried. He cried, ' Woe on me! '
And loosed his hold and sank through the sea.

And soul with soul again in that space
We two were together face to face:

And each knew each, as the moments sped,
Less for one living than for one dead:

And every still star overhead
Seemed an eye that knew we were but dead.

And the hours passed; till the noble's son
Sighed, ' God be thy help! my strength's foredone!

' O farewell, friend, for I can no more! '
' Christ take thee! ' I moaned; and his life was o'er.

Three hundred souls were all lost but one,
And I drifted over the sea alone.

At last the morning rose on the sea
Like an angel's wing that beat tow'rds me.

Sore numbed I was in my sheepskin coat;
Half dead I hung, and might nothing note,
Till I woke sun-warmed in a fisher-boat.

The sun was high o'er the eastern brim
As I praised God and gave thanks to Him.

That day I told my tale to a priest,
Who charged me, till the shrift were releas'd,
That I should keep it in mine own breast.

And with the priest I thence did fare
To King Henry's court at Winchester.

❖ DANTE GABRIEL ROSSETTI ❖

We spoke with the King's high chamberlain,
And he wept and mourned again and again,
As if his own son had been slain:

And round us ever there crowded fast
Great men with faces all aghast:

And who so bold that might tell the thing
Which now they knew to their lord the King?
Much woe I learnt in their communing.

The King had watched with a heart sore stirred
For two whole days, and this was the third:

And still to all his court would he say,
'What keeps my son so long away?'

And they said: 'The ports lie far and wide
That skirt the swell of the English tide;

'And England's cliffs are not more white
Than her women are, and scarce so light
Her skies as their eyes are blue and bright;

'And in some port that he reached from France
The Prince has lingered for his pleasaunce.'

But once the King asked: 'What distant cry
Was that we heard 'twixt the sea and sky?'

And one said: 'With suchlike shouts, pardie!
Do the fishers fling their nets at sea.'

And one: 'Who knows not the shrieking quest
When the sea-mew misses its young from the nest?'

'Twas thus till now they had soothed his dread,
Albeit they knew not what they said:

But who should speak to-day of the thing
That all knew there except the King?

51

Then pondering much they found a way,
And met round the King's high seat that day:

And the King sat with a heart sore stirred,
And seldom he spoke and seldom heard.

'Twas then through the hall the King was 'ware
Of a little boy with golden hair,

As bright as the golden poppy is
That the beach breeds for the surf to kiss:

Yet pale his cheek as the thorn in Spring,
And his garb black like the raven's wing.

Nothing heard but his foot through the hall,
For now the lords were silent all.

And the King wondered, and said, ' Alack!
Who sends me a fair boy dressed in black?

' Why, sweet heart, do you pace through the hall
As though my court were a funeral? '

Then lowly knelt the child at the dais,
And looked up weeping in the King's face.

' O wherefore, black, O King, ye may say,
For white is the hue of death to-day.

' Your son and all his fellowship
Lie low in the sea with the White Ship.'

King Henry fell as a man struck dead;
And speechless still he stared from his bed
When to him next day my rede I read.

There's many an hour must needs beguile
A King's high heart that he should smile, —

Full many a lordly hour, full fain
Of his realm's rule and pride of his reign: —

But this King never smiled again.

By none but me can the tale be told,
The butcher of Rouen, poor Berold.
   (*Lands are swayed by a King on a throne.*)
'Twas a royal train put forth to sea,
Yet the tale can be told by none but me.
   (*The sea hath no King but God alone.*)

THE BALLAD OF DEAD LADIES

François Villon, 1450.

Tell me now in what hidden way is
      Lady Flora the lovely Roman?
Where's Hipparchia, and where is Thaïs,
      Neither of them the fairer woman?
Where is Echo, beheld of no man,
Only heard on river and mere, —
      She whose beauty was more than human? . . .
But where are the snows of yester-year?

Where's Héloise, the learned nun,
      For whose sake Abeillard, I ween,
Lost manhood and put priesthood on?
      (From Love he won such dule and teen!)
And where, I pray you, is the Queen
Who willed that Buridan should steer
      Sewed in a sack's mouth down the Seine? . . .
But where are the snows of yester-year?

White Queen Blanche, like a queen of lilies,
      With a voice like any mermaiden —
Bertha Broadfoot, Beatrice, Alice,
      And Ermengarde the lady of Maine, —
And that good Joan whom Englishmen
At Rouen doomed and burned her there, —
      Mother of God, where are they then?
But where are the snows of yester-year?

Nay, never ask this week, fair lord,
      Where they are gone, nor yet this year,
Except with this for an overword, —
      But where are the snows of yester-year?

MARY MAGDALENE

AT THE DOOR OF SIMON THE PHARISEE.

(For a Drawing.)

Why wilt thou cast the roses from thine hair?
　　Nay, be thou all a rose, — wreath, lips, and cheek.
　　Nay, not this house, — that banquet-house we seek;
See how they kiss and enter; come thou there.
This delicate day of love we two will share
　　Till at our ear love's whispering night shall speak.
　　What, sweet one, — hold'st thou still the foolish freak?
Nay, when I kiss thy feet they'll leave the stair.'

'Oh, loose me! See'st thou not my Bridegroom's face
　　That draws me to Him? For His feet my kiss,
　　My hair, my tears He craves to-day — and oh!
What words can tell what other day and place
　　Shall see me clasp those blood-stained feet of His?
　　He needs me, calls me, loves me: let me go!'

FOR A VENETIAN PASTORAL

By Giorgione.

(In the Louvre.)

Water, for anguish of the solstice: — nay,
　　But dip the vessel, slowly, — nay, but lean
　　And hark how at its verge the wave sighs in,
Reluctant. Hush! beyond all depth away
The heat lies silent at the brink of day;
　　Now the hand trails upon the viol-string
　　That sobs, and the brown faces cease to sing,
Sad with the whole of pleasure. Whither stray
Her eyes now, from whose mouth the slim pipes creep
　　And leave it pouting, while the shadowed grass
　　Is cool against her naked side? Let be: —
Say nothing now unto her lest she weep,
　　Nor name this ever. Be it as it was, —
　　Life touching lips with Immortality.

THE HOUSE OF LIFE

BRIDAL BIRTH

As when desire, long darkling, dawns, and first
  The mother looks upon the new-born child,
Even so my Lady stood at gaze and smiled
When her soul knew at length the Love it nurs'd.
Born with her life, creature of poignant thirst
  And exquisite hunger, at her heart Love lay
  Quickening in darkness, till a voice that day
Cried on him, and the bonds of birth were burst.

Now, shadowed by his wings, our faces yearn
  Together, as his full-grown feet now range
  The grove, and his warm hands our couch prepare:
Till to his song our bodiless souls in turn
  Be born his children, when Death's nuptial change
  Leaves us for light the halo of his hair.

LOVESIGHT

When do I see thee most, beloved one?
  When in the light the spirits of mine eyes
  Before thy face, their altar, solemnize
The worship of that Love through thee made known?
Or when in the dusk hours, (we two alone,)
  Close-kissed and eloquent of still replies
  Thy twilight-hidden glimmering visage lies,
And my soul only sees thy soul its own?

O love, my love! if I no more should see
Thyself, nor on the earth the shadow of thee,
  Nor image of thine eyes in any spring, —
How then should sound upon Life's darkening slope
The ground-whirl of the perished leaves of Hope,
  The wind of Death's imperishable wing?

55

SUPREME SURRENDER

To all the spirits of Love that wander by
　Along his love-sown harvest-field of sleep
　My lady lies apparent; and the deep
Calls to the deep; and no man sees but I.
The bliss so long afar, at length so nigh,
　Rests there attained. Methinks proud Love must weep
　When Fate's control doth from his harvest reap
The sacred hour for which the years did sigh.

First touched, the hand now warm around my neck
　Taught memory long to mock desire: and lo!
　Across my breast the abandoned hair doth flow,
Where one shorn tress long stirred the longing ache:
And next the heart that trembled for its sake
　Lies the queen-heart in sovereign overthrow.

THE BIRTH–BOND

Have you not noted, in some family
　Where two were born of a first marriage-bed,
　How still they own their gracious bond, though fed
And nursed on the forgotten breast and knee? —
How to their father's children they shall be
　In act and thought of one goodwill; but each
　Shall for the other have, in silence speech,
And in a word complete community?

Even so, when first I saw you, seemed it, love,
　That among souls allied to mine was yet
One nearer kindred than life hinted of.
　O born with me somewhere that men forget,
　And though in years of sight and sound unmet,
Known for my soul's birth-partner well enough!

✣ DANTE GABRIEL ROSSETTI ✣

GENIUS IN BEAUTY

Beauty like hers is genius. Not the call
  Of Homer's or of Dante's heart sublime, —
  Not Michael's hand furrowing the zones of time, —
Is more with compassed mysteries musical;
Nay, not in Spring's or Summer's sweet footfall
  More gathered gifts exuberant Life bequeathes
  Than doth this sovereign face, whose love-spell breathes
Even from its shadowed contour on the wall.

As many men are poets in their youth,
  But for one sweet-strung soul the wires prolong
  Even through all change the indomitable song;
So in like wise the envenomed years, whose tooth
  Rends shallower grace with ruin void of ruth,
  Upon this beauty's power shall wreak no wrong.

SILENT NOON

Your hands lie open in the long, fresh grass, —
  The finger-points look through like rosy blooms:
  Your eyes smile peace. The pasture gleams and glooms
'Neath billowing skies that scatter and amass.
All round our nest, far as the eye can pass,
  Are golden kingcup-fields with silver edge
  Where the cow-parsley skirts the hawthorn hedge.
'Tis visible silence, still as the hour-glass.

Deep in the sun-searched growths the dragon-fly
Hangs like a blue thread loosened from the sky: —
  So this wing'd hour is dropt to us from above.
Oh! clasp we to our hearts, for deathless dower,
This close-companioned inarticulate hour
  When twofold silence was the song of love.

LOVE–SWEETNESS

Sweet dimness of her loosened hair's downfall
   About thy face; her sweet hands round thy head
  In gracious fostering union garlanded;
Her tremulous smiles; her glances' sweet recall
Of love; her murmuring sighs memorial;
   Her mouth's culled sweetness by thy kisses shed
  On cheeks and neck and eyelids, and so led
Back to her mouth which answers there for all: —

What sweeter than these things, except the thing
  In lacking which all these would lose their sweet: —
  The confident heart's still fervour: the swift beat
And soft subsidence of the spirit's wing,
Then when it feels in cloud-girt wayfaring,
   The breath of kindred plumes against its feet?

WILLOWWOOD

I

I sat with Love upon a woodside well,
  Leaning across the water, I and he;
   Nor ever did he speak nor looked at me,
But touched his lute wherein was audible
The certain secret thing he had to tell:
   Only our mirrored eyes met silently
   In the low wave; and that sound came to be
The passionate voice I knew; and my tears fell.

And at their fall, his eyes beneath grew hers;
And with his foot and with his wing-feathers
   He swept the spring that watered my heart's drouth.
Then the dark ripples spread to waving hair,
And as I stooped, her own lips rising there
   Bubbled with brimming kisses at my mouth.

II

And now Love sang: but his was such a song,
   So meshed with half-remembrance hard to free,
   As souls disused in death's sterility
May sing when the new birthday tarries long.
And I was made aware of a dumb throng
   That stood aloof, one form by every tree,
   All mournful forms, for each was I or she,
The shades of those our days that had no tongue.

They looked on us, and knew us and were known;
   While fast together, alive from the abyss,
   Clung the soul-wrung implacable close kiss;
And pity of self through all made broken moan
Which said, ' For once, for once, for once alone! '
   And still Love sang, and what he sang was this: —

III

O ye, all ye that walk in Willowwood,
   That walk with hollow faces burning white;
What fathom-depth of soul-struck widowhood,
   What long, what longer hours, one lifelong night,
Ere ye again, who so in vain have wooed
   Your last hope lost, who so in vain invite
Your lips to that their unforgotten food,
   Ere ye, ere ye again shall see the light!

Alas! the bitter banks in Willowwood,
   With tear-spurge wan, with blood-wort burning red:
Alas! if ever such a pillow could
   Steep deep the soul in sleep till she were dead, —
Better all life forget her than this thing,
That Willowwood should hold her wandering! '

IV

So sang he: and as meeting rose and rose
　　Together cling through the wind's wellaway
　Nor change at once, yet near the end of day
The leaves drop loosened where the heart-stain glows, —
So when the song died did the kiss unclose;
　　And her face fell back drowned, and was as grey
　As its grey eyes; and if it ever may
Meet mine again I know not if Love knows.

Only I know that I leaned low and drank
A long draft from the water where she sank,
　Her breath and all her tears and all her soul:
And as I leaned, I know I felt Love's face
Pressed on my neck with moan of pity and grace,
　Till both our heads were in his aureole.

TRUE WOMAN

I. HERSELF

To be a sweetness more desired than Spring;
　　A bodily beauty more acceptable
　Than the wild rose-tree's arch that crowns the fell;
To be an essence more environing
Than wine's drained juice; a music ravishing
　　More than the passionate pulse of Philomel; —
　To be all this 'neath one soft bosom's swell
That is the flower of life: — how strange a thing!

How strange a thing to be what Man can know
　　But as a sacred secret! Heaven's own screen
Hides her soul's purest depth and loveliest glow;
　　Closely withheld, as all things most unseen, —
　　The wave-bowered pearl, — the heart-shaped seal of
　　　green
That flecks the snowdrop underneath the snow.

THE CHOICE

I

Eat thou and drink; to-morrow thou shalt die.
  Surely the earth, that's wise being very old,
  Needs not our help. Then loose me, love, and hold
Thy sultry hair up from my face; that I
May pour for thee this golden wine, brim-high,
  Till round the glass thy fingers glow like gold.
  We'll drown all hours: thy song, while hours are toll'd,
Shall leap, as fountains veil the changing sky.

Now kiss, and think that there are really those,
  My own high-bosomed beauty, who increase
    Vain gold, vain lore, and yet might choose our way!
    Through many years they toil; then on a day
  They die not, — for their life was death, — but cease;
And round their narrow lips the mould falls close.

II

Watch thou and fear; to-morrow thou shalt die.
  Or art thou sure thou shalt have time for death?
  Is not the day which God's word promiseth
To come man knows not when? In yonder sky,
Now while we speak, the sun speeds forth: can I
  Or thou assure him of his goal? God's breath
  Even at this moment haply quickeneth
The air to a flame; till spirits, always nigh
Though screened and hid, shall walk the daylight here.
  And dost thou prate of all that man shall do?
    Canst thou, who hast but plagues, presume to be
    Glad in his gladness that comes after thee?
  Will *his* strength slay *thy* worm in Hell? Go to:
Cover thy countenance, and watch, and fear.

III

Think thou and act; to-morrow thou shalt die.
   Outstretched in the sun's warmth upon the shore,
Thou say'st: ' Man's measured path is all gone o'er:
Up all his years, steeply, with strain and sigh,
Man clomb until he touched the truth; and I,
   Even I, am he whom it was destined for.'
   How should this be? Art thou then so much more
Than they who sowed, that thou shouldst reap thereby?

Nay, come up hither. From this wave-washed mound
   Unto the furthest flood-brim look with me;
Then reach on with thy thought till it be drown'd.
   Miles and miles distant though the last line be,
And though thy soul sail leagues and leagues beyond, —
   Still, leagues beyond those leagues, there is more sea.

SOUL'S BEAUTY

Under the arch of Life, where love and death,
   Terror and mystery, guard her shrine, I saw
   Beauty enthroned; and though her gaze struck awe,
I drew it in as simply as my breath.
Hers are the eyes which, over and beneath,
   The sky and sea bend on thee, — which can draw,
   By sea or sky or woman, to one law,
The allotted bondman of her palm and wreath.

This is that Lady Beauty, in whose praise
   Thy voice and hand shake still, — long known to thee
      By flying hair and fluttering hem, — the beat
      Following her daily of thy heart and feet,
   How passionately and irretrievably,
In what fond flight, how many ways and days!

✤ DANTE GABRIEL ROSSETTI ✤

BODY'S BEAUTY

Of Adam's first wife, Lilith, it is told
(The witch he loved before the gift of Eve,)
That, ere the snake's, her sweet tongue could deceive,
And her enchanted hair was the first gold.
And still she sits, young while the earth is old,
And, subtly of herself contemplative,
Draws men to watch the bright web she can weave,
Till heart and body and life are in its hold.

The rose and poppy are her flowers; for where
Is he not found, O Lilith, whom shed scent
And soft-shed kisses and soft sleep shall snare?
Lo! as that youth's eyes burned at thine, so went
Thy spell through him, and left his straight neck bent
And round his heart one strangling golden hair.

LOST DAYS

The lost days of my life until to-day,
What were they, could I see them on the street
Lie as they fell? Would they be ears of wheat
Sown once for food but trodden into clay?
Or golden coins squandered and still to pay?
Or drops of blood dabbling the guilty feet?
Or such spilt water as in dreams must cheat
The undying throats of Hell, athirst alway?

I do not see them here; but after death
God knows I know the faces I shall see,
Each one a murdered self, with low last breath.
'I am thyself, — what hast thou done to me?'
'And I — and I — thyself,' (lo! each one saith,)
'And thou thyself to all eternity!'

THE ONE HOPE

When vain desire at last and vain regret
    Go hand in hand to death, and all is vain,
    What shall assuage the unforgotten pain
And teach the unforgetful to forget?
Shall Peace be still a sunk stream long unmet, —
    Or may the soul at once in a green plain
    Stoop through the spray of some sweet life-fountain
And cull the dew-drenched flowering amulet?

Ah! when the wan soul in that golden air
    Between the scriptured petals softly blown
    Peers breathless for the gift of grace unknown, —
Ah! let none other alien spell soe'er
But only the one Hope's one name be there, —
    Not less nor more, but even that word alone.

COVENTRY PATMORE
1823–1896

Coventry Kersey Dighton Patmore, born in 1823, was the son of a well-to-do father who dabbled in literature, and encouraged the talents of his precocious son. Coventry grew up with little in the way of regular education, but with the fixed idea that he would be a poet. His first volume, *Poems by Coventry Patmore,* appeared in 1844. It was harshly reviewed by professional critics, but attracted the attention of a few lovers of poetry. He came to know the eager young spirits of the Pre-Raphaelite Brotherhood and contributed to *The Germ* a little poem of true Pre-Raphaelite detail and verisimilitude. His prospects were suddenly dashed by the financial ruin of his father and he was forced to turn from poetry to journalism and sank into such poverty that he found himself at one time with less than half a crown in his pocket. Monckton Milnes, friend of all poets in distress, rescued Patmore from this struggle with the wolf and secured a post for him in the library of the British Museum which he held for twenty years. Within a year he married a lady whose beauty has been immortalized on canvas by Millais and in verse (*A Portrait*) by Browning. Their married life seems to have been most happy and it was while she lived that Patmore began his long poem in praise of married love that appeared in installments, *The Betrothal* in 1854, *The Espousals* in 1856, *Faithful Forever* in 1860, and *The Victories of Love* in 1862. The first two of these, often corrected and enlarged, constitute his best known work, *The Angel in the House* (the Angel, it might be said in passing, is *not* the wife, but the living spirit of love). Mrs. Patmore died in 1862 after a lingering illness and the shock of her death left an ineffaceable impression upon Patmore's work, revealed in such poems as *The Departure* and *The Azalea.*

Patmore's fierce hatred of the liberalizing movement of his age combined with a fervid religious instinct had long been leading him Romeward, and in 1864 he entered the Roman Church, the first of many nineteenth-century poets who fled to that haven, and shortly after married a lady of that faith. To the end of his life Patmore remained a devout, but stubbornly individualistic Catholic. He detested priests; 'All Poets and all Prophets,' he once wrote, 'have always hated Priests — as a class, and it has been their vocation from the beginning to expose Ecclesiasticism.' His *Arbor Vitae* is no very flattering picture of the church to which he had gone over, yet he made pilgrimages to Lourdes and was buried in the habit of the Franciscan order. He was as vigorous and outspoken in his political as in his religious opinions. The advance of democracy in his day was to him little more than ' the amorous and vehement drift of man's herd hellward.'

In 1868 Patmore printed privately a tiny volume of nine *Odes* which marked the transition from his earlier to his later period both in theme and manner. His *Angel* had become by this time perhaps the most popular book of contemporary verse; the *Odes* seem to have received no notice at all, not even the notice of abuse. Patmore, we are told, burnt all the copies that were left on his hands. But he was not discouraged and after long delay and much meditation published in 1877 his greatest work, *The Unknown Eros,* a collection of odes in his new manner of extreme metrical freedom and profound mystical thought. *Amelia,* his own favourite poem, appeared in 1878 and a number of odes were added to later editions of his work. After this Patmore wrote little or no verse. He published some critical and metrical studies, plunged deep into mystical theology, and completed a prose work, *Sponsa Dei,* so daring an exposition of his peculiar views of the identity of physical and spiritual love that his religious advisers frowned upon it and he committed it to the flames before his death. He lived long enough to see a renewed interest and appreciation of his work and died of heart failure in 1896.

Patmore is first and last the poet of Love. Love is the theme that inspires all his best verse and links the simple narrative poems of his first period to the mystical exaltation of his later lyrics. At first sight there appears a sharp and startling contrast between these phases. It seems almost incredible that the poet who began by writing:

66

My queen was crouching at my side,
By love unsceptred and brought low,
Her awful garb of maiden pride
All melted into tears like snow.

should have gone on to write:

Beautiful habitations, auras of delight!
Who shall bewail the crags and bitter foam
And angry sword-blades flashing left and right
Which guard your glittering height
That none thereby may come!

But the truth is that, as a contemporary critic once remarked,
'this laureate of the tea-table with his humdrum stories of
girls that smell of bread and butter, is in his inmost heart the
most arrogant and visionary of mystics.' The *Angel in the
House* is, so far as story goes, the simplest of tales, a story of
true love running smoothly to the end in marriage. It is as
full of the details of English country life as a novel of Trol-
lope's, without the interest of plot or character which keeps
Trollope's novels alive. But Patmore was not interested in
plot or character; the sweet and simple story which made his
poem popular in its day was to him only a peg on which to
hang a robe in praise of Love, a robe embroidered with
delicate touches of psychological observation, of gentle ad-
monition, of religious reverence. For to Patmore Love was
holy, even the most conventional wooing and wedding in the
most conventional of surroundings. To-day it is not the story
that attracts the infrequent reader, but the preludes, the com-
mentary, packed as it is with Patmore's love of Love. There
is, to be sure, little that is profound or transcendent in this
early work; Patmore's own courtship and marriage had been
at once too conventional and too happy to reveal to him the
deeper mysteries of his theme. But his bereavement opened to
him the doors of the temple in whose forecourt he had knelt,
and the neophyte was transformed into the mystic hierophant.
For now Love is no longer the Angel in the House, but the
Unknown Eros, 'sire of awful bliss.' Earthly love is the sign
and symbol of Love Divine. The old myth of Cupid and
Psyche takes on a new meaning for the poet as a parable of
the union of God with the human soul. Patmore was not of

67

those mystics who despise the body to exalt the soul. His ode *To the Body* celebrates it as ' Creation's and Creator's crowning good,'

> Little sequestr'd pleasure-house
> For God and for His Spouse.

It is not a matter for wonder that Patmore's friends and religious advisers were startled and sometimes shocked by the fervour of his rhapsodies and his daring assimilation of the two Loves.

Patmore's form changed in this later period to correspond with the change in subject matter. His earlier verse is for the most part of an extreme simplicity, quatrains or couplets in an iambic measure with slight but skillful variations; his *Odes,* written in what he called ' catalectic metre,' are, in a sense, ' free verse,' free at least from all restraint of stanzaic pattern, length of line, or recurrent regularity of rhyme. The rhythm rises and falls, pauses and hurries on, to correspond with the varying intensity of the emotion. The diction is, as a rule, simple, direct, and vivid; Patmore attains at times extraordinary effects by the use of the homeliest English words, as in the opening lines of *The Toys*. It is on this later verse, free, fluctuant, intense, pregnant with human emotion, exalted in mystical vision, that Patmore's claim to high rank among the lyric poets of England rests. It is not likely that he will ever have a large following; an audience ' fit but few ' is what he would himself have desired. He was a lonely, proud, and conscious artist, and the best summary of his achievement may be given in his own words. ' I have written little, but it is all my best; I have never spoken when I had nothing to say, nor spared time or labour to make my words true. I have respected posterity; and should there be a posterity which cares for letters, I dare to hope that it will respect me.'

THE ANGEL IN THE HOUSE

THE POET'S CONFIDENCE

The richest realm of all the earth
　　Is counted still a heathen land:
Lo, I, like Joshua, now go forth
　　To give it into Israel's hand.

I will not hearken blame or praise;
   For so should I dishonour do
To that sweet Power by which these Lays
   Alone are lovely, good, and true;
Nor credence to the world's cries give,
   Which ever preach and still prevent
Pure passion's high prerogative
   To make, not follow, precedent.
From love's abysmal ether rare
   If I to men have here made known
New truths, they, like new stars, were there
   Before, though not yet written down.
Moving but as the feelings move,
   I run, or loiter with delight,
Or pause to mark where gentle Love
   Persuades the soul from height to height,
Yet, know ye, though my words are gay
   As David's dance, which Michal scorn'd,
If kindly you receive the Lay,
   You shall be sweetly help'd and warn'd.

UNTHRIFT

Ah, wasteful woman, she who may
   On her sweet self set her own price,
Knowing man cannot choose but pay,
   How has she cheapen'd paradise;
How given for nought her priceless gift,
   How spoil'd the bread and spill'd the wine,
Which, spent with due, respective thrift,
   Had made brutes men, and men divine.

THE REVELATION

An idle poet, here and there,
   Looks round him; but, for all the rest,
The world, unfathomably fair,
   Is duller than a witling's jest.
Love wakes men, once a lifetime each;
   They lift their heavy lids, and look;

And, lo, what one sweet page can teach,
   They read with joy, then shut the book.
And some give thanks, and some blaspheme,
   And most forget; but, either way,
That and the Child's unheeded dream
   Is all the light of all their day.

THE MARRIED LOVER

Why, having won her, do I woo?
   Because her spirit's vestal grace
Provokes me always to pursue,
   But, spirit-like, eludes embrace;
Because her womanhood is such
   That, as on court-days subjects kiss
The Queen's hand, yet so near a touch
   Affirms no mean familiarness,
Nay, rather marks more fair the height
   Which can with safety so neglect
To dread, as lower ladies might,
   That grace could·meet with disrespect,
Thus she with happy favour feeds
   Allegiance from a love so high
That thence no false conceit proceeds
   Of difference bridged, or state put by;
Because, although in act and word
   As lowly as a wife can be,
Her manners, when they call me lord,
   Remind me 'tis by courtesy;
Not with her least consent of will,
   Which would my proud affection hurt,
But by the noble style that still
   Imputes an unattain'd desert;
Because her gay and lofty brows,
   When all is won which hope can ask,
Reflect a light of hopeless snows
   That bright in virgin ether bask;
Because, though free of the outer court
   I am, this Temple keeps its shrine
Sacred to heaven; because, in short,
   She's not and never can be mine.

✣ COVENTRY PATMORE ✣

THE UNKNOWN EROS

WINTER

I singularly moved
　To love the lovely that are not beloved,
Of all the Seasons, most
Love Winter, and to trace
The sense of the Trophonian pallor on her face.
It is not death, but plenitude of peace;
And the dim cloud that does the world enfold
Hath less the characters of dark and cold
Than warmth and light asleep,
And correspondent breathing seems to keep
With the infant harvest, breathing soft below
Its eider coverlet of snow.
Nor is in field or garden anything
But, duly look'd into, contains serene
The substance of things hoped for, in the Spring,
And evidence of Summer not yet seen.
On every chance-mild day
That visits the moist shaw,
The honeysuckle, 'sdaining to be crost
In urgance of sweet life by sleet or frost,
'Voids the time's law
With still increase
Of leaflet new, and little, wandering spray;
Often, in sheltering brakes,
As one from rest disturb'd in the first hour,
Primrose or violet bewilder'd wakes,
And deems 'tis time to flower;
Though not a whisper of her voice he hear,
The buried bulb does know
The signals of the year,
And hails far Summer with his lifted spear.
The gorse-field dark, by sudden, gold caprice,
Turns, here and there, into a Jason's fleece;
Lilies, that soon in Autumn slipp'd their gowns of green,
And vanish'd into earth,
And came again, ere Autumn died, to birth,
Stand full-array'd, amidst the wavering shower,

71

And perfect for the Summer, less the flower;
In nook of pale or crevice of crude bark,
Thou canst not miss,
If close thou spy, to mark
The ghostly chrysalis,
That, if thou touch it, stirs in its dream dark;
And the flush'd Robin, in the evenings hoar.
Does of Love's Day, as if he saw it, sing;
But sweeter yet than dream or song of Summer or Spring
Are Winter's sometime smiles, that seem to well
From infancy ineffable;
Her wandering, languorous gaze,
So unfamiliar, so without amaze,
On the elemental, chill adversity,
The uncomprehended rudeness; and her sigh
And solemn, gathering tear,
And look of exile from some great repose, the sphere
Of ether, moved by ether only, or
By something still more tranquil.

THE AZALEA

There, where the sun shines first
   Against our room,
She train'd the gold Azalea, whose perfume
She, Spring-like, from her breathing grace dispersed.
Last night the delicate crests of saffron bloom,
For this their dainty likeness watch'd and nurst,
Were just at point to burst.
At dawn I dream'd, O God, that she was dead,
And groan'd aloud upon my wretched bed,
And waked, ah, God, and did not waken her,
But lay, with eyes still closed,
Perfectly bless'd in the delicious sphere
By which I knew so well that she was near,
My heart to speechless thankfulness composed.
Till 'gan to stir
A dizzy somewhat in my troubled head —
It *was* the azalea's breath, and she *was* dead!
The warm night had the lingering buds disclosed,
And I had fall'n asleep with to my breast

A chance-found letter press'd
In which she said,
' So, till tomorrow eve, my Own, adieu!
Parting's well-paid with soon again to meet,
Soon in your arms to feel so small and sweet,
Sweet to myself that am so sweet to you! '

DEPARTURE

It was not like your great and gracious ways!
  Do you, that have nought other to lament,
Never, my Love, repent
Of how, that July afternoon,
You went,
With sudden, unintelligible phrase,
And frighten'd eye,
Upon your journey of so many days,
Without a single kiss or a good-bye?
I knew, indeed, that you were parting soon;
And so we sate, within the low sun's rays,
You whispering to me, for your voice was weak,
Your harrowing praise.
Well, it was well,
To hear you such things speak,
And I could tell
What made your eyes a growing gloom of love,
As a warm South-wind sombres a March grove.
And it was like your great and gracious ways
To turn your talk on daily things, my Dear,
Lifting the luminous, pathetic lash
To let the laughter flash,
Whilst I drew near,
Because you spoke so low that I could scarcely hear.
But all at once to leave me at the last,
More at the wonder than the loss aghast,
With huddled, unintelligible phrase,
And frighten'd eye,
And go your journey of all days
With not one kiss, or a good-bye,
And the only loveless look the look with which you pass'd:
'Twas all unlike your great and gracious ways.

THE TOYS

My little Son, who looked from thoughtful eyes,
  And moved and spoke in quiet grown-up wise,
Having my law the seventh time disobey'd,
I struck him, and dismiss'd
With hard words and unkiss'd,
His Mother, who was patient, being dead.
Then, fearing lest his grief should hinder sleep,
I visited his bed,
But found him slumbering deep,
With darken'd eyelids, and their lashes yet
From his late sobbing wet.
And I, with moan,
Kissing away his tears, left others of my own;
For, on a table drawn beside his head,
He had put, within his reach,
A box of counters and a red-vein'd stone,
A piece of glass abraded by the beach
And six or seven shells,
A bottle with bluebells
And two French copper coins, ranged there with careful art,
To comfort his sad heart.
So when that night I pray'd
To God, I wept, and said:
' Ah, when at last we lie with tranced breath,
Not vexing Thee in death,
And Thou rememberest of what toys
We made our joys,
How weakly understood,
Thy great commanded good,
Then, fatherly not less
Than I whom Thou hast moulded from the clay,
Thou'lt leave Thy wrath, and say,
" I will be sorry for their childishness." '

✤ COVENTRY PATMORE ✤

MAGNA EST VERITAS

Here, in this little Bay,
    Full of tumultuous life and great repose,
Where, twice a day,
The purposeless, glad ocean comes and goes,
Under high cliffs, and far from the huge town,
I sit me down.
For want of me the world's course will not fail:
When all its work is done, the lie shall rot;
The truth is great, and shall prevail,
When none cares whether it prevail or not.

A FAREWELL

With all my will, but much against my heart,
    We two now part.
My Very Dear,
Our solace is, the sad road lies so clear.
It needs no art,
With faint, averted feet
And many a tear,
In our opposed paths to persevere.
Go thou to East, I West.
We will not say
There's any hope, it is so far away.
But, O, my Best,
When the one darling of our widowhead,
The nursling Grief,
Is dead,
And no dews blur our eyes
To see the peach-bloom come in evening skies,
Perchance we may,
Where now this night is day,
And even through faith of still averted feet,
Making full circle of our banishment,
Amazed meet;
The bitter journey to the bourne so sweet
Seasoning the termless feast of our content
With tears of recognition never dry.

' IF I WERE DEAD '

If I were dead, you'd sometimes say, Poor Child!'
   The dear lips quiver'd as they spake,
And the tears brake
From eyes which, not to grieve me, brightly smiled.
Poor Child, poor Child!
I seem to hear your laugh, your talk, your song.
It is not true that Love will do no wrong.
Poor Child!
And did you think, when you so cried and smiled,
How I, in lonely nights, should lie awake,
And of those words your full avengers make?
Poor Child, poor Child!
And now, unless it be
That sweet amends thrice told are come to thee,
O God, have Thou *no* mercy upon me!
Poor Child!

TO THE BODY

Creation's and Creator's crowning good;
   Wall of infinitude;
Foundation of the sky,
In Heaven forecast
And long'd for from eternity,
Though laid the last;
Reverberating dome,
Of music cunningly built home
Against the void and indolent disgrace
Of unresponsive space;
Little, sequester'd pleasure-house
For God and for His Spouse;
Elaborately, yea, past conceiving, fair,
Since, from the graced decorum of the hair,
Ev'n to the tingling, sweet
Soles of the simple, earth-confiding feet,
And from the inmost heart
Outwards unto the thin
Silk curtains of the skin,
Every least part

Astonish'd hears
And sweet replies to some like region of the spheres;
Form'd for a dignity prophets but darkly name,
Lest shameless men cry ' Shame! '
So rich with wealth conceal'd
That Heaven and Hell fight chiefly for this field;
Clinging to everything that pleases thee
With indefectible fidelity;
Alas, so true
To all thy friendships that no grace
Thee from thy sin can wholly disembrace;
Which thus 'bides with thee as the Jebusite,
That, maugre all God's promises could do,
The chosen People never conquer'd quite;
Who therefore lived with them,
And that by formal truce and as of right,
In metropolitan Jerusalem.
For which false fealty
Thou needs must, for a season, lie
In the grave's arms, foul and unshriven,
Albeit, in Heaven,
Thy crimson-throbbing Glow
Into its old abode aye pants to go,
And does with envy see
Enoch, Elijah, and the Lady, she
Who left the roses in her body's lieu.
O, if the pleasures I have known in thee
But my poor faith's poor first-fruits be,
What quintessential, keen, ethereal bliss
Then shall be his
Who has thy birth-time's consecrating dew
For death's sweet chrism retain'd,
Quick, tender, virginal, and unprofaned!

AMELIA

REGINA COELI

Say, did his sisters wonder what could Joseph see
In a mild, silent little Maid like thee?
And was it awful, in that narrow house,
With God for Babe and Spouse?

Nay, like thy simple, female sort, each one
Apt to find Him in Husband and in Son,
Nothing to thee came strange in this.
Thy wonder was but wondrous bliss:
Wondrous, for, though
True Virgin lives not but does know,
 (Howbeit none ever yet confess'd) ,
That God lies really in her breast,
Of thine He made His special nest!
And so
All mothers worship little feet,
And kiss the very ground they've trod;
But, ah, thy little Baby sweet
Who was indeed thy God!

CHRISTINA ROSSETTI

1830–1894

Christina Georgina Rossetti was the youngest of the four children of the Italian patriot and exile in England, Gabriele Rossetti. Though she was reared in the midst of talent and genius, she developed her abilities in her own way and became the first of the associates of the Pre-Raphaelite Brotherhood to receive the public's approval. The exterior events of her life require small attention from a biographer. Twice she loved and each time she renounced. Her famous brother Gabriel was, in spite of her admiration for his work, something of a trial to her for she possessed enough of her mother's hard sense not to be pleased with his irregular life. William, the civil servant, editor, socialist, and family archivist was, next her mother, the human being who made life endurable for her. In religion she found emotional release and, we may suppose, her only real solace. If we disregard a volume published by her grandfather Polidori when she was seventeen and her fugitive contributions to *The Germ,* her first collection of verse was issued by Macmillan in 1862. *Goblin Market* gave the book its title and inspired Gabriel to an enchanting frontispiece of the beasts who were paid with the golden curl. Fourteen other volumes of verse the most important of which are *The Prince's Progress,* 1866; *A Pageant and other Poems,* 1881, short stories and pious exhortation appeared before her death. Since then her almost subterranean reputation has grown and attained the high place which it is not likely to be forced to abdicate.

In the National Portrait Gallery hangs a pastel by Dante Gabriel Rossetti of his mother and his sister Christina. The two faces, alike in many particulars, are grave and dreaming. The mother's eyes brood gently on the vicissitudes and rewards of her life. The daughter's features are wider, sharper, the chin firmer and a little raised. But the most remarkable trait is a quietude approaching almost to languor. This trait can be

observed in other likenesses of Christina which her brother
made and might therefore be suspected as an interpretation of
her character imposed by him on the picture. But a photo-
graph of Christina made by Lewis Carroll in 1863 corroborates
the impression. There can be no doubt that whatever the look
betokens, it is there.

We can be sure from her poetry that it does not betoken
languor or apathy. Life was not sweet to Christina Rossetti.
She frankly says it will be sweet one day ' to shut our eyes and
die.' But she required herself to endure and contemplate her
sorrow. What we mistake for languor is weariness, the weari-
ness of one who has fought to win a measure of tranquillity.
The heroic nature of that struggle we can easily fail to see be-
cause her victory has been so complete.

We must not be deceived because again and again the sound
of old tears intrudes. She has made her choice, wrestled with
her weakness, reproached herself for the folly which makes
her alike unfit ' for healthy joy and salutary pain '; yet always
the insistent cry returns. Can she have subdued her heart when
it will not be still; with what right may one say she has been
victorious? Surely to have passed through purgatory so that
misery is only remembered, no matter how vividly, is to have
put down sorrow. One cannot say how self-conscious is the
aspiration of her *In Progress,* but the temptation to read sig-
nificance from it is irresistible.

> Ten years ago it seemed impossible
>   That she should ever grow so calm as this,
>   With self-remembrance in her warmest kiss
> And dim dried eyes like an exhausted well.
> Slow-speaking when she has some fact to tell,
>   Silent with long-unbroken silences,
>   Centred in self yet not unpleased to please,
> Gravely monotonous like a passing bell.
> Mindful of drudging daily common things,
>   Patient at pastime, patient at her work,
>   Wearied perhaps, but strenuous certainly.
>   Sometimes I fancy we may one day see
> Her head shoot forth seven stars from where they lurk
> And her eyes lightnings and her shoulders wings.

To most women the religious scruples which kept her from marrying Charles Cayley would seem slight barriers set in the way of a happy life. Her renunciation, though a less conscientious generation may think it needless, is, indirectly at least, responsible for much of her finest poetry. The lovers are nameless who walk in her lines, but their love is frustrate here on earth and expects fulfillment in heaven.

The burden of her song is love. It is also the anticipated joy of the life everlasting. She speaks of heavenly sights with the certainty and clear perception with which worldly poets speak of nature's beauty. Her religion is positive and demands an eloquent expression of its mysteries. Like all true mystics she experienced periods of ' dryness ' when she felt that the ' strangling load ' would never be torn away. But the doubts which assaulted her then never really overcame her, not even in the agony of her deathbed. She trusted these remembered and anticipated mystic communions, and her trust accounts for the tone of exultation in her religious verse.

Her faith did not, however, quiet the horror she felt at the idea of physical dissolution. The colours and the scents of earth were dear. In childhood she had delighted in all near-by objects, in gardens and the flight of birds and small eft-things, and the animals that lurk under hedges and about stones. Her early poetry is full of the joy of realizing in verse these impressions of the physical world. It is easy to see how, when her existence narrowed and she saw her own life fading, she should think of death in terms of physical decay. This trait brings her close to Webster and Tourneur and the other Jacobeans whose verse smells of mortality.

This preoccupation with the macabre is not her only link with the song writers of Shakespeare's time. The musical qualities of her lyrics make her seem almost an incarnation of some lutenist or writer of madrigals of Elizabeth's court. It is a curious and seldom observed fact that English possesses few real songs. Reflective poetry of the highest order it has; ballads and lyrics of a subjective kind. But its pure songs are not numerous after 1610. Christina Rossetti, though not a musician herself, wrote songs so delicately cadenced, so phrased and balanced, that an air seems to sing itself out of them.

IN AN ARTIST'S STUDIO

One face looks out from all his canvases,
    One selfsame figure sits or walks or leans:
  We found her hidden just behind those screens,
That mirror gave back all her loveliness.
A queen in opal or in ruby dress,
    A nameless girl in freshest summer-greens,
    A saint, an angel — every canvas means
The same one meaning, neither more nor less.
He feeds upon her face by day and night,
    And she with true kind eyes looks back on him,
Fair as the moon and joyful as the light:
    Not wan with waiting, not with sorrow dim;
  Not as she is, but was when hope shone bright;
  Not as she is, but as she fills his dream.

ITALIA, IO TI SALUTO

To come back from the sweet South, to the North
    Where I was born, bred, look to die;
  Come back to do my day's work in its day,
        Play out my play —
    Amen, amen, say I.

To see no more the country half my own,
    Nor hear the half familiar speech,
  Amen, I say; I turn to that bleak North
        Whence I came forth —
    The South lies out of reach.

But when our swallows fly back to the South,
    To the sweet South, to the sweet South,
  The tears may come again into my eyes
        On the old wise,
    And the sweet name to my mouth.

A BIRTHDAY

My heart is like a singing bird
   Whose nest is in a watered shoot:
My heart is like an apple-tree
   Whose boughs are bent with thickset fruit;
My heart is like a rainbow shell
   That paddles in a halcyon sea;
My heart is gladder than all these
   Because my love is come to me.

Raise me a dais of silk and down;
   Hang it with vair and purple dyes;
Carve it in doves and pomegranates,
   And peacocks with a hundred eyes;
Work it in gold and silver grapes,
   In leaves and silver fleurs-de-lys;
Because the birthday of my life
   Is come, my love is come to me.

ECHO

Come to me in the silence of the night;
   Come in the speaking silence of a dream;
Come with soft rounded cheeks and eyes as bright
   As sunlight on a stream;
     Come back in tears,
O memory, hope, love of finished years.

O dream how sweet, too sweet, too bitter sweet,
   Whose wakening should have been in Paradise,
Where souls brimfull of love abide and meet;
   Where thirsting longing eyes
     Watch the slow door
That opening, letting in, lets out no more.

Yet come to me in dreams, that I may live
   My very life again though cold in death:
Come back to me in dreams, that I may give
   Pulse for pulse, breath for breath:
     Speak low, lean low,
As long ago, my love, how long ago.

THREE SEASONS

A cup for hope! ' she said,
  In springtime ere the bloom was old;
The crimson wine was poor and cold
  By her mouth's richer red.

'A cup for love! ' how low,
How soft the words; and all the while
Her blush was rippling with a smile
  Like summer after snow.

'A cup for memory! '
Cold cup that one must drain alone:
While autumn winds are up and moan
  Across the barren sea.

Hope, memory, love:
Hope for fair morn, and love for day,
And memory for the evening grey
  And solitary dove.

SONG

When I am dead, my dearest,
  Sing no sad songs for me;
Plant thou no roses at my head,
  Nor shady cypress tree:
Be the green grass above me
  With showers and dewdrops wet:
And if thou wilt, remember,
  And if thou wilt, forget.

I shall not see the shadows,
  I shall not feel the rain;
I shall not hear the nightingale
  Sing on as if in pain:
And dreaming through the twilight
  That doth not rise nor set,
Haply I may remember,
  And haply may forget.

THE BOURNE

Underneath the growing grass,
  Underneath the living flowers,
Deeper than the sound of showers:
There we shall not count the hours
By the shadows as they pass.

Youth and health will be but vain,
  Beauty reckoned of no worth:
  There a very little girth
  Can hold round what once the earth
Seemed too narrow to contain.

REMEMBER

Remember me when I am gone away,
  Gone far away into the silent land;
  When you can no more hold me by the hand,
Nor I half turn to go yet turning stay.
Remember me when no more day by day
  You tell me of our future that you plann'd.
  Only remember me; you understand
It will be late to counsel then or pray.
Yet if you should forget me for a while
  And afterwards remember, do not grieve:
  For if the darkness and corruption leave
  A vestige of the thoughts that once I had,
Better by far you should forget and smile
  Than that you should remember and be sad.

AFTER DEATH

The curtains were half drawn, the floor was swept
  And strewn with rushes, rosemary and may
Lay thick upon the bed on which I lay,
Where through the lattice ivy-shadows crept.

85

He leaned above me, thinking that I slept
   And could not hear him; but I heard him say,
    ' Poor child, poor child '; and as he turned away
Came a deep silence, and I knew he wept.
He did not touch the shroud, or raise the fold
   That hid my face, or take my hand in his,
     Or ruffle the smooth pillows for my head:
     He did not love me living; but once dead
   He pitied me; and very sweet it is
To know he still is warm though I am cold.

A PAUSE

They made the chamber sweet with flowers and leaves,
   And the bed sweet with flowers on which I lay;
   While my soul, love bound, loitered on its way.
I did not hear the birds about the eaves,
Nor hear the reapers talk about the sheaves:
   Only my soul kept watch from day to day,
   My thirsty soul kept watch for one away: —
Perhaps he loves, I thought, remembers, grieves.
At length there came the step upon the stair,
   Upon the lock the old familiar hand:
Then first my spirit seemed to scent the air
   Of Paradise; then first the tardy sand
Of time ran golden; and I felt my hair
   Put on a glory, and my soul expand.

REST

O Earth, lie heavily upon her eyes;
   Seal her sweet eyes weary of watching, Earth;
   Lie close around her; leave no room for mirth
With its harsh laughter, nor for sound of sighs.
She hath no questions, she hath no replies,
   Hushed in and curtained with a blessed dearth
   Of all that irked her from the hour of birth;
With stillness that is almost Paradise.
Darkness more clear than noonday holdeth her,
   Silence more musical than any song;

Even her very heart has ceased to stir:
Until the morning of Eternity
Her rest shall not begin nor end, but be;
    And when she wakes she will not think it long.

TWO PURSUITS

A voice said, ' Follow, follow ': and I rose
  And followed far into the dreamy night,
  Turning my back upon the pleasant light.
It led me where the bluest water flows,
And would not let me drink: where the corn grows
  I dared not pause, but went uncheered by sight
  Or touch: until at length in evil plight
It left me, wearied out with many woes.
Some time I sat as one bereft of sense:
  But soon another voice from very far
    Called, ' Follow, follow ': and I rose again.
  Now on my night has dawned a blessed star:
    Kind steady hands my sinking steps sustain,
And will not leave me till I shall go hence.

A PORTRAIT

1

She gave up beauty in her tender youth,
  Gave up her hope and joy and pleasant ways;
  She covered up her eyes lest they should gaze
On vanity, and chose the bitter truth.
Harsh towards herself, towards others full of ruth,
  Servant of servants, little known to praise,
  Long prayers and fasts trenched on her nights and days:
She schooled herself to sights and sounds uncouth
That with the poor and stricken she might make
  A home, until the least of all sufficed
Her wants; her own self learned she to forsake,
Counting all earthly gain but hurt and loss.
So with calm will she chose and bore the cross
  And hated all for love of Jésus Christ.

2

They knelt in silent anguish by her bed,
  And could not weep; but calmly there she lay.
  All pain had left her; and the sun's last ray
Shone through upon her, warming into red
The shady curtains. In her heart she said:
  ' Heaven opens; I leave these and go away;
  The Bridegroom calls, — shall the Bride seek to stay? '
Then low upon her breast she bowed her head.
O lily flower, O gem of priceless worth,
  O dove with patient voice and patient eyes,
O fruitful vine amid a land of dearth,
  O maid replete with loving purities,
Thou bowedst down thy head with friends on earth
  To raise it with the saints in Paradise.

VANITY OF VANITIES

Ah woe is me for pleasure that is vain,
  Ah woe is me for glory that is past!
  Pleasure that bringeth sorrow at the last,
Glory that at the last bringeth no gain.
So saith the sinking heart; and so again
  It shall say till the mighty angel-blast
  Is blown, making the sun and moon aghast,
And showering down the stars like sudden rain.
And evermore men shall go fearfully,
  Bending beneath their weight of heaviness;
And ancient men shall lie down wearily,
  And strong men shall rise up in weariness:
Yea even the young shall answer sighingly,
  Saying one to another: ' How vain it is! '

LIFE AND DEATH

Life is not sweet. One day it will be sweet
  To shut our eyes and die;
Nor feel the wild flowers blow, nor birds dart by
  With flitting butterfly,
Nor grass grow long above our heads and feet,

Nor hear the happy lark that soars sky-high,
Nor sigh that spring is fleet and summer fleet,
   Nor mark the waxing wheat,
Nor know who sits in our accustomed seat.

Life is not good. One day it will be good
   To die, then live again;
To sleep meanwhile; so, not to feel the wane
   Of shrunk leaves dropping in the wood,
Nor hear the foamy lashing of the main,
Nor mark the blackened bean-fields, nor where stood
   Rich ranks of golden grain,
Only dead refuse stubble clothe the plain:
   Asleep from risk, asleep from pain.

AMOR MUNDI

Oh where are you going with your lovelocks flowing,
   On the west wind blowing along this valley track?'
'The downhill path is easy, come with me an it please ye,
   We shall escape the uphill by never turning back.'

So they two went together in glowing August weather,
   The honey-breathing heather lay to their left and right;
And dear she was to doat on, her swift feet seemed to float on
   The air like soft twin pigeons too sportive to alight.

'Oh what is that in heaven where grey cloud-flakes are seven,
   Where blackest clouds hang riven just at the rainy skirt?'
'Oh that's a meteor sent us, a message dumb, portentous,
   An undeciphered solemn signal of help or hurt.'

'Oh what is that glides quickly where velvet flowers grow
   thickly,
   Their scent comes rich and sickly?' 'A scaled and hooded
   worm.'
'Oh what's that in the hollow, so pale I quake to follow?'
   'Oh that's a thin dead body which waits the eternal term.'

'Turn again, O my sweetest, — turn again, false and fleetest:
   This beaten way thou beatest, I fear, is hell's own track.'

' Nay, too steep for hill mounting; nay, too late for cost
counting:
This downhill path is easy, but there's no turning back.'

THE THREE ENEMIES

THE FLESH

Sweet, thou art pale.'
                 ' More pale to see,
Christ hung upon the cruel tree
And bore His Father's wrath for me.'

' Sweet, thou art sad.'
                 ' Beneath a rod
More heavy, Christ for my sake trod
The winepress of the wrath of God.'

' Sweet, thou art weary.'
                 ' Not so Christ,
Whose mighty love of me sufficed
For Strength, Salvation, Eucharist.'

' Sweet, thou art footsore.'
                 'If I bleed,
His feet have bled; yea in my need
His Heart once bled for mine indeed.'

THE WORLD

' Sweet, thou art young.'
                 ' So He was young
Who for my sake in silence hung
Upon the Cross with Passion wrung.'

'Look   thou art fair.'
                 ' He was more fair
'T ᵃ n, Who deigned for me to wear
A   marred beyond compare.'

'And thou hast riches.'
                              'Daily bread:
All else is His: Who, living, dead,
For me lacked where to lay His Head.'

'And life is sweet.'
                          'It was not so
To Him, Whose Cup did overflow
With mine unutterable woe.'

THE DEVIL

'Thou drinkest deep.'
                              'When Christ would sup
He drained the dregs from out my cup:
So how should I be lifted up?'

'Thou shalt win Glory.'
                              'In the skies,
Lord Jesus, cover up mine eyes
Lest they should look on vanities.'

'Thou shalt have Knowledge.'
                                    'Helpless dust!
In thee, O Lord, I put my trust:
Answer Thou for me, Wise and Just.'

'And Might.' —
                    'Get thee behind me. Lord,
Who hast redeemed and not abhorred
My soul, oh keep it by Thy Word.'

TO THE END

There are lilies for her sisters —
    (Who so cold as they?) —
And heartsease for one I must not name
    When I am far away.
I shall pluck the lady lilies
    And fancy all the rest:

I shall pluck the bright-eyed heartsease
  For her sake I love the best:
As I wander on with weary feet
  Toward the twilight shadowy west.

  O bird that flyest eastward
  Unto that sunny land,
Oh wilt thou light on lilies white
  Beside her whiter hand?
  Soft summer wind that breathest
  Of perfumes and sweet spice,
Ah tell her what I dare not tell
  Of watchful waiting eyes,
Of love that yet may meet again
  In distant Paradise.

  I go from earth to heaven
  A dim uncertain road,
A houseless pilgrim through the world
  Unto a sure abode:
  While evermore an Angel
  Goes with me day and night,
  A ministering spirit
  From the land of light,
My holy fellow-servant sent
  To guide my steps aright.

  I wonder if the Angels
  Love with such love as ours,
If for each other's sake they pluck
  And keep eternal flowers.
  Alone I am and weary,
  Alone yet not alone:
Her soul talks with me by the way
  From tedious stone to stone,
A blessed Angel treads with me
  The awful paths unknown.

When will the long road end in rest
  The sick bird perch and brood?
When will my Guardian fold his wings
  At rest in the finished good?

Lulling, lulling me off to sleep:
  While Death's strong hand doth roll
  My sins behind his back,
  And my life up like a scroll,
Till through sleep I hear kind Angels
  Rejoicing at the goal.

If her spirit went before me
  Up from night to day,
It would pass me like the lightning
  That kindles on its way.
I should feel it like the lightning
  Flashing fresh from heaven:
I should long for heaven sevenfold more,
  Yea and sevenfold seven:
Should pray as I have not prayed before,
  And strive as I have not striven.

She will learn new love in heaven,
  Who is so full of love;
She will learn new depths of tenderness
  Who is tender like a dove.
  Her heart will no more sorrow,
  Her eyes will weep no more:
Yet it may be she will yearn
And look back from far before:
Lingering on the golden threshold
  And leaning from the door.

DREAM LAND

Where sunless rivers weep
  Their waves into the deep,
She sleeps a charmèd sleep:
  Awake her not.
Led by a single star,
She came from very far
To seek where shadows are
  Her pleasant lot.

She left the rosy morn,
She left the fields of corn,
For twilight cold and lorn
   And water springs.
Through sleep, as through a veil,
She sees the sky look pale,
And hears the nightingale
   That sadly sings.

Rest, rest, a perfect rest
Shed over brow and breast;
Her face is toward the west,
   The purple land.
She cannot see the grain
Ripening on hill and plain,
She cannot feel the rain
   Upon her hand.

Rest, rest, for evermore
Upon a mossy shore;
Rest, rest at the heart's core
   Till time shall cease:
Sleep that no pain shall wake;
Night that no morn shall break,
Till joy shall overtake
   Her perfect peace.

OLD AND NEW YEAR DITTIES

3

Passing away, saith the World, passing away:
   Chances, beauty, and youth, sapped day by day:
Thy life never continueth in one stay.
Is the eye waxen dim, is the dark hair changing to grey
That hath won neither laurel nor bay?
I shall clothe myself in Spring and bud in May:
Thou, root-stricken, shalt not rebuild thy decay
On my bosom for aye.
Then I answered: Yea.

✤ CHRISTINA ROSSETTI ✤

Passing away, saith my Soul, passing away:
With its burden of fear and hope, of labour and play,
Hearken what the past doth witness and say:
Rust in thy gold, a moth is in thine array,
A canker is in thy bud, thy leaf must decay.
At midnight, at cockcrow at morning, one certain day
Lo the Bridegroom shall come and shall not delay;
Watch thou and pray.
Then I answered: Yea.

Passing away, saith my God, passing away:
Winter passeth after the long delay:
New grapes on the vine, new figs on the tender spray,
Turtle calleth turtle in Heaven's May.
Though I tarry, wait for Me, trust Me, watch and pray:
Arise, come away, night is past and lo it is day,
My love, My sister, My spouse, thou shalt hear Me say.
Then I answered: Yea.

A BETTER RESURRECTION

I have no wit, no words, no tears;
   My heart within me like a stone
Is numbed too much for hopes or fears.
   Look right, look left, I dwell alone;
I lift mine eyes, but dimmed with grief
   No everlasting hills I see;
My life is in the falling leaf:
   O Jesus, quicken me.

My life is like a faded leaf,
   My harvest dwindled to a husk:
Truly my life is void and brief
   And tedious in the barren dusk;
My life is like a frozen thing,
   No bud nor greenness can I see;
Yet rise it shall — the sap of Spring;
   O Jesus, rise in me.

My life is like a broken bowl,
  A broken bowl that cannot hold
One drop of water for my soul
  Or cordial in the searching cold;
Cast in the fire the perished thing;
  Melt and remold it, till it be
A royal cup for Him, my King:
  O Jesus, drink of me.

UP–HILL

Does the road wind up-hill all the way?
  Yes, to the very end.
Will the day's journey take the whole long day?
  From morn to night, my friend.

But is there for the night a resting-place?
  A roof for when the slow dark hours begin.
May not the darkness hide it from my face?
  You cannot miss that inn.

Shall I meet other wayfarers at night?
  Those who have gone before.
Then must I knock, or call when just in sight?
  They will not keep you standing at that door.

Shall I find comfort, travel-sore and weak?
  Of labour you shall find the sum.
Will there be beds for me and all who seek?
  Yea, beds for all who come.

HEAVEN OVERARCHES

Heaven overarches earth and sea,
  Earth-sadness and sea-bitterness.
Heaven overarches you and me:
A little while and we shall be —
Please God — where there is no more sea
  Nor barren wilderness.

❖ CHRISTINA ROSSETTI ❖

Heaven overarches you and me
   And all earth's gardens and her graves.
Look up with me, until we see
The day break and the shadows flee.
What though to-night wrecks you and me
   If so to-morrow saves?

WILLIAM MORRIS
1834–1896

William Morris, the greatest of arts-craftsmen, was born at Walthamstow near London in 1834, the son of a prosperous billbroker. He was sent to school at Marlborough and later to Exeter College, Oxford. He came to the University with the purpose of taking holy orders but soon abandoned this idea. At Oxford the tide of the Tractarian Movement had sunk to a low ebb and the new enthusiasm for science and exact scholarship had not yet gained ground. At Exeter, Morris tells us, there was neither teaching nor discipline. But Morris was too energetic a character to waste his time in idleness. He read assiduously: the *Morte D'Arthur*, Carlyle, Kingsley, and Ruskin whose chapter on the nature of Gothic became a sort of gospel to him. He formed a close friendship with Burne-Jones and became the center of a little group of students more interested in literature and art than in the university curriculum. Before long he was himself writing verses to the delight of his friends and somewhat to his own amazement. 'If this is poetry,' he said, 'it is very easy to write.' There speaks the craftsman, for poetry throughout his life was to Morris one of the many arts which he practised with the ease and skill of a master.

Inheriting a considerable fortune when he came of age, he founded and endowed *The Oxford and Cambridge Magazine* to which he contributed a number of poems and stories and in which some of Rossetti's loveliest early work appeared. For by this time he had met Rossetti and had come completely under the spell of that dominating personality. He set himself to draw, to paint, to write, all more or less in the Pre-Raphaelite fashion. This is most plainly visible in his first volume, *The Defence of Guenevere* (1858). His marriage, the cares of a family, the founding of the famous firm of Morris and Company, artists and decorators, tended to draw him slowly away from Rossetti, and his second volume, *The*

Life and Death of Jason (1867), marked his complete independence.

From this time on Morris's life was uneventful but filled to overflowing with activity. He designed patterns for wallpaper and tapestry, rediscovered and practised old crafts of dyeing and weaving, and revived printing as a fine art in the beautiful books that issued from his Kelmscott Press. More and more dissatisfied with the conditions of modern industrialism, he became an active Socialist, trained himself to speak on streetcorners, founded the *Commonweal* as the organ of his party and wrote for it his socialistic romance, *The Dream of John Ball* and his vision of a utopian England, *News from Nowhere*. Driven out by envy and intrigue from the Socialist organization, he busied himself in his last years with a series of prose romances, a way of escape from a hostile world into the *Glittering Plain* and the *Wood beyond the World*. He died in 1896, someone said, simply of being William Morris and trying to pack into one life the work of half a dozen men. Poetry was only part of Morris's activity, but it was a very important part. *Jason* was followed in 1868–70 by a three-volume collection of tales in verse, *The Earthly Paradise*. Then came *Love is Enough* (1873), *Sigurd the Volsung* (1877), translations of old epics — the *Odyssey,* the *Aeneid* and *Beowulf,* and last of all his *Poems by the Way* (1891).

Morris is the sanest, simplest, and most virile character of his group of friends and fellow-workers, a burly, red blooded, vigorous Englishman. Delightful tales are told of his wild outbursts of temper, breaking of furniture, kicking in of doorpanels, followed by peals of Homeric laughter. He was very much in love with life, an apostle of joy. ' Art,' he said, ' is the expression of man's joy in labour.' Poetry was to him rather a delightful art than a message or a mission. He scoffed at the notion of poetic inspiration; ' If a man can't compose an epic while he is weaving tapestry, he had better shut up.' By universal consent he is the best teller of verse-tales since Chaucer, but even his best tales lack Chaucer's humour, Scott's vigour, and Byron's passion. His characters are, for the most part, figures in a decorative tapestry rather than creatures of flesh and blood. The charm of his tales lies in the telling, in the even flow of the verse and the atmosphere of other-worldliness which hangs about them. On the other hand there is in

Morris's early work, as in some of his latest, a sharp and even passionate realism that is absent in his longer poems. Arthur's Queen in *The Defence of Guenevere* and *King Arthur's Tomb* is a great and glorious lady very different from the reluctant, repentant sinner of Tennyson's *Idylls*. Such a little master-piece as *The Haystack in the Floods* shows plainly enough that, lover of all things medieval as he was, Morris had no illusions about them, but realized their cruelty as fully as he did their beauty. And in his *Sigurd* and his few Socialistic poems Morris reveals himself as something more than 'the idle singer of an empty day,' as a poet well aware of the tragic seriousness of life.

There is another side of Morris too often forgotten. He was a lover of nature as well as of art; he rejoiced above all things in the quiet beauty of the English countryside. The prologue and the interludes of *The Earthly Paradise* are full of little English landscapes painted with the tender realism of one who loved them well; and the landscapes of his romantic tales in prose and verse are always bits of England.

And finally Morris was a true singer. From the first 'grinds,' as his Oxford companions called them, to his last songs of labour, there rings a lyric note, often clear and fresh, some-times slow and sad, always a singer's voice. The song from *Ogier the Dane* has an Elizabethan lilt; the carol in *The Land East of the Sun* might have been sung by a band of medieval waits; *The Eve of Crecy* is a knightly song of love and fame. Joy in life; sorrow that life passes and love along with it; these are the notes most often struck in the lyrics of Morris.

Craftsman of verse, not, perhaps, one of the great poets, he left behind him a treasury of lovely things, old tales re-told with fresh beauty, pictures of his well-loved land, and a wealth of song — no mean bequest to posterity. The man, no doubt, was greater than his work in verse, but it will be a heavy loss to English-speaking men if ever the poetry of William Morris is neglected or forgotten.

❖ WILLIAM MORRIS ❖

THE EVE OF CRECY

Gold on her head, and gold on her feet,
  And gold where the hems of her kirtle meet,
And a golden girdle round my sweet; —
  Ah! qu'elle est belle La Marguerite.

Margaret's maids are fair to see,
Freshly dressed and pleasantly;
Margaret's hair falls down to her knee; —
  Ah! qu'elle est belle La Marguerite.

If I were rich I would kiss her feet,
I would kiss the place where the gold hems meet,
And the golden kirtle round my sweet —
  Ah! qu'elle est belle La Marguerite.

Ah me! I have never touch'd her hand;
When the arriere-ban goes through the land,
Six basnets under my pennon stand; —
  Ah! qu'elle est belle La Marguerite.

And many an one grins under his hood:
' Sir Lambert du Bois, with all his men good,
Has neither food nor firewood; ' —
  Ah! qu'elle est belle La Marguerite.

If I were rich I would kiss her feet,
And the golden girdle of my sweet,
And thereabouts where the gold hems meet; —
  Ah! qu'elle est belle La Marguerite.

Yet even now it is good to think,
While my few poor varlets grumble and drink
In my desolate hall, where the fires sink, —
  Ah! qu'elle est belle La Marguerite.

Of Margaret sitting glorious there,
In glory of gold and glory of hair,
And glory of glorious face most fair; —
  Ah! qu'elle est belle La Marguerite.

Likewise to-night I make good cheer,
Because this battle draweth near:
For what have I to lose or fear? —
 Ah! qu'elle est belle La Marguerite.

For, look you, my horse is good to prance
A right fair measure in this war-dance,
Before the eyes of Philip of France; —
 Ah! qu'elle est belle La Marguerite.

And sometime it may hap, perdie,
While my new towers stand up three and three,
And my hall gets painted fair to see —
 Ah! qu'elle est belle La Marguerite.

That folks may say: ' Times change, by the rood,
For Lambert, banneret of the wood,
Has heaps of food and firewood; —
 Ah! qu'elle est belle La Marguerite.

' And wonderful eyes, too, under the hood
Of a damsel of right noble blood: '
St. Ives, for Lambert of the Wood! —
 Ah! qu'elle est belle La Marguerite.

THE GILLIFLOWER OF GOLD

A golden gilliflower to-day
I wore upon my helm alway,
And won the prize of this tourney.
 Hah! hah! la belle jaune giroflée.

However well Sir Giles might sit,
His sun was weak to wither it;
Lord Miles's blood was dew on it:
 Hah! hah! la belle jaune giroflée.

Although my spear in splinters flew,
From John's steel-coat, my eye was true;
I wheel'd about, and cried for you,
 Hah! hah! la belle jaune giroflée.

Yea, do not doubt my heart was good,
Though my sword flew like rotten wood,
To shout, although I scarcely stood,
 Hah! hah! la belle jaune giroflée.

My hand was steady too, to take
My axe from round my neck, and break
John's steel-coat up for my love's sake.
 Hah! hah! la belle jaune giroflée.

When I stood in my tent again,
Arming afresh, I felt a pain
Take hold of me, I was so fain —
 Hah! hah! la belle jaune giroflée.

To hear ' *Honneur aux fils des preux!* '
Right in my ears again, and shew
The gilliflower blossomed new.
 Hah! hah! la belle jaune giroflée.

The Sieur Guillaume against me came,
His tabard bore three points of flame
From a red heart: with little blame —
 Hah! hah! la belle jaune giroflée.

Our tough spears crackled up like straw;
He was the first to turn and draw
His sword, that had nor speck nor flaw, —
 Hah! hah! la belle jaune giroflée.

But I felt weaker than a maid,
And my brain, dizzied and afraid,
Within my helm a fierce tune play'd, —
 Hah! hah! la belle jaune giroflée.

Until I thought of your dear head,
Bow'd to the gilliflower bed,
The yellow flowers stain'd with red; —
 Hah! hah! la belle jaune giroflée.

Crash! how the swords met, ' *giroflée!* '
The fierce tune in my helm would play,
' *La belle! la belle! jaune giroflée!* '
    Hah! hah! la belle jaune giroflée.

Once more the great swords met again,
' *La belle! la belle!* ' but who fell then?
Le Sieur Guillaume, who struck down ten; —
    Hah! hah! la belle jaune giroflée.

And as with mazed and unarm'd face
Toward my own crown and the Queen's place,
They led me at a gentle pace —
    Hah! hah! la belle jaune giroflée.

I almost saw your quiet head
Bow'd o'er the gilliflower bed,
The yellow flowers stain'd with red.
    Hah! hah! la belle jaune giroflée.

THE JUDGMENT OF GOD

Swerve to the left, son Roger,' he said,
    ' When you catch his eyes through the helmet-slit,
Swerve to the left, then out at his head,
    And the Lord God give you joy of it! '

The blue owls on my father's hood
    Were a little dimm'd as I turn'd away;
This giving up of blood for blood
    Will finish here somehow to-day.

So — when I walk'd out from the tent,
    Their howling almost blinded me;
Yet for all that I was not bent
    By any shame. Hard by, the sea

Made a noise like the aspens where
    We did that wrong, but now the place
Is very pleasant, and the air
    Blows cool on any passer's face.

And all the wrong is gather'd now
    Into the circle of these lists —
Yea, howl out, butchers! tell me how
    His hands were cut off at the wrists;

And how Lord Roger bore his face
    A league above his spear-point, high
Above the owls, to that strong place
    Among the waters — yea, yea, cry:

'What a brave champion we have got!
    Sir Oliver, the flower of all
The Hainault knights.' The day being hot,
    He sat beneath a broad white pall.

White linen over all his steel;
    What a good knight he look'd! his sword
Laid thwart his knees; he liked to feel
    Its steadfast edge clear as his word.

And he look'd solemn; how his love
    Smiled whitely on him, sick with fear!
How all the ladies up above
    Twisted their pretty hands! so near

The fighting was — Ellayne! Ellayne!
    They cannot love like you can, who
Would burn your hands off, if that pain
    Could win a kiss — am I not true

To you for ever? therefore I
    Do not fear death or anything;
If I should limp home wounded, why
    While I lay sick you would but sing,

And soothe me into quiet sleep.
    If they spat on the recreant knight,
Threw stones at him, and cursed him deep,
    Why then — what then; your hand would light

So gently on his drawn-up face,
　And you would kiss him, and in soft
Cool scented clothes would lap him, pace
　The quiet room and weep oft, — oft

Would turn and smile, and brush his cheek
　With your sweet chin and mouth; and in
The order'd garden you would seek
　The biggest roses — any sin.

And these say: ' No more now my knight,
　Or God's knight any longer ' — you,
Being than they so much more white,
　So much more pure and good and true,

Will cling to me for ever — there,
　Is not that wrong turn'd right at last
Through all these years, and I wash'd clean?
　Say, yea, Ellayne; the time is past,

Since on that Christmas-day last year
　Up to your feet the fire crept,
And the smoke through the brown leaves sere
　Blinded your dear eyes that you wept;

Was it not I that caught you then,
　And kiss'd you on the saddle bow?
Did not the blue owl mark the men
　Whose spears stood like the corn a-row?

This Oliver is a right good knight,
　And must needs beat me, as I fear,
Unless I catch him in the fight,
　My father's crafty way — John, here!

Bring up the men from the south gate,
　To help me if I fall or win,
For even if I beat, their hate
　Will grow to more than this mere grin.

✤ WILLIAM MORRIS ✤

THE LITTLE TOWER

Up and away through the drifting rain!
  Let us ride to the Little Tower again,

Up and away from the council-board!
Do on the hauberk, gird on the sword.

The king is blind with gnashing his teeth,
Change gilded scabbard to leather sheath:

Though our arms are wet with the slanting rain,
This is joy to ride to my love again:

I laugh in his face when he bids me yield;
Who knows one field from the other field,

For the grey rain driveth all astray? —
Which way through the floods, good carle, I pray?

' The left side yet! the left side yet!
Till your hand strikes on the bridge parapet.'

' Yea so: the causeway holdeth good
Under the water?' ' Hard as wood;

Right away to the uplands; speed, good knight.'
Seven hours yet before the light.

Shake the wet off on the upland road;
My tabard has grown a heavy load.

What matter? up and down hill after hill;
Dead grey night for five hours still.

The hill-road droppeth lower again,
Lower, down to the poplar plain.

No furlong farther for us to-night,
The Little Tower draweth in sight;

They are ringing the bells, and the torches glare,
Therefore the roofs of wet slate stare.

There she stands, and her yellow hair slantingly
Drifts the same way that the rain goes by.

Who will be faithful to us to-day,
With little but hard glaive-strokes for pay?

The grim king fumes at the council-board:
' Three more days, and then the sword;

Three more days, and my sword through his head;
And above his white brows, pale and dead,

A paper crown on the top of the spire;
And for her the stake and the witches' fire.'

Therefore though it be long ere day,
Take axe and pick and spade, I pray.

Break the dams down all over the plain:
God send us three more days such rain:

Block all the upland roads with trees;
The Little Tower with no great ease

Is won, I warrant; bid them bring
Much sheep and oxen, everything

The spits are wont to turn with; wine
And wheaten bread, that we may dine

In plenty each day of the siege;
Good friends, ye know me no hard liege;

My lady is right fair, see ye!
Pray God to keep you frank and free.

Love Isabeau, keep goodly cheer;
The Little Tower will stand well here

Many a year when we are dead,
And over it our green and red,
Barred with the Lady's golden head;
From mere old age when we are dead.

SHAMEFUL DEATH

There were four of us about that bed;
 The mass-priest knelt at the side,
I and his mother stood at the head,
 Over his feet lay the bride;
We were quite sure that he was dead,
 Though his eyes were open wide.

He did not die in the night,
 He did not die in the day,
But in the morning twilight
 His spirit passed away,
When neither sun nor moon was bright,
 And the trees were merely grey.

He was not slain with the sword,
 Knight's axe, or the knightly spear,
Yet spoke he never a word
 After he came in here;
I cut away the cord
 From the neck of my brother dear.

He did not strike one blow,
 For the recreants came behind,
In a place where the hornbeams grow,
 A path right hard to find,
For the hornbeam boughs swing so
 That the twilight makes it blind.

They lighted a great torch then,
 When his arms were pinion'd fast,
Sir John the knight of the Fen,
 Sir Guy of the Dolorous Blast,
With knights threescore and ten,
 Hung brave Lord Hugh at last.

I am threescore and ten,
  And my hair is all turn'd grey,
But I met Sir John of the Fen,
  Long ago on a summer day,
And am glad to think of the moment when
  I took his life away.

I am threescore and ten,
  And my strength is mostly pass'd,
But long ago I and my men,
  When the sky was overcast,
And the smoke roll'd over the reeds of the fen,
  Slew Guy of the Dolorous Blast.

And now, knights all of you,
  I pray you pray for Sir Hugh,
A good knight and a true,
  And for Alice, his wife, pray too.

THE HAYSTACK IN THE FLOODS

Had she come all the way for this,
  To part at last without a kiss?
Yea, had she borne the dirt and rain
That her own eyes might see him slain
Beside the haystack in the floods?

  Along the dripping leafless woods,
The stirrup touching either shoe,
She rode astride as troopers do;
With kirtle kilted to her knee,
To which the mud splash'd wretchedly;
And the wet dripp'd from every tree
Upon her head and heavy hair,
And on her eyelids broad and fair;
The tears and rain ran down her face.
By fits and starts they rode apace,
And very often was his place
Far off from her; he had to ride
Ahead, to see what might betide

When the roads cross'd; and sometimes, when
There rose a murmuring from his men,
Had to turn back with promises;
Ah me! she had but little ease;
And often for pure doubt and dread
She sobb'd, made giddy in the head
By the swift riding; while, for cold,
Her slender fingers scarce could hold
The wet reins; yea, and scarcely, too,
She felt the foot within her shoe
Against the stirrup: all for this,
To part at last without a kiss
Beside the haystack in the floods.

For when they near'd that old soak'd hay,
They saw across the only way
That Judas, Godmar, and the three
Red running lions dismally
Grinn'd from his pennon, under which,
In one straight line along the ditch,
They counted thirty heads.
                                    So then,
While Robert turn'd round to his men,
She saw at once the wretched end,
And, stooping down, tried hard to rend
Her coif the wrong way from her head,
And hid her eyes; while Robert said:
'Nay, love, 'tis scarcely two to one,
At Poictiers where we made them run
So fast — why, sweet my love, good cheer.
The Gascon frontier is so near,
Nought after this.'
                              But ' O ' she said,
' My God! my God! I have to tread
The long way back without you; then
The court at Paris; those six men;
The gratings of the Chatelet;
The swift Seine on some rainy day
Like this, and people standing by,
And laughing, while my weak hands try
To recollect how strong men swim.

111

All this, or else a life with him,
For which I should be damned at last,
Would God that this next hour were past! '

He answered not, but cried his cry,
' St. George for Marny! ' cheerily;
And laid his hand upon her rein.
Alas! no man of all his train
Gave back that cheery cry again;
And, while for rage his thumb beat fast
Upon his sword-hilts, someone cast
About his neck a kerchief long,
And bound him.

        Then they went along
To Godmar; who said: ' Now, Jehane,
Your lover's life is on the wane
So fast, that, if this very hour
You yield not as my paramour,
He will not see the rain leave off —
Nay, keep your tongue from gibe and scoff,
Sir Robert, or I slay you now.'

She laid her hand upon her brow,
Then gazed upon the palm, as though
She thought her forehead bled, and — ' No.'
She said, and turn'd her head away,
As there were nothing else to say,
And everything were settled: red
Grew Godmar's face from chin to head:
' Jehane, on yonder hill there stands
My castle, guarding well my lands:
What hinders me from taking you,
And doing that I list to do
To your fair willful body, while
Your knight lies dead? '

        A wicked smile
Wrinkled her face, her lips grew thin,
A long way out she thrust her chin:
' You know that I should strangle you
While you were sleeping; or bite through

Your throat, by God's help — ah! ' she said,
' Lord Jesus, pity your poor maid!
For in such wise they hem me in,
I cannot choose but sin and sin,
Whatever happens: yet I think
They could not make me eat or drink,
And so should I just reach my rest.'
' Nay, if you do not my behest,
O Jehane! though I love you well,'
Said Godmar, ' would I fail to tell
All that I know? ' ' Foul lies,' she said.
' Eh? lies, my Jehane? by God's head,
At Paris folks would deem them true!
Do you know, Jehane, they cry for you,
" Jehane the brown! Jehane the brown!
Give us Jehane to burn or drown! " —
Eh — gag me Robert! — sweet my friend,
This were indeed a piteous end
For those long fingers, and long feet,
And long neck, and smooth shoulders sweet;
An end that few men would forget
That saw it — So, an hour yet:
Consider, Jehane, which to take
Of life or death! '

So, scarce awake,
Dismounting, did she leave that place,
And totter some yards: with her face
Turn'd upward to the sky she lay,
Her head on a wet heap of hay,
And fell asleep: and while she slept,
And did not dream, the minutes crept
Round to the twelve again; but she,
Being waked at last, sigh'd quietly,
And strangely childlike came, and said:
' I will not.' Straightway Godmar's head,
As though it hung on strong wires, turn'd
Most sharply round, and his face burn'd.

For Robert — both his eyes were dry,
He could not weep, but gloomily

He seem'd to watch the rain; yea, too,
His lips were firm; he tried once more
To touch her lips; she reach'd out, sore
And vain desire so tortured them,
The poor grey lips, and now the hem
Of his sleeve brush'd them.

                With a start
Up Godmar rose, thrust them apart;
From Robert's throat he loosed the bands
Of silk and mail; with empty hands
Held out, she stood and gazed, and saw,
The long bright blade without a flaw
Glide out from Godmar's sheath, his hand
In Robert's hair; she saw him bend
Back Robert's head; she saw him send
The thin steel down; the blow told well,
Right backward the knight Robert fell,
And moan'd as dogs do, being half dead,
Unwitting, as I deem: so then
Godmar turn'd grinning to his men,
Who ran, some five or six, and beat
His head to pieces at their feet.

Then Godmar turn'd again and said:
' So, Jehane, the first fitte is read!
Take note, my lady, that your way
Lies backward to the Chatelet! '
She shook her head·and gazed awhile
At her cold hands with a rueful smile,
As though this thing had made her mad.

This was the parting that they had
Beside the haystack in the floods.

THE EARTHLY PARADISE

AN APOLOGY

Of Heaven or Hell I have no power to sing,
    I cannot ease the burden of your fears,
Or make quick-coming death a little thing,
Or bring again the pleasure of past years,

Nor for my words shall ye forget your tears,
Or hope again for aught that I can say,
The idle singer of an empty day.

But rather, when aweary of your mirth,
From full hearts still unsatisfied ye sigh,
And, feeling kindly unto all the earth,
Grudge every minute as it passes by,
Made the more mindful that the sweet days die —
— Remember me a little then I pray,
The idle singer of an empty day.

The heavy trouble, the bewildering care
That weighs us down who live and earn our bread,
These idle verses have no power to bear;
So let me sing of names remembered,
Because they, living not, can ne'er be dead,
Or long time take their memory quite away
From us poor singers of an empty day.

Dreamer of dreams, born out of my due time,
Why should I strive to set the crooked straight?
Let it suffice me that my murmuring rhyme
Beats with light wing against the ivory gate,
Telling a tale not too importunate
To those who in the sleepy region stay,
Lulled by the singer of an empty day.

Folk say, a wizard to a northern king
At Christmas-tide such wondrous things did show,
That through one window men beheld the spring,
And through another saw the summer glow,
And through a third the fruited vines a-row,
While still, unheard, but in its wonted way,
Piped the drear wind of that December day.

So with this Earthly Paradise it is,
If ye will read aright, and pardon me,
Who strive to build a shadowy isle of bliss
Midmost the beating of the steely sea,
Where tossed about all hearts of men must be;
Whose ravening monsters mighty men shall slay,
Not the poor singer of an empty day.

MARCH

Slayer of the winter, art thou here again?
   O welcome, thou that bring'st the summer nigh!
The bitter wind makes not thy victory vain,
Nor will we mock thee for thy faint blue sky.
Welcome, O March! whose kindly days and dry
Make April ready for the throstle's song,
Thou first redresser of the winter's wrong!

Yea, welcome March! and though I die ere June,
Yet for the hope of life I give thee praise,
Striving to swell the burden of the tune
That even now I hear thy brown birds raise,
Unmindful of the past or coming days;
Who sing: ' O joy! a new year is begun:
What happiness to look upon the sun! '

   Ah, what begetteth all this storm of bliss
But Death himself, who crying solemnly,
E'en from the heart of sweet Forgetfulness,
Bids us, ' Rejoice, lest pleasureless ye die.
Within a little time must ye go by.
Stretch forth your open hands, and while ye live
Take all the gifts that Death and Life may give.'

JUNE

O June, O June, that we desired so,
   Wilt thou not make us happy on this day?
Across the river thy soft breezes blow
Sweet with the scent of beanfields far away,
Above our heads rustle the aspens grey,
Calm is the sky with harmless clouds beset,
No thought of storm the morning vexes yet.

See, we have left our hopes and fears behind
To give our very hearts up unto thee;
What better place than this, then, could we find
By this sweet stream that knows not of the sea,

That guesses not the city's misery,
This little stream whose hamlets scarce have names,
This far-off, lonely mother of the Thames?

Here then, O June, thy kindness will we take;
And if indeed but pensive men we seem,
What should we do? thou wouldst not have us wake
From out the arms of this rare happy dream
And wish to leave the murmur of the stream,
The rustling boughs, the twitter of the birds,
And all thy thousand peaceful happy words.

OCTOBER

O love, turn from the unchanging sea, and gaze
Down these grey slopes upon the year grown old,
A-dying mid the autumn-scented haze,
That hangeth o'er the hollow in the wold,
Where the wind-bitten ancient elms enfold
Grey church, long barn, orchard, and red-roofed stead,
Wrought in dead days for men a long while dead.

Come down, O love; may not our hands still meet,
Since still we live to-day, forgetting June,
Forgetting May, deeming October sweet —
— O hearken, hearken! through the afternoon,
The grey tower sings a strange old tinkling tune!
Sweet, sweet, and sad, the toiling year's last breath,
Too satiate of life to strive with death.

And we too — will it not be soft and kind,
That rest from life, from patience and from pain;
That rest from bliss we know not when we find;
That rest from Love which ne'er the end can gain? —
— Hark, how the tune swells, that erewhile did wane!
Look up, love! — ah, cling close and never move!
How can I have enough of life and love?

SONG FROM
THE STORY OF CUPID AND PSYCHE

O pensive, tender maid, downcast and shy,
  Who turnest pale e'en at the name of love,
And with flushed face must pass the elm-tree by,
Ashamed to hear the passionate grey dove
Moan to his mate, thee too the god shall move,
Thee too the maidens shall ungird one day,
And with thy girdle put thy shame away.

   What then, and shall white winter ne'er be done
Because the glittering frosty morn is fair?
Because against the early-setting sun
Bright show the gilded boughs, though waste and bare?
Because the robin singeth free from care?
Ah! these are memories of a better day
When on earth's face the lips of summer lay.

   Come then, beloved one, for such as thee
Love loveth, and their hearts he knoweth well,
Who hoard their moments of felicity,
As misers hoard the medals that they tell,
Lest on the earth but paupers they should dwell:
' We hide our love to bless another day;
The world is hard, youth passes quick,' they say.

   Ah, little ones, but if ye could forget
Amidst your outpoured love that you must die,
Then ye, my servants, were death's conquerors yet,
And love to you should be eternity,
How quick soever might the days go by:
Yes, ye are made immortal on the day
Ye cease the dusty grains of time to weigh.

   Thou hearkenest, love? O, make no semblance then
That thou art loved, but as thy custom is
Turn thy grey eyes away from eyes of men.
With hands down-dropped, that tremble with thy bliss,
With hidden eyes, take thy first lover's kiss;
Call this eternity which is to-day,
Nor dream that this our love can pass away.

SONG FROM *OGIER THE DANE*

Hæc

In the white-flowered hawthorn brake,
Love, be merry for my sake;
Twine the blossoms in my hair,
Kiss me where I am most fair —
Kiss me, love! for who knoweth
What thing cometh after death?

Ille

Nay, the garlanded gold hair
Hides thee where thou art most fair;
Hides the rose-tinged hills of snow —
Ay, sweet love, I have thee now!
Kiss me, love! for who knoweth
What thing cometh after death?

Hæc

Shall we weep for a dead day,
Or set Sorrow in our way?
Hidden by my golden hair,
Wilt thou weep that sweet days wear?
Kiss me, love! for who knoweth
What thing cometh after death?

Ille

Weep, O love, the days that flit,
Now, while I can feel thy breath;
Then may I remember it
Sad and old, and near my death.
Kiss me, love! for who knoweth
What thing cometh after death?

SONG FROM *THE LAND EAST OF THE SUN AND WEST OF THE MOON*

Outlanders, whence come ye last?
The snow in the street and the wind on the door.
Through what green seas and great have ye passed?
Minstrels and maids, stand forth on the floor.

From far away, O masters mine,
The snow in the street and the wind on the door.
We come to bear you goodly wine,
Minstrels and maids, stand forth on the floor.

From far away we come to you,
The snow in the street and the wind on the door.
To tell of great tidings strange and true.
Minstrels and maids, stand forth on the floor.

News, news of the Trinity,
The snow in the street and the wind on the door.
And Mary and Joseph from over the sea!
Minstrels and maids, stand forth on the floor.

For as we wandered far and wide,
The snow in the street and the wind on the door.
What hap do ye deem there should us betide!
Minstrels and maids, stand forth on the floor.

Under a bent when the night was deep,
The snow in the street and the wind on the door.
There lay three shepherds tending their sheep.
Minstrels and maids, stand forth on the floor.

'O ye shepherds, what have ye seen,
The snow in the street and the wind on the door.
To slay your sorrow, and heal your teen?'
Minstrels and maids, stand forth on the floor.

'In an ox-stall this night we saw,
The snow in the street and the wind on the door.
A babe and a maid without a flaw.
Minstrels and maids, stand forth on the floor.

'There was an old man there beside,
The snow in the street and the wind on the door.
His hair was white and his hood was wide.
Minstrels and maids, stand forth on the floor.

And as we gazed this thing upon,
The snow in the street and the wind on the door.
Those twain knelt down to the Little One.
Minstrels and maids, stand forth on the floor.

And a marvellous song we straight did hear,
The snow in the street and the wind on the door.
That slew our sorrow and healed our care.'
Minstrels and maids, stand forth on the floor.

News of a fair and a marvellous thing,
The snow in the street and the wind on the door.
Nowell, nowell, nowell, we sing!
Minstrels and maids, stand forth on the floor.

SONG FROM
THE STORY OF ACONTIUS AND CYDIPPE

Fair is the night and fair the day,
  Now April is forgot of May,
Now into June May falls away;
Fair day, fair night. O give me back
The tide that all fair things did lack
Except my love, except my sweet!

  Blow back, O wind! thou art not kind,
Though thou art sweet; thou hast no mind
Her hair about my sweet to wind;
O flowery sward, though thou art bright,
I praise thee not for thy delight,
Thou hast not kissed her silver feet.

  Thou know'st her not, O rustling tree,
What dost thou then to shadow me,
Whose shade her breast did never see?
O flowers, in vain ye bow adown!
Ye have not felt her odorous gown
Brush past your heads my lips to meet.

  Flow on, great river — thou mayst deem
That far away, a summer stream,
Thou sawest her limbs amidst thee gleam,

121

And kissed her foot, and kissed her knee,
Yet get thee swift unto the sea!
With nought of truth thou wilt me greet.

And thou that men call by my name,
O helpless one, hast thou no shame
That thou must even look the same,
As while agone, as while agone,
When thou and she were left alone,
And hands, and lips, and tears did meet?

Grow weak and pine, lie down to die,
O body in thy misery,
Because short time and sweet goes by;
O foolish heart, how weak thou art!
Break, break, because thou needs must part
From thine own love, from thine own sweet!

SONG FROM *THE HILL OF VENUS*

Before our lady came on earth
Little there was of joy or mirth;
About the borders of the sea
The sea-folk wandered heavily;
About the wintry river side
The weary fishers would abide.

Alone within the weaving-room
The girls would sit before the loom,
And sing no song, and play no play;
Alone from dawn to hot mid-day,
From mid-day unto evening,
The men afield would work, nor sing,
'Mid weary thoughts of man and God,
Before thy feet the wet ways trod.

Unkissed the merchant bore his care,
Unkissed the knights went out to war,
Unkissed the mariner came home,
Unkissed the minstrel men did roam.

Or in the stream the maids would stare,
Nor know why they were made so fair;
Their yellow locks, their bosoms white,
Their limbs well wrought for all delight,
Seemed foolish things that waited death,
As hopeless as the flowers beneath
The weariness of unkissed feet:
No life was bitter then, or sweet.

Therefore, O Venus, well may we
Praise the green ridges of the sea
O'er which, upon a happy day,
Thou cam'st to take our shame away.
Well may we praise the curdling foam
Amidst the which thy feet did bloom,
Flowers of the gods; the yellow sand
They kissed atwixt the sea and land;
The bee-beset, ripe-seeded grass,
Through which thy fine limbs first did pass;
The purple-dusted butterfly,
First blown against thy quivering thigh;
The first red rose that touched thy side,
And over-blown and fainting died;
The flickering of the orange shade,
Where first in sleep thy limbs were laid;
The happy day's sweet life and death,
Whose air first caught thy balmy breath —
Yea, all these things well praised may be,
But with what words shall we praise thee —
O Venus, O thou love alive,
Born to give peace to souls that strive?

FROM *THE LIFE AND DEATH OF JASON*

I know a little garden-close
Set thick with lily and red rose,
Where I would wander if I might
From dewy dawn to dewy night,
And have one with me wandering.

And though within it no birds sing,
And though no pillared house is there,
And though the apple boughs are bare
Of fruit and blossom, would to God,
Her feet upon the green grass trod,
And I beheld them as before.

There comes a murmur from the shore,
And in the close two fair streams are,
Drawn from the purple hills afar,
Drawn down unto the restless sea;
The hills whose flowers ne'er fed the bee,
The shore no ship has ever seen,
Still beaten by the billows green,
Whose murmur comes unceasingly
Unto the place for which I cry.

For which I cry both day and night,
For which I let slip all delight,
That maketh me both deaf and blind,
Careless to win, unskilled to find,
And quick to lose what all men seek.

Yet tottering as I am, and weak,
Still have I left a little breath
To seek within the jaws of death
An entrance to that happy place,
To seek the unforgotten face
Once seen, once kissed, once reft from me
Anigh the murmuring of the sea.

THE VOICE OF TOIL

I heard men saying, Leave hope and praying,
All days shall be as all have been;
To-day and to-morrow bring fear and sorrow,
The never-ending toil between.

When Earth was younger mid toil and hunger,
In hope we strove, and our hands were strong;
Then great men led us, with words they fed us,
And bade us right the earthly wrong.

❖ WILLIAM MORRIS ❖

Go read in story their deeds and glory,
Their names amidst the nameless dead;
Turn then from lying to us slow-dying
In that good world to which they led;

Where fast and faster our iron master,
The thing we made, forever drives,
Bids us grind treasure and fashion pleasure
For other hopes and other lives.

Where home is a hovel and dull we grovel,
Forgetting that the world is fair;
Where no babe we cherish, lest its very soul perish;
Where mirth is crime, and love a snare.

Who now shall lead us, what God shall heed us
As we lie in the hell our hands have won?
For us are no rulers but fools and befoolers,
The great are fallen, the wise men gone.

I heard men saying, Leave tears and praying,
The sharp knife heedeth not the sheep;
Are we not stronger than the rich and the wronger,
When day breaks over dreams and sleep?

Come, shoulder to shoulder, ere the world grows older!
Help lies in naught but thee and me;
Hope is before us, the long years that bore us
Bore leaders more than men may be.

Let dead hearts tarry and trade and marry,
And trembling nurse their dreams of mirth,
While we the living our lives are giving
To bring the bright new world to birth.

Come, shoulder to shoulder ere Earth grows older!
The Cause spreads over land and sea;
Now the world shaketh, and fear awaketh,
And joy at last for thee and me.

THE DAY IS COMING

Come hither, lads, and hearken,
    for a tale there is to tell,
Of the wonderful days a-coming, when all
    shall be better than well.

And the tale shall be told of a country,
    a land in the midst of the sea,
And folk shall call it England
    in the days that are going to be.

There more than one in a thousand
    in the days that are yet to come,
Shall have some hope of the morrow,
    some joy of the ancient home.

For then laugh not, but listen
    to this strange tale of mine,
All folk that are in England
    shall be better lodged than swine.

Then a man shall work and bethink him,
    and rejoice in the deeds of his hand,
Nor yet come home in the even
    , too faint and weary to stand.

Men in that time a-coming
    shall work and have no fear
For to-morrow's lack of earning
    and the hunger-wolf anear.

I tell you this for a wonder,
    that no man then shall be glad
Of his fellow's fall and mishap
    to snatch at the work he had.

For that which the worker winneth
    shall then be his indeed,
Nor shall half be reaped for nothing
    by him that sowed no seed.

❖ WILLIAM MORRIS ❖

O strange new wonderful justice!
  but for whom shall we gather the gain?
For ourselves and for each of our fellows,
  and no hand shall labour in vain.

Then all Mine and all Thine shall be Ours,
  and no more shall any man crave
For riches that serve for nothing
  but to fetter a friend for a slave.

And what wealth then shall be left us
  when none shall gather gold
To buy his friend in the market,
  and pinch and pine the sold?

Nay, what save the lovely city,
  and the little house on the hill,
And the wastes and the woodland beauty,
  and the happy fields we till;

And the homes of ancient stories,
  the tombs of the mighty dead;
And the wise men seeking out marvels,
  and the poet's teeming head;

And the painter's hand of wonder;
  and the marvellous fiddle-bow,
And the banded choirs of music:
  all those that do and know.

For all these shall be ours and all men's,
  nor shall any lack a share
Of the toil and the gain of living
  in the days when the world grows fair.

Ah! such are the days that shall be!
  But what are the deeds of to-day
In the days of the years we dwell in,
  that wear our lives away?

Why, then, and for what are we waiting?
    There are three words to speak;
WE WILL IT, and what is the foeman
    but the dream-strong wakened and weak?

O why and for what are we waiting?
    while our brothers droop and die,
And on every wind of the heavens
    a wasted life goes by.

How long shall they reproach us
    where crowd on crowd they dwell,
Poor ghosts of the wicked city,
    the gold-crushed hungry hell?

Through squalid life they laboured,
    in sordid grief they died,
Those sons of a mighty mother,
    those props of England's pride.

They are gone; there is none can undo it,
    nor save our souls from the curse;
But many a million cometh,
    and shall they be better or worse?

It is we must answer and hasten,
    and open wide the door
For the rich man's hurrying terror,
    and the slow-foot hope of the poor.

Yea, the voiceless wrath of the wretched,
    and their unlearned discontent,
We must give it voice and wisdom
    till the waiting-tide be spent.

Come, then, since all things call us,
    the living and the dead,
And o'er the weltering tangle
    a glimmering light is shed.

❖ WILLIAM MORRIS ❖

Come, then, let us cast off fooling,
    and put by ease and rest,
For the Cause alone is worthy
    till the good days bring the best.

Come, join in the only battle
    wherein no man can fail,
Where whoso fadeth and dieth,
    yet his deed shall still prevail.

Ah! come, cast off all fooling,
    for this, at least, we know:
That the Dawn and the Day is coming,
    and forth the Banners go.

ALGERNON CHARLES SWINBURNE
1837–1909

Algernon Charles Swinburne, ' the singing rebel ' was born in London in 1837. His ancestry on both sides was aristocratic; the Swinburnes had in past centuries given, to use the poet's words, ' their blood like water and their lands like dust for the Stuarts.' His grandfather Sir John, born and brought up in France, was an outspoken republican and a personal friend of Mirabeau. From his gentle mother Swinburne inherited his love of books and in particular his early partiality for French and Italian poetry.

A slight and delicate child he was none the less a very active one; ' that lad is a flame of fire,' said an early observer. He was a daring swimmer, ' the salt of the sea must have been in my veins before I was born,' he said, and a reckless rider over the Northumbrian moors. Throughout his life a highly nervous organization found outlet in restless bodily activity.

His formal education began at Eton at the age of twelve, where he read prodigiously and laid the foundation of that knowledge of literature, ancient and modern, that was to make him after Milton the most ' bookish ' of English poets. From Eton he went to Balliol at Oxford. He seems to have been far from happy at college. He neglected his studies to work at interminable imitations of English poets and dramatists: he offended convention by his outspoken republicanism, and angered the authorities by his irregular habits. At last on the advice of Jowett he was withdrawn from college in order, Jowett said, that Balliol might not incur the disgrace of expelling a poet as University College had once expelled Shelley. One thing at least Oxford gave him, a group of friends who stimulated and enriched his growing genius; he was intimate with Walter Pater and Addington Symonds, and came into the circle of Morris, Burne-Jones and Rossetti.

Shortly after leaving Oxford he published in 1860 his first work, two poetic plays, *The Queen Mother and Rosamond,* dedicated to Dante Gabriel Rossetti. It fell quite still-born from the press. On a trip to Italy in 1864 he met one of the gods of his hero-worship, Walter Savage Landor, and a year after his return he dedicated to Landor his *Atalanta in Calydon,* perhaps the finest reproduction in English of the form, if not the spirit, of Greek tragedy. *Atalanta* gained immediate recognition, if no great popular success; the brilliance of the verse seems to have blinded readers and reviewers to the rebellious spirit of the play.

The appearance of *Poems and Ballads,* 1866, marks a critical point in Swinburne's life. So far he had been a young poet whose genius, recognized by a small circle of friends, was hidden from the world; overnight he became the most talked-of, not to say notorious, figure in British letters. This was due not so much to the book itself as to a furious review of an advance copy. Curiously enough, considering that the reviewer was the liberal-radical, John Morley, little attention was paid to the revolutionary poems, but unstinted vials of wrath were poured out on those which dealt with abnormal phases of sex, poems which could only proceed, the reviewer asserted, 'from a mind all aflame with the feverish carnality of a school-boy,' and he stigmatized the writer as ' the libidinous leader of a pack of satyrs,' mocking and jeering ' like an unclean fiery imp from the pit.' Swinburne's publisher, panic-stricken by the outcry, at once withdrew the book from circulation, and it took all the efforts of the poet's influential friends to induce another bookseller to risk a public prosecution. Swinburne himself professed profound indifference to the censure of professional and prudish moralists, but the harm was done, and for years to come the name of Swinburne was to all sober-minded Englishmen a synonym for a scandalous sensualist. On the other hand as the book gained circulation it was received with rapture by the younger generation; ' we all went about,' said a poet in later years, ' chanting to one another these new astonishing melodies.'

The next ten or twelve years of Swinburne's life were crowded with work. *Songs before Sunrise,* his noblest single book, appeared in 1871 and marked his shift from the erotic themes of *Poems and Ballads* to the cause of human liberty. It was followed by *Bothwell* (1874), *Erectheus* (1875) another Greek tragedy in English verse, and by the second series of *Poems and Ballads* (1878) which contains some of Swin-

burne's loveliest elegiac poetry. Along with this went a mass
of prose, critical and controversial, marked by the same flu-
ency and redundance of expression that characterized his
verse. By 1879 his feverish activity combined with a most ir-
regular habit of life brought him to the verge of complete
collapse. Swinburne was not in the ordinary sense a dissi-
pated man, but his nervous system could not withstand the
stimulus of a very small draught of alcohol, and his epileptic
tendency took on from time to time the form of most alarm-
ing seizures. From premature wreck and death he was rescued
by a friend, Watts-Dunton, who laid kind but forcible hands
upon him, took him to his home in a London suburb, and
kept him there for thirty years under a gentle restraint.

There is little to record of these years. Early in the period
Swinburne completed and published work already begun,
Mary Stuart (1881) and *Tristram of Lyonesse* (1882), his
greatest love-poem. He died peacefully after a brief illness in
1909 — a strange close for such a meteoric beginning.

No one can speak of Swinburne's work without speaking
first of his mastery of the technique of verse, and it is almost
impossible to speak of this without falling into the language
of uncritical eulogy. By common consent Swinburne exerted
a profound liberating influence upon English verse. ' He freed
it from the tyranny of the iambic; ' ' his marvellous metrical
inventiveness was without parallel in English ' — these are
phrases used by later poets and critics. From the point of view
of expression solely, regardless of content, Swinburne is per-
haps the greatest of English lyrical poets. For he was from the
beginning a lyrist, a singer. Whether he is writing drama or
narrative or elegiac poetry his verses sing and dance with a
lilt and freedom unknown in English since the age of Eliza-
beth. He is a musical composer in verse as Rossetti is a
painter. His power as a composer is shown perhaps most fully
in his mastery of musical patterns from the formal complex-
ity of his odes to the intricate beauty of his stanzaic struc-
tures and the plain but effective simplicity of his ballads.
Sometimes, indeed, especially in his later work, this musical
facility runs away with him. As some technician of the piano
may execute variations on a theme with such mastery and
brilliance that the theme itself and its meaning are lost in a
maze of varying sound, so Swinburne's prodigious flow of

words and mastery of rhythm tend to bury his underlying thought.

But it is worse than wrong, it is foolish, to think of Swinburne as a mere artificer in diction and rhythm. Underneath all his best poetry there lies what Rossetti called 'fundamental brain-work.' In other words Swinburne's magnificent and elaborately ornamented structure of verse is built up on a foundation of fixed principles. These are in part negative, in part positive. In the first place, he is the legitimate successor of the Revolutionary school of Byron, Shelley, and Landor, the bitter enemy of kings, priests, and all forms of tyranny. His most extravagant work appears in his denunciation of social and religious convention. The poems that caused such scandal in his early work are those directed against Victorian conceptions of sex relations and of religion. But Swinburne is something more than a reckless rebel. He has his own ideal, and this is Liberty, political, social, and individual. As a poet of political liberty he hailed the Italian struggle for unity and independence and cursed Louis Napoleon as the wrecker of the French Republic. But he is not primarily interested in contemporary events; they are to him only phases in the progress of humanity to its final goal, the Mater Triumphalis, the worldwide republic of man.

Further Swinburne is the poet of social liberty, especially in the relation of the sexes. His early erotic poetry explores with hitherto unknown freedom of expression strange and abnormal phases of sexual passion. His superb Prelude to *Tristram* glorifies love as the motive force of life. And Love, to Swinburne, is something more than the attraction between the sexes; it includes the hero-worship of youth for age, and the adoration of age for the beauty and innocence of childhood. It includes, in a sense, his love of nature, his passion, in particular, for the sea. Over and over again in the work of Swinburne the sea is personified as an object of love and worship, for the sea is the freest of all earthly elements, and in the swimmer's struggle against and conquest of the sea man gains his most immediate consciousness of strength.

And finally Swinburne is supremely the poet of individual liberty. In his belief all that is best in man emerges in the struggle against repressive power, call it as he does in varying moods, Tyranny, Fate or 'the supreme evil God.' The goal of this struggle is the complete emancipation of 'the holy spirit of man.' Swinburne is a thorough and uncompromising pagan. He recognizes no power or powers above man; his quarrel with revealed religion in all its forms, especially the Christian, is that it substitutes for man's own self-conscious effort a light outside of and above man as a guide through life. To Swinburne

> Man's soul is man's God still
> What winds soever waft his will
> Across the waves of day and night
> To port or shipwreck, left or right,
> Save his own soul's light overhead
> None leads him and none ever led.

CHORUS FROM *ATALANTA IN CALYDON*

Before the beginning of years
   There came to the making of man
Time, with a gift of tears;
   Grief, with a glass that ran;
Pleasure, with pain for leaven;
   Summer, with flowers that fell;
Remembrance fallen from heaven,
   And madness risen from hell;
Strength without hands to smite;
   Love that endures for a breath;
Night, the shadow of light,
   And life, the shadow of death.

And the high gods took in hand
   Fire, and the falling of tears,
And a measure of sliding sand
   From under the feet of the years;
And froth and drift of the sea;
   And dust of the labouring earth;
And bodies of things to be
   In the houses of death and of birth;
And wrought with weeping and laughter,
   And fashioned with loathing and love
With life before and after
   And death beneath and above,

For a day and a night and a morrow,
  That his strength might endure for a span
With travail and heavy sorrow,
  The holy spirit of man.

From the winds of the north and the south
  They gathered as unto strife;
They breathed upon his mouth,
  They filled his body with life;
Eyesight and speech they wrought
  For the veils of the soul therein,
A time for labour and thought,
  A time to serve and to sin;
They gave him light in his ways,
  And love, and a space for delight,
And beauty and length of days,
  And night, and sleep in the night.
His speech is a burning fire;
  With his lips he travaileth;
In his heart is a blind desire,
  In his eyes foreknowledge of death;
He weaves, and is clothed with derision;
  Sows, and he shall not reap;
His life is a watch or a vision
  Between a sleep and a sleep.

HYMN TO PROSERPINE

(AFTER THE PROCLAMATION IN ROME OF THE CHRISTIAN FAITH)

VICISTI, GALIÆE

I have lived long enough, having seen one thing, that love
  hath an end;
Goddess and maiden and queen, be near me now and befriend.
Thou art more than the day or the morrow, the seasons that
  laugh or that weep;
For these give joy and sorrow; but thou, Proserpina, sleep.
Sweet is the treading of wine, and sweet the feet of the dove;
But a goodlier gift is thine than foam of the grapes or love.
Yea, is not even Apollo, with hair and harp-string of gold,
A bitter God to follow, a beautiful God to behold?

I am sick of singing: the bays burn deep and chafe: I am fain
To rest a little from praise and grievous pleasure and pain.
For the Gods we know not of, who give us our daily breath,
We know they are cruel as love or life, and lovely as death.
O Gods dethroned and deceased, cast forth, wiped out in a
day!
From your wrath is the world released, redeemed from your
chains, men say.
New Gods are crowned in the city; their flowers have broken
your rods;
They are merciful, clothed with pity, the young compassionate
Gods.
But for me their new device is barren, the days are bare;
Things long past over suffice, and men forgotten that were.
Time and the Gods are at strife; ye dwell in the midst thereof,
Draining a little life from the barren breasts of love.
I say to you, cease, take rest; yea, I say to you all, be at peace,
Till the bitter milk of her breast and the barren bosom shall
cease.
Wilt thou yet take all, Galilean? but these thou shalt not take,
The laurel, the palms, and the pæan, the breasts of the nymphs
in the brake;
Breasts more soft than a dove's, that tremble with tenderer
breath;
And all the wings of the Loves, and all the joy before death;
All the feet of the hours that sound as a single lyre,
Dropped and deep in the flowers, with strings that flicker like
fire.
More than these wilt thou give, things fairer than all these
things?
Nay, for a little we live, and life hath mutable wings.
A little while and we die; shall life not thrive as it may?
For no man under the sky lives twice, outliving his day.
And grief is a grievous thing, and a man hath enough of his
tears:
Why should he labour, and bring fresh grief to blacken his
years?
Thou hast conquered, O pale Galilean; the world has grown
grey from thy breath;
We have drunken of things Lethean, and fed on the fullness of
death.

Laurel is green for a season, and love is sweet for a day;
But love grows bitter with treason, and laurel outlives not
　　May.
Sleep, shall we sleep after all? for the world is not sweet in the
　　end;
For the old faiths loosen and fall, the new years ruin and rend.
Fate is a sea without shore, and the soul is a rock that abides;
But her ears are vexed with the roar and her face with the
　　foam of the tides.
O lips that the live blood faints in, the leavings of racks and
　　rods!
O ghastly glories of saints, dead limbs of gibbeted Gods!
Though all men abase them before you in spirit, and all knees
　　bend,
I kneel not, neither adore you, but standing, look to the end.
All delicate days and pleasant, all spirits and sorrows are cast
Far out with the foam of the present that sweeps to the surf
　　of the past:
Where beyond the extreme sea-wall, and between the remote
　　sea-gates,
Waste water washes, and tall ships founder, and deep death
　　waits:
Where, mighty with deepening sides, clad about with the seas
　　as with wings,
And impelled of invisible tides, and fulfilled of unspeakable
　　things,
White-eyed and poisonous-finned, shark-toothed and serpen-
　　tine-curled,
Rolls, under the whitening wind of the future, the wave of the
　　world.
The depths stand naked in sunder behind it, the storms flee
　　away;
In the hollow before it the thunder is taken and snared as a
　　prey;
In its sides is the north-wind bound; and its salt is of all men's
　　tears,
With light of ruin, and sound of changes, and pulse of years:
With travail of day after day, and with trouble of hour upon
　　hour;
And bitter as blood is the spray; and the crests are as fangs
　　that devour:

And its vapour and storm of its steam as the sighing of spirits
to be;

And its noise as the noise in a dream; and its depths as the
roots of the sea:

And the height of its heads as the height of the utmost stars of
the air:

And the ends of the earth at the might thereof tremble, and
time is made bare.

Will ye bridle the deep sea with reins, will ye chasten the high
sea with rods?

Will ye take her to chain her with chains, who is older than all
ye Gods?

All ye as a wind shall go by, as a fire shall ye pass and be past;

Ye are Gods, and behold, ye shall die, and the waves be upon
you at last.

In the darkness of time, in the deeps of the years, in the
changes of things,

Ye shall sleep as a slain man sleeps, and the world shall forget
you for kings.

Though the feet of thine high priests tread where thy lords
and our forefathers trod,

Though these that were Gods are dead, and thou being dead
art a God,

Though before thee the throned Cytherean be fallen, and hid-
den her head,

Yet thy kingdom shall pass, Galilean, thy dead shall go down
to thee dead.

Of the maiden thy mother men sing as a goddess with grace
clad around;

Thou art throned where another was king; where another was
queen she is crowned.

Yea, once we had sight of another: but now she is queen, say
these.

Not as thine, not as thine was our mother, a blossom of flower-
ing seas,

Clothed round with the world's desire as with raiment, and
fair as the foam,

And fleeter than kindled fire, and a goddess, and mother of
Rome.

For thine came pale and a maiden, and sister to sorrow; but
ours,

138

Her deep hair heavily laden with odour and colour of flowers,
White rose of the rose-white water, a silver splendour, a flame,
Bent down unto us that besought her, and earth grew sweet
with her name.
For thine came weeping, a slave among slaves, and rejected;
but she
Came flushed from the full-flushed wave, and imperial, her
foot on the sea.
And the wonderful waters knew her, the winds and the view-
less ways,
And the roses grew rosier, and bluer the sea-blue stream of the
bays.
Ye are fallen, our lords, by what token? we wist that ye should
not fall.
Ye were all so fair that are broken; and one more fair than ye
all.
But I turn to her still, having seen she shall surely abide in the
end;
Goddess and maiden and queen, be near me now and befriend.
O daughter of earth, of my mother, her crown and blossom of
birth,
I am also, I also, thy brother; I go as I came unto earth.
In the night where thine eyes are as moons are in heaven, the
night where thou art,
Where the silence is more than all tunes, where sleep overflows
from the heart,
Where the poppies are sweet as the rose in our world, and the
red rose is white,
And the wind falls faint as it blows with the fume of the flow-
ers of the night,
And the murmur of spirits that sleep in the shadow of Gods
from afar
Grows dim in thine ears and deep as the deep dim soul of a
star,
In the sweet low light of thy face, under heavens untrod by the
sun,
Let my soul with their souls find place, and forget what is
done and undone.
Thou art more than the Gods who number the days of our
temporal breath;
For these give labour and slumber; but thou, Proserpina, death.

Therefore now at thy feet I abide for a season in silence. I
    know
I shall die as my fathers died, and sleep as they sleep; even so.
For the glass of the years is brittle wherein we gaze for a span;
A little soul for a little bears up this corpse which is man.
So long I endure, no longer; and laugh not again, neither
    weep.
For there is no God found stronger than death; and death is a
    sleep.

ITYLUS

Swallow, my sister, O sister swallow,
    How can thine heart be full of the spring?
      A thousand summers are over and dead.
What hast thou found in the spring to follow?
    What hast thou found in thine heart to sing?
      What wilt thou do when the summer is shed?

O swallow, sister, O fair swift swallow,
    Why wilt thou fly after spring to the south,
      The soft south whither thine heart is set?
Shall not the grief of the old time follow?
    Shall not the song thereof cleave to thy mouth?
      Hast thou forgotten ere I forget?

Sister, my sister, O fleet sweet swallow,
    Thy way is long to the sun and the south;
      But I, fulfilled of my heart's desire,
Shedding my song upon height, upon hollow,
    From tawny body and sweet small mouth
      Feed the heart of the night with fire.

I the nightingale all spring through,
    O swallow, sister, O changing swallow,
      All spring through till the spring be done,
Clothed with the light of the night on the dew,
    Sing, while the hours and the wild birds follow,
      Take flight, and follow and find the sun.

Sister, my sister, O soft light swallow,
    Though all things feast in the spring's guest-chamber,
      How hast thou heart to be glad thereof yet?

For where thou fliest I shall not follow,
  Till life forget and death remember,
    Till thou remember and I forget.

Swallow, my sister, O singing swallow,
  I know not how thou hast heart to sing.
    Hast thou the heart? is it all past over?
Thy lord the summer is good to follow,
  And fair the feet of thy lover the spring:
    But what wilt thou say to the spring thy lover?

O swallow, sister, O fleeting swallow,
  My heart in me is a molten ember,
    And over my head the waves have met.
But thou wouldst tarry or I would follow,
  Could I forget or thou remember,
    Couldst thou remember and I forget.

O sweet stray sister, O shifting swallow,
  The heart's division divideth us.
    Thy heart is light as a leaf of a tree;
But mine goes forth among sea-gulfs hollow
  To the place of the slaying of Itylus,
    The feast of Daulis, the Thracian sea.

O swallow, sister, O rapid swallow,
  I pray thee sing not a little space.
    Are not the roofs and the lintels wet?
The woven web that was plain to follow,
  The small slain body, the flowerlike face,
    Can I remember if thou forget?

O sister, sister, thy first-begotten!
  The hands that cling and the feet that follow,
    The voice of the child's blood crying yet
Who hath remembered me? who hath forgotten?
  Thou hast forgotten, O summer swallow,
    But the world shall end when I forget.

FROM *THE TRIUMPH OF TIME*

I will go back to the great sweet mother,
  Mother and lover of men, the sea.
I will go down to her, I and none other,
  Close with her, kiss her, and mix her with me;
Cling to her, strive with her, hold her fast:
O fair white mother, in days long past
Born without sister, born without brother,
  Set free my soul as thy soul is free.

O fair green-girdled mother of mine,
  Sea, that art clothed with the sun and the rain,
Thy sweet hard kisses are strong like wine,
  Thy large embraces are keen like pain.
Save me and hide me with all thy waves,
Find me one grave of thy thousand graves,
Those pure cold populous graves of thine
  Wrought without hand in a world without stain.

I shall sleep, and move with the moving ships,
  Change as the winds change, veer in the tide;
My lips will feast on the foam of thy lips,
  I shall rise with thy rising, with thee subside;
Sleep, and not know if she be, if she were,
Filled full with life to the eyes and hair,
As a rose is fulfilled to the roseleaf tips
  With splendid summer and perfume and pride.

This woven raiment of nights and days,
  Were it once cast off and unwound from me,
Naked and glad would I walk in thy ways,
  Alive and aware of thy ways and thee;
Clear of the whole world, hidden at home,
Clothed with the green and crowned with the foam,
A pulse of the life of thy straits and bays,
  A vein in the heart of the streams of the sea.

Fair mother, fed with the lives of men,
  Thou art subtle and cruel of heart, men say.
Thou hast taken, and shalt not render again;
  Thou art full of thy dead, and cold as they.

But death is the worst that comes of thee;
Thou art fed with our dead, O mother, O sea,
But when hast thou fed on our hearts? or when,
   Having given us love, hast thou taken away?

O tender-hearted, O perfect lover,
   Thy lips are bitter, and sweet thine heart.
The hopes that hurt and the dreams that hover,
   Shall they not vanish away and apart?
But thou, thou art sure, thou art older than earth;
Thou art strong for death and fruitful of birth;
Thy depths conceal and thy gulfs discover;
   From the first thou wert; in the end thou art.

   .   .   .   .

DOLORES

(Notre-Dame des Sept Douleurs)

Cold eyelids that hide like a jewel
   Hard eyes that grow soft for an hour;
The heavy white limbs, and the cruel
   Red mouth like a venomous flower;
When these are gone by with their glories,
   What shall rest of thee then, what remain,
O mystic and somber Dolores,
   Our Lady of Pain?

Seven sorrows the priests give their Virgin;
   But thy sins, which are seventy times seven,
Seven ages would fail thee to purge in,
   And then they would haunt thee in heaven:
Fierce midnights and famishing morrows,
   And the loves that complete and control
All the joys of the flesh, all the sorrows
   That wear out the soul.

O garment not golden but gilded,
   O garden where all men may dwell,
O tower not of ivory, but builded
   By hands that reach heaven from hell;

143

O mystical rose of the mire,
   O house not of gold but of gain,
O house of unquenchable fire,
   Our Lady of Pain!

. . . .

We shift and bedeck and bedrape us,
   Thou art noble and nude and antique;
Libitina thy mother, Priapus
   Thy father, a Tuscan and Greek.
We play with light loves in the portal,
   And wince and relent and refrain;
Loves die, and we know thee immortal,
   Our Lady of Pain.

. . . .

Could you hurt me, sweet lips, though I hurt you?
   Men touch them, and change in a trice
The lilies and languors of virtue
   For the raptures and roses of vice;
Those lie where thy foot on the floor is,
   These crown and caress thee and chain,
O splendid and sterile Dolores,
   Our Lady of Pain.

. . . .

Ah beautiful passionate body
   That never has ached with a heart!
On thy mouth though the kisses are bloody,
   Though they sting till it shudder and smart,
More kind than the love we adore is,
   They hurt not the heart or the brain,
O bitter and tender Dolores,
   Our Lady of Pain.

. . . .

Ah, thy people, thy children, thy chosen,
   Marked cross from the womb and perverse!
They have found out the secret to cozen
   The gods that constrain us and curse;

They alone, they are wise, and none other;
    Give me place, even me, in their train,
O my sister, my spouse, and my mother,
    Our Lady of Pain.

For the crown of our life as it closes
    Is darkness, the fruit thereof dust;
No thorns go as deep as a rose's,
    And love is more cruel than lust.
Time turns the old days to derision,
    Our loves into corpses or wives;
And marriage and death and division
    Make barren our lives.

.   .   .   .

Dost thou dream, in a respite of slumber,
    In a lull of the fires of thy life,
Of the days without name, without number,
    When thy will stung the world into strife;
When, a goddess, the pulse of thy passion
    Smote kings as they revelled in Rome;
And they hailed thee re-risen, O Thalassian,
    Foam-white, from the foam?

When thy lips had such lovers to flatter,
    When the city lay red from thy rods,
And thine hands were as arrows to scatter
    The children of change and their gods;
When the blood of thy foemen made fervent
    A sand never moist from the main,
As one smote them, their lord and thy servant,
    Our Lady of Pain.

On sands by the storm never shaken,
    Nor wet from the washing of tides;
Nor by foam of the waves overtaken,
    Nor winds that the thunder bestrides;
But red from the print of thy paces,
    Made smooth for the world and its lords,
Ringèd round with a flame of fair faces,
    And splendid with swords.

145

There the gladiator, pale for thy pleasure,
    Drew bitter and perilous breath;
There torments laid hold on the treasure
    Of limbs too delicious for death;
When thy gardens were lit with live torches;
    When the world was a steed for thy rein;
When the nations lay prone in thy porches,
    Our Lady of Pain.

When, with flame all around him aspirant,
    Stood flushed, as a harp-player stands,
The implacable beautiful tyrant,
    Rose-crowned, having death in his hands;
And a sound as the sound of loud water
    Smote far through the flight of the fires,
And mixed with the lightning of slaughter
    A thunder of lyres.

Dost thou dream of what was and no more is,
    The old kingdoms of earth and the kings?
Dost thou hunger for these things, Dolores,
    For these, in a world of new things?
But thy bosom no fasts could emaciate,
    No hunger compel to complain
Those lips that no bloodshed could satiate,
    Our Lady of Pain.

.   .   .   .

Cry aloud; for the old world is broken:
    Cry out; for the Phrygian is priest,
And rears not the bountiful token
    And spreads not the fatherly feast.
From the midmost of Ida, from shady
    Recesses that murmur at morn,
They have brought and baptized her, Our Lady,
    A goddess new-born.

.   .   .   .

Out of Dindymus heavily laden
    Her lions draw bound and unfed
A mother, a mortal, a maiden,
    A queen over death and the dead.

She is cold, and her habit is lowly,
  Her temple of branches and sods;
Most fruitful and virginal, holy,
  A mother of gods.

She hath wasted with fire thine high places,
  She hath hidden and marred and made sad
The fair limbs of the Loves, the fair faces
  Of gods that were goodly and glad.
She slays, and her hands are not bloody;
  She moves as a moon in the wane,
White-robed, and thy raiment is ruddy,
  Our Lady of Pain.

They shall pass and their places be taken,
  The gods and the priests that are pure.
They shall pass, and shalt thou not be shaken?
  They shall perish, and shalt thou endure?
Death laughs, breathing close and relentless
  In the nostrils and eyelids of lust,
With a pinch in his fingers of scentless
  And delicate dust.

.   .   .   .

What ails us to fear overmeasure,
  To praise thee with timorous breath,
O mistress and mother of pleasure,
  The one thing as certain as death?
We shall change as the things that we cherish,
  Shall fade as they faded before,
As foam upon water shall perish,
  As sand upon shore.

We shall know what the darkness discovers,
  If the grave-pit be shallow or deep;
And our fathers of old, and our lovers,
  We shall know if they sleep not or sleep.
We shall see whether hell be not heaven,
  Find out whether tares be not grain,
And the joys of thee seventy times seven,
  Our Lady of Pain.

147

THE GARDEN OF PROSERPINE

Here, where the world is quiet,
  Here, where all trouble seems
Dead winds' and spent waves' riot
  In doubtful dreams of dreams;
I watch the green field growing
For reaping folk and sowing,
For harvest-time and mowing,
  A sleepy world of streams.

I am tired of tears and laughter,
  And men that laugh and weep,
Of what may come hereafter
  For men that sow to reap:
I am weary of days and hours,
Blown buds of barren flowers,
Desires and dreams and powers
  And everything but sleep.

Here life has death for neighbour,
  And far from eye or ear
Wan waves and wet winds labour,
  Weak ships and spirits steer;
They drive adrift, and whither
They wot not who make thither;
But no such winds blow hither,
  And no such things grow here.

No growth of moor or coppice,
  No heather-flower or vine,
But bloomless buds of poppies,
  Green grapes of Proserpine,
Pale beds of blowing rushes
Where no leaf blooms or blushes
Save this whereout she crushes
  For dead men deadly wine.

Pale, without name or number,
  In fruitless fields of corn,
They bow themselves and slumber
  All night till light is born;

And like a soul belated,
In hell and heaven unmated,
By cloud and mist abated
   Comes out of darkness morn.

Though one were strong as seven,
   He too with death shall dwell,
Nor wake with wings in heaven,
   Nor weep for pains in hell;
Though one were fair as roses,
His beauty clouds and closes;
And well though love reposes,
   In the end it is not well.

Pale, beyond porch and portal,
   Crowned with calm leaves, she stands
Who gathers all things mortal
   With cold immortal hands;
Her languid lips are sweeter
Than love's who fears to greet her
To men that mix and meet her
   From many times and lands.

She waits for each and other,
   She waits for all men born;
Forgets the earth her mother,
   The life of fruits and corn;
And spring and seed and swallow
Take wing for her and follow
Where summer song rings hollow
   And flowers are put to scorn.

There go the loves that wither,
   The old loves with wearier wings;
And all dead years draw thither,
   And all disastrous things;
Dead dreams of days forsaken,
Blind buds that snows have shaken,
Wild leaves that winds have taken,
   Red strays of ruined springs.

We are not sure of sorrow,
 And joy was never sure;
To-day will die to-morrow;
 Time stoops to no man's lure;
And love, grown faint and fretful
With lips but half regretful
Sighs, and with eyes forgetful
 Weeps that no loves endure.

From too much love of living,
 From hope and fear set free,
We thank with brief thanksgiving
 Whatever gods may be
That no life lives forever;
That dead men rise up never;
That even the weariest river
 Winds somewhere safe to sea.

Then star nor sun shall waken,
 Nor any change of light:
Nor sound of waters shaken,
 Nor any sound or sight:
Nor wintry leaves nor vernal,
Nor days nor things diurnal;
Only the sleep eternal
 In an eternal night.

SAPPHICS

All the night sleep came not upon my eyelids,
 Shed not dew nor shook nor unclosed a feather,
Yet with lips shut close and with eyes of iron
 Stood and beheld me.

Then to me so lying awake a vision
Came without sleep over the seas and touched me,
Softly touched mine eyelids and lips; and I too,
 Full of the vision,

Saw the white implacable Aphrodite,
Saw the hair unbound and the feet unsandalled
Shine as fire of sunset on western waters;
 Saw the reluctant

Feet, the straining plumes of the doves that drew her,
Looking always, looking with necks reverted,
Back to Lesbos, back to the hills whereunder
　　Shone Mitylene;

Heard the flying feet of the Loves behind her
Make a sudden thunder upon the waters,
As the thunder flung from the strong unclosing
　　Wings of a great wind.

So the goddess fled from her place, with awful
Sound of feet and thunder of wings around her;
While behind a clamour of singing women
　　Severed the twilight.

·　·　·　·　·　·　·　·　·　·　·　·

IN MEMORY OF WALTER SAVAGE LANDOR

Back to the flower-town, side by side,
　　The bright months bring,
New-born, the bridegroom and the bride,
　　Freedom and spring.

The sweet land laughs from sea to sea,
　　Filled full of sun;
All things come back to her, being free;
　　All things but one.

In many a tender wheaten plot
　　Flowers that were dead
Live, and old suns revive; but not
　　That holier head.

By this white wandering waste of sea,
　　Far north, I hear
One face shall never turn to me
　　As once this year:

Shall never smile and turn and rest
　　On mine as there,
Nor one most sacred hand be prest
　　Upon my hair.

I came as one whose thoughts half linger,
  Half run before;
The youngest to the oldest singer
  That England bore.

I found him whom I shall not find
  Till all grief end,
In holiest age our mightiest mind,
  Father and friend.

But thou, if anything endure,
  If hope there be,
O spirit that man's life left pure,
  Man's death set free,

Not with disdain of days that were
  Look earthward now;
Let dreams revive the reverend hair,
  The imperial brow;

Come back in sleep, for in the life
  Where thou art not
We find none like thee. Time and strife
  And the world's lot,

Move thee no more; but love at least
  And reverent heart
May move thee, royal and released,
  Soul, as thou art.

And thou, his Florence, to thy trust
  Receive and keep,
Keep safe his dedicated dust,
  His sacred sleep.

So shall thy lovers, come from far,
  Mix with thy name
As morning-star with evening-star
  His faultless fame.

✤ ALGERNON CHARLES SWINBURNE ✤

AVE ATQUE VALE

IN MEMORY OF CHARLES BAUDELAIRE

Nous devrions pourtant pour lui porter quelques fleurs;
Les morts, les pauvres morts, ont de grandes douleurs,
Et quand Octobre souffle, émondeur des vieux arbres,
Son vent mélancolique à l'entour de leurs marbres,
Certe, ils doivent trouver les vivants bien ingrats.

Les Fleurs du Mal.

I

Shall I strew on thee rose or rue or laurel,
    Brother, on this that was the veil of thee?
    Or quiet sea-flower molded by the sea,
Or simplest growth of meadow-sweet or sorrel,
    Such as the summer-sleepy Dryads weave,
    Waked up by snow-soft sudden rains at eve?
Or wilt thou rather, as on earth before,
    Half-faded fiery blossoms, pale with heat
    And full of bitter summer, but more sweet
To thee than gleanings of a northern shore
    Trod by no tropic feet?

II

For always thee the fervid languid glories
    Allured of heavier suns in mightier skies;
    Thine ears knew all the wandering watery sighs
Where the sea sobs round Lesbian promontories,
    The barren kiss of piteous wave to wave
    That knows not where is that Leucadian grave
Which hides too deep the supreme head of song.
    Ah, salt and sterile as her kisses were,
    The wild sea winds her and the green gulfs bear
Hither and thither, and vex and work her wrong,
    Blind gods that cannot spare.

III

Thou sawest, in thine old singing season, brother,
　　Secrets and sorrows unbeheld of us:
　　Fierce loves, and lovely leaf-buds poisonous,
Bare to thy subtler eye, but for none other
　　Blowing by night in some unbreathed-in clime;
　　The hidden harvest of luxurious time,
Sin without shape, and pleasure without speech;
　　And where strange dreams in a tumultuous sleep
　　Make the shut eyes of stricken spirits weep;
And with each face thou sawest the shadow on each,
　　Seeing as men sow men reap.

IV

O sleepless heart and sombre soul unsleeping,
　　That were athirst for sleep and no more life
　　And no more love, for peace and no more strife!
Now the dim gods of death have in their keeping
　　Spirit and body and all the springs of song,
　　Is it well now where love can do no wrong,
Where stingless pleasure has no foam or fang
　　Behind the unopening closure of her lips?
　　Is it not well where soul from body slips
And flesh from bone divides without a pang
　　As dew from flower-bell drips?

V

It is enough; the end and the beginning
　　Are one thing to thee, who art past the end.
　　O hand unclasped of unbeholden friend,
For thee no fruits to pluck, no palms for winning,
　　No triumph and no labour and no lust,
　　Only dead yew-leaves and a little dust.
O quiet eyes wherein the light saith nought,
　　Whereto the day is dumb, nor any night
　　With obscure finger silences your sight,
Nor in your speech the sudden soul speaks thought,
　　Sleep, and have sleep for light.

VI

Now all strange hours and all strange loves are over,
  Dreams and desires and sombre songs and sweet,
  Hast thou found place at the great knees and feet
Of some pale Titan-woman like a lover,
  Such as thy vision here solicited,
  Under the shadow of her fair vast head,
The deep division of prodigious breasts,
  The solemn slope of mighty limbs asleep,
  The weight of awful tresses that still keep
The savour and shade of old-world pine-forests
  Where the wet hill-winds weep?

VII

Hast thou found any likeness for thy vision?
  O gardener of strange flowers, what bud, what bloom,
  Hast thou found sown, what gathered in the gloom?
What of despair, of rapture, of derision,
  What of life is there, what of ill or good?
  Are the fruits grey like dust or bright like blood?
Does the dim ground grow any seed of ours,
  The faint fields quicken any terrene root,
  In low lands where the sun and moon are mute
And all the stars keep silence? Are there flowers
  At all, or any fruit?

VIII

Alas, but though my flying song flies after,
  O sweet strange elder singer, thy more fleet
  Singing, and footprints of thy fleeter feet,
Some dim derision of mysterious laughter
  From the blind tongueless warders of the dead,
  Some gainless glimpse of Proserpine's veiled head,
Some little sound of unregarded tears
  Wept by effaced unprofitable eyes,
  And from pale mouths some cadence of dead sighs —
These only, these the hearkening spirit hears,
  Sees only such things rise.

IX

Thou art far too far for wings of words to follow,
    Far too far off for thought or any prayer.
    What ails us with thee, who art wind and air?
What ails us gazing where all seen is hollow?
    Yet with some fancy, yet with some desire,
    Dreams pursue death as winds a flying fire,
Our dreams pursue our dead and do not find.
    Still, and more swift than they, the thin flame flies,
    The low light fails us in elusive skies,
Still the foiled earnest ear is deaf, and blind
    Are still the eluded eyes.

X

Not thee, O never thee, in all time's changes,
    Not thee, but this the sound of thy sad soul,
    The shadow of thy swift spirit, this shut scroll
I lay my hand on, and not death estranges
    My spirit from communion of thy song —
    These memories and these melodies that throng
Veiled porches of a Muse funereal —
    These I salute, these touch, these clasp and fold
    As though a hand were in my hand to hold,
Or through mine ears a mourning musical
    Of many mourners rolled.

XI

I among these, I also, in such station
    As when the pyre was charred, and piled the sods,
    And offering to the dead made, and their gods,
The old mourners had, standing to make libation,
    I stand, and to the gods and to the dead
    Do reverence without prayer or praise and shed
Offering to these unknown, the gods of gloom,
    And what of honey and spice my seedlands bear,
    And what I may of fruits in this chilled air,
And lay, Orestes-like, across the tomb
    A curl of severed hair.

XII

But by no hand nor any treason stricken,
   Not like the low-lying head of Him, the King,
   The flame that made of Troy a ruinous thing,
Thou liest, and on this dust no tears could quicken
   There fall no tears like theirs that all men hear
   Fall tear by sweet imperishable tear
Down the opening leaves of holy poets' pages.
   Thee not Orestes, not Electra mourns;
   But bending us-ward with memorial urns
The most high Muses that fulfil all ages
   Weep, and our God's heart yearns.

XIII

For, sparing of his sacred strength, not often
   Among us darkling here the lord of light
   Makes manifest his music and his might
In hearts that open and in lips that soften
   With the soft flame and heat of songs that shine.
   Thy lips indeed he touched with bitter wine,
And nourished them indeed with bitter bread;
   Yet surely from his hand thy soul's food came,
   The fire that scarred thy spirit at his flame
Was lighted, and thine hungering heart he fed
   Who feeds our hearts with fame.

XIV

Therefore he too now at thy soul's sunsetting,
   God of all suns and songs, he too bends down
   To mix his laurel with thy cypress crown,
And save thy dust from blame and from forgetting.
   Therefore he too, seeing all thou wert and art,
   Compassionate, with sad and sacred heart,
Mourns thee of many his children the last dead,
   And hallows with strange tears and alien sighs
   Thine unmelodious mouth and sunless eyes,
And over thine irrevocable head
   Sheds light from the under skies.

XV

And one weeps with him in the ways Lethean,
   And stains with tears her changing bosom chill;
   That obscure Venus of the hollow hill,
That thing transformed which was the Cytherean,
   With lips that lost their Grecian laugh divine
   Long since, and face no more called Erycine;
A ghost, a bitter and luxurious god.
   Thee also with fair flesh and singing spell
   Did she, a sad and second prey, compel
Into the footless places once more trod,
   And shadows hot from hell.

XVI

And now no sacred staff shall break in blossom,
   No choral salutation lure to light
   A spirit sick with perfume and sweet night
And love's tired eyes and hands and barren bosom.
   There is no help for these things; none to mend
   And none to mar; not all our songs, O friend,
Will make death clear or make life durable.
   Howbeit with rose and ivy and wild vine
   And with wild notes about this dust of thine
At least I fill the place where white dreams dwell
   And wreathe an unseen shrine.

XVII

Sleep; and if life was bitter to thee, pardon,
   If sweet, give thanks; thou hast no more to live;
   And to give thanks is good, and to forgive.
Out of the mystic and the mournful garden
   Where all day through thine hands in barren braid
   Wove the sick flowers of secrecy and shade,
Green buds of sorrow and sin, and remnants grey,
   Sweet-smelling, pale with poison, sanguine-hearted,
   Passions that sprang from sleep and thoughts that started,
Shall death not bring us all as thee one day
   Among the days departed?

XVIII

For thee, O now a silent soul, my brother,
  Take at my hands this garland, and farewell.
  Thin is the leaf, and chill the wintry smell,
And chill the solemn earth, a fatal mother,
  With sadder than the Niobean womb,
  And in the hollow of her breasts a tomb.
Content thee, howsoe'er, whose days are done:
  There lies not any troublous thing before,
  Nor sight nor sound to war against thee more,
For whom all winds are quiet as the sun,
  All waters as the shore.

AT PARTING

For a day and a night Love sang to us, played with us,
  Folded us round from the dark and the light;
And our hearts were fulfilled of the music he made with us,
Made with our hearts and our lips while he stayed with us,
  Stayed in mid passage his pinions from flight
        For a day and a night.

From his foes that kept watch with his wings had he hidden
    us,
  Covered us close from the eyes that would smite,
From the feet that had tracked and the tongues that had chid-
    den us,
Sheltering in shade of the myrtles forbidden us
  Spirit and flesh growing one with delight
        For a day and a night.

But his wings will not rest and his feet will not stay for us:
  Morning is here in the joy of its might;
With his breath has he sweetened a night and a day for us;
Now let him pass, and the myrtles make way for us;
  Love can but last in us here at his height
        For a day and a night.

RELICS

This flower that smells of honey and the sea,
White laurustine, seems in my hand to be
   A white star made of memory long ago
Lit in the heaven of dear times dead to me.

A star out of the skies love used to know
Here held in hand, a stray left yet to show
   What flowers my heart was full of in the days
That are long since gone down dead memory's flow.

Dead memory that revives on doubtful ways,
Half hearkening what the buried season says
   Out of the world of the unapparent dead
Where the lost Aprils are, and the lost Mays.

Flower, once I knew thy star-white brethren bred
Nigh where the last of all the land made head
   Against the sea, a keen-faced promontory,
Flowers on salt wind and sprinkled sea-dews fed.

Their hearts were glad of the free place's glory;
The wind that sang them all his stormy story
   Had talked all winter to the sleepless spray,
And as the sea's their hues were hard and hoary.

Like things born of the sea and the bright day,
They laughed out at the years that could not slay,
   Live sons and joyous of unquiet hours,
And stronger than all storms that range for prey.

And in the close indomitable flowers
A keen-edged odour of the sun and showers
   Was as the smell of the fresh honeycomb
Made sweet for mouths of none but paramours.

Out of the hard green wall of leaves that clomb
They showed like windfalls of the snow-soft foam,
   Or feathers from the weary south-wind's wing,
Fair as the spray that it came shoreward from.

❖ ALGERNON CHARLES SWINBURNE ❖

And thou, as white, what word hast thou to bring?
If my heart hearken, whereof wilt thou sing?
    For some sign surely thou too hast to bear,
Some word far south was taught thee of the spring.

White like a white rose, not like these that were
Taught of the wind's mouth and the winter air,
    Poor tender thing of soft Italian bloom,
Where once thou grewest, what else for me grew there?

Born in what spring and on what city's tomb,
By whose hand wast thou reached, and plucked for whom?
    There hangs about thee, could the soul's sense tell,
An odour as of love and of love's doom.

Of days more sweet than thou wast sweet to smell,
Of flower-soft thoughts that came to flower and fell,
    Of loves that lived a lily's life and died,
Of dreams now dwelling where dead roses dwell.

O white birth of the golden mountain-side
That for the sun's love makes its bosom wide
    At sunrise, and with all its woods and flowers
Takes in the morning to its heart of pride!

Thou hast a word of that one land of ours,
And of the fair town called of the Fair Towers,
    A word for me of my San Gimignan,
A word of April's greenest-girdled hours.

Of the breached walls whereon the wallflowers ran
Called of Saint Fina, breachless now of man,
    Though time with soft feet break them stone by stone,
Who breaks down hour by hour his own reign's span.

Of the cliff overcome and overgrown
That all that flowerage clothed as flesh clothes bone,
    That garment of acacias made for May,
Whereof here lies one witness overblown.

The fair brave trees with all their flowers at play,
How king-like they stood up into the day!
  How sweet the day was with them, and the night!
Such words of message have dead flowers to say.

This that the winter and the wind made bright,
And this that lived upon Italian light,
  Before I throw them and these words away,
Who knows but I what memories too take flight?

TRISTRAM OF LYONESSE

PRELUDE: TRISTRAM AND ISEULT

Love, that is first and last of all things made,
  The light that has the living world for shade,
The spirit that for temporal veil has on
The souls of all men woven in unison,
One fiery raiment with all lives inwrought
And lights of sunny and starry deed and thought,
And alway through new act and passion new
Shines the divine same body and beauty through,
The body spiritual of fire and light
That is to worldly noon as noon to night;
Love, that is flesh upon the spirit of man
And spirit within the flesh whence breath began;
Love, that keeps all the choir of lives in chime;
Love, that is blood within the veins of time;
That wrought the whole world without stroke of hand,
Shaping the breadth of sea, the length of land,
And with the pulse and motion of his breath
Through the great heart of the earth strikes life and death,
The sweet twain chords that make the sweet tune live
Through day and night of things alternative,
Through silence and through sound of stress and strife,
And ebb and flow of dying death and life;
Love, that sounds loud or light in all men's ears,
Whence all men's eyes take fire from sparks of tears,
That binds on all men's feet or chains or wings;
Love, that is root and fruit of terrene things;
Love, that the whole world's waters shall not drown,

The whole world's fiery forces not burn down;
Love, that what time his own hands guard his head
The whole world's wrath and strength shall not strike dead;
Love, that if once his own hands make his grave
The whole world's pity and sorrow shall not save;
Love, that for very life shall not be sold,
Nor bought nor bound with iron nor with gold;
So strong that heaven, could love bid heaven farewell,
Would turn to fruitless and unflowering hell;
So sweet that hell, to hell could love be given,
Would turn to splendid and sonorous heaven;
Love that is fire within thee and light above,
And lives by grace of nothing but of love;
Through many and lovely thoughts and much desire
Led these twain to the life of tears and fire;
Through many and lovely days and much delight
Led these twain to the lifeless life of night.
    Yea, but what then? albeit all this were thus,
And soul smote soul and left it ruinous,
And love led love as eyeless men lead men,
Through chance by chance to deathward — Ah, what then?
Hath love not likewise led them further yet,
Out through the years where memories rise and set,
Some large as suns, some moon-like warm and pale,
Some starry-sighted, some through clouds that sail
Seen as red flame through spectral float of fume,
Each with the blush of its own special bloom
On the fair face of its own coloured light,
Distinguishable in all the host of night,
Divisible from all the radiant rest
And separable in splendour? Hath the best
Light of love's all, of all that burn and move,
A better heaven than heaven is? Hath not love
Made for all these their sweet particular air
To shine in, their own beams and names to bear,
Their ways to wander and their wards to keep,
Till story and song and glory and all things sleep?
Hath he not plucked from death of lovers dead
Their musical soft memories, and kept red
The rose of their remembrance in men's eyes,
The sunsets of their stories in his skies,

The blush of their dead blood in lips that speak
Of their dead lives, and in the listener's cheek
That trembles with the kindling pity lit
In gracious hearts for some sweet fever-fit,
A fiery pity enkindled of pure thought
By tales that make their honey out of nought,
The faithless faith that lives without belief
Its light life through, the griefless ghost of grief?
Yea, as warm night refashions the sear blood
In storm-struck petal or in sun-struck bud,
With tender hours and tempering dew to cure
The hunger and thirst of day's distemperature
And ravin of the dry discolouring hours,
Hath he not bid relume their flameless flowers
With summer fire and heat of lamping song,
And bid the short-lived things, long dead, live long,
And thought remake their wan funereal fames,
And the sweet shining signs of women's names
That mark the months out and the weeks anew
He moves in changeless change of seasons through
To fill the days up of his dateless year
Flame from Queen Helen to Queen Guenevere?
For first of all the sphery signs whereby
Love severs light from darkness, and most high,
In the white front of January there glows
The rose-red sign of Helen like a rose:
And gold-eyed as the shore-flower shelterless
Whereon the sharp-breathed sea blows bitterness,
A storm-star that the seafarers of love
Strain their wind-wearied eyes for glimpses of,
Shoots keen through February's grey frost and damp
The lamplike star of Hero for a lamp;
The star that Marlowe sang into our skies
With mouth of gold, and morning in his eyes;
And in clear March across the rough blue sea
The signal sapphire of Alcyone
Makes bright the blown brows of the wind-foot year;
And shining like a sunbeam-smitten tear
Full ere it fall, the fair next sign in sight
Burns opal-wise with April-coloured light
When air is quick with song and rain and flame,

My birth-month star that in love's heaven hath name
Iseult, a light of blossom and beam and shower,
My singing sign that makes the song-tree flower;
Next like a pale and burning pearl beyond
The rose-white sphere of flower-named Rosamond
Signs the sweet head of Maytime; and for June
Flares like an angered and storm-reddening moon
Her signal sphere, whose Carthaginian pyre
Shadowed her traitor's flying sail with fire;
Next, glittering as the wine-bright jacinth-stone,
A star south-risen that first to music shone,
The keen girl-star of golden Juliet bears
Light northward to the month whose forehead wears
Her name for flower upon it, and his trees
Mix their deep English song with Veronese;
And like an awful sovereign chrysolite
Burning the supreme fire that blinds the night,
The hot gold head of Venus kissed by Mars,
A sun-flower among small sphered flowers of stars,
The light of Cleopatra fills and burns
The hollow of heaven whence ardent August yearns;
And fixed and shining as the sister-shed
Sweet tears for Phaethon disorbed and dead,
The pale bright autumn's amber-coloured sphere,
That through September sees the saddening year
As love sees change through sorrow, hath to name
Francesca's; and the star that watches flame
The embers of the harvest overgone
Is Thisbe's, slain of love in Babylon,
Set in the golden girdle of sweet signs
A blood-bright ruby; last save one light shines
An eastern wonder of sphery chrysopras,
The star that made men mad, Angelica's;
And latest named and lordliest, with a sound
Of swords and harps in heaven that ring it round,
Last love-light and last love-song of the year's
Gleams like a glorious emerald Guenevere's.
These are the signs wherethrough the year sees move,
Full of the sun, the sun-god which is love,
A fiery body blood-red from the heart
Outward, with fire-white wings made wide apart,

That close not and unclose not, but upright
Steered without wind by their own light and might
Sweep through the flameless fire of air that rings
From heaven to heaven with thunder of wheels and wings
And antiphones of motion-moulded rhyme
Through spaces out of space and timeless time.

. . . .

    They have the night, who had like us the day;
We, whom day binds, shall have the night as they.
We, from the fetters of the light unbound,
Healed of our wound of living, shall sleep sound.
All gifts but one the jealous God may keep
From our soul's longing, one he cannot — sleep.
This, though he grudge all other grace to prayer,
This grace his closed hand cannot choose but spare.
This, though his ear be sealed to all that live,
Be it lightly given or lothly, God must give.
We, as the men whose name on earth is none,
We too shall surely pass out of the sun;
Out of the sound and eyeless light of things,
Wide as the stretch of life's time-wandering wings,
Wide as the naked world and shadowless,
And long-lived as the world's own weariness.
Us too, when all the fires of time are cold,
The heights shall hide us and the depths shall hold.
Us too, when all the tears of time are dry,
The night shall lighten from her tearless eye.
Blind is the day and eyeless all its light,
But the large unbewildered eye of night
Hath sense and speculation; and the sheer
Limitless length of lifeless life and clear,
The timeless space wherein the brief worlds move
Clothed with light life and fruitful with light love,
With hopes that threaten, and with fears that cease,
Past fear and hope, hath in it only peace.

. . . .

A SONG IN TIME OF ORDER
1852.

Push hard across the sand,
    For the salt wind gathers breath;
Shoulder and wrist and hand,
    Push hard as the push of death.

The wind is as iron that rings,
    The foam-heads loosen and flee;
It swells and welters and swings,
    The pulse of the tide of the sea.

And up on the yellow cliff
    The long corn flickers and shakes;
Push, for the wind holds stiff,
    And the gunwale dips and rakes.

Good hap to the fresh fierce weather,
    The quiver and beat of the sea!
While three men hold together,
    The kingdoms are less by three.

Out to the sea, with her there,
    Out with her over the sand;
Let the kings keep the earth for their share!
    We have done with the sharers of land.

They have tied the world in a tether,
    They have bought over God with a fee;
While three men hold together,
    The kingdoms are less by three.

We have done with the kisses that sting,
    The thief's mouth red from the feast,
The blood on the hands of the king
    And the lie at the lips of the priest.

Will they tie the winds in a tether,
    Put a bit in the jaws of the sea?
While three men hold together,
    The kingdoms are less by three.

Let our flag run out straight in the wind!
  The old red shall be floated again
When the ranks that are thin shall be thinned,
  When the names that were twenty are ten;

When the devil's riddle is mastered
  And the galley-bench creaks with a Pope,
We shall see Buonaparte the bastard
  Kick heels with his throat in a rope.

While the shepherd sets wolves on his sheep
  And the emperor halters his kine,
While Shame is a watchman asleep
  And Faith is a keeper of swine,

Let the wind shake our flag like a feather,
  Like the plumes of the foam of the sea!
While three men hold together,
  The kingdoms are less by three.

All the world has its burdens to bear,
  From Cayenne to the Austrian whips;
Forth, with the rain in our hair
  And the salt sweet foam in our lips;

In the teeth of the hard glad weather,
  In the blown wet face of the sea;
While three men hold together,
  The kingdoms are less by three.

MATER TRIUMPHALIS

Mother of man's time-travelling generations,
  Breath of his nostrils, heartblood of his heart,
God above all Gods worshipped of all nations,
  Light above light, law beyond law, thou art.

Thy face is as a sword smiting in sunder
  Shadows and chains and dreams and iron things;
The sea is dumb before thy face, the thunder
  Silent, the skies are narrower than thy wings.

✤ ALGERNON CHARLES SWINBURNE ✤

Angels and Gods, spirit and sense, thou takest
  In thy right hand as drops of dust or dew;
The temples and the towers of time thou breakest,
  His thoughts and words and works, to make them new.

All we have wandered from thy ways, have hidden
  Eyes from thy glory and ears from calls they heard:
Called of thy trumpets vainly, called and chidden,
  Scourged of thy speech and wounded of thy word.

We have known thee and have not known thee; stood beside
    thee,
  Felt thy lips breathe, set foot where thy feet trod,
Loved and renounced and worshipped and denied thee,
  As though thou wert but as another God.

' One hour for sleep,' we said, ' and yet one other;
  All day we served her, and who shall serve by night? '
Not knowing of thee, thy face not knowing, O mother,
  O light wherethrough the darkness is as light.

Men that forsook thee hast thou not forsaken,
  Races of men that knew not hast thou known;
Nations that slept thou hast doubted not to waken
  Worshippers of strange Gods to make thine own.

All old grey histories hiding thy clear features,
  O secret spirit and sovereign, all men's tales,
Creeds woven of men thy children and thy creatures,
  They have woven for vestures of thee and for veils.

Thine hands, without election or exemption,
  Feed all men fainting from false peace or strife,
O thou, the resurrection and redemption,
  The godhead and the manhood and the life.

Thy wings shadow the waters; thine eyes lighten
  The horror of the hollows of the night;
The depths of the earth and the dark places brighten
  Under thy feet, whiter than fire is white.

Death is subdued to thee, and hell's band's broken;
    Where thou art only is heaven; who hears not thee,
Time shall not hear him; when men's names are spoken,
    A nameless sign of death shall his name be.

Deathless shall be the death, the name be nameless;
    Sterile of stars his twilight time of breath;
With fire of hell shall shame consume him shameless,
    And dying, all the night darken his death.

The years are as thy garments, the world's ages
    As sandals bound and loosed from thy swift feet;
Time serves before thee, as one that hath for wages
    Praise or shame only, bitter words or sweet.

Thou sayest 'Well done,' and all a century kindles;
    Again thou sayest 'Depart from sight of me,'
And all the light of face of all men dwindles,
    And the age is as the broken glass of thee.

The night is as a seal set on men's faces,
    On faces fallen of men that take no light
Nor give light in the deeps of the dark places,
    Blind things, incorporate with the body of night.

Their souls are serpents winterbound and frozen,
    Their shame is as a tame beast; at their feet
Couched; their cold lips deride thee and thy chosen,
    Their lying lips made grey with dust for meat.

Then when their time is full and days run over,
    The splendour of thy sudden brow made bare
Darkens the morning; thy bared hands uncover
    The veils of light and night and the awful air.

And the world naked as a new-born maiden
    Stands virginal and splendid as at birth,
With all thine heaven of all its light unladen,
    Of all its love unburdened all thine earth.

✤ ALGERNON CHARLES SWINBURNE ✤

For the utter earth and the utter air of heaven
    And the extreme depth is thine and the extreme height;
Shadows of things and veils of ages riven
    Are as men's kings unkingdomed in thy sight.

Through the iron years, the centuries brazen-gated,
    By the ages' barred impenetrable doors,
From the evening to the morning have we waited,
    Should thy foot haply sound on the awful floors.

The floors untrodden of the sun's feet glimmer,
    The star-unstricken pavements of the night;
Do the lights burn inside? the light was dimmer
    On festal faces withering out of sight.

The crowned heads lose the light on them; it may be
    Dawn is at hand to smite the loud feast dumb;
To blind the torch-lit centuries till the day be,
    The feasting kingdoms till thy kingdom come.

Shall it not come? deny they or dissemble,
    Is it not even as lightning from on high
Now? and though many a soul close eyes and tremble,
    How should they tremble at all who love thee as I?

I am thine harp between thine hands, O mother!
    All my strong chords are strained with love of thee.
We grapple in love and wrestle, as each with other
    Wrestle the wind and the unreluctant sea.

I am no courtier of thee sober-suited,
    Who loves a little for a little pay.
Me not thy winds and storms nor thrones disrooted
    Nor molten crowns nor thine own sins dismay.

Sinned hast thou sometime, therefore art thou sinless;
    Stained hast thou been, who art therefore without stain;
Even as man's soul is kin to thee, but kinless
    Thou, in whose womb Time sows the all-various grain.

I do not bid thee spare me, O dreadful mother!
  I pray thee that thou spare not, of thy grace.
How were it with me then, if ever another
  Should come to stand before thee in this my place?

I am the trumpet at thy lips, thy clarion
  Full of thy cry, sonorous with thy breath;
The graves of souls born worms and creeds grown carrion
  Thy blast of judgment fills with fires of death.

Thou art the player whose organ-keys are thunders,
  And I beneath thy foot the pedal prest;
Thou art the ray whereat the rent night sunders,
  And I the cloudlet borne upon thy breast.

I shall burn up before thee, pass and perish,
  As haze in sunrise on the red sea-line;
But thou from dawn to sunsetting shalt cherish
  The thoughts that led and souls that lighted mine.

Reared between night and noon and truth and error,
  Each twilight-travelling bird that trills and screams
Sickens at midday, nor can face for terror
  The imperious heaven's inevitable extremes.

I have no spirit of skill with equal fingers
  At sign to sharpen or to slacken strings;
I keep no time of song with gold-perched singers
  And chirp of linnets on the wrists of kings.

I am thy storm-thrush of the days that darken,
  Thy petrel in the foam that bears thy bark
To port through night and tempest; if thou hearken,
  My voice is in thy heaven before the lark.

My song is in the mist that hides thy morning,
  My cry is up before the day for thee;
I have heard thee and beheld thee and give warning,
  Before thy wheels divide the sky and sea.

Birds shall wake with thee voiced and feathered fairer,
　　To see in summer what I see in spring;
I have eyes and heart to endure thee, O thunder-bearer,
　　And they shall be who shall have tongues to sing.

I have love at least, and have not fear, and part not
　　From thine unnavigable and wingless way;
Thou tarriest, and I have not said thou art not,
　　Nor all thy night long have denied thy day.

Darkness to daylight shall lift up thy paean,
　　Hill to hill thunder, vale cry back to vale
With wind-notes as of eagles Æschylean,
　　And Sappho singing in the nightingale.

Sung to by mighty sons of dawn and daughters,
　　Of this night's songs thine ear shall keep but one;
That supreme song which shook the channelled waters,
　　And called thee skyward as God calls the sun.

Come, though all heaven again be fire above thee;
　　Though death before thee come to clear the sky;
Let us but see in his thy face who love thee;
　　Yea, though thou slay us, arise and let us die.

HERTHA

I am that which began;
　　Out of me the years roll;
Out of me God and man;
　　I am equal and whole;
God changes, and man, and the form of them bodily; I am the
　　soul.

Before ever land was,
　　Before ever the sea,
Or soft hair of the grass,
　　Or fair limbs of the tree,
Or the flesh-coloured fruit of my branches, I was, and thy soul
　　was in me.

First life on my sources
   First drifted and swam;
Out of me are the forces
   That save it or damn;
Out of me man and woman, and wild-beast and bird; before
   God was, I am.

Beside or above me
   Naught is there to go;
Love or unlove me,
   Unknow me or know,
I am that which unloves me and loves; I am stricken, and I am
   the blow.

I the mark that is missed
   And the arrows that miss,
I the mouth that is kissed
   And the breath in the kiss,
The search, and the sought, and the seeker, the soul and the
   body that is.

I am that thing which blesses
   My spirit elate;
That which caresses
   With hands uncreate
My limbs unbegotten that measure the length of the measure
   of fate.

But what thing dost thou now,
   Looking Godward, to cry,
' I am I, thou art thou,
   I am low, thou art high.' ?
I am thou, whom thou seekest to find him; find thou but thy-
   self, thou art I.

I the grain and the furrow,
   The plough-cloven clod
And the ploughshare drawn thorough,
   The germ and the sod,
The deed and the doer, the seed and the sower, the dust which
   is God.

Hast thou known how I fashioned thee,
    Child, underground?
Fire that impassioned thee,
    Iron that bound,
Dim changes of water, what thing of all these hast thou known
    of or found?

Canst thou say in thine heart
    Thou has seen with thine eyes
With what cunning of art
    Thou wast wrought in what wise,
By what force of what stuff thou wast shapen, and shown on
    my breast to the skies?

Who hath given, who hath sold it thee,
    Knowledge of me?
Hath the wilderness told it thee?
    Hast thou learnt of the sea?
Hast thou communed in spirit with night? have the winds
    taken counsel with thee?

Have I set such a star
    To show light on thy brow
That thou sawest from afar
    What I show to thee now?
Have ye spoken as brethren together, the sun and the moun-
    tains and thou?

What is here, dost thou know it?
    What was, hast thou known?
Prophet nor poet
    Nor tripod nor throne
Nor spirit nor flesh can make answer, but only thy mother
    alone.

Mother, not maker,
    Born, and not made;
Though her children forsake her,
    Allured or afraid,
Praying prayers to the God of their fashion, she stirs not for
    all that have prayed.

A creed is a rod,
 And a crown is of night;
But this thing is God,
 To be man with thy might,
To grow straight in the strength of thy spirit, and live out thy
 life as the light.

I am in thee to save thee,
 As my soul in thee saith;
Give thou as I gave thee,
 Thy life-blood and breath,
Green leaves of thy labour, white flowers of thy thought, and
 red fruit of thy death.

Be the ways of thy giving
 As mine were to thee;
The free life of thy living,
 Be the gift of it free;
Not as servant to lord, nor as master to slave, shalt thou give
 thee to me.

O children of banishment,
 Souls overcast,
Were the lights ye see vanish meant
 Alway to last,
Ye would know not the sun overshining the shadows and stars
 overpast.

I that saw where ye trod
 The dim paths of the night
Set the shadow called God
 In your skies to give light;
But the morning of manhood is risen, and the shadowless soul
 is in sight.

The tree many-rooted
 That swells to the sky
With frondage red-fruited,
 The life-tree am I;
In the buds of your lives is the sap of my leaves: ye shall live
 and not die.

But the Gods of your fashion
That take and that give,
In their pity and passion
That scourge and forgive,
They are worms that are bred in the bark that falls off; they
shall die and not live.

My own blood is what stanches
The wounds in my bark;
Stars caught in my branches
Make day of the dark,
And are worshiped as suns till the sunrise shall tread out their
fires as a spark.

Where dead ages hide under
The live roots of the tree,
In my darkness the thunder
Makes utterance of me;
In the clash of my boughs with each other ye hear the waves
sound of the sea.

That noise is of Time,
As his feathers are spread
And his feet set to climb
Through the boughs overhead,
And my foliage rings round him and rustles, and branches are
bent with his tread.

The storm-winds of ages
Blow through me and cease,
The war-wind that rages,
The spring-wind of peace,
Ere the breath of them roughen my tresses, ere one of my
blossoms increase.

All sounds of all changes,
All shadows and lights
On the world's mountain-ranges
And stream-riven heights,
Whose tongue is the wind's tongue and language of storm-
clouds on earth-shaking nights;

All forms of all faces,
    All works of all hands
In unsearchable places
    Of time-stricken lands,
All death and all life, and all reigns and all ruins, drop
    through me as sands.

Though sore be my burden
    And more than ye know,
And my growth have no guerdon
    But only to grow,
Yet I fail not of growing for lightnings above me or death-
    worms below.

These too have their part in me,
    As I too in these;
Such fire is at heart in me,
    Such sap is this tree's,
Which hath in it all sounds and all secrets of infinite lands
    and of seas.

In the spring-coloured hours
    When my mind was as May's,
There brake forth of me flowers
    By centuries of days,
Strong blossoms with perfume of manhood, shot out from my
    spirit as rays.

And the sound of them springing
    And smell of their shoots
Were as warmth and sweet singing
    And strength to my roots;
And the lives of my children made perfect with freedom of
    soul were my fruits.

I bid you but be;
    I have need not of prayer;
I have need of you free
    As your mouths of mine air;
That my heart may be greater within me, beholding the fruits
    of me fair.

More fair than strange fruit is
 Of faiths ye espouse;
In me only the root is
 That blooms in your boughs;
Behold now your God that ye made you, to feed him with
faith of your vows.

In the darkening and whitening
 Abysses adored,
With dayspring and lightning
 For lamp and for sword,
God thunders in heaven, and his angels are red with the wrath
of the Lord.

O my sons, O too dutiful
 Toward Gods not of me,
Was not I enough beautiful?
 Was it hard to be free?
For behold, I am with you, am in you and of you; look forth
now and see.

Lo, winged with world's wonders,
 With miracles shod,
With the fires of his thunders
 For raiment and rod,
God trembles in heaven, and his angels are white with the ter-
ror of God.

For his twilight is come on him,
 His anguish is here;
And his spirits gaze dumb on him,
 Grown grey from his fear;
And his hour taketh hold on him stricken, the last of his in-
finite year.

Thought made him and breaks him,
 Truth slays and forgives;
But to you, as time takes him,
 This new thing it gives,
Even love, the beloved Republic, that feeds upon freedom and
lives.

For truth only is living,
    Truth only is whole,
And the love of his giving
    Man's polestar and pole;
Man, pulse of my centre, and fruit of my body, and seed of my
    soul.

One birth of my bosom;
    One beam of mine eye;
One topmost blossom
    That scales the sky;
Man, equal and one with me, man that is made of me, man
    that is I.

THE OBLATION

Ask nothing more of me, sweet;
    All I can give you I give.
    Heart of my heart, were it more,
More would be laid at your feet:
    Love that should help you to live,
    Song that should spur you to soar.

All things were nothing to give,
    Once to have sense of you more,
    Touch you and taste of you, sweet,
Think you and breathe you and live,
    Swept of your wings as they soar,
    Trodden by chance of your feet.

I that have love and no more
    Give you but love of you, sweet:
    He that hath more, let him give;
He that hath wings, let him soar,
    Mine is the heart at your feet
    Here, that must love you to live.

THE WINDS

O weary fa' the east wind,
  And weary fa' the west:
And gin I were under the wan waves wide
  I wot weel wad I rest.

O weary fa' the north wind,
  And weary fa' the south:
The sea went ower my good lord's head
  Or ever he kissed my mouth.

Weary fa' the windward rocks,
  And weary fa' the lee:
They might hae sunken sevenscore ships,
  And let my love's gang free.

And weary fa' ye, mariners a',
  And weary fa' the sea:
It might hae taken an hundred men,
  And let my ae love be.

A JACOBITE'S FAREWELL
1716.

There's nae mair lands to tyne, my dear,
  And nae mair lives to gie:
Though a man think sair to live nae mair,
  There's but one day to die.

For a' things come and a' days gane,
  What needs ye rend your hair?
But kiss me till the morn's morrow,
  Then I'll kiss ye nae mair.

O lands are lost and life's losing,
  And what were they to gie?
Fu' mony a man gives all he can,
  But nae man else gives ye.

181

Our king wons ower the sea's water,
    And I in prison sair;
But I'll win out the morn's morrow,
    And ye'll see me nae mair.

CHILDREN

O f such is the kingdom of heaven.
        No glory that ever was shed
From the crowning star of the seven
    That crown the north world's head,

No word that ever was spoken
    Of human or godlike tongue,
Gave ever such godlike token
    Since human harps were strung.

No sign that ever was given
    To faithful or faithless eyes
Showed ever beyond clouds riven
    So clear a Paradise.

Earth's creeds may be seventy times seven
    And blood have defiled each creed:
If of such be the kingdom of heaven,
    It must be heaven indeed.

SONGS FROM *THE SISTERS*

I

LOVE AND SORROW

L ove and Sorrow met in May
    Crowned with rue and hawthorn-spray,
    And Sorrow smiled.
Scarce a bird of all the spring
Durst between them pass and sing,
    And scarce a child.

Love put forth his hand to take
Sorrow's wreath for sorrow's sake,
   Her crown of rue.
Sorrow cast before her down
Even for love's sake Love's own crown,
   Crowned with dew.

Winter breathed again, and spring
Cowered and shrank with wounded wing
   Down out of sight.
May, with all her loves laid low,
Saw no flowers but flowers of snow
   That mocked her flight.

Love rose up with crownless head
Smiling down on springtime dead,
   On wintry May.
Sorrow, like a cloud that flies,
Like a cloud in clearing skies,
   Passed away.

II

THERE'S NAE LARK

There's nae lark loves the lift, my dear,
   There's nae ship loves the sea,
There's nae bee loves the heather-bells,
  That loves as I love thee, my love,
  That loves as I love thee.

The whin shines fair upon the fell
  The blithe broom on the lea:
The muirside wind is merry at heart:
  It's a' for love of thee, my love,
  It's a' for love of thee.

JAMES THOMSON (B.V.)

1834–1882

James Thomson, ' the poet of despair,' was born in Port Glasgow in 1834. His father, a Scotch sea-captain, strong and hearty, with a weakness for Scotch drink, was stricken with paralysis during the poet's childhood. His mother, a devout but rather melancholy follower of a fanatical sect, was unable to support the family and the boy was sent to an asylum for Scotch children in London. Shortly after his admission his mother died, the first of the many blows that fell on him during his unhappy life.

He received a good education in the asylum and later at a normal school where he prepared for the profession of army schoolmaster. Entering the army he was sent to a post in Ireland where he formed a close friendship with Charles Bradlaugh, later famous as a radical freethinker, then serving as a private in the army. It is probable that his association with Bradlaugh marks the beginning of Thomson's drift from the strict Calvinism in which he had been trained toward his later negation of all belief. It was at this time also that, while little more than a boy, he fell passionately in love with a beautiful girl even younger than himself. His love was returned and Thomson was looking forward to a career, marriage, and a happy life, when her sudden death fell on him like a thunderbolt. For days, we are told, he refused to eat and lay about his room like a man physically stunned. Although in later life Thomson formed many friendships with women, he never had another love, and the memory of his lost sweetheart flits like a vision of delight through much of his work, especially his early poems.

In 1862 Thomson became involved in a petty quarrel with an army officer, was court-marshalled and discharged. It is not unlikely that the habit of occasional intemperance to which as years went on he became more and more a victim had something to do with this affair.

184

❖ JAMES THOMSON ❖

For the next twenty years Thomson led an irregular and desultory life. Bradlaugh took him into his home for a time and assisted him to find work. He visited Colorado as the secretary of a worthless mining company and was cheated of his pay. He served as a war-correspondent for the New York *World* in one of the many civil wars in Spain, and was discharged for incompetence. He secured a post as chief contributor to *Cope's Tobacco Plant,* an advertising periodical which varied its eulogies of Cope's product with sketches, essays, and poems. Meanwhile he set to work to perfect himself as a poet. His earliest verses appeared under various pseudonyms, of which the one finally adopted was B.V., initials which stood for Bysshe Vanolis, a name adopted to show his reverence for Shelley and the German poet, Novalis. To Bradlaugh's freethinking journal, *The National Reformer,* he contributed some of his best work in prose and verse. *The City of Dreadful Night* on which he had been engaged for several years, was published in this paper in 1874. Thomson's association with the dreaded radical Bradlaugh and his own frankly avowed atheistic opinions stood in the way of his obtaining popular recognition and it was not until 1880 that the strenuous advocacy of his friend, Bertram Dobell, secured the publication of his first volume of verse, *The City of Dreadful Night and Other Poems,* which was followed in 1881 by *Vane's Story,* a more or less autobiographical record in verse of his life and thought. The moderate success which these volumes brought him came too late. He experienced a late brief flowering time, a lyric outburst after ' seven songless years ' — 1874–1881 — and then the cloud of melancholia settled down upon him darker and deadlier than before. And melancholia brought with it night after night of sleepless hours. The tragic poem *Insomnia,* written a few months before his death, is a dreadful revelation of his sufferings. A long stay with friends in the country ended in a fashion only too well known to his acquaintances, the miserable sequence of melancholia, insomnia, and the temporary oblivion of drunkenness. Shamed and sick at heart Thomson fled back to London, to cut loose from all friends, wander homeless through the streets, and kill himself in a long bout of wild intoxication. He was found at last, a dying man, and carried to a hospital, where he passed away in the early summer of 1882.

Thomson's career is one of the tragedies of English litera-
ture. Intelligent and highly gifted, widely read and keenly
critical, capable of passionate love and devoted friendship, he
might have risen to unknown heights. Inherited tendencies
to drink and melancholia, combined with a series of misfor-
tunes and disappointments, brought about what he himself
called ' this long defeat my life.' Sleepless, poor, and often hun-
gry, he wandered through London, every street of which was
to him a stony-hearted step-mother. Thomson is essentially a
poet of the town but of a town such as, happily, no other Eng-
lish poet ever knew, in sad truth a city of dreadful night.

A serious and philosophic thinker he replaced his early
faith, not by the stoicism of Arnold or Swinburne's religion
of humanity, but by the strictest materialism of an age when
the new science seemed to be sweeping aside alike old super-
stition, prejudice, and faith. He came to believe that:

> The world rolls round forever like a mill;
> It grinds out death and life and good and ill;
> It has no purpose, heart or mind or will.

It is little wonder that life in such a world seemed to him no
better than ' a tragic farce ' and death a boon to be desired.

Yet after all no man can live out a life of nearly fifty years
under the shadow of unbroken gloom, and there is evidence to
show that in Thomson's case the ever deepening shadow lifted
from time to time to allow brief glimpses of joy and beauty.
Thomson was known to a small but devoted circle as the best
of friends, amiable, sympathetic, and generous. More than most
English poets he was a passionate lover of music. He had an
eye to see and a heart to feel the beauties of the English coun-
tryside and to share the joy of the Londoner who escaped
from the turmoil of the town for a *Sunday up the River*. And
of all this Thomson has left a record in his work.

Two styles in his poetry correspond to the two moods of the
poet. The lighter mood is embodied in lyric verse. It is not
lyric of the highest order, yet it has some affinities with the
lighter verse of Heine whom Thomson admired and trans-
lated, and it foreshadows a certain tendency in later poetry
to celebrate the pleasures of the ' mob ' — to use Thomson's
own word — in realistic verse. In the best of it there is a fine,

frank joy in life, alien it may seem to the poet of despair, but Thomson would never have sunk to such depths of gloom if he had not realized and enjoyed to the full the sensuous pleasures which life was slowly and surely withdrawing from him.

Charming as much of his lighter verse is, it is not to this that Thomson's repute is due, but to the poems that give expression, with an accent peculiarly his own and with a force unparalleled in English, to what was, after all, more than a mood with him, rather a firm conviction, a 'pessimism stubborn as adamant.' These poems are for the most part descriptive, dramatic, and, if the word may be used without derogation, rhetorical. We hear at times a resonance, a clangour as of a blast from a brazen trumpet. The 'sharp and clashing noise' which breaks in upon his vision of the angel and the sphinx echoes and re-echoes throughout the poem. Nothing is easier than for work of this sort to fall below the level of true poetry. What saves and ennobles Thomson's work is his splendid technique, his firm grasp of the thing seen, his picturesque diction, and above all his profound sincerity. Here is no Childe Harold parading the pageant of his bleeding heart, but a voice crying from the very depths a message, if not of comfort, at least of fellowship to comrades in the 'all-disastrous fight.' For the pessimism of Thomson was absolute and all-embracing. To him there was no God, no life beyond the grave, no progress in the world of man, only perpetual change with the final prospect of annihilation and oblivion for the human race. Here, it would seem, is the *ne plus ultra* of despair.

There is no need to discuss, to affirm or deny Thomson's philosophy. It represents a certain outlook on life not unfamiliar since the days of the Jew who wrote *Ecclesiastes* or the Roman who composed *De Rerum Natura;* and neither the Jew nor the Roman has given a fuller, loftier, and sincerer expression of

> The sense that every struggle brings defeat
>   Because Fate holds no prize to crown success;
> That all the oracles are dumb or cheat
>   Because they have no secret to express;
> That none can pierce the vast black veil uncertain
>   Because there is no light beyond the curtain;
>   That all is vanity and nothingness.

SUNDAY UP THE RIVER

AN IDYLL OF COCKAIGNE

XV

Give a man a horse he can ride,
　Give a man a boat he can sail;
And his rank and wealth, his strength and health,
　On sea nor shore shall fail.

Give a man a pipe he can smoke,
　Give a man a book he can read;
And his home is bright with a calm delight,
　Though the room be poor indeed.

Give a man a girl he can love,
　As I, O my Love, love thee;
And his heart is great with the pulse of Fate,
　At home, on land, on sea.

XVII

Let my voice ring out and over the earth,
　Through all the grief and strife,
With a golden joy in a silver mirth:
　　Thank God for Life!

Let my voice swell out through the great abyss
　To the azure dome above,
With a chord of faith in the harp of bliss:
　　Thank God for Love!

Let my voice thrill out beneath and above,
　The whole world through:
O my Love and Life, O my Life and Love,
　　Thank God for you!

XVIII

The wine of Love is music,
　And the feast of Love is song:
And when Love sits down to the banquet,
　　Love sits long:

Sits long and ariseth drunken,
    But not with the feast and the wine;
He reeleth with his own heart,
    That great rich Vine.

SUNDAY AT HAMPSTEAD

(AN IDLE IDYLL BY A VERY HUMBLE MEMBER OF THE GREAT AND
NOBLE LONDON MOB.)

I

This is the Heath of Hampstead,
    There is the dome of Saint Paul's;
Beneath, on the serried house-tops,
A chequered lustre falls:

And the mighty city of London,
Under the clouds and the light,
Seems a low wet beach, half shingle,
With a few sharp rocks upright.

Here will we sit, my darling,
And dream an hour away:
The donkeys are hurried and worried,
But we are not donkeys to-day:

Through all the weary week, dear,
We toil in the murk down there,
Tied to a desk and a counter,
A patient stupid pair!

But on Sunday we slip our tether,
And away from the smoke and the smirch;
Too grateful to God for His Sabbath
To shut its hours in a church.

Away to the green, green country,
Under the open sky;
Where the earth's sweet breath is incense
And the lark sings psalms on high.

On Sunday we're Lord and Lady,
With ten times the love and glee
Of those pale and languid rich ones
Who are always and never free.

They drawl and stare and simper,
So fine and cold and staid,
Like exquisite waxwork figures
That must be kept in the shade:

We can laugh out loud when merry,
We can romp at kiss-in-the-ring,
We can take our beer at a public,
We can loll on the grass and sing. . . .

Would you grieve very much, my darling,
If all yon low wet shore
Were drowned by a mighty flood-tide,
And we never toiled there more?

Wicked? — there is no sin, dear,
In an idle dreamer's head;
He turns the world topsy-turvy
To prove that his soul's not dead.

I am sinking, sinking, sinking;
It is hard to sit upright!
Your lap is the softest pillow!
Good night, my Love, good night!

X

As we rush, as we rush in the Train,
    The trees and the houses go wheeling back,
But the starry heavens above the plain
    Come flying on our track.

All the beautiful stars of the sky,
    The silver doves of the forest of Night,
Over the dull earth swarm and fly,
    Companions of our flight.

We will rush ever on without fear;
  Let the goal be far, the flight be fleet!
For we carry the Heavens with us, Dear,
  While the Earth slips from our feet!

RICHARD FOREST'S MIDSUMMER NIGHT

VIII

Oh, how the nights are short,
    These heavenly nights of June!
The long day all amort
With toil, the time to court
    So stinted in its boon!

In winter brief work-days,
  Long rest-nights dark and cold,
Dank mists and miry ways,
Black boughs and leafless sprays,
  No sweet birds singing bold.

I find this order strange,
  And not at all the right;
Not thus would I arrange:
May I propose a change
  In seasons, day and night?

Cold days, warm nights, be long,
  Cold nights, warm days, be brief:
Warm nights of scent and song,
Nights long as love is strong, —
  Oh, Love should have relief!

Yet some days we would spare,
  Long days of love and rest,
So long, so rich, so rare,
When but to breathe the air
  Is to be fully blest.

When deep in fern we lie
  With golden gorse above;
Deep sapphire sea and sky,
Ringing of larks on high,
  Our whole world breathing love.

Long days of perfect rest!
Long days of infinite bliss!
Your head upon my breast;
Possessing and possessed,
Dissolving in a kiss.

THE FIRE THAT FILLED MY HEART OF OLD

I

The fire that filled my heart of old
Gave lustre while it burned;
Now only ashes grey and cold
Are in its silence urned.
Ah! better was the furious flame,
The splendour with the smart:
I never cared for the singer's fame,
But, oh! for the singer's heart
Once more —
The burning fulgent heart!

II

No love, no hate, no hope, no fear,
No anguish and no mirth;
Thus life extends from year to year,
A flat of sullen dearth.
Ah! life's blood creepeth cold and tame,
Life's thought plays no new part:
I never cared for the singer's fame,
But, oh! for the singer's heart
Once more —
The bleeding passionate heart!

WILLIAM BLAKE

He came to the desert of London town
Grey miles long;
He wandered up and he wandered down,
Singing a quiet song.

He came to the desert of London town,
    Mirk miles broad;
He wandered up and he wandered down,
    Ever alone with God.

There were thousands and thousands of human kind
    In this desert of brick and stone:
But some were deaf and some were blind,
    And he was there alone.

At length the good hour came; he died
    As he had lived, alone:
He was not missed from the desert wide,
    Perhaps he was found at the Throne.

THE CITY OF DREADFUL NIGHT

    ' Per me si va nella città dolente.'
                    — Dante

    ' Poi di tanto adoprar, di tanti moti
    D'ogni celeste, ogni terrena cosa,
    Girando senza posa,
    Per tornar sempre là donde son mosse;
    Uso alcuno, alcun frutto
    Indovinar no so.'

    ' Sola nel mondo eterna, a cui si volve
    Ogni creata cosa,
    In te, morte, si posa
    Nostra ignuda natura;
    Lieta no, ma sicura
    Dell'antico dolor. . . .
    Però ch' esser beato
    Nega ai mortali e nega a' morti il fato.'
                    — Leopardi

PROEM

Lo, thus, as prostrate, ' In the dust I write
    My heart's deep languor and my soul's sad tears.'
Yet why evoke the spectres of black night
    To blot the sunshine of exultant years?

Why disinter dead faith from mouldering hidden?
Why break the seals of mute despair unbidden,
  And wail life's discords into careless ears?

Because a cold rage seizes one at whiles
  To show the bitter old and wrinkled truth
Stripped naked of all vesture that beguiles,
  False dreams, false hopes, false masks and modes of youth:
Because it gives some sense of power and passion
In helpless impotence to try to fashion
  Our woe in living words howe'er uncouth.

Surely I write not for the hopeful young,
  Or those who deem their happiness of worth,
Or such as pasture and grow fat among
  The shows of life and feel nor doubt nor dearth,
Or pious spirits with a God above them
To sanctify and glorify and love them,
  Or sages who foresee a heaven on earth.

For none of these I write, and none of these
  Could read the writing if they deigned to try:
So may they flourish, in their due degrees,
  On our sweet earth and in their unplaced sky.
If any cares for the weak words here written,
It must be someone desolate, Fate-smitten,
  Whose faith and hope are dead, and who would die.

Yes, here and there some weary wanderer
  In that same city of tremendous night,
Will understand the speech, and feel a stir
  Of fellowship in all-disastrous fight;
' I suffer mute and lonely, yet another
Uplifts his voice to let me know a brother
  Travels the same wild paths though out of sight.'

O sad Fraternity, do I unfold
  Your dolorous mysteries shrouded from of yore?
Nay, be assured; no secret can be told
  To any who divined it not before:
None uninitiate by many a presage
Will comprehend the language of the message,
  Although proclaimed aloud for evermore.

✤ JAMES THOMSON ✤

I

The City is of Night; perchance of Death,
   But certainly of Night; for never there
Can come the lucid morning's fragrant breath
   After the dewy dawning's cold grey air;
The moon and stars may shine with scorn or pity;
The sun has never visited that city,
   For it dissolveth in the daylight fair.

Dissolveth like a dream of night away;
   Though present in distempered gloom of thought
And deadly weariness of heart all day.
   But when a dream night after night is brought
Throughout a week, and such weeks few or many
Recur each year for several years, can any
   Discern that dream from real life in aught?

For life is but a dream whose shapes return,
   Some frequently, some seldom, some by night
And some by day, some night and day: we learn,
   The while all change and many vanish quite,
In their recurrence with recurrent changes
A certain seeming order; where this ranges
   We count things real; such is memory's might.

A river girds the city west and south,
   The main north channel of a broad lagoon.
Regurging with the salt tides from the moutn;
   Waste marshes shine and glister to the moon
For leagues, then moorland black, then stony ridges;
Great piers and causeways, many noble bridges,
   Connect the town and islet suburbs strewn.

Upon an easy slope it lies at large,
   And scarcely overlaps the long curved crest
Which swells out two leagues from the river marge.
   A trackless wilderness rolls north and west,
Savannahs, savage woods, enormous mountains,
Bleak uplands, black ravines with torrent fountains;
   And eastward rolls the shipless sea's unrest.

The city is not ruinous, although
   Great ruins of an unremembered past,
With others of a few short years ago,
   More sad, are found within its precincts vast.
The street-lamps always burn; but scarce a casement
In house or palace front from room to basement
   Doth glow or gleam athwart the mirk air cast.

The street-lamps burn amidst the baleful glooms,
   Amidst the soundless solitudes immense
Of rangèd mansions dark and still as tombs.
   The silence which benumbs or strains the sense
Fulfils with awe the soul's despair unweeping:
Myriads of habitants are ever sleeping,
   Or dead, or fled from nameless pestilence!

Yet as in some necropolis you find
   Perchance one mourner to a thousand dead,
So there; worn faces that look deaf and blind
   Like tragic masks of stone. With weary tread,
Each wrapped in his own doom, they wander, wander,
Or sit foredone and desolately ponder
   Through sleepless hours with heavy drooping head.

Mature men chiefly, few in age or youth,
   A woman rarely, now and then a child:
A child! If here the heart turns sick with ruth
   To see a little one from birth defiled,
Or lame or blind, as preordained to languish
Through youthless life, think how it bleeds with anguish
   To meet one erring in that homeless wild.

They often murmur to themselves, they speak
   To one another seldom, for their woe
Broods maddening inwardly and scorns to wreak
   Itself abroad; and if at whiles it grow
To frenzy which must rave, none heeds the clamour,
Unless there waits some victim of like glamour,
   To rave in turn, who lends attentive show.

The City is of Night, but not of Sleep;
   There sweet sleep is not for the weary brain;
The pitiless hours like years and ages creep,
   A night seems termless hell. This dreadful strain
Of thought and consciousness which never ceases,
Or which some moments' stupor but increases,
   This, worse than woe, makes wretches there insane.

They leave all hope behind who enter there:
   One certitude while sane they cannot leave,
One anodyne for torture and despair;
   The certitude of Death, which no reprieve
Can put off long; and which, divinely tender,
But waits the outstretched hand to promptly render
   That draught whose slumber nothing can bereave.

IV

He stood alone within the spacious square,
   Declaiming from the central grassy mound,
With head uncovered and with streaming hair,
   As if large multitudes were gathered round:
A stalwart shape, the gestures full of might,
The glances burning with unnatural light: —

As I came through the desert thus it was,
As I came through the desert: All was black,
In heaven no single star, on earth no track;
A brooding hush without a stir or note,
The air so thick it clotted in my throat;
And thus for hours; then some enormous things
Swooped past with savage cries and clanking wings:
    But I strode on austere;
    No hope could have no fear.

As I came through the desert thus it was,
As I came through the desert: Eyes of fire
Glared at me throbbing with a starved desire;
The hoarse and heavy and carnivorous breath
Was hot upon me from deep jaws of death;

Sharp claws, swift talons, fleshless fingers cold
Plucked at me from the bushes, tried to hold:
    But I strode on austere;
    No hope could have no fear.

As I came through the desert thus it was,
As I came through the desert: Lo you, there,
That hillock burning with a brazen glare;
Those myriad dusky flames with points a-glow
Which writhed and hissed and darted to and fro;
A Sabbath of the Serpents, heaped pell-mell
For Devil's roll-call and some *fête* of hell:
    Yet I strode on austere;
    No hope could have no fear.

As I came through the desert thus it was,
As I came through the desert: Meteors ran
And crossed their javelins on the black sky-span;
The zenith opened to a gulf of flame,
The dreadful thunderbolts jarred earth's fixed frame;
The ground all heaved in waves of fire that surged
And weltered round me sole there unsubmerged:
    Yet I strode on austere;
    No hope could have no fear.

As I came through the desert thus it was,
As I came through the desert: Air once more,
And I was close upon a wild sea-shore;
Enormous cliffs arose on either hand,
The deep tide thundered up a league-broad strand;
White foambelts seethed there, wan spray swept and flew;
The sky broke, moon and stars and clouds and blue:
    And I strode on austere;
    No hope could have no fear.

As I came through the desert thus it was,
As I came through the desert: On the left
The sun arose and crowned a broad crag-cleft;
There stopped and burned out black, except a rim,
A bleeding, eyeless socket, red and dim;

❖ JAMES THOMSON ❖

Whereon the moon fell suddenly south-west,
And stood above the right-hand cliffs at rest:
    Still I strode on austere;
    No hope could have no fear.

As I came through the desert thus it was,
As I came through the desert: From the right
A shape came slowly with a ruddy light;
A woman with a red lamp in her hand,
Bareheaded and barefooted on that strand;
O desolation moving with such grace!
O anguish with such beauty in thy face!
    I fell as on my bier,
    Hope travailed with such fear.

As I came through the desert thus it was,
As I came through the desert: I was twain,
Two selves distinct that cannot join again;
One stood apart and knew but could not stir,
And watched the other stark in swoon and her;
And she came on, and never turned aside,
Between such sun and moon and roaring tide:
    And as she came more near
    My soul grew mad with fear.

As I came through the desert thus it was,
As I came through the desert: Hell is mild
And piteous matched with that accursèd wild;
A large black sign was on her breast that bowed,
A broad black band ran down her snow-white shroud;
That lamp she held was her own burning heart,
Whose blood-drops trickled step by step apart:
    The mystery was clear;
    Mad rage had swallowed fear.

As I came through the desert thus it was,
As I came through the desert: By the sea
She knelt and bent above that senseless me;
Those lamp-drops fell upon my white brow there,
She tried to cleanse them with her tears and hair;

199

She murmured words of pity, love, and woe,
She heeded not the level rushing flow:
    And mad with rage and fear,
    I stood stonebound so near.

As I came through the desert thus it was,
As I came through the desert: When the tide
Swept up to her there kneeling by my side,
She clasped that corpse-like me, and they were borne
Away, and this vile me was left forlorn;
I know the whole sea cannot quench that heart,
Or cleanse that brow, or wash those two apart:
    They love; their doom is drear,
    Yet they nor hope nor fear;
    But I, what do I here?

XIV

Large glooms were gathered in the mighty fane,
    With tinted moongleams slanting here and there;
And all was hush: no swelling organ-strain,
    No chant, no voice or murmuring of prayer;
No priests came forth, no tinkling censers fumed,
And the high altar space was unillumed.

Around the pillars and against the walls
    Leaned men and shadows; others seemed to brood
Bent or recumbent in secluded stalls.
    Perchance they were not a great multitude
Save in that city of so lonely streets
Where one may count up every face he meets.

All patiently awaited the event
    Without a stir or sound, as if no less
Self-occupied, doomstricken, while attent.
    And then we heard a voice of solemn stress
From the dark pulpit, and our gaze there met
Two eyes which burned as never eyes burned yet.

✥ JAMES THOMSON ✥

Two steadfast and intolerable eyes
  Burning beneath a broad and rugged brow;
The head behind it of enormous size.
  And as black fir-groves in a large wind bow,
Our rooted congregation, gloom-arrayed,
By that great sad voice deep and full were swayed: —

O melancholy Brothers, dark, dark, dark!
O battling in black floods without an ark!
  O spectral wanderers of unholy Night!
My soul hath bled for you these sunless years,
With bitter blood-drops running down like tears:
  Oh, dark, dark, dark, withdrawn from joy and light!

My heart is sick with anguish for your bale;
Your woe hath been my anguish; yea, I quail
  And perish in your perishing unblest.
And I have searched the highths and depths, the scope
Of all our universe, with desperate hope
  To find some solace for your wild unrest.

And now at last authentic word I bring,
Witnessed by every dead and living thing;
  Good tidings of great joy for you, for all:
There is no God; no Fiend with names divine
Made us and tortures us; if we must pine,
  It is to satiate no Being's gall.

It was the dark delusion of a dream,
That living Person conscious and supreme,
  Whom we must curse for cursing us with life;
Whom we must curse because the life He gave
Could not be buried in the quiet grave,
  Could not be killed by poison or by knife.

This little life is all we must endure,
The grave's most holy peace is ever sure,
  We fall asleep and never wake again;
Nothing is of us but the mouldering flesh,
Whose elements dissolve and merge afresh
  In earth, air, water, plants, and other men.

We finish thus; and all our wretched race
Shall finish with its cycle, and give place
   To other beings, with their own time-doom:
Infinite æons ere our kind began;
Infinite æons after the last man
   Has joined the mammoth in earth's tomb and womb.

We bow down to the universal laws,
Which never had for man a special clause
   Of cruelty or kindness, love or hate:
If toads and vultures are obscene to sight,
If tigers burn with beauty and with might,
   Is it by favour or by wrath of fate?

All substance lives and struggles evermore
Through countless shapes continually at war,
   By countless interactions interknit:
If one is born a certain day on earth,
All times and forces tended to that birth,
   Not all the world could change or hinder it.

I find no hint throughout the Universe
Of good or ill, of blessing or of curse;
   I find alone Necessity Supreme;
With infinite Mystery, abysmal, dark,
Unlighted ever by the faintest spark
   For us the flitting shadows of a dream.

O Brothers of sad lives! they are so brief;
A few short years must bring us all relief:
   Can we not bear these years of labouring breath?
But if you would not this poor life fulfil,
Lo, you are free to end it when you will
   Without the fear of waking after death. —

The organ-like vibrations of his voice
   Thrilled through the vaulted aisles and died away;
The yearning of the tones which bade rejoice
   Was sad and tender as a requiem lay:
Our shadowy congregation rested still
As brooding on that ' End it when you will.'

XX

I sat me weary on a pillar's base,
    And leaned against the shaft; for broad moonlight
O'erflowed the peacefulness of cloistered space,
    A shore of shadow slanting from the right:
The great cathedral's western front stood there,
A wave-worn rock in that calm sea of air.

Before it, opposite my place of rest,
    Two figures faced each other, large, austere;
A couchant sphinx in shadow to the breast,
    An angel standing in the moonlight clear;
So mighty by magnificence of form,
They were not dwarfed beneath that mass enorm.

Upon the cross-hilt of a naked sword
    The angel's hands, as prompt to smite, were held;
His vigilant, intense regard was poured
    Upon the creature placidly unquelled,
Whose front was set at level gaze which took
No heed of aught, a solemn trance-like look.

And as I pondered these opposèd shapes
    My eyelids sank in stupor, that dull swoon
Which drugs and with a leaden mantle drapes
    The outworn to worse weariness. But soon
A sharp and clashing noise the stillness broke,
And from the evil lethargy I woke.

The angel's wings had fallen, stone on stone,
    And lay there shattered; hence the sudden sound:
A warrior leaning on his sword alone
    Now watched the sphinx with that regard profound;
The sphinx unchanged looked forthright, as aware
Of nothing in the vast abyss of air.

Again I sank in that repose unsweet,
    Again a clashing noise my slumber rent;
The warrior's sword lay broken at his feet:
    An unarmed man with raised hands impotent
Now stood before the sphinx, which ever kept
Such mien as if with open eyes it slept.

My eyelids sank in spite of wonder grown;
   A louder crash upstartled me in dread:
The man had fallen forward, stone on stone,
   And lay there shattered, with his trunkless head
Between the monster's large quiescent paws,
Beneath its grand front changeless as life's laws.

The moon had circled westward full and bright,
   And made the temple-front a mystic dream,
And bathed the whole enclosure with its light,
   The sworded angel's wrecks, the sphinx supreme:
I pondered long that cold majestic face
Whose vision seemed of infinite void space.

XXI

Anear the centre of that northern crest
   Stands out a level upland bleak and bare,
From which the city east and south and west
   Sinks gently in long waves; and thronèd there
An Image sits, stupendous, superhuman,
The bronze colossus of a wingèd Woman,
   Upon a graded granite base foursquare.

Low-seated she leans forward massively,
   With cheek on clenched left hand, the forearm's might
Erect, its elbow on her rounded knee;
   Across a clasped book in her lap the right
Upholds a pair of compasses; she gazes
With full set eyes, but wandering in thick mazes
   Of sombre thought beholds no outward sight.

Words cannot picture her; but all men know
   That solemn sketch the pure sad artist wrought
Three centuries and threescore years ago,
   With phantasies of his peculiar thought:
The instruments of carpentry and science
Scattered about her feet, in strange alliance
   With the keen wolf-hound sleeping undistraught;

Scales, hour-glass, bell, and magic-square above;
  The grave and solid infant perched beside,
With open winglets that might bear a dove,
  Intent upon its tablets, heavy-eyed;
Her folded wings as of a mighty eagle,
But all too impotent to lift the regal
  Robustness of her earth-born strength and pride;

And with those wings, and that light wreath which seems
  To mock her grand head and the knotted frown
Of forehead charged with baleful thoughts and dreams,
  The household bunch of keys, the housewife's gown
Voluminous, indented, and yet rigid
As if a shell of burnished metal frigid,
  The feet thick shod to tread all weakness down;

The comet hanging o'er the waste dark seas,
  The massy rainbow curved in front of it,
Beyond the village with the masts and trees;
  The snaky imp, dog-headed, from the Pit,
Bearing upon its batlike leathern pinions
Her name unfolded in the sun's dominions,
  The ' MELENCOLIA ' that transcends all wit.

Thus has the artist copied her, and thus
  Surrounded to expound her form sublime,
Her fate heroic and calamitous;
  Fronting the dreadful mysteries of Time,
Unvanquished in defeat and desolation,
Undaunted in the hopeless conflagration
  Of the day setting on her baffled prime.

Baffled and beaten back she works on still,
  Weary and sick of soul she works the more,
Sustained by her indomitable will:
  The hands shall fashion and the brain shall pore,
And all her sorrow shall be turned to labour,
Till death, the friend-foe, piercing with his sabre
  That mighty heart of hearts ends bitter war.

But as if blacker night could dawn on night,
  With tenfold gloom on moonless night unstarred,
A sense more tragic than defeat and blight,
  More desperate than strife with hope debarred,
More fatal than the adamantine Never
Encompassing her passionate endeavour,
  Dawns glooming in her tenebrous regard:

The sense that every struggle brings defeat
  Because Fate holds no prize to crown success;
That all the oracles are dumb or cheat
  Because they have no secret to express;
That none can pierce the vast black veil uncertain
Because there is no light beyond the curtain;
  That all is vanity and nothingness.

Titanic from her high throne in the north,
  That City's sombre Patroness and Queen,
In bronze sublimity she gazes forth.
  Over her Capital of teen and threne,
Over the river with its isles and bridges,
The marsh and moorland, to the stern rock-ridges,
  Confronting them with a coëval mien.

The moving moon and stars from east to west
  Circle before her in the sea of air;
Shadows and gleams glide round her solemn rest.
  Her subjects often gaze up to her there:
The strong to drink new strength of iron endurance,
The weak new terrors; all, renewed assurance
  And confirmation of the old despair.

THOMAS EDWARD BROWN
1830–1897

A compressed account of the life of T. E. Brown can convey little of the richness of his nature. On the surface — to publishers and critics — it was a staid and useful life of school-mastering and occasional preaching and verse-making, and at the end a quiet drifting into old age among the Manxmen on the island he knew and loved. But then Dr. Johnson's life makes in outline a tedious brief chronicle. Nor is the comparison inept for Brown's influence, like Johnson's, was at least as great as his literary performance; his wit and sympathy and downrightness, his deep though reserved religious fervour, remind one of the lexicographer. His first sally into the livelier world outside his native island was to Christ Church, Oxford, where he endured a servitorship — a medieval survival whereby poor boys obtained on sufferance of the dons and gentlemen commoners such an education as the authorities condescended to give them. Though Brown took a high place in the final schools, his own college refused to acknowledge his brilliance with a fellowship, a wound that he never forgave. Oriel was glad to receive him, but he soon turned his back on academic honours and became a schoolmaster, first on the Isle of Man, then finally at Clifton, where generations of boys came under his spirited leadership.

Though he was a master such as the public schools can seldom keep in the mill, his life was, as he privately confessed, 'steadfastly or normally rebellious against the calling to which circumstances' had compelled him. His solace and escape was poetry — the 'inner work' which he belatedly realized he had been destined to produce. As he grew confident of his talent, his life took on a new radiance and he began to plan and dream like a man of twenty. At fifty-seven he upbraids the young for lacking 'insanity.' It is somewhat startling to overhear a history master confessing to a friend: 'I only need a very slight hint to set me off on the road to sheer and untamable and dissolute heathenism.' He chafes under the inherited

207

prejudices which swathe and *encaudle* him. He wishes he might repair the mistake he made in allowing himself to be 'born into the professional class.'

His poetry let off the steam of these desires and ambitions while he was still at Clifton. When he finally cut loose from duty, to settle on the island which he hoped to make famous again by his tales of her seamen and 'pazons' (parsons) and fisherfolk, he refused the honour of the archdeaconry of Man and asked that he be allowed to become a 'smug, bucolic, thriving Manx farmer, guiltless of ideas, incubating repose, a peaceful centre of lambs, rooks, and incipient turnips.'

Before his death in 1897 he had published *Fo'c's'le Yarns* (1881), *The Doctor and other Poems* (1887), *The Manx Witch and other Poems* (1889), *Old John and other Poems* (1893). *The Collected Poems,* with an introduction by his old pupil W. E. Henley, was issued in 1900.

It is probably well to begin with an apology for including T. E. Brown in a collection of poetry which in the main represents the revolt against the laurelled verse of Victoria's reign. Did not Brown believe, heart-whole, in God and the Empire, the wisdom of the public-school system, the necessary and inviolable purity of womanhood? And does not his poetry, as a reviewer said of it, tend to urge upon the young the stainless moral life? If it comes to a flat yes or no, the answer is yes. But, let us quickly subjoin, it need not come to that, for he wore his rue with a difference. He generally took these important matters for granted and went on to more interesting concerns, such as spring in the Manx glens and the tragi-comedy of island life. It is only the critics in respectable quarterlies who could think of nothing else to say who linger over Brown's 'morality' and 'sanity.' We are able to like him for quite different reasons.

The truth is, and no one has yet blurted it out, that he is 'the best spinner of yarns since Burns and has no one to challenge his supremacy in these times except Masefield. His first poem, *Betsy Lee,* contains that most cruelly wronged of lovers Tom Baynes, and the tale he tells is the first of many in his repertory. He ought to be as famous as his much duller contemporary Enoch Arden, but his Anglo-Manx lingo has kept lazy people from making his acquaintance. Tom is Brown as he wanted to be: ' I never stopped for a moment to think what

Tom Baynes should be like: he simply is I, just such a crabbed text, blurred with scholia " in the margent." . . . So when I am alone, I think and speak to myself always as he does.'

Brown knew Manx history, geography, folklore, and genealogy as no one else. His favourite Virgilian ' *antiquam exquirite* ' in which his love of deep, rich living is summed up, he most completely carried out in his absorption of the life of his people. His imagination teemed with characters and scenes. He felt the island quivering and trembling all over with stories — ' they are like leaves on a tree. . . . The people are always telling them to one another, and any morning or evening you hear, whether you like it or not, innumerable anecdotes and sayings, tragedies, comedies — I wonder whether they lie fearfully? ' So faithful are his characters to their originals that ' jus' the shy' in them stirred up a trace of resentment towards Brown for having exposed them naked to the world. They trusted him at their harvest-homes with some apprehension.

One marks instantly in Brown's lyric verse a full-blooded quality which characterized all that he did. In this he is akin to Browning. The great difference between them, aside from the obvious point of the styles they adopted, depends from Brown's terse, aphoristic cast of mind. The much derided *My Garden,* generally taken as a pretty Victorian sentiment, shows this well. Here, as often in his verse, the heartiness and assurance which might irritate a modern ear, are saved by the abrupt and even humorous turn of phrase. Brown never completely let himself go in irony, but he saw the world through that glass.

> For though the heavens are still,
> God sits upon His hill,
> And sees the shadows fly;
> And if He laughs at fools, why should He not?

CLIFTON

I'm here at Clifton, grinding at the mill
　　My feet for thrice nine barren years have trod;
But there are rocks and waves at Scarlett still,
　　And gorse runs riot in Glen Chass — thank God!

Alert, I seek exactitude of rule,
 I step, and square my shoulders with the squad;
But there are blaeberries on old Barrule,
 And Langness has its heather still — thank God!

There is no silence here: the truculent quack
 Insists with acrid shriek my ears to prod,
And, if I stop them, fumes; but there's no lack
 Of silence still on Carraghyn — thank God!

Pragmatic fibs surround my soul, and bate it
 With measured phrase, that asks the assenting nod;
I rise, and say the bitter thing, and hate it —
 But Wordsworth's castle's still at Peel — thank God!

O broken life! O wretched bits of being,
 Unrhythmic, patched, the even and the odd!
But Bradda still has lichens worth the seeing,
 And thunder in her caves — thank God! thank God!

THE DHOON

Leap from the crags, brave boy!
 The musing hills have kept thee long,
But they have made thee strong,
And fed thee with the fulness of their joy,
And given direction that thou might'st return
To me who yearn
At foot of this great steep —
Leap! leap! '

So the stream leapt
Into his mother's arms,
Who wept
A space,
Then calmed her sweet alarms,
And smiled to see him as he slept,
Wrapt in that dear embrace:
And with the brooding of her tepid breast
Cherished his mountain chillness —
O, then — what rest!
O, everywhere what stillness!

SALVE!

To live within a cave — it is most good.
　　But, if God make a day,
　　And some one come, and say: —
' Lo! I have gathered faggots in the wood! '
　　E'en let him stay,
And light a fire, and fan a temporal mood!

So sit till morning! When the light is grown
　　That he the path can read,
　　Then bid the man God-speed!
His morning is not thine; yet must thou own
They have a cheerful warmth — those ashes on the stone.

MY GARDEN

A garden is a lovesome thing, God wot!
　　Rose plot,
Fringed pool,
Ferned grot —
The veriest school
Of peace; and yet the fool
Contends that God is not —
Not God! in gardens! when the eve is cool?
Nay, but I have a sign;
'Tis very sure God walks in mine.

IN THE COACH

V. — THE PAZONS

What's the gud of these Pazons? They're the most despard
　　rubbage go'n',
Reg'lar humbugs they are. Show me a Pazon, show me a drone!
Livin' on the fat of the land, livin' on the people's money
The same's the drones is livin' on the beeses honey.
Aw bless ye! the use of them? not the smallest taste in the
　　world, no!
Grindin' down the honest workin' man, just so;

Suckin' the blood of the poor and needy,
And as greedy's greedy.
See the tithes, see the fees, see the glebes and all;
What's the call
For the lek? and their wives go'n a takin' for ladies, and their
    childhar go'n sendin' to College
Like the fuss of the land. Aw, it bates all knowledge
The uprisement of the lek! And fingerin' with their piannas,
Them that shud be singin' their hosannahs
To the King of glory constant. Clap them in the pulfit theer,
What can they do! Aw, come down the steer! come down the
    steer,
And don't be disgracin' yourself that way! That's what I've
    been thinking many a time —
And let a praecher take his turn, a local, aye, just try'm!
Aw, give your people a chance to get salvation.
' Blow ye the trumpet in Zion! ' That's the style, and the pres-
    piration
Pourin' out all over his body! See the wrestlin',
And the poor Pazon with his collec' and his pestlin'
And his gosp'lin'. *Gospel!* Let it sound abroad,
The rael gospel of God!
Aw then the happy I am!
Give us the Lamb! give us the Lamb!
But he can't, I tell ye, he can't —
What's that young man sayin' theer — rant?
Rant indeed, is that what he's learnin'
At Oxfoot College, to revile the spirit that's burnin'
In the hearts of the faithful? Aye, and let it burn, let it blaze!
But here's the Pazon, if ye plaze,
Cocked up with his little twinkle of a farlin' rush,
And'll hauk and blush,
And his snips and his snaps
And his scrips and his scraps,
And endin' up with the Lord's Prayer quite sudden
Lek the ould woman's sauce to give a notion of a puddin', . . .
Aye, puddin', and drabbin' with their swishups and dishups
Of the stale ould broth of the law! If all the hands of all the
    bishops
Was goin' crookin' over his head, he wudn' be a preacher,
Not him, *nor* a taecher.

You can't be married without a Pazon? Can't I though?
Can't I, Masther Crow?
Give me the chance: I'm a married man with a fam'ly comin',
But if it plazed the Lord to take Mrs. Creer, d'ye think there's
    a woman
'd refuse to go with me before the High Bailiff down
At Castletown,
And ger' a slick of matrimony put upon us?
Honest?
Yes, honest thallure: *but holy, ' holy matrimony,' they're
    say'n —*
Holy your grandmother! — At laste, I mane,
And astin' your pardon, Mrs. Clague!
But the idikkilis people is about the lek o'yandhar — Aisy with
    your leg,
Masthar Callow; thank ye! that'll do —
Yis, Mrs. Clague, and crizzenin's and funarls too —
Shuperstition, just shuperstition, the whole kit,
Most horrid, just popery, clane popery, that's it —
Aye, popery and schamin' and a lie and a delusion and snares
To get money out of the people, which is the Lord's and not
    theirs!
Money, money every turn,
Money, money — pay or burn!
And where does it come from? I said it before, and I say it
    again,
Out of the sweat of the workin' man,
Aw these priests! these priests! these priests —
Down with them, I say. The brute beasts
Has more sense till us, that's willin' to pay blackmail
To a set of rascals, to a pack of — Good evenin', Pazon Gale!
Good evenin', sir, good evenin'! Step up, sir! Make room,
Make room for our respected Vicar — And may I presume
To ax how is Mrs. Gale, sir, and the family?
Does this weather agree —
Rather damp, I dessay! And the Governor's got knighted?
I'm delighted to see you, sir, delighted, delighted!

CHALSE A KILLEY

TO CHALSE IN HEAVEN

So you are gone, dear Chalse!
Ah! well: it was enough —.
The ways were cold, the ways were rough —
O Heaven! O home!
No more to roam —
Chalse, poor Chalse.

And now it's all so plain, dear Chalse!
So plain —
The wildered brain,
The joy, the pain —
The phantom shapes that haunted,
The half-born thoughts that daunted —
All, all is plain
Dear Chalse!
All is plain.

Yet where you're now, dear Chalse,
Have you no memory
Of land and sea,
Of vagrant liberty?
Through all your dreams
Come there no gleams
Of morning sweet and cool
On old Barrule?
Breathes there no breath,
Far o'er the hills of Death,
Of a soft wind that dallies
Among the Curragh sallies —
Shaking the perfumed gold-dust on the streams?
Chalse, poor Chalse!

Or is it all forgotten Chalse?
A fever fit that vanished with the night —
Has God's great light
Pierced through the veiled delusions,
The errors and confusions;
And pointed to the tablet, where
In quaint and wayward character,

As of some alien clime,
His name was graven all the time?
All the time!
O Chalse! poor Chalse.

Such music as you made, dear Chalse!
With that crazed instrument
That God had given you here for use —
You will not wonder now if it did loose
Our childish laughter, being writhen and bent
From native function — was it not, sweet saint?
But when such music ceases,
'Tis God that takes to pieces
The inveterate complication,
And makes a restoration
Most subtle in its sweetness,
Most strong in its completeness,
Most constant in its meetness;
And gives the absolute tone,
And so appoints your station
Before the throne —
Chalse, poor Chalse.

And yet while you were here, dear Chalse,
You surely had more joy than sorrow:
Even from your weakness you did borrow
A strength to mock
The frowns of fortune, to decline the shock
Of rigorous circumstance,
To weave around your path a dance
Of ' airy nothings,' Chalse; and while your soul,
Dear Chalse! was dark
As an o'erwanèd moon from pole to pole,
Yet had you still an arc
Forlorn, a silvery rim
Of the same light wherein the cherubim
Bathe their glad brows, and veer
On circling wings above the starry sphere —
Chalse, poor Chalse.

Yes, you had joys, dear Chalse! as when forsooth,
Right valiant for the truth,

You crossed the Baldwin hills,
And at the Union Mills,
Inspired with sacred fury,
You helped good Parson Drury,
To ' put the *Romans* out,'
A champion brave and stout —
Ah! now, dear Chalse, of all the radiant host,
Who loves you most?
I think I know him, kneeling on his knees —
Is it Saint Francis of Assise?
Chalse, poor Chalse.

Great joy was yours, dear Chalse! when first I met you
In that old Vicarage
That shelters under Bradda: we did get you
By stratagem most sage
Of youthful mischief — got you all unweeting
Of mirthful toys —
A merry group of girls and boys,
To hold a missionary meeting;
And you did stand upon a chair,
In the best parlour there;
And dear old Parson Corrin was from home,
And I did play a tune upon a comb;
And unto us
You did pronounce a speech most marvellous,
Dear Chalse! and then you said
And *sthrooghed* the head —
' If there'll be no objection,
We'll now *purseed* to the collection ' —
Chalse, poor Chalse!

And do you still remember, Chalse,
How at the Dhoor —
Near Ramsey, *to be sure* —
I got two painters painting in the chapel
To make with me a congregation?
And you did mount the pulpit, and did grapple
With a tremendous text, and warn the nation
Of drunkenness; and in your hand
Did wave an empty bottle, so that we,

By palpable typology,
Might understand —
Dear Chalse, you never had
An audience more silent or more sad!

And have you met him Chalse,
Whom you did long to meet?
You used to call him *dear and sweet* —
Good Bishop Wilson — has he *taken you*
In hand, dear Chalse? And is he true,
And is he kind,
And do you tell him all your mind,
Dear Chalse —
All your mind?
And have you yet set up the press;
And is the type in readiness,
Founded with gems
Of living sapphire, dipped
In blood of molten rubies, diamond-tipped?
And, *with the sanction of the Governor,*
Do you, a proud compositor,
Stand forth, and *prent the Hemns?* —
Chalse, poor Chalse!

THE ORGANIST IN HEAVEN

When Wesley died, the Angelic orders,
   To see him at the state,
Pressed so incontinent that the warders
   Forgot to shut the gate.
So I, that hitherto had followed
   As one with grief o'ercast,
Where for the doors a space was hollowed,
   Crept in, and heard what passed.
And God said: — ' Seeing thou hast given
   Thy life to my great sounds,
Choose thou through all the cirque of Heaven
   What most of bliss redounds.'
Then Wesley said: — ' I hear the thunder
   Low growling from Thy seat —
Grant me that I may bind it under
   The trampling of my feet.'

And Wesley said: — ' See, lightning quivers
   Upon the presence walls —
Lord, give me of it four great rivers,
   To be my manuals.'
And then I saw the thunder chidden
   As slave to his desire;
And then I saw the space bestridden
   With four great bands of fire;
And stage by stage, stop stop subtending,
   Each lever strong and true,
One shape inextricable blending,
   The awful organ grew.
Then certain angels clad the Master
   In very marvellous wise,
Till clouds of rose and alabaster
   Concealed him from mine eyes.
And likest to a dove soft brooding,
   The innocent figure ran;
So breathed the breath of his preluding,
   And then the fugue began —
Began; but, to his office turning,
   The porter swung his key;
Wherefore, although my heart was yearning,
   I had to go; but he
Played on; and, as I downward clomb,
   I heard the mighty bars
Of thunder-gusts, that shook heaven's dome,
   And moved the balanced stars.

FROM *CLEVEDON VERSES*

DORA

She knelt upon her brother's grave,
   My little girl of six years old —
He used to be so good and brave,
   The sweetest lamb of all our fold;
He used to shout, he used to sing,
Of all our tribe the little king —
And so unto the turf her ear she laid,
To hark if still in that dark place he played.

No sound! no sound!
Death's silence was profound;
And horror crept
Into her aching heart, and Dora wept.
If this is as it ought to be,
My God, I leave it unto Thee.

THE INTERCEPTED SALUTE

A little maiden met me in the lane,
And smiled a smile so very fain,
So full of trust and happiness,
I could not choose but bless
The child, that she should have such grace
To laugh into my face.

She never could have known me; but I thought
It was the common joy that wrought
Within the little creature's heart
As who should say: — ' Thou art
As I; the heaven is bright above us;
And there is God to love us.
And I am but a little gleeful maid,
And thou art big, and old, and staid;
But the blue hills have made thee mild
As is a little child.
Wherefore I laugh that thou may'st see —
O, laugh! O, laugh with me! '

A pretty challenge! Then I turned me round,
And straight the sober truth I found.
For I was not alone; behind me stood,
Beneath his load of wood,
He that of right the smile possessed —
Her father manifest.

O, blest be God! that such an overplus
Of joy is given to us:
That the sweet innocent
Gave me the gift she never meant,
A gift secure and permanent!
For, howsoe'er the smile had birth,
It is an added glory on the earth.

O GOD TO THEE I YIELD

O God to Thee I yield
    The gift Thou givest most precious, most divine!
Yet to what field
I must resign
His little feet
That wont to be so fleet,
I muse. O, joy to think
On what soft brink
Of flood he plucks the daffodils,
On what empurpled hills
He stands, Thy kiss all fresh upon his brow,
And wonders, if his father sees him now!

ANDREW LANG
1844–1912

Andrew Lang, for all his years of residence in England, never belied his Scottish origin. A good share of his literary activity was devoted to singing her natural beauty and setting straight her tangled history. From the universities of St. Andrews and Glasgow he migrated to Oxford. His achievements there earned him a fellowship at Merton College but, longing for a life which would allow his various talents scope, he tore himself from academic comforts and settled in London. To many, even to his friends, he seemed a most amiable dilettante. As a matter of fact he was a prodigious worker. His novels, volumes of verse, belletristic essays, biographies, historical monographs, studies in anthropology and Homeric origins, mount up well towards a hundred. He probably wrote too much, but certain of his accomplishments are solid. The great fight of his life — to save Homer from the theorists who believed the *Iliad* and *Odyssey* the work of many hands — it appears that he won. Of his verse the notable volumes are: *Ballads and Lyrics of Old France* (1872), *Ballades in Blue China* (1880), *Helen of Troy* (1882), *Grass of Parnassus* (1888).

As a result of the polite but undemonstrative reception given his *Helen of Troy* (a Tennysonian version in stanzas of the Iliad story), Lang never properly valued his own poetic abilities. His critics and his friends, as is usually the case, were content to accept his self-judgment and file him away as a writer of ingratiating occasional verse, a man of letters who resorted to poetastering for recreation as naturally as to fishing and golfing. His contemporary reputation was, actually, subject to the freakishness of poetic taste. During his early years you could be poetically respectable in two ways. You might imitate Tennyson, though this pursuit entailed an eventual non-plus because no matter how good you might be, you could never excel your master. Lang fouled on this snag through his long poem about Helen. It was a good bit of work, everyone agreed, but of course, not so good a poem as the Laureate might have turned off in a few lazy hours. You could also venture for fame, and here more safely because in selecter company, among recondite emotions, overweighting poetry's 'singing chaplet with the snows and showers,' as Lang put it.

> The songs are all of bale and blight;
> Alas! I do not need them,
> For almost every one can write,
> And *nobody* can read them.

Lang felt no impulse to travel either of these fashionable roads. But instead of proclaiming that his way to poetic excellence was as direct as another's, he abided by the general verdict and, somewhat ruefully but with a good grace, pitched his camp on the lower slopes of Parnassus.

> Grass of Parnassus, flower of my delight,
> How gladly with the unpermitted bay —
> Garlands not mine, and leaves that not decay —
> How gladly would I twine thee if I might!

He admired two unfashionable heroes, Scott and Longfellow, and it is easy to see why he liked them. They knew how to touch the many; they never went up to the high altar to communicate their experiences to the private ear of God. A remark of Lang's about Longfellow reveals, by inference, his own poetic ideal.

" Longfellow is exactly the antithesis of Poe, who, with all his science of verse and ghostly skill, has no humanity, or puts none of it into his lines. One is the poet of Life, and every-day life; the other is the poet of Death and of *bizarre* shapes of death, from which Heaven deliver us."

Lang has humanity. Whatever he enjoyed in human relationships, whatever manifestations of human life well and fully lived he found in books, he communicated as easily as he breathed. The trait of gentle, shrewd humanity in his poetry sets him beyond the writers of light verse with whom his name was associated. He is not a Bab-balladist or a nonsense-rhymer because there is so much of himself in his lines. Since he believed that a poet (because each minute of his life is worth turning into song) need not cease to be a poet when he puts

aside his singing robes and talks to a friend, his own poetry
touches the deeper moments, as well as the gayer, wherever his
own life touched them. He was more of a poet in the austere
and traditional sense of the word than he and his critics would
grant. Though the bays on Parnassus grew then farther up the
slope than they do now, Lang plucked at least enough for a
wreath.

ALMAE MATRES

(St. Andrews, 1862. Oxford, 1865.)

St. Andrews by the Northern sea,
 A haunted town it is to me!
A little city, worn and grey,
 The grey North Ocean girds it round.
And o'er the rocks, and up the bay,
 The long sea-rollers surge and sound.
And still the thin and biting spray
 Drives down the melancholy street,
And still endure, and still decay,
 Towers that the salt winds vainly beat.
Ghost-like and shadowy they stand
Dim mirrored in the wet sea-sand.

St. Leonard's chapel, long ago
 We loitered idly where the tall
Fresh budded mountain ashes blow
 Within thy desecrated wall:
The tough roots rent the tomb below,
 The April birds sang clamorous,
We did not dream, we could not know
 How hardly Fate would deal with us!

O, broken minster, looking forth
 Beyond the bay, above the town,
O, winter of the kindly North,
 O, college of the scarlet gown,
And shining sands beside the sea,
 And stretch of links beyond the sand,
Once more I watch you, and to me
 It is as if I touched his hand!

And therefore art thou yet more dear,
   O, little city, grey and sere,
Though shrunken from thine ancient pride
   And lonely by thy lonely sea,
Than these fair halls on Isis' side,
   Where Youth an hour came back to me!

A land of waters green and clear,
   Of willows and of poplars tall,
And, in the spring time of the year,
   The white may breaking over all,
And Pleasure quick to come at call.
   And summer rides by marsh and wold,
And Autumn with her crimson pall
   About the towers of Magdalen rolled;
And strange enchantments from the past,
   And memories of the friends of old,
And strong Tradition, binding fast
   The ' flying terms ' with bands of gold —

All these hath Oxford: all are dear,
   But dearer far the little town,
The drifting surf, the wintry year,
   The college of the scarlet gown,
     St. Andrews by the Northern sea,
     That is a haunted town to me!

TWILIGHT ON TWEED

Three crests against the saffron sky,
   Beyond the purple plain,
The kind remembered melody
   Of Tweed once more again.

Wan water from the border hills,
   Dear voice from the old years,
Thy distant music lulls and stills,
   And moves to quiet tears.

Like a loved ghost thy fabled flood
   Fleets through the dusky land;
Where Scott, come home to die, has stood,
   My feet returning stand.

A mist of memory broods and floats,
    The Border waters flow;
The air is full of ballad notes,
    Borne out of long ago.

Old songs that sung themselves to me,
    Sweet through a boy's day-dream,
While trout below the blossom'd tree
    Plashed in the golden stream.

.   .   .   .

Twilight, and Tweed, and Eildon Hill,
    Fair and too fair you be;
You tell me that the voice is still
    That should have welcomed me.

THE ODYSSEY

As one that for a weary space has lain
    Lulled by the song of Circe and her wine
In gardens near the pale of Proserpine,
Where that Ægæan isle forgets the main,
And only the low lutes of love complain,
    And only shadows of wan lovers pine —
    As such an one were glad to know the brine
Salt on his lips, and the large air again —
So gladly from the songs of modern speech
    Men turn, and see the stars, and feel the free
        Shrill wind beyond the close of heavy flowers;
        And through the music of the languid hours
They hear like ocean on a western beach
    The surge and thunder of the Odyssey.

OF HIS LADY'S OLD AGE

RONSARD

When you are very old, at evening
    You'll sit and spin beside the fire, and say,
Humming my songs, ' Ah well, ah well-a-day!
When I was young, of me did Ronsard sing.'

None of your maidens that doth hear the thing,
  Albeit with her weary task foredone,
    But wakens at my name, and calls you one
Blest, to be held in long remembering.

I shall be low beneath the earth, and laid
On sleep, a phantom in the myrtle shade,
  While you beside the fire, a grandame grey,
My love, your pride, remember and regret;
Ah, love me, love! we may be happy yet,
  And gather roses, while 'tis called to-day.

MARTIAL IN TOWN

Last night, within the stifling train,
  Lit by the foggy lamp o'erhead,
  Sick of the sad Last News, I read
Verse of that joyous child of Spain,

Who dwelt when Rome was waxing cold,
  Within the Roman din and smoke.
  And like my heart to me they spoke,
These accents of his heart of old: —

Brother, had we but time to live,
  And fleet the careless hours together,
With all that leisure has to give
  Of perfect life and peaceful weather,

The Rich Man's halls, the anxious faces,
The weary Forum, courts, and cases
  Should know us not; but quiet nooks,
But summer shade by field and well,
  But country rides, and talk of books,
At home, with these, we fain would dwell!

Now neither lives, but day by day
  Sees the suns wasting in the west,
And feels their flight, and doth delay
  To lead the life he loveth best.

So from thy city prison broke,
    Martial, thy wail for life misspent,
And so, through London's noise and smoke
    My heart replies to the lament.

For dear as Tagus with his gold,
    And swifter Salo, were to thee,
So dear to me the woods that fold
    The streams that circle Fernielea!

MELEAGER

HELIODORE

Pour wine, and cry, again, again, again,
    To Heliodore!
And mingle the sweet word ye call in vain
    With that ye pour:
And bring to me her wreath of yesterday,
    That's dank with myrrh;
Hesternae Rosae, ah, my friends, but they
    Remember her.
Lo! the kind roses, loved of lovers, weep,
    As who repine;
For if on any breast they see her sleep,
    It is not mine.

SCYTHE SONG

Mowers, weary and brown, and blithe,
    What is the word methinks ye know,
Endless over-word that the Scythe
    Sings to the blades of the grass below?
Scythes that swing in the grass and clover,
    Something, still, they say as they pass;
What is the word that, over and over,
    Sings the Scythe to the flowers and grass?

Hush, ah hush, the Scythes are saying,
    Hush, and heed not, and fall asleep;
Hush, they say to the grasses swaying;
    Hush, they sing to the clover deep!

227

Hush — 'tis the lullaby Time is singing —
  Hush, and heed not, for all things pass;
Hush, ah hush! and the Scythes are swinging
  Over the clover, over the grass!

NIGHTINGALE WEATHER

' Serai-je nonnette, oui ou non?
Serai-je nonnette? je crois que non.
Derrière chez mon père
Il est un bois taillis,
Le rossignol y chante
Et le jour et la nuit.
Il chante pour les filles
Qui n'ont pas d'ami;
Il ne chant pas pour moi,
J'en ai un, Dieu merci.' — OLD FRENCH

I'll never be a nun, I trow,
  While apple bloom is white as snow,
    But far more fair to see;
I'll never wear nun's black and white
While nightingales make sweet the night
    Within the apple tree.

Ah, listen! 'tis the nightingale,
And in the wood he makes his wail,
    Within the apple tree;
He singeth of the sore distress
Of many ladies loverless;
    Thank God, no song for me.

For when the broad May moon is low,
A gold fruit seen where blossoms blow
    In the boughs of the apple tree,
A step I know is at the gate;
Ah love, but it is long to wait
    Until night's noon bring thee!

Between lark's song and nightingale's
A silent space, while dawning pales.
    The birds leave still and free
For words and kisses musical,
For silence and for sighs that fall
    In the dawn, 'twixt him and me.

BALLADE OF HIS CHOICE OF A SEPULCHRE

Here I'd come when weariest!
        Here the breast
Of the Windburg's tufted over
Deep with bracken; here his crest
        Takes the west,
Where the wide-winged hawk doth hover.

Silent here are lark and plover;
        In the cover
Deep below the cushat best
Loves his mate and croons above her
        O'er their nest,
Where the wide-winged hawk doth hover!

Bring me here, Life's tired out guest,
        To the blest
Bed that waits the weary rover,
Here should failure be confessed;
        Ends my quest
Where the wide-winged hawk doth hover!

ENVOY

Friend, or stranger kind, or lover,
Ah, fulfil a last behest,
        Let me rest
Where the wide-winged hawk doth hover!

AUSTIN DOBSON

1840–1921

Austin Dobson left definite instructions to his executors that no one should write about him any form of memoir. Perhaps this was because he himself had written so many biographies, perhaps because of his quite genuine modesty or, still more probable, his consciousness of the utter lack of identity between the lives of Henry Austin Dobson, civil servant, and Austin Dobson, poet and essayist.

At sixteen Dobson obtained a post as clerk in the Board of Trade in London and there he worked until he was sixty, rising steadily through the various ranks to Principal, but those years have left no trace upon his poems. He formed firm friendships with two of his associates, Cosmo Monkhouse, the art critic, and Sir Edmund Gosse, yet neither these nor his many other literary acquaintances nor his domestic relationships are recorded in his verse. He published no lines to his wife and he successfully conceals ten unpoetical children. The young ladies of his poetic love affairs are obviously imaginary, ' divine, demure ' and frequently deceased in youth. *Vignettes in Rhyme* and *Proverbs in Porcelain,* the titles of his first volumes, suggest their native element. In *Old-World Idylls,* which followed, *At the Sign of the Lyre* and *Poems on Several Occasions* there is no record of personal experience or emotion. The first collected edition of his poems was published in 1897 (the *Complete Poetical Works* in 1923) but from 1885 onward Dobson devoted himself almost exclusively to prose, eighteenth century biographies and essays, as far removed from his daily life as his verses are.

Austin Dobson wrote about the eighteenth century because he did not like the nineteenth. It was too noisy, too excited, far too energetic. Even the mild routine of the Board of Trade and the quiet of his garden at Ealing were insufficient barriers. For a time he explored that country of escape imagined by the Pre-Raphaelites and, under the influence of Morris, wrote *The*

Dying of Tanneguy du Bois and other experiments in that kind but he soon abandoned that alien land, wisely, for what he missed from the nineteenth century was not so much beauty as peace. He did not crave scarlets and purples but the warm browns, the greens and golden haze of Gainsborough landscapes. He found his home in the eighteenth century. One fancies, from the pleasure with which he writes of him, that there was none of his imaginary companions with whom he would so gladly have exchanged bodies as Ralph Allen, the Bath Postmaster who expended his riches in beautifying the city of his heart and in agreeably entertaining distinguished men of letters. That is the way Dobson would have liked to live. He enjoyed the company of writers because the talk he liked best was of books and of the details of the making of books. His care for perfection made him always singularly amenable to critical suggestions about his own work. When the Laureate demanded sepulchrally: ' Are you a classic? Then become one! Read Horace every day of your life! ' Dobson set to work obediently ipon the *Odes* and *Epistles* in a prolonged study whose influence is apparent in his prose as well as in his verse. The critical advice of lesser men than Tennyson he considered with courteous seriousness and in 1874 he read and was strongly influenced by Théodore de Banville's discussion, in the *Petit Traité de Poésie Française,* of the rondeau and other elaborate French forms.

Dobson could afford to work in conventional patterns and to listen to the ideas of other men because he had a definitely original mind. One of the chief delights in his poetry is the sudden flashing from a formal, even commonplace, setting of an unexpected figure or idea. But he did not strive for singularity. ' *Sat est scripisse,*' he wrote in one of his rare personal utterances:

> They knew not, nor cared greatly, if they were spark or star;
> They knew to move is somewhat, although the goal be far;
> And larger light or lesser, this thing at least is clear,
> They served the Muses truly, — their service was sincere.

The true and quiet service Dobson offered the Muses was very far from dull. He had a wit which was frequently ' pretty ' and frequently a good deal more, but it is never forced; indeed one has frequently the sense that he is holding himself down; that he might have been far more severe if good manners had not tempered him and that second thought without which he never published. Dobson took his time. He declined to be whirled off by the nineteenth century conviction that there was ' so little done, so much to do.' Born into an age whose standards he could not recognize, he had the courage to erect his own and then to pursue them through a long life, unhurried, happy, steadfast, and serene.

THE LADIES OF ST. JAMES'S

A PROPER NEW BALLAD OF THE COUNTRY AND THE TOWN

Phyllida amo ante alias. — VIRG.

The ladies of St. James's
  Go swinging to the play;
Their footmen run before them,
  With a ' Stand by! Clear the way! '
But Phyllida, my Phyllida!
  She takes her buckled shoon,
When we go out a-courting
  Beneath the harvest moon.

The ladies of St. James's
  Wear satin on their backs;
They sit all night at *Ombre,*
  With candles all of wax:
But Phyllida, my Phyllida!
  She dons her russet gown,
And runs to gather May dew
  Before the world is down.

The ladies of St. James's!
  They are so fine and fair,
You'd think a box of essences
  Was broken in the air:
But Phyllida, my Phyllida!
  The breath of heath and furze,
When breezes blow at morning,
  Is not so fresh as hers.

The ladies of St. James's!
　　They're painted to the eyes;
Their white it stays forever,
　　Their red it never dies.
But Phyllida, my Phyllida!
　　Her colour comes and goes;
It trembles to a lily, —
　　It wavers to a rose.

The ladies of St. James's!
　　You scarce can understand
The half of all their speeches,
　　Their phrases are so grand;
But Phyllida, my Phyllida!
　　Her shy and simple words
Are clear as after rain-drops
　　The music of the birds.

The ladies of St. James's!
　　They have their fits and freaks;
They smile on you — for seconds;
　　They frown on you — for weeks:
But Phyllida, my Phyllida!
　　Come either storm or shine,
From Shrove-tide unto Shrove-tide,
　　Is always true — and mine.

My Phyllida! my Phyllida!
　　I care not though they heap
The hearts of all St. James's,
　　And give me all to keep;
I care not whose the beauties
　　Of all the world may be,
For Phyllida — for Phyllida
　　Is all the world to me!

233

A DEAD LETTER

' À cœur blessé — l'ombre et le silence.'
— H. DE BALZAC.

I

I drew it from its china tomb; —
    It came out feebly scented
With some thin ghost of past perfume
    That time and years had lent it.

An old, old letter — folded still!
    To read with due composure
I sought the sun-lit window-sill
    Above the grey enclosure,

That glimmering in the sultry haze,
    Faint-flowered, dimly shaded,
Slumbered like Goldsmith's Madam Blaize,
    Bedizened and brocaded.

A queer old place! You'd surely say
    Some tea-board garden-maker
Had planned it in Dutch William's day
    To please some florist Quaker,

So trim it was. The yew-trees still,
    With pious care perverted,
Grew in the same grim shapes; and still
    The lipless dolphin spurted;

Still in his wonted state abode
    The broken-nosed Apollo;
And still the cypress-arbour showed
    The same umbrageous hollow.

Only, — as fresh young Beauty gleams
    From coffee-coloured laces, —
So peeped from its old-fashioned dreams
    The fresher modern traces;

For idle mallet, hoop, and ball
  Upon the lawn were lying;
A magazine, a tumbled shawl,
  Round which the swifts were flying;

And, tossed beside the Guelder rose,
  A heap of rainbow knitting,
Where, blinking in her pleased repose,
  A Persian cat was sitting.

' A place to love in, — live, — for aye,
  If we too, like Tithonus,
Could find some god to stretch the grey
  Scant life that Fates have thrown us;

' But now by steam we run our race
  With buttoned heart and pocket;
Our Love's a gilded, surplus grace, —
  Just like an empty locket.

' " The time is out of joint." Who will
  May strive to make it better;
For me, this warm old window-sill,
  And this old dusty letter.'

II

' Dear *John* (the letter ran) , it can't, can't be,
  For Father's gone to *Chorley Fair* with *Sam,*
And Mother's storing Apples, — *Prue* and Me
  Up to our Elbows making Damson Jam:
But we shall meet before a Week is gone, —
  " 'Tis a long Lane that has no Turning," *John!*

' Only till Sunday next, and then you'll wait
  Behind the White-Thorn, by the broken Stile —
We can go round and catch them at the Gate,
  All to Ourselves, for nearly one long Mile;
Dear *Prue* won't look, and Father he'll go on,
And *Sam's* two Eyes are all for *Cissy, John!*

235

' *John,* she's so smart — with every Ribbon new,
    Flame-coloured Sack, and Crimson Padesoy;
As proud as proud; and has the Vapours too,
    Just like My Lady; — calls poor *Sam* a Boy,
And vows no Sweetheart's worth the Thinking-on
Till he's past Thirty . . . I know better, *John!*

' My Dear, I don't think that I thought of much
    Before we knew each other, I and you;
And now, why, *John,* your least, least Finger-touch
    Gives me enough to think a Summer through.
See, for I send you Something! There, 'tis gone!
Look in this corner, — mind you find it, *John!* '

III

This was the matter of the note, —
    A long-forgot deposit,
Dropped in an Indian dragon's throat,
    Deep in a fragrant closet,

Piled with a dapper Dresden world, —
    Beaux, beauties, prayers, and poses, —
Bonzes with squat legs undercurled,
    And great jars filled with roses.

Ah, heart that wrote! Ah, lips that kissed!
    You had no thought or presage
Into what keeping you dismissed
    Your simple old-world message!

A reverent one. Though we to-day
    Distrust beliefs and powers,
The artless, ageless things you say
    Are fresh as May's own flowers,

Starring some pure primaeval spring,
    Ere Gold had grown despotic, —
Ere Life was yet a selfish thing,
    Or Love a mere exotic!

I need not search too much to find
    Whose lot it was to send it,
That feel upon me yet the kind
    Soft hand of her who penned it;

And see, through two score years of smoke,
    In by-gone, quaint apparel,
Shine from yon time-black Norway oak
    The face of Patience Caryl, —

The pale, smooth forehead, silver-tressed;
    The grey gown, primly flowered;
The spotless, stately coif whose crest
    Like Hector's horse-plume towered;

And still the sweet half-solemn look
    Where some past thought was clinging,
As when one shuts a serious book
    To hear the thrushes singing.

I kneel to you! Of those you were,
    Whose kind old hearts grow mellow, —
Whose fair old faces grow more fair
    As Point and Flanders yellow;

Whom some old store of garnered grief,
    Their placid temples shading,
Crowns like a wreath of autumn leaf
    With tender tints of fading.

Peace to your soul! You died unwed —
    Despite this loving letter.
And what of John? The less that 's said
    Of John, I think, the better.

A POSTSCRIPT TO 'RETALIATION'

[*After the Fourth Edition of* DR. GOLDSMITH's Retaliation
*was printed, the Publisher received a supplementary Epitaph
on the Wit and Punster* Caleb Whitefoord. *Though it is found
appended to the later issues of the Poem, it has been suspected
that* Whitefoord *wrote it himself. It may be that the following
which has recently come to light is another forgery.*]

Here Johnson is laid. Have a care how you walk;
   If he stir in his sleep, in his sleep he will talk.
Ye gods! how he talk'd! What a torrent of sound,
His hearers, invaded, encompass'd, and — drown'd!
What a banquet of memory, fact, illustration,
In that innings-for-one that he call'd *conversation!*
Can't you hear his sonorous ' Why no, Sir! ' and ' Stay, Sir!
Your premise is wrong,' or ' You don't see your way, Sir! '
How he silenc'd a prig, or a slip-shod romancer!
How he pounc'd on a fool with a knock-me-down answer!

But peace to his slumbers! Tho' rough in the rind,
The heart of the giant was gentle and kind:
What signifies now, if in bouts with a friend,
When his pistol miss'd fire, he would use the butt-end?
If he trampled your flow'rs, like a bull in a garden,
What matter for that? he was sure to ask pardon;
And you felt on the whole, tho' he'd tossed you and gor'd you,
It was something, at least, that he had not ignor'd you,
Yes! the outside was rugged. But test him within,
You found he had nought of the bear but the skin;
And for bottom and base to his *anfractuosity,*
A fund of fine feeling, good taste, generosity.
He was true to his conscience, his King, and his duty;
And he hated the *Whigs,* and he soften'd to Beauty.

Turn now to his Writings. I grant, in his tales,
That he made little fishes talk vastly like whales;
I grant that his language was rather emphatic,
Nay, even — to put the thing plainly — dogmatic;
But read him for Style, — and dismiss from your thoughts,
The crowd of compilers who copied his faults, —

Say, where is there English so full and so clear,
So weighty, so dignified, manly, sincere?
So strong in expression, conviction, persuasion?
So prompt to take colour from place and occasion?
So widely remov'd from the doubtful, the tentative;
So truly — and in the best sense — argumentative?
You may talk of your BURKES and your GIBBONS so clever,
But I hark back to him with a 'JOHNSON for ever!'
And I feel as I muse on his ponderous figure,
Tho' he's great in this age, in the next he'll grow bigger;
And still while . . . (*Cætera desunt.*)

POT–POURRI

Si jeunesse savait! —

I plunge my hand among the leaves:
(An alien touch but dust perceives,
    Nought else supposes;)
For me those fragrant ruins raise
Clear memory of the vanished days
    When they were roses.

'If youth but knew!' Ah, 'if,' in truth? —
I can recall with what gay youth,
    To what light chorus,
Unsobered yet by time or change,
We roamed the many-gabled Grange
    All life before us;

Braved the old clock-tower's dust and damp,
To catch the dim Arthurian camp
    In misty distance;
Peered at the still-room's sacred stores,
Or rapped at walls for sliding doors
    Of feigned existence.

What need had we for thoughts or cares!
The hot sun parched the old parterres
    And 'flowerful closes';

We roused the rooks with rounds and glees,
Played hide-and-seek behind the trees, —
    Then plucked these roses.

Louise was one — light, glib Louise,
So freshly freed from school decrees
    You scarce could stop her;
And Bell, the Beauty, unsurprised
At fallen locks that scandalized
    Our dear ' Miss Proper '; —

Shy Ruth, all heart and tenderness,
Who wept — like Chaucer's Prioress,
    When Dash was smitten;
Who blushed before the mildest men,
Yet waxed a very Corday when
    You teased her kitten.

I loved them all. Bell first and best;
Louise the next — for days of jest
    Or madcap masking;
And Ruth, I thought, — why, failing these,
When my High-Mightiness should please,
    She'd come for asking.

.   .   .   .

Louise was grave when last we met;
Bell's beauty, like a sun, has set;
    And Ruth, Heaven bless her,
Ruth that I wooed, — and wooed in vain, —
Has gone where neither grief nor pain
    Can now distress her.

A GENTLEMAN OF THE OLD SCHOOL

He lived in that past Georgian day,
    When men were less inclined to say
That ' Time is Gold,' and overlay
    With toil their pleasure;
He held some land, and dwelt thereon, —
Where, I forget, — the house is gone;
His Christian name, I think, was John, —
    His surname, Leisure.

Reynolds has painted him, — a face
Filled with a fine, old-fashioned grace,
Fresh-coloured, frank, with ne'er a trace
    Of trouble shaded;
The eyes are blue, the hair is drest
In plainest way, — one hand is prest
Deep in a flapped canary vest,
    With buds brocaded.

He wears a brown old Brunswick coat,
With silver buttons, — round his throat
A soft cravat; — in all you note
    An elder fashion, —
A strangeness, which, to us who shine
In shapely hats, — whose coats combine
All harmonies of hue and line, —
    Inspires compassion.

He lived so long ago, you see!
Men were untravelled then, but we
Like Ariel, post o'er land and sea
    With careless parting;
He found it quite enough for him
To smoke his pipe in ' garden trim,'
And watch, about the fish-tank's brim,
    The swallows darting.

He liked the well-wheel's creaking tongue, —
He liked the thrush that fed her young, —
He liked the drone of flies among
    His netted peaches;
He liked to watch the sunlight fall
Athwart his ivied orchard wall;
Or pause to catch the cuckoo's call
    Beyond the beeches.

His were the times of Paint and Patch,
And yet no Ranelagh could match
The sober doves that round his thatch
    Spread tails and sidled;

He liked their ruffling, puffed content, —
For him their drowsy wheelings meant
More than a Mall of Beaux that bent,
 Or Belles that bridled.

Not that, in truth, when life began,
He shunned the flutter of the fan;
He too had maybe ' pinked his man '
 In Beauty's quarrel;
But now his ' fervent youth ' had flown
Where lost things go; and he was grown
As staid and slow-paced as his own
 Old hunter, Sorrel.

Yet still he loved the chase, and held
That no composer's score excelled
The merry horn, when Sweetlip swelled
 Its jovial riot;
But most his measured words of praise
Caressed the angler's easy ways, —
His idly meditative days, —
 His rustic diet.

Not that his ' meditating ' rose
Beyond a sunny summer doze;
He never troubled his repose
 With fruitless pryings;
But held, as law for high and low,
What God withholds no man can know,
And smiled away inquiry so,
 Without replying.

We read — alas, how much we read!
The jumbled strifes of creed and creed
With endless controversies feed
 Our groaning tables;
His books — and they sufficed him — were
Cotton's ' Montaigne,' ' The Grave ' of Blair,
A ' Walton ' — much the worse for wear —
 And ' Æsop's Fables.'

One more, — ' The Bible.' Not that he
Had searched its page as deep as we;
No sophistries could make him see
    Its slender credit;
It may be that he could not count
The sires and sons to Jesse's fount, —
He liked the ' Sermon on the Mount,' —
    And more, he read it.

Once he had loved, but failed to wed,
A red-cheeked lass who long was dead;
His ways were far too slow, he said,
    To quite forget her;
And still when time had turned him gray
The earliest hawthorn buds in May
Would find his lingering feet astray,
    Where first he met her.

' *In Coelo Quies* ' heads the stone
On Leisure's grave, — now little known,
A tangle of wild-rose has grown
    So thick across it;
The ' Benefactions ' still declare
He left the clerk an elbow-chair,
And ' 12 Pence Yearly to Prepare
    A Christmas Posset.'

Lie softly, Leisure! Doubtless you
With too serene a conscience drew
Your easy breath, and slumbered through
    The gravest issue;
But we, to whom our age allows
Scarce space to wipe our weary brows,
Look down upon your narrow house,
    Old friend, and miss you!

'GOOD–NIGHT, BABETTE!'

'Si vieillesse pouvait! —'

SCENE. — *A small neat Room. In a high Voltaire Chair sits a white-haired old Gentleman.*

MONSIEUR VIEUXBOIS.   BABETTE.

M. VIEUXBOIS *(turning querulously).*

D ay of my life! Where *can* she get?
BABETTE! I say! BABETTE! — BABETTE!

BABETTE *(entering hurriedly).*

Coming, M'sieu'! If M'sieu' speaks
So loud, he won't be well for weeks!

M. VIEUXBOIS

Where have you been?

BABETTE

Why, M'sieu' knows: —
April! . . . Ville d'Avray! . . . Ma'am'selle ROSE!

M. VIEUXBOIS

Ah! I am old — and I forget.
Was the place growing green, BABETTE?

BABETTE

But of a greenness! — yes, M'sieu'!
And then the sky so blue! — so blue!
And when I dropped my *immortelle,*
How the birds sang!

(Lifting her apron to her eyes.)
This poor Ma'am'selle!

M. VIEUXBOIS

You're a good girl, BABETTE, but she, —
She was an angel, verily.
Sometimes I think I see her yet

❖ AUSTIN DOBSON ❖

Stand smiling by the cabinet;
And once, I know, she peeped and laughed
Betwixt the curtains . . .

　　　　　Where's the draught?

(She gives him a cup.)

Now I shall sleep, I think, BABETTE; —
Sing me your Norman *chansonnette.*

BABETTE *(sings).*

' *Once at the Angelus*
　(Ere I was dead),
Angels all glorious
　Came to my Bed;
Angels in blue and white
　Crowned on the Head.'

M. VIEUXBOIS *(drowsily).*

' She was an Angel ' . . . ' Once she laughed '. . .
What, was I dreaming?

　　　　　Where's the draught?

BABETTE *(showing the empty cup).*

The draught, M'sieu'?

M. VIEUXBOIS

　　　　　How I forget!

I am so old! But sing, BABETTE!

BABETTE *(sings).*

' *One was the Friend I left*
　Stark in the Snow;
One was the Wife that died
　Long, — long ago;
One was the Love I lost . . .
　How could she know?'

M. VIEUXBOIS *(murmuring).*

Ah, PAUL! . . . old PAUL! . . . EULALIE too!
And ROSE . . . And O! ' the sky so blue! '

BABETTE (*sings*).

' One had my Mother's eyes
Wistful and mild;
One had my Father's face;
One was a Child:
All of them bent to me,—
Bent down and smiled! '

(He is asleep!)

M. VIEUXBOIS (*almost inaudibly*).

' How I forget! '
' I am so old! ' . . . *' Good night,* BABETTE! *'*

A FANCY FROM FONTENELLE

De mémoires de Roses on n'a point vu mourir le Jardinier

The Rose in the garden slipped her bud,
    And she laughed in the pride of her youthful blood
As she thought of the Gardener standing by —
' He is old, — so old! And he soon must die! '

The full Rose waxed in the warm June air,
And she spread and spread till her heart lay bare;
And she laughed once more as she heard his tread —
' He is older now! He will soon be dead! '

But the breeze of the morning blew, and found
That the leaves of the blown Rose strewed the ground
And he came at noon, that Gardener old,
And he raked them gently under the mould.

And I wove the thing to a random rhyme,
For the Rose is Beauty, the Gardener, Time.

TO A MISSAL OF THE THIRTEENTH
CENTURY

Missal of the Gothic age,
Missal with the blazoned page,
Whence, O Missal, hither come,
From what dim scriptorium?

Whose the name that wrought thee thus,
Ambrose or Theophilus,
Bending, through the waning light,
O'er thy vellum scraped and white;

Weaving 'twixt thy rubric lines
Sprays and leaves and quaint designs;
Setting round thy border scrolled
Buds of purple and of gold?

Ah! — a wondering brotherhood,
Doubtless, by that artist stood,
Raising o'er his careful ways
Little choruses of praise;

Glad when his deft hand would paint
Strife of Sathanas and Saint,
Or in secret coign entwist
Jest of cloister humorist.

Well the worker earned his wage,
Bending o'er the blazoned page!
Tired the hand and tired the wit
Ere the final *Explicit!*

Not as ours the books of old —
Things that steam can stamp and fold,
Not as ours the books of yore —
Rows of type, and nothing more.

Then a book was still a Book,
Where a wistful man might look,
Finding something through the whole,
Beating, — like a human soul.

In that growth of day by day,
When to labour was to pray,
Surely something vital passed
To the patient page at last;

Something that one still perceives
Vaguely present in the leaves;
Something from the worker lent;
Something mute — but eloquent!

A BALLAD OF ANTIQUARIES

The days decay as flowers of grass,
    The years as silent waters flow;
All things that are depart, alas!
    As leaves the winnowing breezes strow;
    And still while yet, full-orbed and slow,
New suns the old horizon climb,
    Old Time must reap, as others sow:
We are the gleaners after Time!

We garner all the things that pass,
    We harbour all the winds may blow;
As misers we up-store, amass
    All gifts the hurrying Fates bestow;
    Old chronicles of feast and show,
Old waifs of by-gone rune and rhyme,
    Old jests that made old banquets glow: —
We are the gleaners after Time!

We hoard old lore of lad and lass,
    Old flowers that in old gardens grow,
Old records writ on tomb and brass,
    Old spoils of arrow-head and bow,
    Old wrecks of old worlds' overthrow,
Old relics of Earth's primal slime,
    All drift that wanders to and fro: —
We are the gleaners after Time!

ENVOY

Friends, that we know not and we know!
We pray you, by this Christmas chime,
Help us to save the things that go:
We are the gleaners after Time.

THE BALLAD OF PROSE AND RHYME

When the ways are heavy with mire and rut,
In November fogs, in December snows,
When the North Wind howls, and the doors are shut, —
There is place and enough for the pains of prose;
But whenever a scent from the whitethorn blows,
And the jasmine-stars at the casement climb,
And a Rosalind-face at the lattice shows,
Then hey! — for the ripple of laughing rhyme!

When the brain gets dry as an empty nut,
When the reason stands on its squarest toes,
When the mind (like a beard) has a ' formal cut,' —
There is place and enough for the pains of prose;
But whenever the May-blood stirs and glows,
And the young year draws to the ' golden prime,'
And Sir Romeo sticks in his ear a rose, —
Then hey! — for the ripple of laughing rhyme!

In a theme where the thoughts have a pedant-strut,
In a changing quarrel of ' Ayes ' and ' Noes,'
In a starched procession of ' If ' and ' But,' —
There is place and enough for the pains of prose;
But whenever a soft glance softer grows
And the light hours dance to the trysting-time,
And the secret is told ' that no one knows,' —
Then hey! — for the ripple of laughing rhyme!

ENVOY

In the work-a-day world, — or its needs and woes,
There is place and enough for the pains of prose;
But whenever the May-bells clash and chime,
Then hey! — for the ripple of laughing rhyme!

A SONG OF THE FOUR SEASONS

When Spring comes laughing
    By vale and hill,
By wind-flower walking
    And daffodil, —
Sing stars of morning,
    Sing morning skies,
Sing blue of speedwell, —
    And my Love's eyes.

When comes the Summer,
    Full-leaved and strong,
And gay birds gossip
    The orchard long, —
Sing hid, sweet honey
    That no bee sips;
Sing red, red roses, —
    And my Love's lips.

When Autumn scatters
    The leaves again,
And piled sheaves bury
    The broad-wheeled wain, —
Sing flutes of harvest
    Where men rejoice;
Sing rounds of reapers, —
    And my Love's voice.

But when comes Winter
    With hail and storm,
And red fire roaring
    And ingle warm, —
Sing first sad going
    Of friends that part;
Then sing glad meeting, —
    And my Love's hear

A GARDEN SONG

(TO W. E. H.)

Here, in this sequestered close,
   Bloom the hyacinth and rose;
Here beside the modest stock
Flaunts the flaring hollyhock;
Here, without a pang, one sees
Ranks, conditions, and degrees.

All the seasons run their race
In this quiet resting place;
Peach, and apricot, and fig
Here will ripen, and grow big;
Here is store and overplus, —
More had not Alcinoüs!

Here, in alleys cool and green,
Far ahead the thrush is seen;
Here along the southern wall
Keeps the bee his festival;
All is quiet else — afar
Sounds of toil and turmoil are.

Here be shadows large and long;
Here be spaces meet for song;
Grant, O garden-god, that I,
Now that none profane is nigh, —
Now that mood and moment please, —
Find the fair Pierides!

IN AFTER DAYS

In after days when grasses high
   O'er-top the stone where I shall lie,
      Though ill or well the world adjust
      My slender claim to honoured dust,
I shall not question or reply.

I shall not see the morning sky;
I shall not hear the night-wind sigh;
   I shall be mute, as all men must
      In after days!

But yet, now living, fain were I
That some one then should testify,
   Saying — ' He held his pen in trust
   To Art, not serving shame or lust.'
Will none? — Then let my memory die
      In after days!

ARS VICTRIX

(IMITATED FROM THEOPHILE GAUTIER)

Yes; when the ways oppose —
   When the hard means rebel,
Fairer the work outgrows, —
   More potent far the spell.

O POET, then, forbear
   The loosely-sandalled verse,
Choose rather thou to wear
   The buskin — straight and terse;

Leave to the tiro's hand
   The limp and shapeless style,
See that thy form demand
   The labour of the file.

SCULPTOR, do thou discard
   The yielding clay, — consign
To Paros marble hard
   The beauty of thy line; —

Model thy Satyr's face
   In bronze of Syracuse;
In the veined agate trace
   The profile of thy Muse.

✣ AUSTIN DOBSON ✣

PAINTER, that still must mix
    But transient tints anew,
Thou in the furnace fix
    The firm enamel's hue;

Let the smooth tile receive
    Thy dove-drawn Erycine;
Thy Sirens blue at eve
    Coiled in a wash of wine.

All passes. ART alone
    Enduring stays to us;
The Bust outlasts the throne, —
    The Coin, Tiberius;

Even the gods must go;
    Only the lofty Rhyme
Not countless years o'erthrow, —
    Not long array of time.

Paint, chisel, then, or write;
    But, that the work surpass,
With the hard fashion fight, —
    With the resisting mass.

ERNEST DOWSON
1867–1900

After an uneventful sojourn at Queen's College, Oxford, Dowson came to London and joined the group of young poets of the Rhymers' Club whose shining lights were Arthur Symons, John Davidson, Lionel Johnson and W. B. Yeats. Three volumes of verse appeared during his lifetime: *Verses* (1896), *The Pierrot of the Minute* (1897), a verse drama, and *Decorations* (1899). Dowson eked out his existence by hackwork — chiefly translations from the French — by two novels done in collaboration with Arthur Moore, and a volume of short stories, *Dilemmas; Stories and Studies in Sentiment* (1895). In his last days sickness and dissipation so reduced his morale that he lived much of the time on the continent in order to avoid the society of his friends. He was finally rescued by one of them who cared for him during his dying hours.

Ernest Dowson's life has become a legend. The English find it so difficult to understand a man of his temperament that they have explained him too completely. They have heaped on him, as a convenient scapegoat, all the lurid stories of poets and artists which descend from the '90's, with the result that it is difficult to know him as he lived and to judge his poetry fairly. There have been few poets who cared so little for the usual concerns of ordinary people or who lived so much in the memory of past happiness. This detachment from the actual world of everyday baffled chance acquaintances, baffled even his friends, except those few who felt his ' gracious and insistent air of modesty ' and knew how to interpret his diffidence.

One has only to read his poetry to apprehend the world he really lived in. Though squalor surrounded him in his last desperate days, his mind dwelt, as it always had, on sunshine and apple trees in Brittany, on April love and dreamful autumns and the final rest ' there, beside the altar, there.'

England has produced no greater elegist than Dowson,

though *Lycidas* and *Adonais* are greater elegies than any he
has left us. The voice is never quiet which sings in his poetry
of the transience of life, the remembrance of bright youth and
fresh beauty that fades. His text might be from Dante: there
is no greater sadness than to remember past joy in the time of
misery. In *Vesperal* he awaits the angelus when the day's evil
things are done; the Garden of Shadow has grown a wilder-
ness; Yvonne of Brittany does not remember (bitterest of all
sorrows) and he will soon forget. In his few stories as well as
in his love poems this elegiac mood prevails. He cannot love
for long because he cannot endure the idea of a beautiful girl
grown old. He will not risk losing the perfect moment by try-
ing to hold it longer than it can live.

Dowson's friends, sceptics, most of them, and pagans, were
puzzled by his conversion to Rome. One of them ventures to
assert that Dowson did not feel the experience deeply and was
even disappointed that it caused so little change in his life. It
is true that his religion was not achieved as Lionel Johnson's
was, after a patient exploration of creeds; nor was he a mystic
with the conviction of Francis Thompson. But this much we
can say: the Church was to him something fixed in the black
flux of time, a refuge after all the weariness of living has been
endured.

> Strange silence here: without, the sounding street
>   Heralds the world's swift passage to the fire:
> O Benediction, perfect and complete!
>   When shall men cease to suffer and desire?

The impulse which drove him to the Church made him seek
perfection in his art. In a perfect stanza he could catch the
glory and hold it against time. He was the devoted follower of
artists in words like Flaubert and, above all, Verlaine, who
was his hero. He tried to learn from them how to set down in
precise words the moment he wished to hold for himself and
evoke for others. By means of simple and familiar stanzas,
whose cadences are sweet in English ears, and old symbols and
figures sparingly used, he escapes the pretentiousness which
has damaged the fame of many of his contemporaries who
tried to enclose in poetry moods similar to his.

NON SUM QUALIS ERAM BONAE SUB REGNO CYNARAE

Last night, ah, yesternight, betwixt her lips and mine
    There fell thy shadow, Cynara! thy breath was shed
Upon my soul between the kisses and the wine;
And I was desolate and sick of an old passion,
    Yea, I was desolate and bowed my head:
I have been faithful to thee, Cynara! in my fashion.

All night upon mine heart I felt her warm heart beat,
Night-long within mine arms in love and sleep she lay;
Surely the kisses of her bought red mouth were sweet;
But I was desolate and sick of an old passion,
    When I awoke and found the dawn was gray:
I have been faithful to thee, Cynara! in my fashion.

I have forgot much, Cynara! gone with the wind,
Flung roses, roses riotously with the throng,
Dancing, to put thy pale, lost lilies out of mind;
But I was desolate and sick of an old passion,
    Yea, all the time, because the dance was long:
I have been faithful to thee, Cynara! in my fashion.

I cried for madder music and for stronger wine,
But when the feast is finished and the lamps expire,
Then falls thy shadow, Cynara! the night is thine;
And I am desolate and sick of an old passion,
    Yea, hungry for the lips of my desire:
I have been faithful to thee, Cynara! in my fashion.

BEATA SOLITUDO

What land of Silence,
    Where pale stars shine
On apple-blossom
    And dew-drenched vine,
    Is yours and mine?

The silent valley
  That we will find,
Where all the voices
  Of humankind
  Are left behind.

There all forgetting,
  Forgotten quite,
We will repose us,
  With our delight
  Hid out of sight.

The world forsaken,
  And out of mind
Honour and labour,
  We shall not find
  The stars unkind.

And men shall travail,
  And laugh and weep;
But we have vistas
  Of Gods asleep,
  With dreams as deep.

A land of Silence,
  Where pale stars shine
On apple-blossoms
  And dew-drenched vine,
  Be yours and mine!

IN TEMPORE SENECTUTIS

When I am old,
    And sadly steal apart,
Into the dark and cold,
  Friend of my heart!
Remember, if you can,
Not him who lingers, but that other man,
Who loved and sang, and had a beating heart, —
  When I am old!

When I am old,
 And all Love's ancient fire
Be tremulous and cold:
 My soul's desire!
Remember, if you may,
Nothing of you and me but yesterday,
When heart on heart we bid the years conspire
 To make us old.

When I am old,
 And every star above
Be pitiless and cold:
 My life's one love!
Forbid me not to go:
Remember nought of us but long ago,
And not at last, how love and pity strove
 When I grew old!

VITAE SUMMA BREVIS SPEM NOS VETAT INCOHARE LONGAM

They are not long, the weeping and the laughter,
 Love and desire and hate:
I think they have no portion in us after
 We pass the gate.

They are not long, the days of wine and roses:
 Out of a misty dream
Our path emerges for a while, then closes
 Within a dream.

VILLANELLE OF MARGUERITES

A little, passionately, not at all? '
 She casts the snowy petals on the air:
And what care we how many petals fall!

 Nay, wherefore seek the seasons to forestall?
 It is but playing, and she will not care,
 A little, passionately, not at all!

She would not answer us if we should call,
　Across the years: her visions are too fair;
And what care we how many petals fall!

　She knows us not, nor recks if she enthrall
　　With voice and eyes and fashion of her hair,
A little, passionately, not at all!

　Knee-deep she goes in meadow grasses tall,
　　Kissed by the daisies that her fingers tear:
And what care we how many petals fall!

　We pass and go: but she shall not recall
　　What men we were, nor all she made us bear:
　' *A little, passionately, not at all!* '
And what care we how many petals fall!

SAPIENTIA LUNAE

The wisdom of the world said unto me:
　　' *Go forth and run, the race is to the brave;*
Perchance some honour tarrieth for thee! '
　' As tarrieth,' I said, ' for sure, the grave.'
　For I had pondered on a rune of roses,
　Which to her votaries the moon discloses.

The wisdom of the world said: ' *There are bays:*
　　Go forth and run, for victory is good,
After the stress of the laborious days.'
　' Yet,' said I, ' shall I be the worms' sweet food,'
　As I went musing on a rune of roses,
　Which in her hour, the pale, soft moon discloses.

Then said my voices: ' *Wherefore strive or run,*
　　On dusty highways ever, a vain race?
The long night cometh, starless, void of sun,
　　What light shall serve thee like her golden face?'
　For I had pondered on a rune of roses,
　And knew some secrets which the moon discloses.

' Yea,' said I, ' for her eyes are pure and sweet
    As lilies, and the fragrance of her hair
Is many laurels; and it is not meet
      To run for shadows when the prize is here.'
    And I went reading in that rune of roses
    Which to her votaries the moon discloses.

DREGS

The fire is out, and spent the warmth thereof
    (This is the end of every song man sings!)
The golden wine is drunk, the dregs remain,
Bitter as wormwood and as salt as pain;
And health and hope have gone the way of love
Into the drear oblivion of lost things.
Ghosts go along with us until the end;
This was a mistress, this, perhaps, a friend.
With pale, indifferent eyes, we sit and wait
For the dropt curtain and the closing gate:
This is the end of all the songs man sings.

O MORS! QUAM AMARA EST MEMORIA TUA HOMINI PACEM HABENTI IN SUBSTANTIIS SUIS

Exceeding sorrow
    Consumeth my sad heart!
Because to-morrow
    We must depart.
Now is exceeding sorrow
    All my part!

Give over playing,
    Cast thy viol away:
Merely laying
    Thy head my way:
Prithee, give over playing,
    Grave or gay.

Be no word spoken;
   Weep nothing: let a pale
Silence, unbroken
   Silence prevail!
Prithee, be no word spoken,
   Lest I fail!

Forget to-morrow!
   Weep nothing: only lay
In silent sorrow
   Thine head my way:
Let us forget to-morrow,
   This one day!

VENITE DESCENDAMUS

Let be at last; give over words and sighing,
   Vainly were all things said:
Better at last to find a place for lying,
   Only dead.

Silence were best, with songs and sighing over;
   Now be the music mute;
Now let the dead, red leaves of autumn cover
   A vain lute.

Silence is best: for ever and for ever,
   We will go down and sleep,
Somewhere beyond her ken, where she need never
   Come to weep.

Let be at last: colder she grows and colder,
   Sleep and the night were best;
Lying at last where we can not behold her,
   We may rest.

IMPENITENTIA ULTIMA

Before my light goes out for ever if God should give me a choice of graces,
    I would not reck of length of days, nor crave for things to be;
But cry: ' One day of the great lost days, one face of all the faces,
    Grant me to see and touch once more and nothing more to see.

' For, Lord, I was free of all Thy flowers, but I chose the world's sad roses,
    And that is why my feet are torn and mine eyes are blind with sweat,
But at Thy terrible judgment-seat, when this my tired life closes,
    I am ready to reap whereof I sowed, and pay my righteous debt.

' But once before the sand is run and the silver thread is broken,
    Give me a grace and cast aside the veil of dolorous years,
Grant me one hour of all mine hours, and let me see for a token
    Her pure and pitiful eyes shine out, and bathe her feet with tears.'

Her pitiful hands should calm, and her hair stream down and blind me,
    Out of the sight of night, and out of the reach of fear,
And her eyes should be my light whilst the sun went out behind me,
    And the viols in her voice be the last sound in mine ear.

Before the ruining waters fall and my life be carried under,
    And Thine anger cleave me through as a child cuts down a flower,
I will praise Thee, Lord, in Hell, while my limbs are racked asunder,
    For the last sad sight of her face and the little grace of an hour.

BENEDICTIO DOMINI

Without, the sullen noises of the street!
   The voice of London, inarticulate,
Hoarse and blaspheming, surges in to meet
   The silent blessing of the Immaculate.

Dark is the church, and dim the worshippers,
   Hushed with bowed heads as though by some old spell,
While through the incense-laden air there stirs
   The admonition of a silver bell.

Dark is the church, save where the altar stands,
   Dressed like a bride, illustrious with light,
Where one old priest exalts with tremulous hands
   The one true solace of man's fallen plight.

Strange silence here: without, the sounding street
   Heralds the world's swift passage to the fire:
O Benediction, perfect and complete!
   When shall men cease to suffer and desire?

EXTREME UNCTION

Upon the eyes, the lips, the feet,
   On all the passages of sense.
The atoning oil is spread with sweet
   Renewal of lost innocence.

The feet, that lately ran so fast
   To meet desire, are soothly sealed;
The eyes, that were so often cast
   On vanity, are touched and healed.

From troublous sights and sounds set free;
   In such a twilight hour of breath,
Shall one retrace his life, or see,
   Through shadows, the true face of death?

Vials of mercy! Sacring oils!
   I know not where nor when I come,
Nor through what wanderings and toils,
   To crave of you Viaticum.

Yet, when the walls of flesh grow weak.
In such an hour, it well may be,
Through mist and darkness, light will break,
And each anointed sense will see.

LIONEL JOHNSON
1867–1902

At Winchester School Lionel Johnson gave promise of becoming a notable poet and critic. His companions at New College, Oxford, reported in awed tones to the rest of the University that he wrote Latin verse as easily as English and read Plato and Aeschylus for pleasure. Though contemptuous of ordinary university honours, he stood well enough to justify the enthusiasm of his teachers. When he came to London Mr. Kegan Paul, the publisher, made a career possible for him in journalism. For ten years (1890–1900) he was the most distinguished literary critic of his generation. His fellow members of the Rhymers' Club — Mr. Yeats excepted — regarded him as a prose writer who had strayed into poetry. Nevertheless the two volumes published during his life, *Poems* (1895) and *Ireland with Other Poems* (1897), bid fair to survive much of the verse that was composed and declaimed by that rebellious crowd of young poets in their sessions in an upstairs room at the Cheshire Cheese. Johnson's last years were darkened by the effects of excessive drinking. Though his death resulted directly from an accidental fall against the kerb as he was crossing the Strand, alcoholism was responsible for the accident.

The poetry of Lionel Johnson does not make its way immediately to our affection. It lacks, often, the rapture and warmth which ingratiates the work of lesser poets. But it is poetry to which one must come back a second time, and again. The reason cannot be better demonstrated than by applying to him a sentence which he wrote of Arnold: ' The false worship of words, the conventional acceptance of phrases, all the spurious wisdom of the world, he fought against and conquered much of it.'

Even in his Winchester days Johnson broke lances on the shields of the champions of falsehood. By the time he was eighteen he had brought to the bar the various religions by which men can live, judged them, and elected which he would follow. He had worshipped many heroes — Whitman, Emerson, Hugo, Kingsley, Browning, Pater, Newman — and decided which he could safely trust. In poetry he had discovered for himself, at the age when most boys are beginning cautiously to explore the realm of ideas, that ' it is in the expansion of the intellectual enjoyment, together with absolute suppression of intellectual pride, that the Truth has its chiefest glory.' This high intellectual discrimination and probity admits him to the company of the great. His achievements hardly make him the companion there of Milton and Shelley, but he understands their language.

Nature, more certainly than the Catholic Church or the wisdom of his chosen masters in literature, was the dominant impulse of his poetry. The pastoral country about Winchester touched him, as it had earlier moved Keats who wrote the last of his odes under its spell. Johnson speaks fervently in one of his Winchester letters of the autumnal loveliness of the Itchen meads: ' the richest gold on the trees, and mild melancholy air; and I walk by the river, perfectly happy.' But his delight in nature is never a sensuous dream. He is not entranced. He is enlivened. Unlike most poets of nature he seems to feel her beauty with his mind. It is evident from his poetry that he looked on her with the same clearness of vision with which he surveyed ideas. What could be more sharp and direct, more free from the ' false worship of words ' than these opening lines of ' In Falmouth Harbour.'

> The large, calm harbour lies below
> Long, terraced lines of circling light:
> Without, the deep sea currents flow:
> And here are stars, and night.

There is no poet of the ' tragic generation ' who so quickly compels our personal sympathy as Johnson. To maintain the proud austerity of his mind, to achieve the ' image of our desire ' and the serenity which abides ' upon the breast of some divine and windless sea,' the ascetic in him waged unceasing war against the ' dark angel ' of his life. Johnson for all his courage had premonitions of defeat. He clung to the Roman Church with the passionate devotion of a man to whom close human friendship is for some reason impossible. It seemed to him in those terrible struggles when all his resistance to the tempter had melted away, the only ultimate source of strength. Mr. Yeats has saved for us a pitiful picture of him surrounded by drunken men at three in the morning, a childlike figure looking straight before him with head erect and one hand resting on the table. In the midst of the brutish silence he says in a clear, unshaken voice, ' I believe in nothing but the Holy Roman Church.' Not even his faith could save him.

The ' precept of silence ' enjoined him from speaking.

> Some players upon plaintive strings
> Publish their wistfulness abroad:
> I have not spoken of these things,
> Save to one man, and unto God.

A few times only he cries out, and the cry is agonizing. To those who know his story there are no more terrifying poems in English than *Mystic and Cavalier* and *The Dark Angel*.

IN FALMOUTH HARBOUR

To Frank Mathew.

I

The large, calm harbour lies below
　Long, terraced lines of circling light:
Without, the deep sea currents flow:
　And here are stars, and night.

No sight, no sound, no living stir
　But such as perfect the still bay:
So hushed it is, the voyager
　Shrinks at the thought of day.

We glide by many a lanterned mast;
　Our mournful horns blow wild to warn
Yon looming pier: the sailors cast
　Their ropes, and watch for morn.

Strange murmurs from the sleeping town,
　And sudden creak of lonely oars
Crossing the water, travel down
　The roadstead, the dim shores.

A charm is on the silent bay;
Charms of the sea, charms of the land.
Memories of open wind convey
   Peace to this harbour strand.

Far off, Saint David's crags descend
On seas of desolate storm: and far
From this pure rest, the Land's drear End,
   And ruining waters, are.

Well was it worth to have each hour
Of high and perilous blowing wind:
For here, for now, deep peace hath power
   To conquer the worn mind.

I have passed over the rough sea,
And over the white harbour bar:
And this is Death's dreamland to me,
   Led hither by a star.

And what shall dawn be? Hush thee, nay!
Soft, soft is night, and calm and still:
Save that day cometh, what of day
   Knowest thou: good, or ill?

Content thee! Not the annulling light
Of any pitiless dawn is here;
Thou art alone with ancient night:
   And all the stars are clear.

Only the night air, and the dream;
Only the far, sweet-smelling wave;
The stilly sounds, the circling gleam,
   And thine: and thine a grave

❖ LIONEL JOHNSON ❖

WESTWARD

To Roger Fry.

White Land within the West
　　Upon the breast
Of some divine and windless sea:
One of thy musing ghosts make me,
　　Glad and at rest.

White leaves of poplar there
　　Move to an air,
Gracious, and musical, and kind:
Under those leaves, let me too find
　　The cure of care.

But chiefly for their sake,
　　Whom thou didst take;
Lost to me in thine heart, White Land!
Soon bid me sleep, soon hand in hand
　　With them to wake.

TO A FRIEND

Sweet, hard and wise, your choice so early made,
　To cast the world away, a derelict:
To wear within the pure and austere shade
The sacred sable of Saint Benedict.

I give you praise: give me your better prayers.
The nothingness, which you have flung away,
To me seems full of fond delightful cares,
Visions, and dangers of the crowded day.

Give me your prayers: you keep no other wealth,
And therefore are the wealthiest of my friends.
So shall you lure me by an holy stealth
At last into the Land where wandering ends.

MAGIC

To John Myres.

II

They wrong with ignorance a royal choice,
  Who cavil at my loneliness and labour:
For them, the luring wonder of a voice,
The viol's cry for them, the harp and tabour:
    For me divine austerity,
    And voices of philosophy.

Ah! light imaginations, that discern
No passion in the citadel of passion:
Their fancies lie on flowers; but my thoughts turn
To thoughts and things of an eternal fashion:
    The majesty and dignity
    Of everlasting verity.

Mine is the sultry sunset, when the skies
Tremble with strange, intolerable thunder:
And at the dead of an hushed night, these eyes
Draw down the soaring oracles winged with wonder:
    From the four winds they come to me,
    The Angels of Eternity.

Men pity me; poor men, who pity me!
Poor, charitable, scornful souls of pity!
I choose laborious loneliness: and ye
Lead Love in triumph through the dancing city:
    While death and darkness girdle me,
    I grope for immortality.

VINUM DAEMONUM

To Stephen Phillips.

The crystal flame, the ruby flame,
  Alluring, dancing, revelling!
See them: and ask me not, whence came
    This cup I bring.

But only watch the wild wine glow,
But only taste its fragrance: then,
Drink the wild drink I bring, and so
    Reign among men.

Only one sting, and then but joy:
One pang of fire, and thou art free.
Then, what thou wilt, thou canst destroy:
    Save only me!

Triumph in tumult of thy lust:
Wanton in passion of thy will:
Cry *Peace!* to conscience, and it must
    At last be still.

I am the Prince of this World: I
Command the flames, command the fires.
Mine are the draughts, that satisfy
    This World's desires.

Thy longing leans across the brink:
Ah, the brave thirst within thine eyes!
For there is that within this drink,
    Which never dies.

THE DAY OF COMING DAYS

To J. P. Quinn.

Bright seas cast far upon her shore
    White flowers of flying spray:
The blossoms of her fields are more,
    Than blossomed yesterday:
The music of her winds and birds
Alone can tell the triumph words,
    Her children cannot say.

The stars from solemn deeps look down
    In favour and delight:
The glories of her day, they crown
    With splendours of her night:
The queen of the adoring Gael,
Their radiant mother, Inisfail,
    Reigns, by divinest right.

PARNELL

To John McGrath.

The wail of Irish winds,
     The cry of Irish seas:
Eternal sorrow finds
Eternal voice in these.

I cannot praise our dead,
Whom Ireland weeps so well:
Her morning light, that fled;
Her morning star, that fell.

She of the mournful eyes
Waits, and no dark clouds break:
Waits, and her strong son lies
Dead, for her holy sake.

Her heart is sorrow's home,
And hath been from of old:
An host of griefs hath come,
To make that heart their fold.

Ah, the sad autumn day,
When the last sad troop came
Swift down the ancient way,
Keening a chieftain's name!

Gray hope was there, and dread;
Anger, and love in tears:
They mourned the dear and dead,
Dirge of the ruined years.

Home to her heart she drew
The mourning company:
Old sorrows met the new,
In sad fraternity.

A mother, and forget?
Nay! all her children's fate
Ireland remembers yet,
With love insatiate.

She hears the heavy bells:
Hears, and with passionate breath
Eternally she tells
A rosary of death.

Faithful and true is she,
The mother of us all:
Faithful and true! may we
Fail her not, though we fall.

Her son, our brother, lies
Dead, for her holy sake:
But from the dead arise
Voices, that bid us wake.

Not his, to hail the dawn:
His but the herald's part.
Be ours to see withdrawn
Night from our Mother's heart.

TO MORFYDD

A voice on the winds,
   A voice by the waters,
  Wanders and cries:
Oh! what are the winds?
And what are the waters?
  Mine are your eyes!

Western the winds are,
And western the waters,
  Where the light lies:
Oh! what are the winds?
And what are the waters?
  Mine are your eyes!

Cold, cold, grow the winds,
And wild grow the waters,
  Where the sun dies:
Oh! what are the winds?
And what are the waters?
  Mine are your eyes!

273

And down the night winds,
And down the night waters,
   The music flies:
Oh! what are the winds?
And what are the waters?
Cold be the winds,
And wild be the waters,
   So mine be your eyes!

BY THE STATUE OF KING CHARLES AT CHARING CROSS

To William Watson.

Sombre and rich, the skies;
  Great glooms, and starry plains.
Gently the night wind sighs;
Else a vast silence reigns.

The splendid silence clings
Around me: and around
The saddest of all kings
Crowned, and again discrowned.

Comely and calm, he rides
Hard by his own Whitehall:
Only the night wind glides:
No crowds, nor rebels, brawl.

Gone too, his Court: and yet,
The stars his courtiers are:
Stars in their stations set;
And every wandering star.

Alone he rides, alone,
The fair and fatal king:
Dark night is all his own,
That strange and solemn thing.

Which are more full of fate:
The stars; or those sad eyes?
Which are more still and great:
Those brows; or the dark skies?

Although his whole heart yearn
In passionate tragedy:
Never was face so stern
With sweet austerity.

Vanquished in life, his death
By beauty made amends:
The passing of his breath
Won his defeated ends.

Brief life, and hapless? Nay:
Through death, life grew sublime
Speak after sentence? Yea:
And to the end of time.

Armoured he rides, his head
Bare to the stars of doom:
He triumphs now, the dead,
Beholding London's gloom.

Our wearier spirit faints,
Vexed in the world's employ:
His soul was of the saints;
And art to him was joy.

King, tried in fires of woe!
Men hunger for thy grace:
And through the night I go,
Loving thy mournful face.

Yet, when the city sleeps,
When all the cries are still:
The stars and heavenly deeps
Work out a perfect will.

THE DARK ANGEL

Dark Angel, with thine aching lust
   To rid the world of penitence:
Malicious Angel, who still dost
My soul such subtile violence!

Because of thee, no thought, no thing,
Abides for me undesecrate:
Dark Angel, ever on the wing,
Who never reachest me too late!

When music sounds, then changest thou
Its silvery to a sultry fire:
Nor will thine envious heart allow
Delight untortured by desire.

Through thee, the gracious Muses turn
To Furies, O mine Enemy!
And all the things of beauty burn
With flames of evil ecstasy.

Because of thee, the land of dreams
Becomes a gathering place of fears:
Until tormented slumber seems
One vehemence of useless tears.

When sunlight glows upon the flowers,
Or ripples down the dancing sea:
Thou, with thy troop of passionate powers,
Beleaguerest, bewilderest, me.

Within the breath of autumn woods,
Within the winter silences:
Thy venomous spirit stirs and broods,
O Master of impieties!

The ardour of red-flame is thine,
And thine the steely soul of ice:
Thou poisonest the fair design
Of nature, with unfair device.

Apples of ashes, golden bright;
Waters of bitterness, how sweet!
O banquet of a foul delight,
Prepared by thee, dark Paraclete!

❖ LIONEL JOHNSON ❖

Thou art the whisper in the gloom,
The hinting tone, the haunting laugh:
Thou art the adorner of my tomb,
The minstrel of mine epitaph.

I fight thee, in the Holy Name!
Yet, what thou dost, is what God saith:
Tempter! should I escape thy flame,
Thou wilt have helped my soul from Death:

The second Death, that never dies,
That cannot die, when time is dead:
Live Death, wherein the lost soul cries,
Eternally uncomforted.

Dark Angel, with thine aching lust!
Of two defeats, of two despairs:
Less dread, a change to drifting dust,
Than thine eternity of cares.

Do what thou wilt, thou shalt not so,
Dark Angel! triumph over me:
Lonely, unto the Lone I go;
Divine, to the Divinity.

ARTHUR SYMONS
1865–

Mr. Arthur Symons has been the chief apologist of the 'tragic generation.' For eight months he edited their second party organ *The Savoy* (1892), and waved its modernism in the face of horrified British respectability. There has been no more brilliant episode in journalism. Subsequently he has alternated between poetry and criticism, an almost necessary procedure in view of the fact that he holds the poet to be the best critic. His critical interest is by no means confined to the men with whose work he has been intimately associated, such as Verlaine, Wilde, and Beardsley. It extends to the Elizabethans, Blake, the Romantic poets, Browning, and Hardy. Heinemann published a collective edition of his poetry in 1921. Not included in those two volumes are several dramas in verse and *The Fool of the World* (1906), *Knave of Hearts* (1913) and *Lesbia and Other Poems* (1906).

Mr. Symons survives. He must find the literary world of these times a strange place. Most of his companions of the yellow '90's have died; those who remain, like Mr. Yeats, have passed to new phases of activity. He alone reminds us — as he does in an almost annual volume of reminiscence or criticism — of the ambitions and poetic doctrines of the group which helped him make *The Savoy* the best journal of the arts ever published in England.

Symons epitomizes the age which he chooses still to represent, in part because he had thought coherently about the intentions of the 'English Decadents' — as he insists we shall call them — but mainly because he quite consciously desired to be the English equivalent of the French originals whom he so vastly admired. He owns the gift, too, of a remarkable adaptability. One of his friends says of him that he 'more than any man I have ever known, could slip, as it were, into the mind of another.' This power has allowed him to absorb into himself, and to give expression both in poetry and in his peculiar kind

of impressionistic criticism, to the artistic temper of an era
which he outlived.

The articles of his creed have not been amended in forty
years. He still believes, we may be sure, in the cult of beau-
tiful *things;* that there is no necessary difference in artistic
value between a ' good poem about a flower in the hedge and
a good poem about the scent in a sachet '; that there is no dis-
tinction ' between what is called the work of nature and what
is the work of man.' His delight in the stream of varied sensa-
tion has never grown less since the days when he used to haunt
the music hall and the ballet and savour the gaiety of literary
Bohemia at the Café François Premier in the company of Ver-
laine, Moréas and Vignier.

> For in our time we lose so large a part
> In serious trifles, and so oft let slip
> The wine of every moment, at the lip
> Its moment, and the moment of the heart.

He has sought to drain the sensational possibilities of each
moment of life, and he has refused to discriminate among sen-
sations. He admires Verlaine above all the great ones of the
fin de siècle because Verlaine's art is, as he would like his own
to be, ' a delicate waiting upon moods, with that perfect con-
fidence in them as they are, which it is a large part of ordinary
education to discourage in us, and a large part of experience
to repress.'

What sets Symons off from the poets after 1900 is the nar-
row range of his poetry. The things he has felt are myriad, but
they are much the same in kind, or they seem to be so because
his feeling about them is always a little ' perverse ' — to use a
favourite word of his. It is as if he were looking on the dancer
or the crowd or the absinthe-drinker a trifle uneasily; hoping,
almost wistfully, that he is experiencing a not quite normal
sensation. He would like to think he has been deliciously, de-
liriously wicked. When he tries to step beyond pathos and sen-
timent and *souvenir* into tragedy, the emotion will not fill out
the form he has designed for it, and he bogs himself in words.

Yet his services to poetry must be reckoned considerable. He
did much to destroy the romantic and exclusive worship of na-
ture and obtain permission for the poet to write about any ob-

ject or mood which he feels he can transform by his emotion.
The Georgians owe him something for making their way to
simple and intimate subjects easier. Even the Imagists were
forestalled by him, as this poem from the many which might
be taken, will prove:

Pale from the watery west, with the pallor of winter a-cold,
Rays of the afternoon sun in a glimmer across the trees;
Glittering moist underfoot, the long alley. The firs, one by
    one,
Catch and conceal, as I saunter, and flash in a dazzle of gold
Lower and lower the vanishing disc; and the sun alone sees
As I wait for my love in the fir-tree alley alone with the sun.

PROLOGUE: BEFORE THE CURTAIN

We are the puppets of a shadow-play,
    We dream the plot is woven of our hearts,
Passionately we play the self-same parts
Our fathers have played passionately yesterday,
And our sons play to-morrow. There's no speech
In all desire, nor any idle word,
Men have not said and women have not heard;
And when we lean and whisper each to each
Until the silence quickens to a kiss,
Even so the actor and the actress played
The lovers yesterday; when the lights fade
Before our feet, and the obscure abyss
Opens, and darkness falls about our eyes,
'Tis only that some momentary rage
Or rapture blinds us to forget the stage,
Like the wise actor, most in this thing wise.
We pass, and have our gesture; love and pain
And hope and apprehension and regret
Weave ordered lines into a pattern set
Not for our pleasure, and for us in vain.
The gesture is eternal; we who pass
Pass on the gesture; we, who pass, pass on
One after one into oblivion,
As shadows dim and vanish from a glass.

✤ ARTHUR SYMONS ✤

MODERN BEAUTY

I am the torch, she saith, and what to me
  If the moth die of me? I am the flame
Of Beauty, and I burn that all may see
Beauty, and I have neither joy nor shame,
But live with that clear life of perfect fire
Which is to men the death of their desire.

I am Yseult and Helen, I have seen
  Troy burn, and the most loving knight lie dead.
The world has been my mirror, time has been
  My breath upon the glass; and men have said,
Age after age, in rapture and despair,
Love's poor few words, before my image there.

I live, and am immortal; in my eyes
  The sorrow of the world, and on my lips
The joy of life, mingle to make me wise;
  Yet now the day is darkened with eclipse:
Who is there lives for beauty? Still am I
The torch, but where's the moth that still dares die?

EMMY

Emmy's exquisite youth and her virginal air,
  Eyes and teeth in the flash of a musical smile,
Come to me out of the past, and I see her there
  As I saw her once for a while.

Emmy's laughter rings in my ears, as bright,
  Fresh and sweet as the voice of a mountain brook,
And still I hear her telling us tales that night,
  Out of Boccaccio's book.

There, in the midst of the villainous dancing-hall,
  Leaning across the table, over the beer,
While the music maddened the whirling skirts of the ball,
  As the midnight hour drew near,

There with the women, haggard, painted and old,
  One fresh bud in a garland withered and stale,
She, with her innocent voice and her clear eyes, told
  Tale after shameless tale.

281

And ever the witching smile, to her face beguiled,
Paused and broadened, and broke in a ripple of fun,
And the soul of a child looked out of the eyes of a child,
Or ever the tale was done.

O my child, who wronged you first, and began
First the dance of death that you dance so well?
Soul for soul: and I think the soul of a man
Shall answer for yours in hell.

IN FOUNTAIN COURT

The fountain murmuring of sleep,
    A drowsy tune;
The flickering green of leaves that keep
The light of June;
Peace, through a slumbering afternoon,
The peace of June.

A waiting ghost, in the blue sky,
The white curved moon;
June, hushed and breathless, waits, and I
Wait too, with June;
Come, through the lingering afternoon,
Soon, love, come soon.

THE STREET–SINGER

She sings a pious ballad wearily;
    Her shivering body creeps on painful feet
Along the muddy runlets of the street;
The damp is in her throat: she coughs to free
The cracked and husky notes that tear her chest;
From side to side she looks with eyes that grope,
Feverishly hungering in a hopeless hope,
For pence that will not come; and pence mean rest,
The rest that pain may steal at night from sleep,
The rest that hunger gives when satisfied;
Her fingers twitch to handle them; she sings
Shriller; her eyes, too hot with tears to weep,
Fasten upon a window, where, inside,
A sweet voice mocks her with its carollings.

AT THE STAGE–DOOR

Kicking my heels in the street,
    Here at the edge of the pavement I wait, and my feet
Paw at the ground like the horses' hoofs in the street.

Under the archway sheer,
Sudden and black as a hole in the placarded wall,
Faces flicker and veer,
Wavering out of the darkness into the light,
Wavering back into night;
Under the archway, suddenly seen, the curls
And thin, bright faces of girls,
Roving eyes, and smiling lips, and the glance
Seeking, finding perchance,
Here at the edge of the pavement, there by the wall,
One face, out of them all.

Steadily, face after face,
Cheeks with the blush of the paint yet lingering, eyes
Still with their circle of black . . .
But hers, but hers?
Rose-leaf cheeks, and flower-soft lips, and the grace
Of the vanishing Spring come back,
And a child's heart blithe in the sudden and sweet surprise,
Subtly expectant, that stirs
In the smile of her heart to my heart, of her eyes to my eyes.

LA MÉLINITE: MOULIN–ROUGE

Olivier Metra's Waltz of Roses
    Sheds in a rhythmic shower
The very petals of the flower;
And all is roses,
The rouge of petals in a shower.

Down the long hall the dance returning
Rounds the full circle, rounds
The perfect rose of lights and sounds,
The rose returning
Into the circle of its rounds.

Alone, apart, one dancer watches
Her mirrored, morbid grace;
Before the mirror, face to face,
Alone she watches
Her morbid, vague, ambiguous grace.

Before the mirror's dance of shadows
She dances in a dream,
And she and they together seem
A dance of shadows,
Alike the shadows of a dream.

The orange-rosy lamps are trembling
Between the robes that turn;
In ruddy flowers of flame that burn
The lights are trembling:
The shadows and the dancers turn.

And, enigmatically smiling,
In the mysterious night,
She dances for her own delight,
A shadow smiling
Back to a shadow in the night.

JAVANESE DANCERS

Twitched strings, the clang of metal, beaten drums,
Dull, shrill, continuous, disquieting;
And now the stealthy dancer comes
Undulantly with cat-like steps that cling;

Smiling between her painted lids a smile,
Motionless, unintelligible, she twines
Her fingers into mazy lines,
The scarves across her fingers twine the while.

One, two, three, four glide forth, and, to and fro,
Delicately and imperceptibly,
Now swaying gently in a row,
Now interthreading slow and rhythmically,

Still, with fixed eyes, monotonously still,
Mysteriously, with smiles inanimate,
With lingering feet that undulate,
With sinuous fingers, spectral hands that thrill

In measure while the gnats of music whirr,
The little amber-coloured dancers move,
Like painted idols seen to stir
By the idolaters in a magic grove.

OPALS

M y soul is like this cloudy, flaming opal ring.
The fields of earth are in it, green and glimmering,
The waves of the blue sky, night's purple flower of noon,
The vanishing cold scintillations of the moon,
And the red heart that is a flame within a flame.
And as the opal dies, and is reborn the same,
And all the fire that is its life-blood seems to dart
Through the veined variable intricacies of its heart,
And ever wandering ever wanders back again,
So must my swift soul constant to itself remain.
Opal, have I not been as variable as you?
But, cloudy opal flaming green and red and blue,
Are you not ever constant in your varying,
Even as my soul, O captive opal of my ring?

BY THE POOL AT THE THIRD ROSSES

I heard the sighing of the reeds
In the grey pool in the green land,
The sea-wind in the long reeds sighing
Between the green hill and the sand.

I heard the sighing of the reeds
Day after day, night after night;
I heard the whirring wild ducks flying,
I saw the sea-gulls' wheeling flight.

I heard the sighing of the reeds
Night after night, day after day,
And I forgot old age, and dying,
And youth that loves, and love's decay.

I heard the sighing of the reeds
At noontide and at evening,
And some old dream I had forgotten
I seemed to be remembering.

I heard the sighing of the reeds:
Is it in vain, is it in vain
That some old peace I had forgotten
Is crying to come back again?

TO NIGHT

I have loved wind and light,
  And the bright sea,
But, holy and most secret Night,
Not as I love and have loved thee.

God, like all highest things,
Hides light in shade,
And in the night his visitings
To sleep and dreams are clearliest made.

Love, that knows all things well,
Loves the night best;
Joys whereof daylight dares not tell
Are his, and the diviner rest.

And Life, whom day shows plain
His prison-bars,
Feels the close walls and the hard chain
Fade when the darkness brings the stars.

TWILIGHT

The pale grey sea crawls stealthily
   Up the pale lilac of the beach;
A bluer grey, the waters reach
To where the horizon ends the sea.

Flushed with a tinge of dusky rose,
The clouds, a twilit lavender,
Flood the low sky, and duskier
The mist comes flooding in, and flows

Into the twilight of the land,
And darkness, coming softly down,
Rustles across the fading sand
And folds its arms about the town.

REQUIES

O is it death or life
   That sounds like something strangely known
In this subsiding out of strife,
This slow sea-monotone?

A sound, scarce heard through sleep,
Murmurous as the August bees
That fill the forest hollows deep
About the roots of trees.

O is it life or death,
O is it hope or memory,
That quiets all things with this breath
Of the eternal sea?

WANDERER'S SONG

I have had enough of women, and enough of love,
   But the land waits, and the sea waits, and day and night is
     enough;
Give me a long white road, and the grey wide path of the sea,
And the wind's will and the bird's will, and the heart-ache still
     in me.

287

Why should I seek out sorrow, and give gold for strife?
I have loved much and wept much, but tears and love are not
    life;
The grass calls to my heart, and the foam to my blood cries up,
And the sun shines and the road shines, and the wine's in the
    cup.

I have had enough of wisdom, and enough of mirth,
For the way's one and the end's one, and it's soon to the ends
    of the earth;
And it's then good-night and to bed, and if heels or heart ache,
Well, it's sound sleep and long sleep, and sleep too deep to
    wake.

WHITE MAGIC

Against the world I closed my heart,
  And, half in pride and half in fear,
I said to Love and Lust: Depart,
None enters here.

A gipsy witch has glided in,
She takes her seat beside my fire;
Her eyes are innocent of sin,
Mine of desire.

She holds me with an unknown spell,
She folds me in her heart's embrace;
If this be love, I cannot tell:
I watch her face.

Her sombre eyes are happier
Than any joy that found a voice;
Since I am happiness to her,
I too rejoice.

And I have closed the door again,
Against the world I close my heart;
I hold her with my spell; in vain
Would she depart.

I hold her with a surer spell,
Beyond her magic, and above:
If hers be love, I cannot tell,
But mine is love.

WILLIAM BUTLER YEATS
1865–

M r. Yeats has with difficulty learned to live in the modern world of motors, Fabian socialism, Board Schools and sanitary plumbing. That he has been, in spite of his inheritance and training, such a power in the revolution which brought Ireland independence as well as a new literature, is not the least singular of the miracles of the Irish renaissance.

His father, a Pre-Raphaelite painter and a passionate man with a roving intellect, abetted the child's love of the marvellous and encouraged his early fondness for poetry which had been awakened to life by the Orange Rhymes of a stable boy. His mother used to spend hours exchanging stories of pilots and fishing people and village ghosts with their family servant, a fisherman's wife, while the boy listened and stored them away in his memory for later rehearsal in his poems and in *The Celtic Twilight*, a collection of Irish lore. All his dreams were of ships and smugglers, the Sidhe (fairies) and the banshee. His heroes were Manfred and Prince Athanase; their women accompanied their lovers through all manner of wild places, lawless women without homes and without children.

His first poems were dramatic, vast, incoherent, fanciful imitations of Shelley and Spenser into which he poured the Irish legends and strange beliefs he had heard in his childhood and now eagerly collected from every source. Katherine Tynan, one of the first outside the family to listen to his poetry, tells how she used to be awakened in the night, when she was staying at the Yeatses, by the steady, monotonous sound ' of the poet chanting to himself in the watches of the night.' Though he still intended to follow his father as a painter, it was plain that his talent in verse might come to something more valuable than his charcoal sketches promised. He was already meditating a revival of Irish literature founded in the ancient story of his people and breaking with the conventions of Lever and Thomas Moore, the ' convivial Ireland with traditional tear and smile.'

In 1887 the family moved to London and his real training as a poet began. He foregathered at the Cheshire Cheese with the Rhymers; he submitted to Henley's ruthless corrections in his style. His admiration for Morris was so great that he declared he would choose to ' live his life, poetry and all ' rather than his own. When Arthur Symons brought the good news of Symbolism from Paris, he abandoned the ' overcharged colour inherited from the romantic movement,' which suffused the story of the *Wanderings of Oisin* (1899), in a search for symbols which could fire the imagination of the Irish. Might he not create some new *Prometheus Unbound,* Patrick or Columkil, Oisin or Fion, in Prometheus' stead and persuade the educated classes to enjoy the mythology of the illiterate?

Hatred of the scientific realism then fashionable in art, led him to investigate Blake's symbolic system with E. J. Ellis and to play with the mysteries of alchemy and the *Kabbala.* For a time he attended Madame Blavatsky's Theosophist séances, enjoying the absurd *dévots* circling round that amazing woman, but sufficiently impressed to make thaumaturgic experiments of his own.

During the '90's his youthful plans for a new Irish literature began to take definite form. Lady Gregory, who had actually seen the banshee in her own garden and was as great an expert in Irish legend as Yeats himself offered him the few pounds necessary to found a theatre. Mr. George Moore promised to engage actors and do the preliminary rehearsing in London. On the eighth of May 1899 the Irish National Theatre was inaugurated, to the accompaniment of catcalls, in the Antient Concert Rooms in Dublin. The venture uncovered the unsuspected dramatic abilities of Lady Gregory and John Synge, and the struggle of the players and authors against Irish political and religious bigotry gave them a sense of solidarity which a movement subordinating to itself such diverse personalities needed. Though George Moore, Synge, Shaw, George Russell, Dr. Hyde, and Lady Gregory were his adjutants, the Celtic Renaissance, as Mr. Moore generously says, ' rose out of Yeats and returns to Yeats.'

The responsibilities of theatrical management transformed the youthful symbolist and phantom-seeker into a most capable man of affairs, without diminishing the quality of his poetry. He has served the Free State as senator, inspected her schools,

and even censored her cinema with patriotic patience. He
grows old humorously and wisely and as vigorously as his
compatriot Bernard Shaw whose life is so complete a contrast
to his.

Since the early verse, *Poems* (1895), *The Secret Rose*
(1897), *The Wind Among the Reeds* (1899), his chief vol-
umes have been: *The Green Helmet* (1912), *The Wild Swans
at Coole* (1919), and *The Tower* (1928). The plays and prose
have been collected. *Autobiographies,* completed in 1922, con-
tains a most shrewd and sympathetic study of the ' tragic
generation' of the '90's. There is no modern autobiography,
perhaps none in English, which can rival it.

In one of his frequent flashes of critical insight Mr. Yeats
defined genius as the ' crisis that joins [the] buried self for cer-
tain moments to our trivial daily round.' In his own poetry
he has sought from the first to uncover this ' buried self ' which
lies much deeper than a man's own nature, in the hidden sym-
bols of his race. This search is really the sum and substance of
the Irish revival since he and his associates have wished to
fashion a literature in which personal emotion is ' woven by a
sensuous, musical vocabulary into a general pattern of myth
and symbol ' and to bequeath this to later Irish poets.

The Victorians, he maintained, filled their work with ' im-
purities,' curiosities about politics, science, history, and re-
ligion. ' Pure work ' must once more be created, free from
abstractions, anecdotes, and brooding over scientific opinion.
A nation is not united by thought, which is only transitory
and contemporaneous, but by an interchange, among streams
and shadows, of emotions which are molded together after
centuries of use and accretion, into an Image or a bundle
of related Images. These provide the poet with an originating
symbol powerfully provocative of a state of mind.

No Anglo-Saxon can appreciate how the Irish temperament
responds to symbols, waiting for the events of which the sym-
bolic manifestation gives promise, anticipating birth or death
or calamity when the symbols announcing their imminence
have passed by. Not only did Yeats make use of the accumu-
lated symbols of his people, but from his dabbling in magic
and by natural predisposition he came to see all experience
as issuing in signal and sign. Even these personal symbols of
events, he believed, are actually embedded in the great ' mem-

ory' since everything in 'heaven or earth has its association, momentous or trivial . . . and one never knows what forgotten events may have plunged . . . into the great passions.'

Directly allied with his idea of the participation of individual emotion in the emotion of the universal memory is Yeats's doctrine of the Mask. He has asserted that the lyric poet is linked with 'another age, historical or imaginary, where alone he finds images that arouse his energy,' and that only when he has found by a stroke of 'luckless luck' his proper traditional pose, will the accumulated expression of the world open before him. It is possible that this fantastic theory was a necessary rationalization of the poet's to justify his own eagerness to escape from a civilization he did not like. Of late he has said little about the Mask, as his interests have been widened by his active life and his own poetry has approached that ideal genius which he defined as joining the buried self to the trivial daily round.

Yeats has never said which of the half-dozen traditional masks he overtly assumed, whether that of 'lover or saint, sage or sensualist, or mere mocker of all life.' If he once thought of himself as masked behind the bard or seer, his latest verse in *The Tower* reveals a new Mask, that of a happy man who has prepared his peace.

> With learned Italian things
> And the proud stones of Greece,
> Poet's imaginings
> And memories of love,
> Memories of the words of women,
> All those things whereof
> Man makes superhuman
> Mirror-resembling dream.

DOWN BY THE SALLEY GARDENS

Down by the salley gardens my love and I did meet;
    She passed the salley gardens with little snow-white feet.
She bid me take love easy, as the leaves grow on the tree;
But I, being young and foolish, with her would not agree.

In a field by the river my love and I did stand,
And on my leaning shoulder she laid her snow-white hand.
She bid me take life easy, as the grass grows on the weirs;
But I was young and foolish, and now am full of tears.

THE LAKE ISLE OF INNISFREE

I will arise and go now, and go to Innisfree,
    And a small cabin build there, of clay and wattles made;
Nine bean rows will I have there, a hive for the honey bee,
    And live alone in the bee-loud glade.

And I shall have some peace there, for peace comes
        dropping slow,
    Dropping from the veils of the morning to where
        the cricket sings;
There midnight's all a glimmer, and noon a purple glow,
    And evening full of the linnet's wings.

I will arise and go now, for always night and day
    I hear lake water lapping with low sounds by the shore;
While I stand on the roadway, or on the pavements grey,
    I hear it in the deep heart's core.

THE BALLAD OF FATHER GILLIGAN

The old priest Peter Gilligan
    Was weary night and day;
For half his flock were in their beds,
    Or under green sods lay.

Once, while he nodded on a chair,
    At the moth-hour of eve,
Another poor man sent for him,
    And he began to grieve.

' I have no rest, nor joy, nor peace,
    For people die and die ';
And after cried he, ' God forgive!
    My body spake, not I! '

He knelt, and leaning on the chair
He prayed and fell asleep;
And the moth-hour went from the fields,
And the stars began to peep.

They slowly into millions grew,
And leaves shook in the wind;
And God covered the world with shade,
And whispered to mankind.

Upon the time of sparrow chirp
When the moths came once more,
The old priest Peter Gilligan
Stood upright on the floor.

' Mavrone, mavrone! the man has died,
While I slept on the chair ';
He roused his horse out of its sleep,
And rode with little care.

He rode now as he never rode,
By rocky lane and fen;
The sick man's wife opened the door:
' Father! you come again! '

' And is the poor man dead? ' he cried.
' He died an hour ago,'
The old priest Peter Gilligan
In grief swayed to and fro.

' When you were gone, he turned and died
As merry as a bird.'
The old priest Peter Gilligan
He knelt him at that word.

' He who hath made the night of stars
For souls, who tire and bleed,
Sent one of His great angels down
To help me in my need.

' He who is wrapped in purple robes,
With planets in His care,
Had pity on the least of things
Asleep upon a chair.'

WHEN YOU ARE OLD

When you are old and gray and full of sleep,
  And nodding by the fire, take down this book,
And slowly read, and dream of the soft look
Your eyes had once, and of their shadows deep;

How many loved your moments of glad grace,
And loved your beauty with love false or true;
But one man loved the pilgrim soul in you,
And loved the sorrows of your changing face.

And bending down beside the glowing bars
Murmur, a little sadly, how love fled
And paced upon the mountains overhead
And hid his face amid a crowd of stars.

THE LOVER TELLS OF THE ROSE IN
HIS HEART

All things uncomely and broken, all things worn out and
    old,
The cry of a child by the roadway, the creak of a lumbering
    cart,
The heavy steps of the ploughman, splashing the wintry
    mould,
Are wronging your image that blossoms a rose in the deeps of
    my heart.

The wrong of unshapely things is a wrong too great to be told;
I hunger to build them anew and sit on a green knoll apart,
With the earth and the sky and the water, remade, like a cas-
    ket of gold
For my dreams of your image that blossoms a rose in the deeps
    of my heart.

THE SONG OF WANDERING AENGUS

I went out to the hazel wood,
  Because a fire was in my head,
And cut and peeled a hazel wand,
And hooked a berry to a thread;

And when white moths were on the wing,
And moth-like stars were flickering out,
I dropped the berry in a stream
And caught a little silver trout.

When I had laid it on the floor
I went to blow the fire a-flame,
But something rustled on the floor,
And some one called me by my name:
It had become a glimmering girl
With apple blossom in her hair
Who called me by my name and ran
And faded through the brightening air.

Though I am old with wandering
Through hollow lands and hilly lands,
I will find out where she has gone,
And kiss her lips and take her hands;
And walk among long dappled grass,
And pluck till time and times are done,
The silver apples of the moon,
The golden apples of the sun.

THE INDIAN UPON GOD

I passed along the water's edge below the humid trees,
  My spirit rocked in evening light, the rushes round
    my knees,
My spirit rocked in sleep and sighs; and saw the
    moorfowl pace
All dripping on a grassy slope, and saw them cease
    to chase
Each other round in circles, and heard the eldest
    speak:
Who holds the world between His bill and made us
    strong or weak
Is an undying moorfowl, and He lives beyond
    the sky.
The rains are from His dripping wing, the moonbeams
    from His eye.

I passed a little further on and heard a lotus talk:
*Who made the world and ruleth it, He hangeth
    on a stalk,*
*For I am in His image made, and all this tinkling
    tide*
*Is but a sliding drop of rain between His petals
    wide.*
A little way within the gloom a roebuck raised
    his eyes
Brimful of starlight, and he said: *The Stamper
    of the Skies,*
*He is a gentle roebuck; for how else, I pray,
    could He*
*Conceive a thing so sad and soft, a gentle thing
    like me?*
I passed a little further on and heard a peacock
    say:
*Who made the grass and made the worms and made
    my feathers gay,*
*He is a monstrous peacock, and He waveth all
    the night*
*His languid tail above us, lit with myriad spots
    of light.*

INTO THE TWILIGHT

O ut-worn heart, in a time out-worn,
    Come clear of the nets of wrong and right;
Laugh heart again in the gray twilight,
Sigh, heart, again in the dew of the morn.

Your mother Eire is always young,
Dew ever shining and twilight gray;
Though hope fall from you and love decay,
Burning in fires of a slanderous tongue.

Come, heart, where hill is heaped upon hill;
For there the mystical brotherhood
Of sun and moon and hollow and wood
And river and stream work out their will;

❖ WILLIAM BUTLER YEATS ❖

And God stands winding His lonely horn,
And time and the world are ever in flight;
And love is less kind than the gray twilight,
And hope is less dear than the dew of the morn.

GERARD MANLEY HOPKINS
1844–1889

Father Hopkins's reputation as a poet is due to an accident of friendship. Had it not been for the devotion of Robert Bridges to his memory, we should possess little of his work and know little of his artistic progress. Understanding full well that Hopkins's remarkable innovations would meet incomprehension and possibly even abuse in the '90's and early 1900's, Dr. Bridges waited until 1918 before releasing to the world an edition of his friend's poems. This was precisely the right moment for there are affinities, superficial but illuminating between Hopkins's poetry and the prevalent poetic manner of the years after the War. Consequently he leapt into a fame forty years delayed.

Hopkins's conversion to Rome during his undergraduate years was the central event of his life. His brilliance and popularity — he was called the ' Star of Balliol ' — made the occurrence sensational in Oxford. It hurt his family deeply and distressed his Church of England teachers. When he was received into the Society of Jesus, he burned his poems and ' resolved to write no more, as not belonging to [his] profession.' In the winter of 1875 when five Franciscan nuns perished in the wreck of the *Deutschland* off the English coast, at the instance of his rector he memorialized their death in a poem. This is the first of the poems in which he worked out the new ideas of rhythm which is their most notable trait.

Although his vows permitted him little contact with the world, Father Hopkins exercised an influence over his poet friends, Coventry Patmore, Richard Watson Dixon, and Robert Bridges. So completely did Patmore trust his judgment in matters artistic and spiritual, that he threw into the fire a manuscript volume, believing Hopkins did not wish that it should be published.

In 1884 Father Hopkins was elected to a fellowship in the revived Catholic University at Dublin. There the remaining five years of his life were spent.

The discovery of a new poet is the pleasantest of experiences. When Robert Bridges in 1918 introduced Hopkins to the literary world by an edition of his poems, those who were so fortunate as to come on this volume, which was almost immediately out of print, could scarcely believe that poetry so bold and vigorous could have been written in the Victorian age. The 'new' poets claimed him at once as a blood brother and praised him extravagantly. By many, even at so late a time, he was called perversely and uselessly obscure.

Obscure, at least on first reading, he undoubtedly is. But our difficulties do not arise because his inspiration had been indeterminate or because he stumbled into a mode of expression which was inadequate. Actually it takes only a little knowledge of the way in which Hopkins strove to hew thought and feeling out of language in order to be a master of the obscurities in his poetry. We shall be more adept at this than even his close friends, since the newer habits of poetic expression, to which we grow reluctantly accustomed, have made poets like Browning seem transparent. And the effort to understand is rewarding, since it brings us close to a man whose tenderness and frankness and passion make the inanities of much contemporary poetry look futile indeed.

The paradoxical problem of the lyric poet is to put into verse, which by nature requires time for the reading, an experience which may have occupied only an instant. Language, being slow of utterance, especially when it issues in careful sentences with subject and verb and a herd of modifiers, retards the imitation of the shock which characterized the experience. Hopkins tries to evade this paradox and reproduce the emotional impact by reducing sentences to their barest content. He writes, often, in word-clusters instead of clauses or sentences. In reading his poetry one must try to apprehend the experience behind the words, as one gathers the meaning of a painting directly without pausing to frame the elements into neat and logical sentences. In other respects Hopkins as an innovator in language is only doing what all poets have done (and been successively blamed for it) — inventing words where that is necessary and forcing old worn-out words to mean what he requires of them.

When we consider his really wonderful achievements in rhythm, we find our task more difficult.[1] One must be exceed-

[1] Hopkins elucidates his prosody in the 'Author's Preface' included by Bridges in the *Poems*.

ingly dull of ear to miss the breath-taking beauty of *The Wind-hover* which for virtuosity takes a place with the choruses of *Samson Agonistes*. But to explain, except in general terms, how Hopkins has accomplished his aim, would require more space than is available here. Actually what he did was to push to the limit the possibilities of licence in English metre. The result was that he gained a maximum of flexibility, a varia-tion in rhythm for every delicate variation in emotion, while at the same time he retained (what free-verse cannot effect) all the rapturous *stringendo* which a rhythmical pattern gives to poetry.

But it is not necessary to know the how or why in order to feel. If one reads Hopkins aloud — and he wished his poems to be read this way — one cannot escape the fiery force, the rush and swing, the moments of calm and the majestic pace. His poetry possesses one, the best of it, after it is understood. When death took him, he had only just mastered a difficult, self-explored art. The greatest was yet to be. Yet he had carved simplicity from the hard rock of language and had learned how to write

> To him who ever thought with love of me
> Or ever did for my sake some good deed
> I will appear, looking such charity
> And kind compassion, at his life's last need
> That he will out of hand and heartily
> Repent he sinned and all his sins be freed.

TO R. B.

The fine delight that fathers thought; the strong
   Spur, live and lancing like the blowpipe flame,
Breathes once and, quenchèd faster than it came,
Leaves yet the mind a mother of immortal song.
Nine months she then, nay years, nine years she long
Within her wears, bears, cares and moulds the same:
The widow of an insight lost she lives, with aim
Now known and hand at work now never wrong.
   Sweet fire the sire of muse, my soul needs this;
I want the one rapture of an inspiration.

O then if in my lagging lines you miss
The roll, the rise, the carol, the creation,
My winter world, that scarcely breathes that bliss
Now, yields you, with some sighs, our explanation.

BROTHERS

How lovely the elder brother's
    Life all laced in the other's.
Lóve-laced! — what once I well
Witnessed; so fortune fell.
When Shrovetide, two years gone,
Our boys' plays brought on
Part was picked for John,
Young Jóhn: then fear, then joy
Ran revel in the elder boy.
Their night was come now; all
Our company thronged the hall;
Henry, by the wall,
Beckoned me beside him:
I came where called, and eyed him
By meanwhiles; making my play
Turn most on tender byplay.
For, wrung all on love's rack,
My lad, and lost in Jack,
Smiled, blushed, and bit his lip;
Or drove, with a diver's dip,
Clutched hands down through clasped knees —
Truth's tokens tricks like these,
Old telltales, with what stress
He hung on the imp's success.
Now the other was bráss-bóld:
Hé had no work to hold
His heart up at the strain;
Nay, roguish ran the vein.
Two tedious acts were past;
Jack's call and cue at last;
When Henry, heart-forsook,
Dropped eyes and dared not look.
Eh, how áll rúng!

Young dog, he did give tongue!
But Harry — in his hands he has flung
His tear-tricked cheeks of flame
For fond love and for shame.
   Ah Nature, framed in fault,
There's comfort then, there's salt;
Nature, bad, base, and blind,
Dearly thou canst be kind;
There dearly thén, deárly,
I'll cry thou canst be kind.

SPRING AND FALL:

to a young child

Márgarét, are you gríeving
   Over Goldengrove unleaving?
Leáves, líke the things of man, you
With your fresh thoughts care for, can you?
Áh! ás the heart grows older
It will come to such sights colder
By and by, nor spare a sigh
Though worlds of wanwood leafmeal lie;
And yet you wíll weep and know why.
Now no matter, child, the name:
Sórrow's spríngs áre the same,
Nor mouth had, no nor mind, expressed
What heart heard of, ghost guessed:
It ís the blight man was born for,
It is Margaret you mourn for.

THE BUGLER'S FIRST COMMUNION

A bugler boy from barrack (it is over the hill
   There) — boy bugler, born, he tells me, of Irish
         Mother to an English sire (he
Shares their best gifts surely, fall how things will),

This very very day came down to us after a boon he on
My late being there begged of me, overflowing
         Boon in my bestowing,
Came, I say, this to it — to a First Communion.

❖ GERARD MANLEY HOPKINS ❖

Here he knelt then ín regimental red.
Forth Christ from cupboard fetched, how fain I of feet
　　　To his youngster take his treat!
Low-latched in leaf-light housel his too huge godhead.

There! and your sweetest sendings, ah divine,
By it, heavens, befall him! at a heart Christ's darling,
　　　dauntless;
　　　Tongue true, vaunt — and tauntless;
Breathing bloom of a chastity in mansex fine.

Frowning and forefending angel-warder
Squander the hell-rook ranks sally to molest him;
　　　March, kind comrade, abreast him;
Dress his days to a dexterous and starlight order.

How it dóes my heart good, visiting at that bleak hill,
When limber liquid youth, that to all I teach
　　　Yields tender as a pushed peach,
His headstrong to its wellbeing of a self-wise self-will!

Then though I should tread tufts of consolation
Dáys áfter, só I in a sort deserve to
　　　And do serve God to serve to
Just such slips of soldiery Christ's royal ration.

Nothing élse is like it, no, not all so strains
Us: fresh youth fretted in a bloomfall all portending
　　　That sweet's sweeter ending;
Realm both Christ is heir to and thére réigns.

O now well work that sealing sacred ointment!
O for now charms, arms, what bans off bad
　　　And locks love ever in a lad!
Let mé though see no more of him, and not disappointment

Those sweet hopes quell whose least me quickenings lift,
In scarlet or somewhere of some day seeing
　　　That brow and bead of being,
An our day's God's own Galahad. Though this child's drift

305

Seems by a divíne doom chánnelled, nor do I cry
Disaster there; but may he not rankle and roam
      In backwheels though bound home? —
That left to the Lord of the Eucharist, I here lie by;

Recorded only, I have put my lips on pleas
Would brandle adamantine heaven with ride and jar, did
      Prayer go disregarded:
Forward-like, but however, and like favourable heaven heard
    these.

INVERSNAID

This darksome burn, horseback brown,
  His rollrock highroad roaring down,
In coop and in comb the fleece of his foam
Flutes and low to the lake falls home.

A windpuff-bonnet of fáwn-fróth
Turns and twindles over the broth
Of a pool so pitchblack, féll-frówning,
It rounds and rounds Despair to drowning.

Degged with dew, dappled with dew
Are the groins of the braes that the brook treads through,
Wiry heathpacks, flitches of fern,
And the beadbonny ash that sits over the burn.

What would the world be, once bereft
Of wet and of wildness? Let them be left,
Oh, let them be left, wildness and wet;
Long live the weeds and the wilderness yet.

PIED BEAUTY

Glory be to God for dappled things —
    For skies of couple-colour as a brinded cow;
      For rose-moles all in stipple upon trout that swim;
Fresh-firecoal chestnut-falls; finches' wings;
    Landscape plotted and pieced — fold, fallow, and plough;
      And áll trádes, their gear and tackle and trim.

All things counter, original, spare, strange;
    Whatever is fickle, freckled (who knows how?)
    With swift, slow; sweet, sour; adazzle, dim;
He fathers-forth whose beauty is past change:
    Praise him.

I WAKE AND FEEL THE FELL

I wake and feel the fell of dark, not day.
  What hours, O what black hoürs we have spent
This night! what sights you, heart, saw; ways you went!
And more must, in yet longer light's delay.
    With witness I speak this. But where I say
Hours I mean years, mean life. And my lament
Is cries countless, cries like dead letters sent
To dearest him that lives alas! away.

I am gall, I am heartburn. God's most deep decree
Bitter would have me taste: my taste was me;
Bones built in me, flesh filled, blood brimmed the curse.
    Selfyeast of spirit a dull dough sours. I see
The lost are like this, and their scourge to be
As I am mine, their sweating selves; but worse.

THE SEA AND THE SKYLARK

On ear and ear two noises too old to end
  Trench — right, the tide that ramps against the shore;
  With a flood or a fall, low lull-off or all roar,
Frequenting there while moon shall wear and wend.

Left hand, off land, I hear the lark ascend,
  His rash-fresh re-winded new-skeinèd score
  In crisps of curl off wild winch whirl, and pour
And pelt music, till none's to spill nor spend.

How these two shame this shallow and frail town!
  How ring right out our sorbid turbid time,
Being pure! We, life's pride and cared-for crown,

  Have lost that cheer and charm of earth's past prime:
Our make and making break, are breaking, down
  To man's last dust, drain fast towards man's first slime.

PEACE

When will you ever, Peace, wild wooddove, shy wings shut,
　　Your round me roaming end, and under be my boughs?
When, when, Peace, will you, Peace? I'll not play hypocrite
To own my heart: I yield you do come sometimes; but
That piecemeal peace is poor peace. What pure peace allows
Alarms of wars, the daunting wars, the death of it?

O surely, reaving Peace, my Lord should leave in lieu
Some good! And so he does leave Patience exquisite,
That plumes to Peace thereafter. And when Peace here
　　does house
He comes with work to do, he does not come to coo,
　　He comes to brood and sit.

HEAVEN–HAVEN

A nun takes the veil

I have desired to go
　　Where springs not fail,
To fields where flies no sharp and sided hail,
　　And a few lilies blow.

And I have asked to be
　　Where no storms come,
Where the green swell is in the havens dumb,
　　And out of the swing of the sea.

CARRION COMFORT

Not, I'll not, carrion comfort, Despair, not feast on thee;
　　Not untwist — slack they may be — these last strands of
　　man
In me ór, most weary, cry *I can no more.* I can;
Can something, hope, wish day come, not choose not to be.
But ah, but O thou terrible, why wouldst thou rude on me
Thy wring-world right foot rock? lay a lionlimb against me?
　　scan
With darksome devouring eyes my bruisèd bones? and fan,
O in turns of tempest, me heaped there; me frantic to avoid
　　thee and flee?

308

Why? That my chaff might fly; my grain lie, sheer and clear.
Nay in all that toil, that coil, since (seems) I kissed the rod,
Hand rather, my heart lo! lapped strength, stole joy would
    laugh, cheér.
Cheer whom though? the hero whose heaven-handling flung
    me, fóot tród
Me? or me that fought him? O which one? is it each one?
        That night, that year
Of now done darkness I wretch lay wrestling with (my God!)
    my God.

THE WINDHOVER

To Christ our Lord

I caught this morning morning's minion, king-
    dom of daylight's dauphin, dapple-dawn-drawn
      Falcon, in his riding
  Of the rolling level underneath him steady air, and striding
High there, how he rung upon the rein of a wimpling wing
In his ecstasy! then off, off forth on swing,
  As a skate's heel sweeps smooth on a bow-bend: the
    hurl and gliding
Rebuffed the big wind. My heart in hiding
Stirred for a bird, — the achieve of, the mastery of the thing!

Brute beauty and valour and act, oh, air, pride, plume, here
  Buckle! AND the fire that breaks from thee then, a
    billion
Times told lovelier, more dangerous, O my chevalier!

  No wonder of it: shéer plód makes plough down sillion
Shine, and blue-bleak embers,·ah my dear,
  Fall, gall themselves, and gash gold-vermilion.

FRANCIS THOMPSON
1859–1907

In February 1887 Wilfrid Meynell, the editor of a Roman Catholic magazine, *Merry England*, found a soiled and tattered manuscript in his letter-box containing a few poems and an essay on *Paganism Old and New*. Over a year passed before he succeeded in finding the author; and then it was a waif of the streets, unkempt, ragged, and starved, that shuffled hesitatingly into his office. Under his friendly care, Francis Thompson was gradually won back to health and to civilization.

He was a strange impractical man, unable to deal with the ordinary hum-drum details of existence. Some of his waywardness he may have inherited from his mother. His father, a Lancashire doctor, was kind-hearted and patient, but never understood him. He spent seven unhappy years at a Roman Seminary and in the end the authorities decided that he was unfitted for the priesthood. His absent-mindedness, his lack of co-ordination, his queer reticence, they translated as ' a natural indolence,' and reluctantly but definitely dismissed him. His father sent him to Manchester to study medicine. In four years he failed to pass a single examination. In desperation he tried to enlist, but he was already a drug addict, and he was rejected on the grounds of health. With neither hope nor expectation for the future, he travelled to London, where he sank rung by rung down the ladder of destitution, selling newspapers, fetching cabs, hawking pencils and matches, drifting from lodgings to doss-houses, from doss-houses to the Embankment, and saved from the last inroads of consumption only by the virtue of his drug. A bootmaker tried to rescue him and failed. A prostitute befriended him in his direst need. But when the Meynells found him she disappeared. ' They will not understand our friendship,' she said, and without warning moved to strange lodgings. All his life after he hoped that he might meet her in the streets, and though he referred to her seldom in his speech, he paid his tribute to her unselfish devotion in the first section of the *Sister Songs*.

Under the patronage of the Meynells, Francis Thompson published three volumes of verse: *Poems* in 1893, *Sister Songs* in 1895, and *New Poems* in 1896. He lived sometimes in London, sometimes with the monks in Storrington Priory, sometimes at the gates of the monastery at Pantasaph. He met Coventry Patmore, and there grew a deep friendship and admiration between them. He met Cardinal Manning in whose memory his poem *To the Dead Cardinal of Westminster* was written. He met Meredith once, and Henley once, and E. V. Lucas. But he was difficult of friendship, and even in company remained strangely alone. By the turn of the century he had written most of his great poetry. His later years were darkened by a reversion to opium, but the drug staved off his death till 1907.

' To be the poet of the return to Nature is somewhat, but I would be the poet of the return to God.' Thompson's wish is fulfilled in his poetry. The pitiful circumstances of his life drop disregarded from him there and leave the essential mystic. Religion was to him continuously a magnificent and passionate experience; passion and magnificence are everywhere the outstanding qualities of his poetry.

In his religion, at least, and therefore in his poetry, there are none of the confusions and hesitations which characterized his daily life. He had been made possessor of the splendours of Heaven and was fully alive to the responsibilities attached to the gift. He discussed interminably with Coventry Patmore the problem of the mystical poet who must struggle to hold in the coarse net of words a remnant, at least of what he has seen. The contemplative mystic does not try to communicate the intensity of his vision, but when he is by nature also a poet, the two powers, of seeing and of communicating, conflict. His rapt study of the Vulgate and the liturgies of seventeenth century mystics and later of mystical poetry helped Thompson to fashion a vehicle, though even after he had begun to be known, he felt his instrument ' yet too imperfect to profane by it the highest ranges of mysticism.' He excelled, as he naïvely confessed, in the ability to string together striking images and at one time was ready to maintain that the art of poetry demanded no more. But though his lines are al-

ways richly loaded with image, symbol, and conceit, he learned
at length how to weld them at white heat in order to convey
the intensest and most complex feeling.

He is frequently called a belated member of the seventeenth
century school of ' metaphysicals.' As a matter of fact he had
read at the time of his first book little of this poetry — ' just
Crashaw and a little Cowley — and I had formed my style be-
fore I knew Cowley, whom I really did curiously resemble;
though none perceived it because none had read Cowley.' The
point is, of course, that his background and his habit of mind
resembled theirs. The Protestant forgets that the Litany of the
Virgin and the lyrics of St. John of the Cross, to mention
only two sources of inspiration, have been continuously avail-
able to the Catholic poet. It is no more remarkable that
Thompson should have written as he did in 1900 than that a
chasubled priest should next Sunday morning say mass under
the tribune of Westminster Cathedral.

THE POPPY

To Monica

Summer set lip to earth's bosom bare,
And left the flushed print in a poppy there:
Like a yawn of fire from the grass it came,
And the fanning wind puffed it to flapping flame.

With burnt mouth, red like a lion's, it drank
The blood of the sun as he slaughtered sank,
And dipped its cup in the purpurate shine
When the eastern conduits ran with wine.

Till it grew lethargied with fierce bliss,
And hot as a swinked gypsy is,
And drowsed in sleepy savageries,
With mouth wide a-pout for a sultry kiss.

A child and man paced side by side,
Treading the skirts of eventide;
But between the clasp of his hand and her
Lay, felt not, twenty withered years.

She turned, with the rout of her dusk South hair,
And saw the sleeping gypsy there;
And snatched and snapped it in swift child's whim,
With — ' Keep it, long as you live! ' — to him.

And his smile, as nymphs from their laving meres,
Trembled up from a bath of tears;
And joy, like a mew sea-rocked apart,
Tossed on the wave of his troubled heart.

For *he* saw what she did not see,
That — as kindled by its own fervency —
The verge shriveled inward smolderingly:
And suddenly 'twixt his hand and hers
He knew the twenty withered years —
No flower, but twenty shriveled years.

' Was never such thing until this hour,'
Low to his heart he said; ' the flower
Of sleep brings wakening to me,
And of oblivion, memory.'

' Was never this thing to me,' he said,
' Though with bruisèd poppies my feet are red! '
And again to his own heart very low:
' O child! I love, for I love and know;

' But you, who love nor know at all
The diverse chambers in Love's guest-hall,
Where some rise early, few sit long:
In how differing accents hear the throng
His great Pentecostal tongue;

' Who know not love from amity,
Nor my reported self from me;
A fair fit gift is this, meseems,
You give — this withering flower of dreams.

' O frankly fickle, and fickly true,
Do you know what the days will do to you?
To your Love and you what the days will do,
O frankly fickle, and fickly true?

' You have loved me, Fair, three lives — or days:
'Twill pass with the passing of my face.
But where *I* go, your face goes too,
To watch lest I play false to you.

' I am but, my sweet, your foster-lover,
Knowing well when certain years are over
You vanish from me to another;
Yet I know, and love, like the foster-mother.

' So, frankly fickle, and fickly true!
For my brief life-while I take from you
This token, fair and fit, meseems,
For me — this withering flower of dreams.'

The sleep-flower sways in the wheat its head,
Heavy with dreams, as that with bread:
The goodly grain and the sun-flushed sleeper
The reaper reaps, and Time the reaper.

I hang 'mid men my needless head,
And my fruit is dreams, as theirs is bread:
The goodly men and the sun-hazed sleeper
Time shall reap, but after the reaper
The world shall glean of me, me the sleeper.

Love, love! your flower of withered dream
In leavèd rhyme lies safe, I deem,
Sheltered and shut in a nook of rhyme,
From the reaper man, and his reaper Time.

Love! *I* fall into the claws of Time;
But lasts within a leavèd rime
All that the world of me esteems —
My withered dreams, my withered dreams.

TO A SNOWFLAKE

What heart could have thought you? —
　　Past our devisal
(O filigree petal!)
Fashioned so purely,
Fragilely, surely,
From what Paradisal
Imagineless metal,
Too costly for cost?
Who hammered you, wrought you,
From argentine vapour? —
'God was my shaper.
Passing surmisal,
He hammered, He wrought me,
From curled silver vapour,
To lust of His mind: —
Thou could'st not have thought me!
So purely, so palely,
Tinily, surely,
Mightily, frailly,
Insculped and embossed,
With His hammer of wind,
And His graver of frost.'

THE MAKING OF VIOLA

I

The Father of Heaven

Spin, daughter Mary, spin,
　　Twirl your wheel with silver din;
Spin, daughter Mary, spin,
　　Spin a tress for Viola.

Angels

Spin, Queen Mary, a
Brown tress for Viola!

II

The Father of Heaven

Weave, hands angelical,
Weave a woof of flesh to pall —
Weave, hands angelical —
　　Flesh to pall our Viola.

Angels

　Weave, singing brothers, a
　Velvet flesh for Viola!

III

The Father of Heaven

Scoop, young Jesus, for her eyes,
Wood-browned pools of Paradise —
Young Jesus, for the eyes,
　　For the eyes of Viola.

Angels

　Tint, Prince Jesus, a
　Duskèd eye for Viola!

IV

The Father of Heaven

Cast a star therein to drown,
Like a torch in cavern brown,
Sink a burning star to drown
　　Whelmed in eyes of Viola.

Angels

　Lave, Prince Jesus, a
　Star in eyes of Viola!

V

The Father of Heaven

Breathe, Lord Paraclete,
To a bubbled crystal meet —
Breathe, Lord Paraclete —
Crystal soul for Viola.

Angels

Breathe, Regal Spirit, a
Flashing soul for Viola!

VI

The Father of Heaven

Child-angels, from your wings
Fall the roseal hoverings,
Child-angels, from your wings
On the cheeks of Viola.

Angels

Linger, rosy reflex, a
Quenchless stain, on Viola!

VII

*All things being accomplished, saith the Father
of Heaven:*

Bear her down, and bearing, sing,
Bear her down on spyless wing,
Bear her down, and bearing, sing,
With a sound of viola.

Angels

Music as her name is, a
Sweet sound of Viola!

VIII

Wheeling angels, past espial,
Danced her down with sound of viol;
Wheeling angels, past espial,
    Descanting on ' Viola.'

Angels

Sing, in our footing, a
Lovely lilt of ' Viola! '

IX

Baby smiled, mother wailed,
Earthward while the sweetling sailed;
Mother smiled, baby wailed,
    When to earth came Viola.

And her elders shall say:

So soon have we taught you a
Way to weep, poor Viola!

X

Smile, sweet baby, smile,
For you will have weeping-while;
Native in your Heaven is smile, —
    But your weeping, Viola?

Whence your smiles, we know, but ah!
Whence your weeping, Viola? —
Our first gift to you is a
Gift of tears, my Viola!

DAISY

Where the thistle lifts a purple crown
    Six foot out of the turf,
And the harebell shakes on the windy hill —
    O the breath of the distant surf! —

✤ FRANCIS THOMPSON ✤

The hills look over on the South,
  And southward dreams the sea;
And with the sea-breeze hand in hand
  Came innocence and she.

Where 'mid the gorse the raspberry
  Red for the gatherer springs,
Two children did we stray and talk
  Wise, idle, childish things.

She listened with big-lipped surprise,
  Breast-deep mid flower and spine:
Her skin was like a grape whose veins
  Run snow instead of wine.

She knew not those sweet words she spake,
  Nor knew her own sweet way;
But there's never a bird, so sweet a song
  Thronged in whose throat that day.

Oh, there were flowers in Storrington
  On the turf and on the spray;
But the sweetest flower on Sussex hills
  Was the Daisy-flower that day!

Her beauty smoothed earth's furrowed face,
  She gave me tokens three: —
A look, a word of her winsome mouth,
  And a wild raspberry.

A berry red, a guileless look,
  A still word, — strings of sand!
And yet they made my wild, wild heart
  Fly down to her little hand.

For standing artless as the air,
  And candid as the skies,
She took the berries with her hand,
  And the love with her sweet eyes.

The fairest things have fleetest end,
  Their scent survives their close:
But the rose's scent is bitterness
  To him that loved the rose.

She looked a little wistfully,
　　Then went her sunshine way: —
The sea's eye had a mist on it,
　　And the leaves fell from the day.

She went her unremembering way,
　　She went and left in me
The pang of all the partings gone,
　　And partings yet to be.

She left me marvelling why my soul
　　Was sad that she was glad;
At all the sadness in the sweet,
　　The sweetness in the sad.

Still, still I seemed to see her, still
　　Look up with soft replies,
And take the berries with her hand,
　　And the love with her lovely eyes.

Nothing begins, and nothings ends,
　　That is not paid with moan;
For we are born in other's pain,
　　And perish in our own.

DREAM–TRYST

The breaths of kissing night and day
　　Were mingled in the eastern Heaven:
　　Throbbing with unheard melody
Shook Lyra all its star-chord seven:
　　When dusk shrunk cold, and light trod shy,
　　And dawn's grey eyes were troubled grey;
　　And souls went palely up the sky,
　　　And mine to Lucidé.

There was no change in her sweet eyes
　　Since last I saw those sweet eyes shine;
There was no change in her deep heart
　　Since last that deep heart knocked at mine.

Her eyes were clear, her eyes were Hope's,
    Wherein did ever come and go
The sparkle of the fountain-drops
    From her sweet soul below.

The chambers in the house of dreams
    Are fed with so divine an air,
That Time's hoar wings grow young therein,
    And they who walk there are most fair.
        I joyed for me, I joyed for her,
            Who with the Past meet girt about:
        Where our last kiss still warms the air,
            Nor can her eyes go out.

ARAB LOVE–SONG

The hunchèd camels of the night
    Trouble the bright
And silver waters of the moon.
The Maiden of the Morn will soon
Through Heaven stray and sing,
Star gathering.

Now while the dark about our loves is strewn,
Light of my dark, blood of my heart, O come!
And night will catch her breath up, and be dumb.

Leave thy father, leave thy mother
And thy brother;
Leave the black tents of thy tribe apart!
Am I not thy father and thy brother,
And thy mother?
And thou — what needest with thy tribe's black tents
Who hast the red pavilion of my heart?

LINES FOR A DRAWING OF OUR LADY
OF THE NIGHT

This, could I paint my inward sight,
    This were Our Lady of the Night:

She bears on her front's lucency
The starlight of her purity:

For as the white rays of that star
The union of all colours are,

She sums all virtues that may be
In her sweet light of purity.

The mantle which she holds on high
Is the great mantle of the sky.

Think, O sick toiler, when the night
Comes on thee, sad and infinite,

Think, sometimes, 'tis our own Lady
Spreads her blue mantle over thee,

And folds the earth, a wearied thing,
Beneath·its gentle shadowing;

Then rest a little; and in sleep
Forget to weep, forget to weep!

LITTLE JESUS

*Ex ore infantium Deus et lactentium
perfecisti laudem*

Little Jesus, wast Thou shy
    Once, and just so small as I?
And what did it feel like to be
Out of Heaven, and just like me?
Didst Thou sometimes think of *there,*
And ask where all the angels were?
I should think that I would cry
For my house all made of sky;
I would look about the air,
And wonder where my angels were;
And at waking 'twould distress me —
Not an angel there to dress me!
Hadst Thou ever any toys,
Like us little girls and boys?

And didst Thou play in Heaven with all
The angels that were not too tall,
With stars for marbles? Did the things
Play *Can you see me?* through their wings?
And did Thy Mother let Thee spoil
Thy robes, with playing on *our* soil?
How nice to have them always new
In Heaven, because 'twas quite clean blue!

Didst Thou kneel at night to pray,
And didst Thou join Thy hands, this way?
And did they tire sometimes, being young,
And make the prayer seem very long?
And dost Thou like it best, that we
Should join our hands to pray to Thee?
I used to think, before I knew
The prayer not said unless we do.
And did Thy Mother at the night
Kiss Thee, and fold the clothes in right?
And didst Thou feel quite good in bed,
Kissed, and sweet, and Thy prayers said?

Thou canst not have forgotten all
That it feels like to be small:
And Thou know'st I cannot pray
To Thee in my father's way —
When Thou wast so little, say,
Couldst Thou talk Thy Father's way? —

So, a little Child, come down
And hear a child's tongue like Thy own;
Take me by the hand and walk,
And listen to my baby-talk.
To Thy Father show my prayer
 (He will look, Thou art so fair) ,
And say: ' O Father, I, Thy Son,
Bring the prayer of a little one.'

And He will smile, that children's tongue
Has not changed since Thou wast young!

TO THE DEAD CARDINAL
OF WESTMINSTER

I will not perturbate
Thy Paradisal state
    With praise
    Of thy dead days;

To the new-heavened say,
' Spirit, thou wert fine clay ':
    This do,
    Thy praise who knew.

Therefore my spirit clings
Heaven's porter by the wings,
    And holds
    Its gated golds

Apart, with thee to press
A private business; —
    Whence,
    Deign me audience.

Anchorite, who didst dwell
With all the world for cell,
    My soul
    Round me doth roll

A sequestration bare.
Too far alike we were,
    Too far
    Dissimilar.

For its burning fruitage I
Do climb the tree o' the sky;
    Do prize
    Some human eyes.

You smelt the Heaven-blossoms,
And all the sweet embosoms
    The dear
    Uranian year.

✤ FRANCIS THOMPSON ✤

Those Eyes my weak gaze shuns,
Which to the suns are Suns,
     Did
      Not affray your lid.

The carpet was let down
 (With golden moultings strown)
     For you
      Of the angels' blue.

But I, ex-Paradised,
The shoulder of your Christ
     Find high
      To lean thereby.

So flaps my helpless sail,
Bellying with neither gale,
     Of Heaven
      Nor Orcus even.

Life is a coquetry
Of Death, which wearies me,
     Too sure
      Of the amour;

A tiring-room where I
Death's divers garments try,
     Till fit
      Some fashion sit.

It seemeth me too much
I do rehearse for such
     A mean
      And single scene.

The sandy glass hence bear —
Antique remembrancer:
     My veins
      Do spare its pains.

With secret sympathy
My thoughts repeat in me
    Infirm
  The turn o' the worm

Beneath my appointed sod;
The grave is in my blood;
    I shake
  To winds that take

Its grasses by the top;
The rains thereon that drop
    Perturb
  With drip acerb

My subtly answering soul;
The feet across its knoll
    Do jar
  Me from afar.

As sap foretastes the spring;
As Earth ere blossoming
    Thrills
  With far daffodils,

And feels her breast turn sweet
With the unconceivèd wheat;
    So doth
  My flesh foreloathe

The abhorrèd spring of Dis,
With seething presciences
    Affirm
  The preparate worm.

I have no thought that I,
When at the last I die,
    Shall reach
  To gain your speech.

But you, should that be so,
May very well, I know,
    May well
  To me in hell

With recognizing eyes
Look from your Paradise —
    ' God bless
  Thy hopelessness! '

Call, holy soul, O call
The hosts angelical,
    And say —
  ' See, far away

' Lies one I saw on earth;
One stricken from his birth
    With curse
  Of destinate verse.

' What place doth He ye serve
For such sad spirit reserve, —
    Given,
  In dark lieu of Heaven,

' The impitiable Dæmon,
Beauty, to adore and dream on,
    To be
  Perpetually

' Hers, but she never his?
He reapeth miseries;
    Foreknows
  His wages woes;

' He lives detachèd days;
He serveth not for praise;
    For gold
  He is not sold;

' Deaf is he to world's tongue;
He scorneth for his song
    The loud
    Shouts of the crowd;

' He asketh not world's eyes;
Not to world's ears he cries;
    Saith — " These
    Shut, if you please ";

' He measureth world's pleasure,
World's ease, as Saints might measure;
    For hire
    Just love entire

' He asks, not grudging pain;
And knows his asking vain,
    And cries —
    " Love! Love! " and dies,

' In guerdon of long duty,
Unowned by Love or Beauty;
    And goes —
    Tell, tell, who knows!

' Aliens from Heaven's worth,
Fine beasts who nose i' the earth,
    Do there
    Reward prepare.

' But are *his* great desires
Food but for nether fires?
    Ah me,
    A mystery!

' Can it be his alone,
To find, when all is known,
    That what
    He solely sought

'Is lost, and thereto lost
All that its seeking cost?
    That he
    Must finally,

'Through sacrificial tears
And anchoretic years,
    Tryst
    With the sensualist?'

So ask; and if they tell
The secret terrible,
    Good friend,
    I pray thee send

Some high gold embassage
To teach my unripe age.
    Tell!
    Lest my feet walk hell.

THE HOUND OF HEAVEN

I fled Him, down the nights and down the days;
  I fled Him, down the arches of the years;
  I fled Him, down the labyrinthine ways
    Of my own mind; and in the mist of tears
I hid from Him, and under running laughter.
    Up vistaed hopes I sped;
    And shot, precipitated,
Adown Titanic glooms of chasmèd fears,
  From those strong Feet that followed, followed after.
    But with unhurrying chase,
    And unperturbèd pace,
  Deliberate speed, majestic instancy,
    They beat — and a Voice beat
    More instant than the Feet —
'All things betray thee, who betrayest Me.'

I pleaded, outlaw-wise,
By many a hearted casement, curtained red,
  Trellised with intertwining charities;
(For, though I knew His love Who followèd,
    Yet was I sore adread
Lest, having Him, I must have naught beside).
But, if one little casement parted wide,
  The gust of His approach would clash it to.
  Fear wist not to evade, as Love wist to pursue.
Across the margent of the world I fled,
  And troubled the gold gateways of the stars,
  Smiting for shelter on their clangèd bars;
    Fretted to dulcet jars
And silvern chatter the pale ports o' the moon.
I said to Dawn: Be sudden — to Eve: Be soon;
  With thy young skiey blossoms heap me over
    From this tremendous Lover —
Float thy vague veil about me, lest He see!
  I tempted all His servitors, but to find
My own betrayal in their constancy,
In faith to Him their fickleness to me,
  Their traitorous trueness, and their loyal deceit.
To all swift things for swiftness did I sue;
  Clung to the whistling mane of every wind.
    But whether they swept, smoothly fleet,
    The long savannahs of the blue;
      Or whether, Thunder-driven,
      They clanged his chariot 'thwart a heaven
Plashy with flying lightnings round the spurn o' their feet: —
  Fear wist not to evade as Love wist to pursue.
    Still with unhurrying chase,
    And unperturbèd pace,
    Deliberate speed, majestic instancy,
      Came on the following Feet,
      And a Voice above their beat —
  ' Naught shelters thee, who wilt not shelter Me.'

I sought no more that after which I strayed
    In face of man or maid;
But still within the little children's eyes
    Seems something, something that replies,

They at least are for me, surely for me!
I turned me to them very wistfully;
But, just as their young eyes grew sudden fair
    With dawning answers there,
Their angel plucked them from me by the hair.
' Come then, ye other children, Nature's — share
With me ' (said I) ' your delicate fellowship;
    Let me greet you lip to lip,
    Let me twine with you caresses,
      Wantoning
    With our Lady-Mother's vagrant tresses,
      Banqueting
    With her in her wind-walled palace,
    Underneath her azured daïs,
    Quaffing, as your taintless way is,
      From a chalice
Lucent-weeping out of the dayspring.'
    So it was done:
I in their delicate fellowship was one —
Drew the bolt of Nature's secrecies.
    I knew all the swift importings
    On the wilful face of skies;
    I knew how the clouds arise
    Spumèd of the wild sea-snortings;
      All that's born or dies
    Rose and drooped with; made them shapers
Of mine own moods, or wailful or divine;
    With them joyed and was bereaven.
    I was heavy with the even,
    When she lit her glimmering tapers
    Round the day's dead sanctities.
    I laughed in the morning's eyes.
I triumphed and I saddened with all weather,
    Heaven and I wept together,
And its sweet tears were salt with mortal mine;
Against the red throb of its sunset-heart
    I laid my own to beat,
    And share commingling heat;
But not by that, by that, was eased my human smart,
In vain my tears were wet on Heaven's grey cheek.
For ah! we know not what each other says,

These things and I; in sound *I* speak —
Their sound is but their stir, they speak by silences.
Nature, poor stepdame, cannot slake my drouth;
    Let her, if she would owe me,
Drop yon blue bosom-veil of sky, and show me
    The breasts o' her tenderness;
Never did any milk of hers once bless
      My thirsting mouth.
      Nigh and nigh draws the chase,
      With unperturbèd pace,
    Deliberate speed, majestic instancy;
      And past those noisèd Feet
      A voice comes yet more fleet —
' Lo! naught contents thee, who content'st not Me.'

Naked I wait Thy love's uplifted stroke!
My harness piece by piece Thou hast hewn from me,
    And smitten me to my knee;
    I am defenseless utterly.
    I slept, methinks, and woke,
And, slowly gazing, find me stripped in sleep.
In the rash lustihead of my young powers,
    I shook the pillaring hours
And pulled my life upon me; grimed with smears,
I stand amid the dust o' the mounded years —
My mangled youth lies dead beneath the heap.
My days have crackled and gone up in smoke,
Have puffed and burst as sun-starts on a stream.
    Yea, faileth now even dream
The dreamer, and the lute the lutanist;
Even the linked fantasies, in whose blossomy twist
I swung the earth a trinket at my wrist,
Are yielding; cords of all too weak account
For earth with heavy griefs so overplussed.
    Ah! is Thy love indeed
A weed, albeit an amaranthine weed,
Suffering no flowers except its own to mount?
    Ah! must —
    Designer infinite! —
Ah! must Thou char the wood ere Thou canst limn with it?
My freshness spent its wavering shower i' the dust:

And now my heart is as a broken fount,
Wherein tear-drippings stagnate, spilt down ever
   From the dank thoughts that shiver
Upon the sighful branches of my mind.
     Such is; what is to be?
The pulp so bitter, how shall taste the rind?
I dimly guess what Time in mists confounds;
Yet ever and anon a trumpet sounds
From the hid battlements of Eternity;
Those shaken mists a space unsettle, then
Round the half-glimpsèd turrets slowly wash again.
    But not ere him who summoneth
    I first have seen, enwound
With glooming robes purpureal, cypress-crowned;
His name I know, and what his trumpet saith.
Whether man's heart or life it be which yields
    Thee harvest, must Thy harvest fields
    Be dunged with rotten death?

     Now of that long pursuit
     Comes on at hand the bruit;
    That Voice is round me like a bursting sea:
      ' And is thy earth so marred,
      Shattered in shard on shard?
    Lo, all things fly thee, for thou fliest Me!
    Strange, piteous, futile thing!
Wherefore should any set thee love apart?
Seeing none but I makes much of naught ' (He said),
' And human love needs human meriting:
    How hast thou merited —
Of all man's clotted clay the dingiest clot?
    Alack, thou knowest not
How little worthy of any love thou art!
Whom wilt thou find to love ignoble thee
    Save Me, save only Me?
All which I took from thee I did but take,
    Not for thy harms,
But just that thou might'st seek it in My arms.
   All which thy child's mistake
Fancies as lost, I have stored for thee at home;
    Rise, clasp My hand, and come! '

Halts by me that footfall:
Is my gloom, after all,
Shade of His hand, outstretched caressingly?
' Ah, fondest, blindest, weakest,
I am He Whom thou seekest!
Thou dravest love from thee, who dravest Me.'

ENVOY

Go, songs, for ended is our brief, sweet play;
Go, children of swift joy and tardy sorrow:
And some are sung, and that was yesterday,
And some unsung, and that may be to-morrow.

Go forth; and if it be o'er stony way,
Old joy can lend what newer grief must borrow:
And it was sweet, and that was yesterday,
And sweet is sweet, though purchasèd with sorrow.

Go, songs, and come not back from your fair way:
And if men ask you why ye smile and sorrow,
Tell them ye grieve, for your hearts know To-day,
Tell them ye smile, for your eyes know To-morrow.

THE KINGDOM OF GOD

' In no Strange Land '

O world invisible, we view thee,
O world intangible, we touch thee,
O world unknowable, we know thee,
Inapprehensible, we clutch thee!

Does the fish soar to find the ocean,
The eagle plunge to find the air —
That we ask of the stars in motion
If they have rumour of thee there?

Not where the wheeling systems darken,
And our benumbed conceiving soars! —
The drift of pinions, would we hearken,
Beats at our own clay-shuttered doors.

334

❖ FRANCIS THOMPSON ❖

The angels keep their ancient places; —
Turn but a stone, and start a wing!
'Tis ye, 'tis your estrangèd faces,
That miss the many-splendoured thing.

But (when so sad thou canst not sadder)
Cry; — and upon thy so sore loss
Shall shine the traffic of Jacob's ladder
Pitched betwixt Heaven and Charing Cross.

Yes, in the night, my Soul, my daughter,
Cry, — clinging Heaven by the hems;
And lo, Christ walking on the water
Not of Gennesareth, but Thames!

ALICE MEYNELL
1849–1922

M rs. Meynell, born Alice Thompson, stands a singularly aloof figure, cool and reserved amid the flushed excesses of the 1890's. She outlived them, saw the rise of the Georgian poets, passed through the strain of the World War and died in 1922 honoured and beloved as essayist and poet and most of all as an intelligent, sympathetic, spiritual woman. There is little to say of her life. Her mother, a beautiful, highly emotional and musical woman, transmitted something of her temperament and a double portion of her gifts of expression to two daughters, one of whom became a famous painter, the other the one English woman to be named in the same breath with Mrs. Browning and Christina Rossetti. Alice Thompson's childhood was spent on the Continent, especially in the Italy she loved and sang so well. She entered her mother's church, the Catholic, early in life for a very characteristic reason. 'I saw,' she said, ' that a guide in morals was even more necessary than a guide in faith,' and in the Roman Church she found that one sure guide. Matters of dogma, questions and doubts raised by the new science, never troubled her.

A tiny volume of poems, the *Preludes,* appeared in 1875, including the sonnet, *Renouncement,* one of the three finest, said Rossetti, ever written by a woman. She married Wilfrid Meynell in 1877 and took up with him the daily duties of a journalist. Eight children were born to them, and her daughter's *Memoir* gives a charming picture of the household where the ' pencilling mama ' sat surrounded by her lovely and precocious brood, correcting proofs, writing essays and reviews and even paragraphs for the daily press. Not until 1893 did she publish another volume of *Poems.* Meanwhile she had won the intimate friendship of a noble circle. Ruskin praised her early work; Patmore, whom she revered, was in constant correspondence with her; George Meredith called her his Portia; Francis Thompson worshipped her and sang her praise in splendid verse. There was something of the saint about Alice Meynell but nothing of the ascetic; she was full of a sense of the pity of things, resolute, doing what she could to put wrong right, and holding buried in her heart her secret of certain hope.

The slender volume which includes the whole of her poetry collects the *Preludes,* the *Poems* of '93, the *Later Poems* (1901), *A Father of Women and Other Poems* (1918) and the *Last Poems* which appeared after her death. A mere glance at the dates shows how infrequent was her utterance in verse, but her poetry is the finest fruit of a busy, varied, and thoughtful life. Slight as is her contribution to the volume of English poetry her immortality seems assured; here is 'poetry,' said Francis Thompson, 'the spiritual voice of which will become audible when the high noises of to-day have followed the feet that made them.'

Alice Meynell's poetry has been highly praised — possibly overpraised by those who knew her. It must have been hard, perhaps impossible, for a friend to discriminate between the poetess and the living woman, 'saint and sybil, smoking a cigarette in her drawing-room' and breaking her long silences by the apt, the discriminating, the sympathetic word. Yet it is hard to believe that any praise can be too high for her best work, and it was work of a kind unique in her time. Her affiliations were with the lyrists and the metaphysical poets of her beloved seventeenth century rather than with the Victorians or the Georgians. But she never allowed herself to be entangled in the rhapsodies or to fall into the conceits of the 'metaphysicals.' The restraint so eminently characteristic in her life and so evident everywhere in her work checks all overflow of emotion and lends distinction to every utterance. No English poet of her day was more aware of the value of words, their associative significance which implies rather than declares the thought and the feeling that lie behind them. And thought, profound and subtle, is ever present in her verse. All her poems, says one admiring critic, are 'the music of a thought,' and the thought at times is far-ranging in its significance. What other poet has imagined the pilgrimage of Christ through the universe carrying 'a million alien gospels' to 'the Pleiades, the Lyre, the Bear,' or dared to call on God to

' come to our ignorant hearts and be forgiven '? Yet to insist too much upon her thought would be to forget an even higher quality in her verse, her exquisite tenderness. This severe stylist was not a cold or passionless woman. The loving-kindness of her private letters to husband and children now and again breaks through the strict restraint of her verse, nowhere with such felicity of utterance as in the lines *At Night* which bring her poems to their perfect end. This is a poem of earthly love; even more deeply moving are the songs of the divine love which was hers from the beginning. She passed through life strengthened and sustained by a consciousness of the immanent presence of the divine. The visible world with all its appearances and experiences was to her the shadow and symbol of the invisible, the spiritual. She could not see the end but she was sure that her feet were set upon the Way.

A POET OF ONE MOOD

A poet of one mood in all my lays,
   Ranging all life to sing one only love,
   Like a west wind across the world I move,
Sweeping my harp of floods mine own wild ways.

The countries change, but not the west-wind days
   Which are my songs. My soft skies shine above,
   And on all seas the colours of a dove,
And on all fields a flash of silver greys.

I make the whole world answer to my art
   And sweet monotonous meanings. In your ears
I change not ever, bearing, for my part,
   One thought that is the treasure of my years
A small cloud full of rain upon my heart
   And in mine arms, clasped, like a child in tears.

'I AM THE WAY'

Thou art the Way.
　　Hadst Thou been nothing but the goal,
　　　　I cannot say
If Thou hadst ever met my soul.

　　　I cannot see —
I, child of process — if there lies
　　　An end for me,
Full of repose, full of replies.

　　　I'll not reproach
The road that winds, my feet that err.
　　　Access, Approach
Art Thou, Time, Way, and Wayfarer.

CHIMES

Brief, on a flying night,
　　From the shaken tower,
A flock of bells take flight.
　　And go with the hour.

Like birds from the cote to the gales,
　　Abrupt — O hark!
A fleet of bells set sails,
　　And go to the dark.

Sudden the cold airs swing.
　　Alone, aloud,
A verse of bells takes wing
　　And flies with the cloud.

A THRUSH BEFORE DAWN

A voice peals in this end of night
　　A phrase of notes resembling stars,
Single and spiritual notes of light.
　　What call they at my window-bars?
　　　　The South, the past, the day to be,
　　　　An ancient infelicity.

Darkling, deliberate, what sings
   This wonderful one, alone, at peace?
What wilder things than song, what things
   Sweeter than youth, clearer than Greece,
      Dearer than Italy, untold
      Delight, and freshness centuries old?

And first first-loves, a multitude,
   The exaltation of their pain;
Ancestral childhood long renewed;
   And midnights of invisible rain;
      And gardens, gardens, night and day,
      Gardens and childhood all the way.

What Middle Ages passionate,
   O passionless voice! What distant bells
Lodged in the hills, what palace state
   Illyrian! For it speaks, it tells,
      Without desire, without dismay,
      Some morrow and some yesterday.

All-natural things! But more — Whence came
   This yet remoter mystery?
How do these starry notes proclaim
   A graver still divinity?
      This hope, this sanctity of fear?
      O innocent throat! O human ear!

THE WATERSHED

Lines written between Munich and Verona

Black mountains pricked with pointed pine
   A melancholy sky.
Out-distanced was the German vine,
   The sterile fields lay high.
From swarthy Alps I travelled forth
Aloft; it was the north, the north;
   Bound for the Noon was I.

I seemed to breast the streams that day;
    I met, opposed, withstood
The northward rivers on their way,
    My heart against the flood —
My heart that pressed to rise and reach,
And felt the love of altering speech,
    Of frontiers, in its blood.

But O the unfolding South! the burst
    Of summer! O to see
Of all the southward brooks the first!
    The travelling heart went free
With endless streams; that strife was stopped;
And down a thousand vales I dropped,
    I flowed to Italy.

THOUGHTS IN SEPARATION

We never meet; yet we meet day by day
    Upon those hills of life, dim and immense —
The good we love, and sleep, our innocence.
O hills of life, high hills! And, higher than they,

Our guardian spirits meet at prayer and play.
    Beyond pain, joy, and hope, and long suspense,
    Above the summits of our souls, far hence,
An angel meets an angel on the way.

Beyond all good I ever believed of thee,
    Or thou of me, these always love and live.
And though I fail of thy ideal of me,

My angel falls not short. They greet each other.
    Who knows, they may exchange the kiss we give,
Thou to thy crucifix, I to my mother.

RENOUNCEMENT

I must not think of thee; and, tired yet strong,
    I shun the thought that lurks in all delight —
    The thought of thee — and in the blue Heaven's height,
And in the sweetest passage of a song.

O just beyond the fairest thoughts that throng
    This breast, the thought of thee waits, hidden yet bright;
    But it must never, never come in sight;
I must stop short of thee the whole day long.

But when sleep comes to close each difficult day,
    When night gives pause to the long watch I keep,
    And all my bonds I needs must loose apart,

Must doff my will as raiment laid away, —
    With the first dream that comes with the first sleep
    I run, I run, I am gathered to thy heart.

SAN LORENZO'S MOTHER

I had not seen my son's dear face
    (He chose the cloister by God's grace)
    Since it had come to full flower-time.
    I hardly guessed at its perfect prime,
That folded flower of his dear face.

Mine eyes were veiled by mists of tears
When on a day in many years
    One of his Order came. I thrilled,
    Facing, I thought, that face fulfilled.
I doubted, for my mists of tears.

His blessing be with me for ever!
My hope and doubt were hard to sever.
    — That altered face, those holy weeds.
    I filled his wallet and kissed his beads,
And lost his echoing feet for ever.

If to my son my alms were given
I know not, and I wait for Heaven.
    He did not plead for child of mine,
    But for another Child divine,
And unto Him it was surely given.

There is One alone who cannot change;
Dreams are we, shadows, visions strange;
  And all I give is given to One.
  I might mistake my dearest son,
But never the Son who cannot change.

THE LADY POVERTY

The Lady Poverty was fair:
  But she has lost her looks of late,
With change of times and change of air.
Ah slattern! she neglects her hair,
Her gown, her shoes; she keeps no state
As once when her pure feet were bare.

Or — almost worse, if worse can be —
She scolds in parlours, dusts and trims,
Watches and counts. Oh, is this she
Whom Francis met, whose step was free,
Who with Obedience carolled hymns,
In Umbria walked with Chastity?

Where is her ladyhood? Not here,
Not among modern kinds of men;
But in the stony fields, where clear
Through the thin trees, the skies appear,
In delicate spare soil and fen,
And slender landscape and austere.

CHRISTMAS NIGHT

If I cannot see Thee present I will mourn
Thee absent, for this also is a proof of love.
                              THOMAS À KEMPIS

We do not find Him on the difficult earth,
  In surging human-kind,
In wayside death or accidental birth,
  Or in the ' march of mind.'

Nature, her nests, her prey, the fed, the caught,
   Hide Him so well, so well,
His steadfast secret there seems to our thought
   Life's saddest miracle.

He's but conjectured in man's happiness,
   Suspected in man's tears,
Or lurks beyond the long, discouraged guess,
   Grown fainter through the years.

.   .   .   .

But absent, absent now? Ah, what is this,
   Near as in child-birth bed,
Laid on our sorrowful hearts, close to a kiss?
   A homeless childish head.

AT NIGHT

To W. M.

Home, home from the horizon far and clear,
   Hither the soft wings sweep;
Flocks of the memories of the day draw near
   The dovecote doors of sleep.

Oh, which are they that come through sweetest light
   Of all these homing birds?
Which with the straightest and the swiftest flight?
   Your words to me, your words!

WILLIAM ERNEST HENLEY
1849–1903

Against the mauves and yellows and whites of the '90's Henley stands out rugged and vociferous, demanding and defending a new order in poetry with all the belligerency of his energetic spirit. ' To hold views and to publish them, is human,' he once wrote. It is not inappropriate that he should be popularly remembered as a man who was master of his fate and captain of his soul.

His heartiness and pugnacity are ascribable, in part, to a physical origin. At the age of twelve he was attacked by tuberculosis which cost him a foot. When he was advised to allow the other to be amputated, though desperate and penniless, he went to Edinburgh with characteristic determination to beg Lister, then a young practitioner in some disfavour with his profession, to save him from being a helpless cripple. Lister took the challenge and after twenty months in the Old Infirmary, which he later made famous in the sequence of poems, *In Hospital,* Henley emerged with enough of his body to make life endurable. He was never reconciled to his lameness and the usual cheerfulness of the cripple became with him a boisterousness which alternated with savage rage against his fate. In one of his poems appears a significant image of an ' old black rotter of a boat ' abandoned in the mud:

> With a horrid list, a frightening lapse from the line,
> That makes me think of legs and a broken spine.

Stevenson discovered Henley in Edinburgh. The record of the friendship that grew up between them is written on many pages, perhaps most interestingly in the character of Long John Silver whose original was Henley, though he never quite appreciated the compliment; in Henley's *Apparition,* which is a portrait of Stevenson; and in the plays which they wrote in collaboration.

❖ POETRY OF THE TRANSITION ❖

In 1877 Henley assumed the editorship of *London,* his first post in a journalistic career which lasted until 1898. The most influential magazine whose policy he controlled was the *National Observer.* Though Henley posed as a Tory, he jeered at respectability and dullness and spread his blistering wrath over the sacred institutions of Church and State. As an editor he introduced or forced into the hands of the public, Hardy, Swinburne, Stevenson, Kipling, Meredith, Conrad, and H. G. Wells. He rescued the criticism of art from the ignorant triflers and the moralists and made it a creditable profession. His championship of the newer schools did not, one could readily guess, take Aestheticism under its banner. There is a diverting story of an encounter between Henley and the leader of the Decadents. The scene is a half-lighted street in front of a London theatre. As the argument increases in fury, Henley gesticulates more and more wildly. Finally, unable to hold his hate longer, he drives his crutch straight into the bloated paunch of — Oscar Wilde.

Henley's poetry gained favour slowly. His unrhymed verse seemed careless and the subjects too pungent and crude for the delicate sensibilities of the critics. His first volume *A Book of Verses* (1888) was taken by David Nutt after rejection, as he ruefully declared, by every other ' editor of standing in London — I had well-nigh said in the world.' The principal subsequent collections are *London Voluntaries* (1893), *For England's Sake* (1900) and *Hawthorn and Lavender* (1901).

The bulk of Henley's poetry is bound to be forgotten. It was his misfortune that three of his contemporaries excelled him in three kinds of verse to which at different times he devoted himself. Kipling's poetry of the robustious life, Stevenson's glamorous verse, Dobson's essays in old French forms, surpass any of the work in these *genres* which Henley has left. But in the remainder of his poetry he forged ahead into a new style.

Look for a moment at the poem from the hospital series called *Vigil.* The diction is bare. The words are in their natural prose order. Often the syntactical connectives are omitted and the language is that of thought and not of speech. The most notable innovation is the free rhythm, Henley's contribution to English verse. Arnold had shown the way but Henley demonstrated the emotional release

346

which the new flexibility might effect. Notice in the strophe beginning ' All the old time ' how in the first six lines three similar cadences induce a feeling of routine and repetition. In the last three, by means of the pauses, he keeps the silent procession in motion while the sufferer's wakeful mind looks on in utter weariness. In the strophe preceding, a different rhythm describes the intolerable bodily ache; in the following one he catches the spasmodic noises and movements of the night. In the last he slips into the rhythm of an exhausting, restless sleep.

Henley's best work has the excellence of lithography. Its effects arrive with great economy of line and with little or no colour. The few details are selected and powerfully evocative. There is no ornament to obscure the emotion. A paradox in Henley's nature fitted him to write poetry of this concentrated sort; indeed, one might say, made it inevitable that he should discover such a style. Though he worshipped force and bigness, he was incapable of sustained work. His reviews are brief and pointed just as his verse is lyrical and impressionistic. But this desire for an abundant life, this largeness of mind which exhausted his frail body with its excursions into new regions, gave his work power, by showing him the essentials of a scene, while his fastidiousness saves it, except in a few instances where he is carried off by a momentary enthusiasm, from being over-muscled.

IN HOSPITAL

VII

VIGIL

Lived on one's back,
    In the long hours of repose,
Life is a practical nightmare —
Hideous asleep or awake.

Shoulders and loins
Ache . . . !
Ache, and the mattress,
Run into boulders and hummocks,
Glows like a kiln, while the bedclothes —
Tumbling, importunate, daft —

Ramble and roll, and the gas,
Screwed to its lowermost,
An inevitable atom of light,
Haunts, and a stertorous sleeper
Snores me to hate and despair.

All the old time
Surges malignant before me;
Old voices, old kisses, old songs
Blossom derisive about me;
While the new days
Pass me in endless procession:
A pageant of shadows
Silently, leeringly wending
On . . . and still on . . . still on!

Far in the stillness a cat
Languishes loudly. A cinder
Falls, and the shadows
Lurch to the leap of the flame. The next
        man to me
Turns with a moan; and the snorer,
The drug like a rope at his throat,
Gasps, gurgles, snorts himself free, as the
        night-nurse,
Noiseless and strange,
Her bull's eye half-lanterned in apron
(Whispering me, ' Are ye no' sleepin' yet? '),
Passes, list-slippered and peering,
Round . . . and is gone.

Sleep comes at last —
Sleep full of dreams and misgivings —
Broken with brutal and sordid
Voices and sounds that impose on me,
Ere I can wake to it,
The unnatural, intolerable day.

XIV

AVE, CAESAR!

From the winter's gray despair,
From the summer's golden languor,
Death, the lover of Life,
Frees us for ever.

Inevitable, silent, unseen,
Everywhere always,
Shadow by night and as light in the day
Signs she at last to her chosen;
And, as she waves them forth,
Sorrow and Joy
Lay by their looks and their voices,
Set down their hopes, and are made
One in the dim Forever.

Into the winter's gray delight,
Into the summer's golden dream,
Holy and high and impartial,
Death, the mother of Life,
Mingles all men for ever.

XXI

ROMANCE

' Talk of pluck! ' pursued the Sailor,
　Set at euchre on his elbow,
　' I was on the wharf at Charleston,
　Just ashore from off the runner.

' It was gray and dirty weather,
　And I heard a drum go rolling,
　Rub-a-dubbing in the distance,
　Awful dour-like and defiant.

' In and out among the cotton,
　Mud and chains, and stores, and anchors,
　Tramped a squad of battered scarecrows —
　Poor old Dixie's bottom dollar!

' Some had shoes, but all had rifles,
    Them that wasn't bald was beardless,
    And the drum was rolling *Dixie*,
    And they stepped to it like men, sir!

' Rags and tatters, belts and bayonets,
    On they swung, the drum a-rolling,
    Mum and sour. It looked like fighting,
    And they meant it too, by thunder! '

XXV

APPARITION

Thin-legged, thin-chested, slight unspeakably,
Neat-footed and weak-fingered: in his face —
Lean, large-boned, curved of beak, and touched with race,
Bold-lipped, rich-tinted, mutable as the sea,
The brown eyes radiant with vivacity —
There shines a brilliant and romantic grace,
A spirit intense and rare, with trace on trace
Of passion and impudence and energy.
Valiant in velvet, light in ragged luck,
Most vain, most generous, sternly critical,
Buffoon and poet, lover and sensualist:
A deal of Ariel, just a streak of Puck,
Much of Antony, of Hamlet most of all,
And something of the Shorter-Catechist.

XXVIII

DISCHARGED

Carry me out
Into the wind and the sunshine,
Into the beautiful world.

O, the wonder, the spell of the streets!
The stature and strength of the horses,
The rustle and echo of footfalls,
The flat roar and rattle of wheels!
A swift tram floats huge on us . . .
It's a dream?
The smell of the mud in my nostrils
Blows brave — like a breath of the sea!

As of old,
Ambulant, undulant drapery,
Vaguely and strangely provocative,
Flutters and beckons. O, yonder —
Is it? — the gleam of a stocking!
Sudden, a spire
Wedged in the mist! O, the houses,
The long lines of lofty, gray houses,
Cross-hatched with shadow and light!
These are the streets. . . .
Each is an avenue leading
Whither I will!

Free . . . !
Dizzy, hysterical, faint,
I sit, and the carriage rolls on with me
Into the wonderful world.

I. M.

R. T. HAMILTON BRUCE
(1846–1899)

Out of the night that covers me,
    Black as the Pit from pole to pole,
I thank whatever gods may be
    For my unconquerable soul.

In the fell clutch of circumstance
    I have not winced nor cried aloud.
Under the bludgeonings of chance
    My head is bloody, but unbowed.

Beyond this place of wrath and tears
    Looms but the Horror of the shade,
And yet the menace of the years
    Finds, and shall find, me unafraid.

It matters not how strait the gate,
    How charged with punishments the scroll,
I am the master of my fate;
    I am the captain of my soul.

BALLADE
OF DEAD ACTORS

I. M.

EDWARD JOHN HENLEY
(1861–1898)

Where are the passions they essayed,
  And where are the tears they made to flow?
Where the wild humours they portrayed
For laughing worlds to see and know?
Othello's wrath and Juliet's woe?
Sir Peter's whims and Timon's gall?
And Millamant and Romeo?
Into the night go one and all.

Where are the braveries, fresh or frayed?
The plumes, the armours — friend and foe?
The cloth of gold, the rare brocade,
The mantles glittering to and fro?
The pomp, the pride, the royal show?
The cries of war and festival?
The youth, the grace, the charm, the glow?
Into the night go one and all.

The curtain falls, the play is played:
The Beggar packs beside the Beau;
The Monarch troops, and troops the Maid;
The Thunder huddles with the Snow.
Where are the revellers high and low?
The clashing swords? The lover's call?
The dancers gleaming row on row?
Into the night go one and all.

Envoy

Prince, in one common overthrow
The Hero tumbles with the Thrall:
As dust that drives, as straws that blow,
Into the night go one and all.

✣ WILLIAM ERNEST HENLEY ✣

BALLADE
MADE IN THE HOT WEATHER

To C. M.

Fountains that frisk and sprinkle
The moss they overspill;
Pools that the breezes crinkle;
The wheel beside the mill,
With its wet, weedy frill;
Wind-shadows in the wheat;
A water-cart in the street;
The fringe of foam that girds
An islet's ferneries;
A green sky's minor thirds —
To live, I think of these!

Of ice and glass the tinkle,
Pellucid, silver-shrill;
Peaches without a wrinkle;
Cherries and snow at will,
From china bowls that fill
The senses with a sweet
Incuriousness of heat;
A melon's dripping sherds;
Cream-clotted strawberries;
Dust dairies set with curds —
To live, I think of these!

Vale-lily and periwinkle;
Wet stone-crop on the sill;
The look of leaves a-twinkle
With windlets clear and still;
The feel of a forest rill
That wimples fresh and fleet
About one's naked feet;
The muzzles of drinking herds;
Lush flags and bulrushes;
The chirp of rain-bound birds —
To live, I think of these!

Envoy

Dark aisles, new packs of cards,
Mermaidens' tails, cool swards,
Dawn dews and starlit seas,
White marbles, whiter words —
To live, I think of these!

ECHOES

VII

Fill a glass with golden wine,
    And the while your lips are wet
Set their perfume unto mine,
    And forget,
Every kiss we take and give
Leaves us less of life to live.

Yet again! Your whim and mine
In a happy while have met.
All your sweets to me resign,
    Nor regret
That we press with every breath,
Sighed or singing, nearer death.

XVIII

To A. D.

The nightingale has a lyre of gold,
    The lark's is a clarion call,
And the blackbird plays but a boxwood flute,
    But I love him best of all.

For his song is all of the joy of life,
    And we in the mad, spring weather,
We two have listened till he sang
    Our hearts and lips together.

XXIV

The full sea rolls and thunders
  In glory and in glee.
O, bury me not in the senseless earth
  But in the living sea!

Ay, bury me where it surges
  A thousand miles from shore,
And in its brotherly unrest
  I'll range for evermore.

XXIX

To R. L. S.

A child,
  Curious and innocent,
Slips from his Nurse, and rejoicing
Loses himself in the Fair.

Thro' the jostle and din
Wandering, he revels,
Dreaming, desiring, possessing;
Till, of a sudden,
Tired and afraid, he beholds
The sordid assemblage
Just as it is; and he runs
With a sob to his Nurse
  (Lighting at last on him),
And in her motherly bosom
Cries him to sleep.

Thus thro' the World,
Seeing and feeling and knowing,
Goes Man: till at last,
Tired of experience, he turns
To the friendly and comforting breast
Of the old nurse, Death.

XXXIV

To K. De M.

Love blows as the wind blows,
Love blows into the heart.
— Nile Boat-Song.

Life in her creaking shoes
   Goes, and more formal grows,
A round of calls and cues:
Love blows as the wind blows.
Blows! . . . in the quiet close
As in the roaring mart,
By ways no mortal knows
Love blows into the heart.

The stars some cadence use,
Forthright the river flows,
In order fall the dews,
Love blows as the wind blows:
Blows! . . . and what reckoning shows
The courses of his chart?
A spirit that comes and goes,
Love blows into the heart.

XXXV

I. M.

MARGARITAE SORORI
(1886)

A late lark twitters from the quiet skies;
   And from the west,
Where the sun, his day's work ended,
Lingers as in content,
There falls on the old, gray city
An influence luminous and serene,
A shining peace.

The smoke ascends
In a rosy-and-golden haze. The spires
Shine, and are changed. In the valley
Shadows rise. The lark sings on. The sun,
Closing his benediction,
Sinks, and the darkening air
Thrills with a sense of the triumphing night —
Night with her train of stars
And her great gift of sleep.

So be my passing!
My task accomplished and the long day done,
My wages taken, and in my heart
Some late lark singing,
Let me be gathered to the quiet west,
The sundown splendid and serene,
Death.

FROM A WINDOW IN PRINCES STREET

To M. M. M'B.

Above the Crags that fade and gloom
 Starts the bare knee of Arthur's Seat;
Ridged high against the evening bloom,
The Old Town rises, street on street;
With lamps bejewelled, straight ahead,
Like rampired walls the houses lean,
All spired and domed and turreted,
Sheer to the valley's darkling green;
Ranged in mysterious disarray,
The Castle, menacing and austere,
Looms through the lingering last of day;
And in the silver dusk you hear,
Reverberated from crag and scar,
Bold bugles blowing points of war.

RHYMES AND RHYTHMS

III

A desolate shore,
   The sinister seduction of the Moon,
The menace of the irreclaimable Sea.

Flaunting, tawdry and grim,
From cloud to cloud along her beat,
Leering her battered and inveterate leer,
She signals where he prowls in the dark alone.
Her horrible old man,
Mumbling old oaths and warming
His villainous old bones with villainous talk —
The secrets of their grisly housekeeping
Since they went out upon the pad
In the first twilight of self-conscious Time:
Growling, hideous and hoarse,
Tales of unnumbered Ships,
Goodly and strong, Companions of the Advance,
In some vile alley of the night
Waylaid and bludgeoned —
Dead.

Deep cellared in primeval ooze,
Ruined, dishonoured, spoiled,
They lie where the lean water-worm
Crawls free of their secrets, and their broken sides
Bulge with the slime of life. Thus they abide,
Thus fouled and desecrate,
The summons of the Trumpet, and the while
These Twain, their murderers,
Unravined, imperturbable, unsubdued,
Hang at the heels of their children — She aloft
As in the shining streets,
He as in ambush at some accomplice door.

The stalwart Ships,
The beautiful and bold adventurers!

Stationed out yonder in the isle,
The tall Policeman,
Flashing his bull's eye, as he peers
About him in the ancient vacancy,
Tells them this way is safety — this way home.

XII

Some starlit garden gray with dew,
Some chamber flushed with wine and fire,
What matters where, so I and you
    Are worthy our desire?

Behind, a past that scolds and jeers
For ungirt loins and lamps unlit;
In front, the unmanageable years,
    The trap upon the Pit;

Think on the shame of dreams for deeds,
The scandal of unnatural strife,
The slur upon immortal needs,
    The treason done to life:

Arise! no more a living lie,
And with me quicken and control
Some memory that shall magnify
    The universal Soul.

XXIII

To A. C.

Not to the staring Day,
For all the importunate questionings he pursues
In his big, violent voice,
Shall those mild things of bulk and multitude,
The Trees — God's sentinels
Over His gift of live, life-giving air,
Yield of their huge, unutterable selves.
Midsummer-manifold, each one
Voluminous, a labyrinth of life,
They keep their greenest musings, and the dim
    dreams

That haunt their leafier privacies,
Dissembled, baffling the random gapeseed still
With blank full-faces, or the innocent guile
Of laughter flickering back from shine to shade,
And disappearances of homing birds,
And frolicsome freaks
Of little boughs that frisk with little boughs.

But at the word
Of the ancient, sacerdotal Night,
Night of the many secrets, whose effect —
Transfiguring, hierophantic, dread —
Themselves alone may fully apprehend,
They tremble and are changed.
In each, the uncouth individual soul
Looms forth and glooms
Essential, and their bodily presences
Touched with inordinate significance,
Wearing the darkness like the livery
Of some mysterious and tremendous guild,
They brood — they menace — they appal;
Or the anguish of prophecy tears them, and they
        wring
Wild hands of warning in the face
Of some inevitable advance of doom;
Or, each to the other bending, beckoning, signing
As in some monstrous market-place,
They pass the news, these Gossips of the Prime,
In that old speech their forefathers
Learned on the lawns of Eden, ere they heard
The troubled voice of Eve
Naming the wondering folk of Paradise.

Your sense is sealed, or you should hear them tell
The tale of their dim life, with all
Its compost of experience: how the Sun
Spreads them their daily feast,
Sumptuous, of light, firing them as with wine;
Of the old Moon's fitful solicitude
And those mild messages the Stars
Descend in silver silences and dews;

Or what the sweet-breathing West,
Wanton with wading in the swirl of the wheat,
Said, and their leafage laughed;
And how the wet-winged Angel of the Rain
Came whispering . . . whispering; and the gifts
    of the Year
The sting of the stirring sap
Under the wizardry of the young-eyed Spring,
Their summer amplitudes of pomp,
Their rich autumnal melancholy, and the shrill,
Embittered housewifery
Of the lean Winter: all such things,
And with them all the goodness of the Master,
Whose right hand blesses with increase and life,
Whose left hand honours with decay and death.

Thus under the constraint of Night
These gross and simple creatures,
Each in his scores of rings, which rings are years,
A servant of the Will!
And God, the Craftsman, as He walks
The floor of His workshop, hearkens, full of cheer
In thus accomplishing
The aims of His miraculous artistry.

LONDON VOLUNTARIES

III

Scherzando

Down through the ancient Strand
    The spirit of October, mild and boon
And sauntering, takes his way
This golden end of afternoon,
As though the corn stood yellow in all the land,
And the ripe apples dropped to the harvest-moon.

Lo! the round sun, half-down the western slope —
Seen as along an unglazed telescope —
Lingers and lolls, loth to be done with day:
Gifting the long, lean, lanky street
And its abounding confluences of being

With aspects generous and bland;
Making a thousand harnesses to shine
As with new ore from some enchanted mine,
And every horse's coat so full of sheen
He looks new-tailored, and every 'bus feels clean,
And never a hansom but is worth the feeing;
And every jeweler within the pale
Offers a real Arabian Night for sale;
And even the roar
Of the strong streams of toil, that pause and pour
Eastward and westward, sounds suffused —
Seems as it were bemused
And blurred, and like the speech
Of lazy seas on a lotus-haunted beach —
With this enchanted lustrousness,
This mellow magic, that (as a man's caress
Brings back to some faded face, beloved before,
A heavenly shadow of the grace it wore
Ere the poor eyes were minded to beseech)
Old things transfigures, and you hail and bless
Their looks of long-lapsed loveliness once more:
Till Clement's, angular and cold and staid,
Gleams forth in glamour's very stuffs arrayed;
And Bride's, her aëry, unsubstantial charm
Through flight on flight of springing, soaring
        stone
Grown flushed and warm,
Laughs into life full-mooded and fresh-blown;
And the high majesty of Paul's
Uplifts a voice of living light, and calls —
Calls to his millions to behold and see
How goodly this his London Town can be!

For earth and sky and air
Are golden everywhere,
And golden with a gold so suave and fine
The looking on it lifts the heart like wine.
Trafalgar Square
 (The fountains volleying golden glaze)
Shines like an angel-market. High aloft
Over his couchant Lions, in a haze

Shimmering and bland and soft,
A dust of chrysoprase,
Our Sailor takes the golden gaze
Of the saluting sun, and flames superb,
As once he flamed it on his ocean round.

The dingy dreariness of the picture-place,
Turned very nearly bright,
Takes on a luminous transiency of grace,
And shows no more a scandal to the ground.
The very blind man pottering on the kerb
Among the posies and the ostrich feathers
And the rude voices touched with all the weathers
Of the long, varying year,
Shares in the universal alms of light.
The windows, with their fleeting, flickering fires,
The height and spread of frontage shining sheer,
The quiring signs, the rejoicing roofs and spires —
'Tis El Dorado — El Dorado plain,
The Golden City! And when a girl goes by,
Look! as she turns her glancing head,
A call of gold is floated from her ear!
Golden, all golden! In a golden glory,
Long-lapsing down a golden coasted sky,
The day, not dies but, seems
Dispersed in wafts and drifts of gold, and shed
Upon a past of golden song and story
And memories of gold and golden dreams.

EPILOGUE

These, to you now, O, more than ever now —
  Now that the Ancient Enemy
Has passed, and we, we two that are one, have seen
A piece of perfect Life
Turn to so ravishing a shape of Death
The Arch-Discomforter might well have smiled
In pity and pride,
Even as he bore his lovely and innocent spoil
From those home-kingdoms he left desolate!

Poor windlestraws
On the great, sullen, roaring pool of Time
And Chance and Change, I know!
But they are yours, as I am, till we attain
That end for which we make, we two that are one:
A little, exquisite Ghost
Between us, smiling with the serenest eyes
Seen in this world, and calling, calling still
In that clear voice whose infinite subtleties
Of sweetness, thrilling back across the grave,
Break the poor heart to hear: —
      ' Come, Dadsie, come!
Mama, how long — how long! '

ROBERT LOUIS STEVENSON
1850–1894

Stevenson was in his day, perhaps he is still to not a few, the most engaging, the most delightful figure among English men of letters. His dauntless courage, his gay humour, his scorn of the commonplace and love of romance and adventure, came like a draught of heady wine to a generation that was full-fed with the husks of realism and materialism. If he is less read and less loved now, so much the worse, one fancies, for the present generation.

An only child, weak and sickly from his birth, he received an irregular education, but travelled widely with his father about the shores of Scotland, where the elder Stevenson inspected lighthouses that his family had built. He turned away first from the family profession of engineering, then from the law, to follow his heart's desire, the spinning of his thoughts and fancies into words in prose and verse. He became the friend of many of the best known writers of the day, Henry James, Meredith, Henley, Addington Symonds, and Andrew Lang. But his own success was long deferred, and his seeming-idle life and reckless Bohemian ways shocked the proprieties of Edinburgh.

During a sojourn in an artists' colony in France he fell in love with a married woman, an American some years his elder. He followed her across the sea to California and endured the extreme of poverty and sickness while waiting for the divorce that would permit their marriage. Stevenson's wife proved the best of helpmates; she nursed him from the very door of death back to comparative health, reconciled him to his parents, accompanied his wanderings and cared for his well-being for the rest of his life. That rest was short and crowded. The suffering he had endured in California had completely wrecked an always delicate constitution and his remaining years were spent in a vain pursuit of health and strength. He stayed at Davos in the Alps, at Saranac, on the Riviera, and finally embarked on a series of voyages on the Pacific that ended in his settling in Samoa where he made his final home and where he died and was buried in 1894. And always he wrote: books of travel, essays, stories, novels, and verse, dictating when he could not write, correcting endlessly and leaving a mass of unfinished manuscript.

Stevenson's poetry is but a small part of his work, and it is idle to suppose that he will be remembered as a poet rather than as an essayist or a romancer. Yet he is by no means a minor poet. In his best work there is a sincerity, a simplicity and a directness that points on to some of the finest poetry of the present century. Stevenson is in no sense of the word a Victorian; he is untroubled by the major problems that vexed the great Victorians; he is peculiarly and intensely interested in his own, both ethical and aesthetic. He abandons the common topics of Victorian poetry, love, doubt, despair, and human progress, to sing of the joy of the open road, the joy of human friendship, the joy in resolute living in the face of death. And he is a true singer. It has been said that Stevenson was unmusical. It may be true that he could hardly carry a tune, but his best lyrics set themselves to old folk-tunes like those of the greatest of Scottish poets.

Stevenson's incorrigible optimism glows in every line he wrote and not only his optimism, but his whimsical humour, his longing for the homeland that failing health made to him a forbidden country, his rare, but sincere, ethical earnestness — that note of the Shorter Catechist that Henley derided; in short about all that went to make up the fascinating personality of Stevenson himself, expressed more simply and directly, in short more honestly, than in much of his sometimes attitudinizing and often over-elaborated prose. It is as safe a prediction as any in the doubtful field of literary prophecy that so long as the name of Stevenson is remembered and his work read, his poems, at least his best poems, will be treasured for what they tell us of the man.

THE VAGABOND

(To an air of Schubert)

Give to me the life I love,
   Let the lave go by me,
Give the jolly heaven above
   And the byway nigh me.
Bed in the bush with stars to see,
   Bread I dip in the river —
There's the life for a man like me,
   There's the life for ever.

Let the blow fall soon or late,
   Let what will be o'er me;
Give the face of earth around
   And the road before me.
Wealth I seek not, hope nor love,
   Nor a friend to know me;
All I seek the heaven above
   And the road below me.

Or let autumn fall on me
   Where afield I linger,
Silencing the bird on tree,
   Biting the blue finger:
White as meal the frosty field —
   Warm the fireside haven —
Not to autumn will I yield,
   Not to winter even!

Let the blow fall soon or late,
   Let what will be o'er me;
Give the face of earth around,
   And the road before me.
Wealth I ask not, hope nor love,
   Nor a friend to know me.
All I ask the heaven above,
   And the road below me.

A SONG OF THE ROAD

The gauger walked with willing foot,
  And aye the gauger played the flute;
And what should Master Gauger play
But *Over the hills and far away?*

Whene'er I buckle on my pack
And foot it gaily in the track,
O pleasant gauger, long since dead,
I hear you fluting on ahead.

You go with me the self-same way —
The self-same air for me you play;
For I do think and so do you
It is the tune to travel to.

For who would gravely set his face
To go to this or t'other place?
There's nothing under heav'n so blue
That's fairly worth the travelling to.

On every hand the roads begin,
And people walk with zeal therein;
But whereso'er the highways tend,
Be sure there's nothing at the end.

Then follow you, wherever hie
The travelling mountains of the sky.
Or let the streams in civil mode
Direct your choice upon a road;

For one and all, or high or low,
Will lead you where you wish to go;
And one and all go night and day
Over the hills and far away!

IT IS THE SEASON

It is the season now to go
  About the country high and low,
Among the lilacs hand in hand,
And two by two in fairy land.

The brooding boy, the singing maid,
Wholly fain and half afraid,
Now meet along the hazel'd brook
To pass and linger, pause and look.

A year ago, and blithely paired,
Their rough-and-tumble play they shared;
They kissed and quarrelled, laughed and cried,
A year ago at Eastertide.

With bursting heart, with fiery face,
She strove against him in the race;
He unabashed her garter saw,
That now would touch her skirts with awe.

Now by the stile ablaze she stops,
And his demurer eyes he drops;
Now they exchange averted sighs
Or stand and marry silent eyes.

And he to her a hero is
And sweeter she than primroses;
Their common silence dearer far
Than nightingale or mavis are.

Now when they sever wedded hands,
Joy trembles in their bosom-strands,
And lovely laughter leaps and falls
Upon their lips in madrigals.

I WILL MAKE YOU BROOCHES

I will make you brooches and toys for your delight
Of bird-song at morning and star-shine at night.
I will make a palace fit for you and me
Of green days in forests and blue days at sea.

I will make my kitchen, and you shall keep your room,
Where white flows the river and bright blows the broom,
And you shall wash your linen and keep your body white
In rainfall at morning and dewfall at night.

And this shall be for music when no one else is near,
The fine song for singing, the rare song to hear!
That only I remember, that only you admire,
Of the broad road that stretches and the roadside fire.

MY WIFE

Trusty, dusky, vivid, true,
   With eyes of gold and bramble-dew,
   Steel-true and blade-straight,
The great artificer
   Made my mate.

Honour, anger, valour, fire;
A love that life could never tire,
   Death quench or evil stir,
The mighty master
   Gave to her.

Teacher, tender, comrade, wife,
A fellow-farer true through life,
   Heart-whole and soul-free
The august father
   Gave to me.

TO ANDREW LANG

Dear Andrew, with the brindled hair,
  Who glory to have thrown in air,
High over arm, the trembling reed,
By Ale and Kail, by Till and Tweed:
An equal craft of hand you show
The pen to guide, the fly to throw:
I count you happy-starred; for God,
When He with inkpot and with rod
Endowed you, bade your fortune lead
Forever by the crooks of Tweed,
Forever by the woods of song
And lands that to the Muse belong;
Or if in peopled streets, or in
The abhorred pedantic sanhedrim,
It should be yours to wander, still
Airs of the morn, airs of the hill,
The plovery Forest and the seas
That break about the Hebrides,
Should follow over field and plain
And find you at the window pane;
And you again see hill and peel,
And the bright springs gush at your heel.
So went the fiat forth, and so
Garrulous like a brook you go,
With sound of happy mirth and sheen
Of daylight — whether by the green
You fare that moment, or the grey;
Whether you dwell in March or May;
Or whether treat of reels and rods
Or of the old unhappy gods:
Still like a brook your page has shone,
And your ink sings of Helicon.

THE BLAST — 1875

It's rainin'. Weet's the gairden sod,
  Weet the lang roads whaur gangrels plod —
A maist unceevil thing o' God
      In mid July —
If ye'll just curse the sneckdraw, dod!
      An' sae wull I!

He's a braw place in Heev'n, ye ken,
An' lea's us puir, forjaskit men
Clamjamfried in the but and ben
      He ca's the earth —
A wee bit inconvenient den
      No muckle worth;

An' whiles, at orra times, keeks out,
Sees what puir mankind are about;
An' if He can, I've little doubt,
      Upsets their plans;
He hates a' mankind, brainch and root,
      And a' that's man's.

An' whiles, whan they tak' heart again,
An' life i' the sun looks braw an' plain,
Doun comes a jaw o' droukin' rain
      Upon their honours —
God sends a spate out-ower the plain,
      Or mebbe thun'ers.

Lord safe us, life's an unco thing!
Simmer an' Winter, Yule an' Spring,
The damned, dour-heartit seasons bring
      A feck o' trouble.
I wadnae try't to be a king —
      No, nor for double.

But since we're in it, willy-nilly,
We maun be watchfü', wise an' skilly,
An' no mind ony ither billy,
      Lassie nor God.
But drink — that's my best counsel till 'e:
      Sae tak' the nod.

THE SPAEWIFE

Oh, I wad like to ken — to the beggar-wife says I —
  Why chops are guid to brander and nane sae guid to
    fry.
An' siller, that's sae braw to keep, is brawer still to gi'e.
— *It's gey an' easy spierin'*, says the beggar-wife to me.

O, I wad like to ken — to the beggar-wife says I —
Hoo a' things come to be whaur we find them when we try,
The lasses in their claes an' the fishes in the sea.
— *It's gey an' easy spierin'*, says the beggar-wife to me.

O, I wad like to ken — to the beggar-wife says I —
Why lads are a' to sell an' lasses a' to buy;
An' naebody for dacency but barely twa or three.
— *It's gey an' easy spierin'*, says the beggar-wife to me.

O, I wad like to ken — to the beggar-wife says I —
Gin death's as shüre to men as killin' is to kye,
Why God has filled the yearth sae fu' o' tasty things to
    pree.
— *It's gey an' easy spierin'*, says the beggar-wife to me.

Oh, I wad like to ken — to the beggar-wife says I —
The reason o' the cause an' the wherefore o' the why,
Wi' mony anither riddle brings the tear into my e'e.
— *It's gey an' easy spierin'*, says the beggar-wife to me.

WANDERING WILLIE

Home no more home to me, whither must I wander?
  Hunger my driver, I go where I must.
Cold blows the winter wind over hill and heather;
  Thick drives the rain, and my roof is in the dust.
Loved of wise men was the shade of my roof-tree.
  The true word of welcome was spoken in the door —
Dear days of old, with the faces in the firelight,
  Kind folks of old, you come again no more.

373

Home was home then, my dear, full of kindly faces,
  Home was home then, my dear, happy for the child.
Fire and the windows bright glittered on the moorland;
  Song, tuneful song, built a palace in the wild.
Now, when day dawns on the brow of the moorland,
  Lone stands the house, and the chimney-stone is cold.
Lone let it stand, now the friends are all departed,
  The kind hearts, the true hearts, that loved the place of old.

Spring shall come, come again, calling up the moor-fowl,
  Spring shall bring the sun and rain, bring the bees and
    flowers;
Red shall the heather bloom over hill and valley
  Soft flow the stream through the even-flowing hours;
Fair the day shine as it shone on my childhood —
  Fair shine the day on the house with open door;
Birds come and cry there and twitter in the chimney —
  But I go forever and come again no more.

IN THE HIGHLANDS

In the highlands, in the country places,
  Where the old plain men have rosy faces,
And the young fair maidens
  Quiet eyes;
Where essential silence cheers and blesses,
And for ever in the hill-recesses
Her more lovely music
  Broods and dies.

O to mount again where erst I haunted;
Where the old red hills are bird-enchanted,
And the low green meadows
  Bright with sward;
And when even dies, the million-tinted,
And the night has come, and planets glinted,
Lo! the valley hollow,
  Lamp-bestarred.

O to dream, O to awake and wander
There, and with delight to take and render,
Through the trance of silence,
    Quiet breath;
Lo! for there, among the flowers and grasses,
Only the mightier movement sounds and passes,
Only winds and rivers,
    Life and death.

SING ME A SONG

Sing me a song of a lad that is gone,
    Say, could that lad be I?
Merry of soul he sailed on a day
    Over the sea to Skye.

Mull was astern, Rum on the port,
    Egg on the starboard bow;
Glory of youth glowed in his soul:
    Where is that glory now?

Sing me a song of a lad that is gone,
    Say, could that lad be I?
Merry of soul he sailed on a day
    Over the sea to Skye.

Give me again all that was there,
    Give me the sun that shone!
Give me the eyes, give me the soul,
    Give me the lad that's gone!

Sing me a song of a lad that is gone,
    Say, could that lad be I?
Merry of soul he sailed on a day
    Over the sea to Skye.

Billow and breeze, islands and seas,
    Mountains of rain and sun,
All that was good, all that was fair,
    All that was me is gone.

TO S. R. CROCKETT

(In Reply to a Dedication)

Blows the wind to-day, and the sun and the rain are flying,
    Blows the wind on the moors to-day and now,
Where about the graves of the martyrs the whaups are crying,
    My heart remembers how!

Grey recumbent tombs of the dead in desert places,
    Standing stones on the vacant wine-red moor,
Hills of sheep, and the homes of the silent vanished races,
    And winds, austere and pure:

Be it granted me to behold you again in dying
    Hills of home! and to hear again the call;
Hear about the graves of the martyrs the peewees crying,
    And hear no more at all.

I DO NOT FEAR

I do not fear to own me kin
    To the glad clods in which spring flowers begin;
Or to my brothers, the great trees,
That speak with pleasant voices in the breeze,
Loud talkers with the winds that pass;
Or to my sister, the deep grass.

Of such I am, of such my body is,
That thrills to reach its lips to kiss.
That gives and takes with wind and sun and rain
And feels keen pleasure to the point of pain.
Of such are these,
The brotherhood of stalwart trees,
The humble family of flowers,
That make a light of shadowy bowers
Or star the edges of the bent:
They give and take sweet colour and sweet scent
They joy to shed themselves abroad;
And tree and flower and grass and sod
Thrill and leap and live and sing
With silent voices in the Spring.

Hence I not fear to yield my breath,
Since all is still unchanged by death;
Since in some pleasant valley I may be,
Clod beside clod, or tree by tree,
Long ages hence, with her I love this hour;
And feel a lively joy to share
With her the sun and rain and air,
To taste her quiet neighbourhood
As the dumb things of field and wood,
The clod, the tree, the starry flower,
Alone of all things have the power.

IF THIS WERE FAITH

God, if this were enough,
That I see things bare to the buff
And up to the buttocks in mire;
That I ask nor hope nor hire,
Nut in the husk,
Nor dawn beyond the dusk,
Nor life beyond death:
God, if this were faith?

Having felt thy wind in my face
Spit sorrow and disgrace,
Having seen thine evil doom
In Golgotha and Khartoum,
And the brutes, the work of thine hands,
Fill with injustice lands
And stain with blood the sea:
If still in my veins the glee
Of the black night and the sun
And the lost battle, run:
If, an adept,
The iniquitous lists I still accept
With joy, and joy to endure and be withstood,
And still to battle and perish for a dream of good:
God, if that were enough?

If to feel, in the ink of the slough,
And the sink of the mire,

377

Veins of glory and fire
Run through and transpierce and transpire,
And a secret purpose of glory in every part,
And the answering glory of battle fill my heart;
To thrill with the joy of girded men
To go on for ever and fail and go on again,
And be mauled to the earth and arise,
And contend for the shade of a word and a thing not
    seen with the eyes:
With the half of a broken hope for a pillow at night
That somehow the right is the right
And the smooth shall bloom from the rough:
Lord, if that were enough?

THE CELESTIAL SURGEON

If I have faltered more or less
   In my great task of happiness;
If I have moved among my race
And shown no glorious morning face;
If beams from happy human eyes
Have moved me not; if morning skies,
Books, and my food, and summer rain
Knocked on my sullen heart in vain: —
Lord, thy most pointed pleasure take
And stab my spirit broad awake;
Or, Lord, if too obdurate I,
Choose thou, before that spirit die,
A piercing pain, a killing sin,
And to my dead heart run them in!

REQUIEM

Under the wide and starry sky,
   Dig the grave and let me lie.
Glad did I live and gladly die,
   And I laid me down with a will.

This be the verse you grave for me:
Here he lies where he longed to be;
Home is the sailor, home from sea,
   And the hunter home from the hill.

GEORGE MEREDITH
1828–1909

Meredith's life, superficially, contained no more of excitement, pleasure, and pain than falls to the lot of most. Yet a biographer finds it, because of its transmutations in poetry and fiction, extraordinarily rich. At the beginning an amusing puzzle confronts us. Why did Meredith, the anatomist of egoism, keep so carefully concealed all his life the fact of his birth into a family of Portsmouth naval outfitters, while revealing with considerable accuracy in *Evan Harrington* the story of that family and holding up for scorn just such snobbery as he himself was guilty of? The paradox invites speculation. Does it not reveal the proud, romantic youth grown into the disciple of the comic spirit and show how there were combined in him two dominant qualities which his countrymen cannot easily allow to a man unless they are kept carefully discrete?

The boy was sent at fourteen, a forlorn youth whose nickname of "Gentleman George" is an index to his effect on other children, to a remarkable school in Germany. His two years there stamped deep in him a passion for liberty — it was a year of revolutions — and sowed a love of exuberant German romanticism which gives tone to much of his early work. He escaped at Neuwied the conventional exercises in composition imposed on English schoolboys and was allowed to use his native language as his imagination dictated. Neither he nor Browning, who also evaded public school discipline, ever understood the bewilderment of English readers before the ' barbarities ' of their style.

We should not expect that Meredith, on his return to England, would long keep up the pretense of reading Blackstone in a solicitor's office. He knew that he was going to write and set about it as promptly as possible, first by fugitive contributions to the journals and then in 1851 by a volume briefly entitled *Poems*, which Kingsley and Tennyson applauded amid the general silence of the rest of the world.

In the meantime he had married the daughter of Thomas Love Peacock and opened the windows to a flood of rapturous love and new life. It could not last. They were the two snared falcons of *Modern Love*, condemned to do ' the flitting of the bat.' When at last Mary abruptly justified the misery of his growing suspicion by flight to Italy with her lover, Meredith's affection turned to bitterness in his blood and he never allowed her to repent. The memories of the days when he had been carried at full tide into the sunlight of young love he tried to exile from his life, but they are alive for us in *Love in the Valley* and *Richard Feverel*.

The legend persists that Meredith's novels were unpopular. Actually they made their way with an important public and his eminence as a man of letters was soon fixed. He became shortly the member of a group which included not only such writers and artists as Swinburne, Fitzgerald, Watts, and Rossetti, but men of affairs like John Morley. The Meredith of those days tramped the Surrey hills in thirty-mile stretches and kept the table in a roar when the halt for the night was made at a roadside inn; a handsome, generous, high-spirited man, adored by the women on whom he was wont to rely and the loadstone of a troop of friends. In 1864 he crowned his happiness by marrying Marie Vulliamy. Ideas for new work thronged his mind and his wife urged him on. He wrote to a friend: ' I never had such a fit on me since the age of 21; and my good love, waking too [at three in the morning] joyfully assisted by lending notepaper and soothing me for having disturbed her slumbers.'

The public finally made up its several minds that Meredith was a tolerable if eccentric writer of prose. The poetry they would not touch. For a time Meredith published the volumes at his own expense; later on he did not even trouble to send out copies for review. Five books of verse appeared during his life: *Poems* (1851), *Modern Love* (1862), *Odes in Contribution to the Song of French History* (1871), *Poems and Lyrics of the Joy of Earth* (1883), *Ballads and Poems of Tragic Life* (1887), *A Reading of Earth* (1888).

Meredith and Hardy were too honest to try to salvage the ragged creeds of their generation. They saw without flinching that a reading of life which dared not include evolution, even in its more destructive phases, could not satisfy the intelligence of men. Beginning with the same trust in nature,

> Where Life is at her grindstone set
> That she may give us edging keen,

they travelled to quite opposite poles of thought but together they have made old-fashioned the romanticists' view of nature as the healer and the mirror of man's woe.

Meredith clung to earth as the one piece ' of God's handiwork which we possess,' not solely because the season's change delighted him but of a desperate necessity. When we reckon up our life, we find in our hand ' naught save earth.' Only the ' totterknee'd ' cringe before the slights she gives us. We must accept them for they are life and all we shall have of life. No romantic poet looked more gratefully than Meredith through her ' showers, her mists, her streaming gold.' In his efforts to enjoy her life-bringing gifts he stretched the endurance of his body so that he was invalided before old age. But he had proved that the ' spin of the blood is one of the main secrets of Nature, otherwise we breed as the stagnant pools do,' and he had no regrets. A wonder always edged the familiar face, a mystery held him which he inveterately strained to see.

Earth is a triad. She hides joy from her beholder if he divides the trinity of blood and brain and spirit. ' I have written always,' he said to one who asked for a nutshell of philosophy, ' with the perception that there is no life but of the spirit; that the concrete is really the shadowy; yet that the way to spiritual life lies in the complete unfolding of the creature, not in the nipping of his passions. . . . An outrage to Nature helps to extinguish his light. To the flourishing of the spirit then, through the healthy exercise of the sense.'

This is the main theorem. A corollary follows hard upon. Man is unlike the rest of Earth's creatures in that he has developed a faculty of reason.

> Change is on the wing to bud
> Rose in brain from rose in blood.

Sometimes man's power of analyzing his experience overwhelms him and he becomes so devoted to his own fascinating individuality that he is unfit for society. This is the egoist, slave to ' self, the Dragon fowl ' in the Woods of Westermain. To subdue the unnatural monster, let loose the sword of common sense and kill it with the thoughtful laughter of the comic spirit.

> Thou, soul of wakened heads, art armed to warn,
> Restrain, lest we backslide on whence we sprang
> Scarce better than our dwarf beginning shoot.

In the finely tempered man brain evolves from blood and common sense keeps watch over the proportioning.

In a scant space a rehearsal of Meredith's penetrating and comprehensive reading of earth must border on parody. It is doubtful if many of his contemporaries, lacking even an outline of his ideas, got very far with his poetry. They mistook his struggles with the dead matter of language for willful obscurantism and his irony for cynicism. An excessive virtue of Meredith's style is responsible for their main difficulty. He was too uninterruptedly the poet in the sense that he saw the world *sub specie imaginis*. He seems never to have lived at the common level of observation but to have leapt inconsiderately from image to image and from symbol to symbol, demanding of those who essay him that they follow at a breathless pace his metaphorical progress.

Meredith recognized, moreover, that ' thought is tough and dealing with thought produces toughness.' His prescience bewildered his readers for he tumbled them about with ideas which were only shadows to the rest of men. He foresaw, for instance, the effect that machinery would have in standardizing modern life and thought; he prophesied, in a passage in the *Ordeal*, the trend of fiction toward the microscopic analysis of consciousness. The poetry which resulted when his strong emotions ran full tilt against his active mind scarcely made a suitable giftbook ' for the innumerable nuptial curate and his bride.' Meredith wished to write poetry which should be the voice of essential man before the gods. To do that, thought must embrace feeling as the man the woman. ' Then you have the highest in mind with the deepest in nature.'

✤ GEORGE MEREDITH ✤

LOVE IN THE VALLEY

Under yonder beech-tree single on the green-sward,
   Couched, with her arms behind her golden head,
Knees and tresses folded to slip and ripple idly,
   Lies my young love sleeping in the shade.
Had I the heart to slide an arm beneath her,
   Press her parting lips as her waist I gather slow,
Waking in amazement she could not but embrace me:
   Then would she hold me and never let me go?

．　．　．　．　．　．　．　．　．　．

Shy as the squirrel and wayward as the swallow,
   Swift as the swallow along the river's light
Circleting the surface to meet his mirrored winglets,
   Fleeter she seems in her stay than in her flight.
Shy as the squirrel that leaps among the pine-tops,
   Wayward as the swallow overhead at set of sun,
She whom I love is hard to catch and conquer,
   Hard, but O the glory of the winning were she won!

．　．　．　．　．　．　．　．　．　．

When her mother tends her before the laughing mirror,
   Tying up her laces, looping up her hair,
Often she thinks, were this wild thing wedded,
   More love should I have, and much less care.
When her mother tends her before the lighted mirror,
   Loosening her laces, combing down her curls,
Often she thinks, were this wild thing wedded,
   I should miss but one for many boys and girls.

．　．　．　．　．　．　．　．　．　．

Heartless she is as the shadow in the meadows
   Flying to the hills on a blue and breezy noon.
No, she is athirst and drinking up her wonder:
   Earth to her is young as the slip of the new moon.
Deals she an unkindness, 'tis but her rapid measure,
   Even as in a dance; and her smile can heal no less:
Like the swinging May-cloud that pelts the flowers with
     hailstones
   Off a sunny border, she was made to bruise and bless.

．　．　．　．　．　．　．　．　．　．

383

Lovely are the curves of the white owl sweeping
   Wavy in the dusk lit by one large star.
Lone on the fir-branch, his rattle-note unvaried,
   Brooding o'er the gloom, spins the brown eve-jar.
Darker grows the valley, more and more forgetting:
   So were it with me if forgetting could be willed.
Tell the grassy hollow that holds the bubbling well-spring,
   Tell it to forget the source that keeps it filled.

    .   .   .   .

Stepping down the hill with her fair companions,
   Arm in arm, all against the raying West,
Boldly she sings, to the merry tune she marches,
   Brave is her shape, and sweeter unpossessed,
Sweeter, for she is what my heart first awaking
   Whispered the world was; morning light is she.
Love that so desires would fain keep her changeless;
   Fain would fling the net, and fain have her free.

    .   .   .   .

Happy, happy time, when the white star hovers
   Low over dim fields fresh with bloomy dew,
Near the face of dawn, that draws athwart the darkness,
   Threading it with color, like yewberries the yew.
Thicker crowd the shades as the grave East deepens
   Glowing, and with crimson a long cloud swells.
Maiden still the morn is; and strange she is, and secret;
   Strange her eyes; her cheeks are cold as cold sea-shells.

    .   .   .   .

Sunrays, leaning on our southern hills and lighting
   Wild cloud-mountains that drag the hills along,
Oft ends the day of your shifting brilliant laughter
   Chill as a dull face frowning on a song.
Ay, but shows the South-West a ripple-feathered bosom
   Blown to silver while the clouds are shaken and ascend,
Scaling the mid-heavens as they stream, there comes a sunset
   Rich, deep like love in beauty without end.

    .   .   .   .

When at dawn she sighs, and like an infant to the window
   Turns grave eyes craving light, released from dreams,
Beautiful she looks, like a white water-lily
   Bursting out of bud in havens of the streams.

When from bed she rises clothed from neck to ankle
  In her long nightgown sweet as boughs of May,
Beautiful she looks, like a tall garden lily
  Pure from the night, and splendid for the day.

  .   .   .   .

Mother of the dews, dark eye-lashed twilight,
  Low-lidded twilight, o'er the valley's brim,
Rounding on thy breast sings the dew-delighted skylark,
  Clear as though the dewdrops had their voice in him.
Hidden where the rose-flush drinks the rayless planet,
  Fountain-full he pours the spraying fountain-showers.
Let me hear her laughter, I would have her ever
  Cool as dew in twilight, the lark above the flowers.

  .   .   .   .

All the girls are out with their baskets for the primrose;
  Up lanes, woods through, they troop in joyful bands.
My sweet leads: she knows not why, but now she loiters,
  Eyes the bent anemones, and hangs her hands.
Such a look will tell that the violets are peeping,
  Coming the rose: and unaware a cry
Springs in her bosom for odours and for colour,
  Covert and the nightingale; she knows not why.

  .   .   .   .

Kerchiefed head and chin she darts between her tulips,
  Streaming like a willow grey in arrowy rain:
Some bend beaten cheek to gravel, and their angel
  She will be; she lifts them, and on she speeds again.
Black the driving raincloud breasts the iron gateway:
  She is forth to cheer a neighbour lacking mirth.
So when sky and grass met rolling dumb for thunder
  Saw I once a white dove, sole light of earth.

  .   .   .   .

Prim little scholars are the flowers of her garden,
  Trained to stand in rows, and asking if they please.
I might love them well but for loving more the wild ones:
  O my wild ones! they tell me more than these.
You, my wild one, you tell of honeyed field-rose,
  Violet, blushing eglantine in life; and even as they,
They by the wayside are earnest of your goodness,
  You are of life's, on the banks that line the way.

  .   .   .   .

385

Peering at her chamber the white crowns the red rose,
  Jasmine winds the porch with stars two and three.
Parted is the window; she sleeps; the starry jasmine
  Breathes a falling breath that carries thoughts of me.
Sweeter unpossessed, have I said of her my sweetest?
  Not while she sleeps: while she sleeps the jasmine breathes,
Luring her to love; she sleeps; the starry jasmine
  Bears me to her pillow under white rose-wreaths.

.   .   .   .

Yellow with birdfoot-trefoil are the grass-glades;
  Yellow with cinquefoil of the dew-grey leaf;
Yellow with stonecrop; the moss-mounds are yellow;
  Blue-necked the wheat sways, yellowing to the sheaf.
Green-yellow bursts from the copse the laughing yaffle;
  Sharp as a sickle is the edge of shade and shine:
Earth in her heart laughs looking at the heavens,
  Thinking of the harvest: I look and think of mine.

.   .   .   .

This I may know: her dressing and undressing
  Such a change of light shows as when the skies in sport
Shift from cloud to moonlight; or edging over thunder
  Slips a ray of sun; or sweeping into port
White sails furl; or on the ocean borders
  White sails lean along the waves leaping green.
Visions of her shower before me, but from eyesight
  Guarded she would be like the sun were she seen.

.   .   .   .

Front door and back of the mossed old farmhouse
  Open with the morn; and in a breezy link
Freshly sparkles garden to stripe-shadowed orchard,
  Green across a rill where on sand the minnows wink.
Busy in the grass the early sun of summer
  Swarms, and the blackbird's mellow fluting notes —
Call my darling up with round and roguish challenge:
  Quaintest, richest carol of all the singing throats!

.   .   .   .

Cool was the woodside; cool as her white dairy
  Keeping sweet the cream-pan; and there the boys from
    school,

✤ GEORGE MEREDITH ✤

Cricketing below, rushed brown and red with sunshine;
    O the dark translucence of the deep-eyed cool!
Spying from the farm, herself she fetched a pitcher
    Full of milk, and tilted for each in turn the beak.
Then a little fellow, mouth up and on tiptoe,
    Said, ' I will kiss you: ' she laughed and leaned her cheek.

    .   .   .   .

Doves of the fir-wood walling high our red roof
    Through the long noon coo, crooning through the coo.
Loose droop the leaves, and down the sleepy roadway
    Sometimes pipes a chaffinch; loose droops the blue.
Cows flap a slow tail knee-deep in the river,
    Breathless, given up to sun and gnat and fly.
Nowhere is she seen; and if I see her nowhere,
    Lightning may come, straight rains and tiger sky.

    .   .   .   .

O the golden sheaf, the rustling treasure-armful!
    O the nutbrown tresses nodding interlaced!
O the treasure-tresses one another over
    Nodding! O the girdle slack about the waist!
Slain are the poppies that shot their random scarlet
    Quick amid the wheatears: wound about the waist,
Gathered, see these brides of Earth one blush of ripeness!
    O the nutbrown tresses nodding interlaced!

    .   .   .   .

Large and smoky red the sun's cold disk drops,
    Clipped by naked hills, on violet shaded snow:
Eastward large and still lights up a bower of moonrise,
    Whence at her leisure steps the moon aglow.
Nightlong on black print-branches our beech-tree
    Gazes in this whiteness: nightlong could I.
Here may life on death or death on life be painted.
    Let me clasp her soul to know she cannot die!

    .   .   .   .

Gossips count her faults; they scour a narrow chamber
    Where there is no window, read not heaven or her.
' When she was a tiny,' one aged woman quavers,
    Plucks at my heart and leads me by the ear.

Faults she had once as she learned to run and tumbled:
　　Faults of feature some see, beauty not complete.
Yet, good gossips, beauty that makes holy
　　Earth and air, may have faults from head to feet.

．　　．　　．　　．　　．　　．　　．　　．

Hither she comes; she comes to me; she lingers,
　　Deepens her brown eyebrows, while in new surprise
High rise the lashes in wonder of a stranger;
　　Yet am I the light and living of her eyes.
Something friends have told her fills her heart to brimming,
　　Nets her in her blushes, and wounds her, and tames. —
Sure of her haven, O like a dove alighting,
　　Arms up, she dropped: our souls were in our names.

．　　．　　．　　．　　．　　．　　．　　．

Soon will she lie like a white-frost sunrise.
　　Yellow oats and brown wheat, barley pale as rye,
Long since your sheaves have yielded to the thresher,
　　Felt the girdle loosened, seen the tresses fly.
Soon will she lie like a blood-red sunset.
　　Swift with the to-morrow, green-winged Spring!
Sing from the South-West, bring her back the truants,
　　Nightingale and swallow, song and dipping wing.

．　　．　　．　　．　　．　　．　　．　　．

Soft new beech-leaves, up to beamy April
　　Spreading bough on bough a primrose mountain, you
Lucid in the moon, raise lilies to the skyfields,
　　Youngest green transfused in silver shining through:
Fairer than the lily, than the wild white cherry:
　　Fair as in image my seraph love appears
Borne to me by dreams when dawn is at my eyelids:
　　Fair as in the flesh she swims to me on tears.

．　　．　　．　　．　　．　　．　　．　　．

Could I find a place to be alone with heaven,
　　I would speak my heart out: heaven is my need.
Every woodland tree is flushing like the dogwood,
　　Flashing like the whitebeam, swaying like the reed.
Flushing like the dogwood crimson in October;
　　Streaming like the flag-reed South-West blown;
Flashing as in gusts the sudden-lighted whitebeam:
　　All seem to know what is for heaven alone.

❖ GEORGE MEREDITH ❖

JUGGLING JERRY

Pitch here the tent, while the old horse grazes:
   By the old hedge-side we'll halt a stage.
It's nigh my last above the daisies:
   My next leaf'll be man's blank page.
Yes, my old girl! and it's no use crying:
   Juggler, constable, king, must bow.
One that outjuggles all's been spying
   Long to have me, and he has me now.

We've travelled times to this old common:
   Often we've hung our pots in the gorse.
We've had a stirring life, old woman!
   You, and I, and the old grey horse.
Races, and fairs, and royal occasions,
   Found us coming to their call:
Now they'll miss us at our stations:
   There's a Juggler outjuggles all!

Up goes the lark, as if all were jolly!
   Over the duck-pond the willow shakes.
It's easy to think that grieving's folly,
   When the hand's firm as driven stakes!
Ay, when we're strong, and braced, and manful,
   Life's a sweet fiddle: but we're a batch
Born to become the Great Juggler's han'ful:
   Balls he shies up, and is safe to catch.

Here's where the lads of the village cricket:
   I was a lad not wide from here:
Couldn't I whip off the bale from the wicket?
   Like an old world those days appear!
Donkey, sheep, geese and thatched ale-house — I know them!
   They are old friends of my halts, and seem,
Somehow, as if kind thanks I owe them;
   Juggling don't hinder the heart's esteem.

Juggling's no sin, for we must have victual:
   Nature allows us to bait for the fool.
Holding one's own makes us juggle no little;
   But, to increase it, hard juggling's the rule.

389

You that are sneering at my profession,
    Haven't you juggled a vast amount?
There's the Prime Minister, in one Session,
    Juggles more games than my sins'll count.

I've murdered insects with mock thunder:
    Conscience, for that, in men don't quail.
I've made bread from the bump of wonder:
    That's my business, and there's my tale.
Fashion and rank all praised the professor:
    Ay! and I've had my smile from the Queen:
Bravo, Jerry! she meant: God bless her!
    Ain't this a sermon on that scene?

I've studied men from my topsy-turvy
    Close, and, I reckon, rather true.
Some are fine fellows: some, right scurvy:
    Most, a dash between the two.
But it's a woman, old girl, that makes me
    Think more kindly of the race:
And it's a woman, old girl, that shakes me
    When the Great Juggler I must face.

We two were married, due and legal:
    Honest we've lived since we've been one.
Lord! I could then jump like an eagle:
    You danced bright as a bit o' the sun.
Birds in a May-bush we were! right merry!
    All night we kiss'd, we juggled all day.
Joy was the heart of Juggling Jerry!
    Now from his old girl he's juggled away.

It's past parsons to console us:
    No, nor no doctor fetch for me:
I can die without my bolus;
    Two of a trade, lass, never agree!
Parson and Doctor! — don't they love rarely,
    Fighting the devil in other men's fields!
Stand up yourself and match him fairly:
    Then see how the rascal yields!

❖ GEORGE MEREDITH ❖

I, lass, have lived no gypsy, flaunting
  Finery while his poor helpmate grubs:
Coin I've stored, and you won't be wanting:
  You shan't beg from the troughs and tubs.
Nobly you've stuck to me, though in his kitchen
  Many a Marquis would hail you Cook!
Palaces you could have ruled and grown rich in,
  But your old Jerry you never forsook.

Hand up the chirper! ripe ale winks in it;
  Let's have comfort and be at peace.
Once a stout draft made me light as a linnet.
  Cheer up! the Lord must have his lease.
May be — for none see in that black hollow —
  It's just a place where we're held in pawn,
And, when the Great Juggler makes as to swallow,
  It's just the sword-trick — I ain't quite gone!

Yonder came smells of the gorse, so nutty,
  Gold-like and warm: it's the prime of May.
Better than mortar, brick, and putty,
  Is God's house on a blowing day.
Lean me more up the mound; now I feel it:
  All the old heath-smells! Ain't it strange?
There's the world laughing, as if to conceal it,
  But He's by us, juggling the change.

I mind it well, by the sea-beach lying,
  Once — it's long gone — when two gulls we beheld,
Which, as the moon got up, were flying
  Down a big wave that sparked and swelled.
Crack went a gun: one fell: the second
  Wheeled round him twice, and was off for new luck:
There in the dark her white wing beckon'd: —
  Drop me a kiss — I'm the bird dead-struck!

MODERN LOVE

I

By this he knew she wept with waking eyes:
That, at his hand's light quiver by her head,
The strange low sobs that shook their common bed,
Were called into her with a sharp surprise,
And strangled mute, like little gaping snakes,
Dreadfully venomous to him. She lay
Stone-still, and the long darkness flowed away
With muffled pulses. Then, as midnight makes
Her giant heart of Memory and Tears
Drink the pale drug of silence, and so beat
Sleep's heavy measure, they from head to feet
Were moveless, looking through their dead black years,
By vain regret scrawled over the blank wall.
Like sculptured effigies they might be seen
Upon their marriage-tomb, the sword between;
Each wishing for the sword that severs all.

II

It ended, and the morrow brought the task.
Her eyes were guilty gates, that let him in
By shutting all too zealous for their sin:
Each sucked a secret, and each wore a mask.
But, oh, the bitter taste her beauty had!
He sickened as at breath of poison-flowers:
A languid humour stole among the hours,
And if their smiles encountered, he went mad,
And raged deep inward, till the light was brown
Before his vision, and the world, forgot,
Looked wicked as some old dull murder-spot.
A star with lurid beams, she seemed to crown
The pit of infamy: and then again
He fainted on his vengefulness, and strove
To ape the magnanimity of love,
And smote himself, a shuddering heap of pain.

VIII

Yet it was plain she struggled, and that salt
Of righteous feeling made her pitiful.
Poor twisting worm, so queenly beautiful!
Where came the cleft between us? whose the fault?
My tears are on thee, that have rarely dropped
As balm for any bitter wound of mine:
My breast will open for thee at a sign!
But, no: we are two reed-pipes, coarsely stopped:
The God once filled them with his mellow breath;
And they were music till he flung them down,
Used! used! Hear now the discord-loving clown
Puff his gross spirit in them, worse than death!
I do not know myself without thee more:
In this unholy battle I grow base:
If the same soul be under the same face,
Speak, and a taste of that old time restore!

IX

He felt the wild beast in him betweenwhiles
So masterfully rude, that he would grieve
To see the helpless delicate thing receive
His guardianship through certain dark defiles.
Had he not teeth to rend, and hunger too?
But still he spared her. Once: ' Have you no fear?'
He said: ' twas dusk; she in his grasp; none near.
She laughed: ' No, surely; am I not with you?'
And uttering that soft starry ' you,' she leaned
Her gentle body near him, looking up;
And from her eyes, as from a poison-cup,
He drank until the flittering eyelids screened.
Devilish malignant witch! and oh, young beam
Of heaven's circle-glory! Here thy shape
To squeeze like an intoxicating grape —
I might, and yet thou goest safe, supreme.

XIV

What soul would bargain for a cure that brings
Contempt the nobler agony to kill?

393

Rather let me bear on the bitter ill,
And strike this rusty bosom with new stings!
It seems there is another veering fit,
Since on a gold-haired lady's eyeballs pure,
I looked with little prospect of a cure,
The while her mouth's red bow loosed shafts of wit.
Just heaven! can it be true that jealousy
Has decked the woman thus? and does her head
Swim somewhat for possessions forfeited?
Madam, you teach me many things that be.
I open an old book, and there I find,
That ' Women still may love whom they deceive.'
Such love I prize not, madam: by your leave,
The game you play at is not to my mind.

XVII

At dinner, she is hostess, I am host.
Went the feast ever cheerfuller? She keeps
The Topic over intellectual deeps
In buoyancy afloat. They see no ghost.
With sparkling surface-eyes we ply the ball:
It is in truth a most contagious game:
HIDING THE SKELETON shall be its name.
Such play as this the devils might appal!
But here's the greater wonder; in that we,
Enamoured of an acting nought can tire,
Each other, like true hypocrites, admire;
Warm-lighted looks, Love's ephemerioe,
Shoot gayly o'er the dishes and the wine.
We waken envy of our happy lot.
Fast, sweet, and golden, shows the marriage-knot.
Dear guests, you now have seen Love's corpse-light shine.

XX

I am not of those miserable males
Who sniff at vice, and, daring not to snap,
Do therefore hope for heaven. I take the hap
Of all my deeds. The wind that fills my sails,
Propels; but I am helmsman. Am I wrecked,

I know the devil has sufficient weight
To bear: I lay it not on him, or fate.
Besides, he's damned. That man I do suspect
A coward, who would burden the poor deuce
With what ensues from his own slipperiness.
I have just found a wanton-scented tress
In an old desk, dusty for lack of use.
Of days and nights it is demonstrative,
That, like some aged star, gleam luridly.
If for those times I must ask charity,
Have I not any charity to give?

XXI

We three are on the cedar-shadowed lawn;
My friend being third. He who at love once laughed
Is in the weak rib by a fatal shaft
Struck through, and tells his passion's bashful dawn
And radiant culmination, glorious crown,
When ' this ' she said: went ' thus ': most wondrous she.
Our eyes grow white, encountering: that we are three,
Forgetful; then together we look down.
But he demands our blessing; is convinced
That words of wedded lovers must bring good.
We question; if we dare! or if we should!
And pat him, with light laugh. We have not winced.
Next, she has fallen. Fainting points the sign
To happy things in wedlock. When she wakes,
She looks the star that thro' the cedar shakes:
Her lost moist hand clings mortally to mine.

XXII

What may the woman labour to confess?
There is about her mouth a nervous twitch.
'Tis something to be told, or hidden: — which?
I get a glimpse of hell in this mild guess.
She has desires of touch, as if to feel
That all the household things are things she knew.
She stops before the glass. What sight in view?
A face that seems the latest to reveal!

For she turns from it hastily, and tossed
Irresolute, steals shadow-like to where
I stand; and wavering pale before me there,
Her tears fall still as oak-leaves after frost.
She will not speak. I will not ask. We are
League-sundered by the silent gulf between.
You burly lovers on the village green,
Yours is a lower, and a happier star!

XXIX

Am I failing? For no longer can I cast
A glory round about this head of gold.
Glory she wears, but springing from the mould;
Not like the consecration of the Past!
Is my soul beggared? Something more than earth
I cry for still: I cannot be at peace
In having Love upon a mortal lease.
I cannot take the woman at her worth!
Where is the ancient wealth wherewith I clothed
Our human nakedness, and could endow
With spiritual splendour a white brow
That else had grinned at me the fact I loathed?
A kiss is but a kiss now! and no wave
Of a great flood that whirls me to the sea.
But, as you will! we'll sit contentedly,
And eat our pot of honey on the grave.

XXXIV

Madam would speak with me. So, now it comes:
The Deluge or else Fire! She's well; she thanks
My husbandship. Our chain on silence clanks.
Time leers between, above his twiddling thumbs.
Am I quite well? Most excellent in health!
The journals, too, I diligently peruse.
Vesuvius is expected to give news:
Niagara is no noisier. By stealth
Our eyes dart scrutinizing snakes. She's glad
I'm happy, says her quivering under-lip.
' And are not you? ' ' How can I be? ' ' Take ship!
For happiness is somewhere to be had.'

' Nowhere for me! ' Her voice is barely heard.
I am not melted, and make no pretence.
With commonplace I freeze her, tongue and sense.
Niagara or Vesuvius is deferred.

XLVI

At last we parley: we so strangely dumb
In such a close communion! It befell
About the sounding of the Matin-bell,
And lo! her place was vacant, and the hum
Of loneliness was round me. Then I rose,
And my disordered brain did guide my foot
To that old wood where our first love-salute
Was interchanged: the source of many throes!
There did I see her, not alone. I moved
Toward her, and made proffer of my arm.
She took it simply, with no rude alarm;
And that disturbing shadow passed reproved.
I felt the pained speech coming, and declared
My firm belief in her, ere she could speak.
A ghastly morning came into her cheek,
While with a widening soul on me she stared.

XLVII

We saw the swallows gathering in the sky,
And in the osier-isle we heard them noise.
We had not to look back on summer joys,
Or forward to a summer of bright dye:
But in the largeness of the evening earth
Our spirits grew as we went side by side.
The hour became her husband and my bride.
Love, that had robbed us so, thus blessed our dearth!
The pilgrims of the year waxed very loud
In multitudinous chatterings, as the flood
Full brown came from the West, and like pale blood
Expanded to the upper crimson cloud.
Love, that had robbed us of immortal things,
This little moment mercifully gave,
Where I have seen across the twilight wave
The swan sail with her young beneath her wings.

XLIX

He found her by the ocean's moaning verge,
Nor any wicked change in her discerned;
And she believed his old love had returned,
Which was her exultation, and her scourge.
She took his hand, and walked with him, and seemed
The wife he sought, though shadow-like and dry.
She had one terror, lest her heart should sigh,
And tell her loudly she no longer dreamed.
She dared not say, ' This is my breast: look in.'
But there's a strength to help the desperate weak.
That night he learned how silence best can speak
The awful things when Pity pleads for Sin.
About the middle of the night her call
Was heard, and he came wondering to the bed.
' Now kiss me, dear! it may be, now! ' she said.
Lethe had passed those lips, and he knew all.

L

Thus piteously Love closed what he begat:
The union of this ever-diverse pair!
These two were rapid falcons in a snare,
Condemned to do the flitting of the bat.
Lovers beneath the singing sky of May,
They wandered once; clear as the dew on flowers:
But they fed not on the advancing hours:
Their hearts held cravings for the buried day.
Then each applied to each that fatal knife,
Deep questioning, which probes to endless dole.
Ah, what a dusty answer gets the soul
When hot for certainties in this our life! —
In tragic hints here see what evermore
Moves dark as yonder midnight ocean's force,
Thundering like ramping hosts of warrior horse,
To throw that faint thin line upon the shore!

❖ GEORGE MEREDITH ❖

LUCIFER IN STARLIGHT

On a starred night Prince Lucifer uprose.
 Tired of his dark dominion swung the fiend
Above the rolling ball in cloud part screened,
Where sinners hugged their spectre of repose.
Poor prey to his hot fit of pride were those.
And now upon his western wing he leaned,
Now his huge bulk o'er Afric's sands careened,
Now the black planet shadowed Arctic snows.
Soaring through wider zones that pricked his scars
With memory of the old revolt from Awe,
He reached a middle height, and at the stars,
Which are the brain of heaven, he looked, and sank.
Around the ancient track marched, rank on rank,
The army of unalterable law.

DIRGE IN WOODS

A wind sways the pines,
   And below
Not a breath of wild air;
Still as the mosses that glow
On the flooring and over the lines
Of the roots here and there.
The pine-tree drops its dead;
They are quiet, as under the sea.
Overhead, overhead
Rushes life in a race,
As the clouds the clouds chase;
      And we go,
And we drop like the fruits of the tree,
      Even we,
      Even so.

SONG IN THE SONGLESS

They have no song, the sedges dry,
   And still they sing.
It is within my breast they sing,
   As I pass by.

Within my breast they touch a string,
 They wake a sigh.
There is but sound of sedges dry;
 In me they sing.

BREATH OF THE BRIAR

O briar-scents, on yon wet wing
 Of warm South-west wind brushing by,
You mind me of the sweetest thing
That ever mingled frank and shy:
When she and I, by love enticed,
Beneath the orchard-apples met,
In equal halves a ripe one sliced,
And smelt the juices ere we ate.

That apple of the briar-scent,
Among our lost in Britain now,
Was green of rind, and redolent
Of sweetness as a milking cow.
The briar gives it back, well nigh
The damsel with her teeth on it;
Her twinkle between frank and shy,
My thirst to bite where she had bit.

THE YEAR'S SHEDDINGS

The varied colours are a fitful heap:
 They pass in constant service though they sleep;
The self gone out of them, therewith the pain:
Read that, who still to spell our earth remain.

WOODLAND PEACE

Sweet as Eden is the air,
 And Eden-sweet the ray.
No Paradise is lost for them
Who foot by branching root and stem,
And lightly with the woodland share
 The change of night and day.

400

Here all say,
We serve her, even as I:
We brood, we strive to sky,
We gaze upon decay,
We wot of life through death,
How each feeds each we spy;
And is a tangle round,
Are patient; what is dumb,
We question not, nor ask
The silent to give sound,
The hidden to unmask,
The distant to draw near.

And this the woodland saith:
I know not hope or fear;
I take whate'er may come;
I raise my head to aspects fair,
From foul I turn away.

Sweet as Eden is the air,
    And Eden-sweet the ray.

THE LARK ASCENDING

He rises and begins to round,
    He drops the silver chain of sound,
Of many links without a break,
In chirrup, whistle, slur and shake,
All intervolved and spreading wide,
Like water-dimples down a tide
Where ripple ripple overcurls
And eddy into eddy whirls;
A press of hurried notes that run
So fleet they scarce are more than one,
Yet changeingly the trills repeat
And linger ringing while they fleet,
Sweet to the quick o' the ear, and dear
To her beyond the handmaid ear,
Who sits beside our inner springs,
Too often dry for this he brings,
Which seems the very jet of earth

At sight of sun, her music's mirth,
As up he wings the spiral stair,
A song of light, and pierces air
With fountain ardour, fountain play,
To reach the shining tops of day,
And drink in everything discerned,
An ecstasy to music turned,
Impelled by what his happy bill
Disperses; drinking, showering still,
Unthinking save that he may give
His voice the outlet, there to live
Renewed in endless notes of glee,
So thirsty of his voice is he,
For all to hear and all to know
That he is joy, awake, aglow,
The tumult of the heart to hear
Through pureness filtered crystal-clear,
And know the pleasure sprinkled bright
By simple singing of delight,
Shrill, irreflective, unrestrained,
Rapt, ringing, on the jet sustained
Without a break, without a fall,
Sweet-silvery, sheer lyrical,
Perennial, quavering up the chord
Like myriad dews of sunny sward
That trembling into fulness shine,
And sparkle dropping argentine;
Such wooing as the·ear receives
From zephyr caught in choric leaves
Of aspens when their chattering net
Is flushed to white with shivers wet;
And such the water-spirit's chime
On mountain heights in morning's prime,
Too freshly sweet to seem excess,
Too animate to need a stress;
But wider over many heads
The starry voice ascending spreads,
Awakening, as it waxes thin,
The best in us to him akin;
And every face to watch him raised,
Puts on the light of children praised,

❖ GEORGE MEREDITH ❖

So rich our human pleasure ripes
When sweetness on sincereness pipes,
Though nought be promised from the seas,
But only a soft-ruffling breeze
Sweep glittering on a still content,
Serenity in ravishment.

For singing till his heaven fills,
'Tis love of earth that he instills,
And ever winging up and up,
Our valley is his golden cup,
And he the wine which overflows
To lift us with him as he goes:
The woods and brooks, the sheep and kine,
He is, the hills, the human line,
The meadows green, the fallows brown,
The dreams of labour in the town;
He sings the sap, the quickened veins;
The wedding song of sun and rains
He is, the dance of children, thanks
Of sowers, shout of primrose-banks,
And eye of violets while they breathe;
All these the circling song will wreathe,
And you shall hear the herb and tree,
The better heart of men shall see,
Shall feel celestially, as long
As you crave nothing save the song.

Was never voice of ours could say
Our inmost in the sweetest way,
Like yonder voice aloft, and link
All hearers in the song they drink.
Our wisdom speaks from failing blood,
Our passion is too full in flood,
We want the key of his wild note
Of truthful in a tuneful throat,
The song seraphically free
Of taint of personality,
So pure that it salutes the suns,
The voice of one for millions,
In whom the millions rejoice
For giving their one spirit voice.

Yet men have we, whom we revere,
Now names, and men still housing here,
Whose lives, by many a battle-dint
Defaced, and grinding wheels on flint,
Yield substance, though they sing not, sweet
For song our highest heaven to greet:
Whom heavenly singing gives us new,
Enspheres them brilliant in our blue,
From firmest base to farthest leap,
Because their love of Earth is deep,
And they are warriors in accord
With life to serve, and pass reward,
So touching purest and so heard
In the brain's reflex of yon bird:
Wherefore their soul in me, or mine,
Through self-forgetfulness divine,
In them, that song aloft maintains,
To fill the sky and thrill the plains
With showerings drawn from human stores,
As he to silence nearer soars,
Extends the world at wings and dome,
More spacious making more our home,
Till lost on his aërial rings
In light, and then the fancy sings.

A BALLAD OF PAST MERIDIAN

Last night returning from my twilight walk
    I met the grey mist Death, whose eyeless brow
Was bent on me, and from his hand of chalk
He reached me flowers as from a withered bough:
O Death, what bitter nosegays givest thou!

Death said, I gather, and pursued his way.
Another stood by me, a shape in stone,
Sword-hacked and iron-stained, with breasts of clay,
And metal veins that sometimes fiery shone.
O Life, how naked and how hard when known!

Life said, As thou hast carved me, such am I.
Then memory, like the nightjar on the pine,
And sightless hope, a woodlark in night sky,
Joined notes of Death and Life till night's decline.
Of Death, of Life, those inwound notes are mine.

THE QUESTION WHITHER

When we have thrown off this old suit,
    So much in need of mending,
To sink among the naked mute,
    Is that, think you, our ending?
We follow many, more we lead,
    And you who sadly turf us,
Believe not that all living seed
    Must flower above the surface.

Sensation is a gracious gift,
    But were it cramped to station,
The prayer to have it cast adrift,
    Would spout from all sensation.
Enough if we have winked to sun,
    Have sped the plough a season;
There is a soul for labour done,
    Endureth fixed as reason.

Then let our trust be firm in Good,
    Though we be of the fasting;
Our questions are a mortal brood,
    Our work is everlasting.
We children of Beneficence
    Are in its being sharers;
And Whither vainer sounds than Whence,
    For word with such wayfarers.

HARD WEATHER

Bursts from a rending East in flaws
    The young green leaflet's harrier, sworn
To strew the garden, strip the shaws,
And show our Spring with banner torn.

Was ever such virago morn?
The wind has teeth, the wind has claws.
All the wind's wolves through woods are loose,
The wild wind's falconry aloft.
Shrill underfoot the grassblade shrews,
At gallop, clumped, and down the croft
Bestrid by shadows, beaten, tossed;
It seems a scythe, it seems a rod.
The howl is up at the howl's accost;
The shivers greet and the shivers nod.

Is the land ship? we are rolled, we drive
Tritonly, cleaving hiss and hum;
Whirl with the dead, or mount or dive,
Or down in dregs, or on in scum.
And drums the distant, pipes the near,
And vale and hill are grey in grey,
As when the surge is crumbling sheer,
And sea-mews wing the haze of spray.
Clouds — are they bony witches? — swarms,
Darting swift on the robber's flight,
Hurry an infant sky in arms:
It peeps, it becks; 'tis day, 'tis night.
Black while over the loop of blue
The swathe is closed, like shroud on corse.
Lo, as if swift the Furies flew,
The Fates at heel at a cry to horse!

Interpret me the savage whirr:
And is it Nature scourged, or she,
Her offspring's executioner,
Reducing land to barren sea?
But is there meaning in a day
When this fierce angel of the air,
Intent to throw, and haply slay,
Can for what breath of life we bear
Exact the wrestle? Call to mind
The many meanings glistening up
When Nature, to her nurslings kind,
Hands them the fruitage and the cup!

And seek we rich significance
Not otherwhere than with those tides
Of pleasure on the sunned expanse,
Whose flow deludes, whose ebb derides?

Look in the face of men who fare
Lock-mouthed, a match in lungs and thews
For this fierce angel of the air,
To twist with him and take his bruise.
That is the face beloved of old
Of Earth, young mother of her brood:
Nor broken for us shows the mould
When muscle is in mind renewed:
Though farther from her nature rude,
Yet nearer to her spirit's hold.
And though of gentler mood serene,
Still forceful of her fountain-jet.
So shall her blows be shrewdly met,
Be luminously read the scene
Where Life is at her grindstone set,
That she may give us edgeing keen,
String us for battle, till as play
The common strokes of fortune shower.
Such meaning in a dagger-day
Our wits may clasp to wax in power.
Yea, feel us warmer at her breast,
By spin of blood in lusty drill,
Than when her honeyed hands caressed,
And Pleasure, sapping, seemed to fill.

Behold the life at ease; it drifts.
The sharpened life commands its course.
She winnows, winnows roughly; sifts,
To dip her chosen in her source:
Contention is the vital force,
Whence pluck they brain, her prize of gifts,
Sky of the senses! on which height,
Not disconnected, yet released,
They see how spirit comes to light,
Through conquest of the inner beast,
Which Measure tames to movement sane,

407

In harmony with what is fair.
Never is Earth misread by brain:
That is the welling of her, there
The mirror: with one step beyond,
For likewise is it voice; and more,
Benignest kinship bids respond,
When wail the weak, and them restore
Whom days as fell as this may rive,
While Earth sits ebon in her gloom,
Us atomies of life alive
Unheeding, bent on life to come.
Her children of the labouring brain,
These are the champions of the race,
True parents, and the sole humane,
With understanding for their base.
Earth yields the milk, but all her mind
Is vowed to thresh for stouter stock.
Her passion for old giantkind,
That scaled the mount, uphurled the rock,
Devolves on them who read aright
Her meaning and devoutly serve;
Nor in her starlessness of night
Peruse her with the craven nerve:
But even as she from grass to corn,
To eagle high from grubbing mole,
Prove in strong brain her noblest born,
The station for the flight of soul.

MEDITATION UNDER STARS

What links are ours with orbs that are
    So resolutely far:
The solitary asks, and they
Give radiance as from a shield:
    Still at the death of day,
    The seen, the unrevealed.
    Implacable they shine
To us who would of Life obtain
An answer for the life we strain,
    To nourish with one sign.
Nor can imagination throw

The penetrative shaft: we pass
The breath of thought, who would divine
   If haply they may grow
As Earth; have our desire to know;
If life comes there to grain from grass,
And flowers like ours of toil and pain;
   Has passion to beat bar,
   Win space from cleaving brain;
   The mystic link attain,
   Whereby star holds on star.

Those visible immortals beam
   Allurement to the dream:
Ireful at human hungers brook
   No question in the look.
For ever virgin to our sense,
Remote they wane to gaze intense:
Prolong it, and in ruthlessness they smite
The beating heart behind the ball of sight:
   Till we conceive their heavens hoar,
   Those lights they raise but sparkles frore,
And Earth, our blood-warm Earth, a shuddering prey
To that frigidity of brainless ray.

Yet space is given for breath of thought
Beyond our bounds when musing: more
When to that musing love is brought,
And love is asked of love's wherefore.
'Tis Earth's her gift; else have we nought:
Her gift, her secret, here our tie.
And not with her and yonder sky?
Bethink you: were it Earth alone
Breeds love, would not her region be
   The sole delight and throne
   Of generous Deity?

   To deeper than this ball of sight
Appeal the lustrous people of the night.
Fronting yon shoreless, sown with fiery sails,
   It is our ravenous that quails,

Flesh by its craven thirsts and fears distraught.
   The spirit leaps alight,
   Doubts not in them is he,
The binder of his sheaves, the sane, the right:
Of magnitude to magnitude is wrought,
To feel it large of the great life they hold:
In them to come, or vaster intervolved,
The issues known in us, our unsolved solved:
That there with toil Life climbs the self-same Tree,
Whose roots enrichment have from ripeness dropped.
So may we read and little find them cold:
Let it but be the lord of Mind to guide
Our eyes; no branch of Reason's growing lopped;
Nor dreaming on a dream; but fortified
By day to penetrate black midnight; see,
Hear, feel, outside the senses; even that we,
The specks of dust upon a mound of mould,
We who reflect those rays, though low our place,
   To them are lastingly allied.

So may we read, and little find them cold:
Not frosty lamps illuming dead space,
Not distant aliens, not senseless Powers.
The fire is in them whereof we are born;
The music of their motion may be ours.
Spirit shall deem them beckoning Earth and voiced
Sisterly to her, in her beams rejoiced.
Of love, the grand impulsion, we behold
   The love that lends her grace
   Among the starry fold.
Then at new flood of customary morn,
   Look at her through her showers,
   Her mists, her streaming gold,
A wonder edges the familiar face:
She wears no more that robe of printed hours;
Half strange seems Earth, and sweeter than her flowers.

THOMAS HARDY
1840–1928

Thomas Hardy, the most completely and perfectly English of all English men of letters of the late Victorian period, was born in Higher Bockhampton, a little hamlet in Dorset, one of the southern English counties belonging to the district which he was to make world-known as Wessex. When he died in 1928 it was felt that the last link with the Victorian age was broken, yet Hardy, at least on one side of his life and work, belongs to an even earlier time. The England in which he spent his formative years was the old agricultural England little changed since Elizabethan times — Merry England in one sense, for it was a land of folk-song, folk-dance, balladry, church-choirs of fiddle, clarionet, and 'cello, of old tradition, superstition and much friendly neighbourliness. On the other hand life there was often hard and cruel. Hardy knew a shepherd boy who died of sheer starvation; he saw a man sitting in the village stocks and stood beside the gallows on which a woman was hanged. Until he was of age Hardy never left his native district for long; he came to know his Wessex as Sir Walter knew Edinburgh and the Scottish Border and he has left an imperishable record in prose and verse of a world that has vanished into what seems to us almost a historic past.

His ancestors traditionally traced their descent back to the son of a Clement le Hardy, Bailif of the Isle of Jersey, who settled in Dorset in the fifteenth century. Once a well-to-do and influential family they had come down in the world — like Tess's D'Urbervilles; his father was a small land-owner and local contractor; his mother was brought up in a household of poverty and hard work. But his father was a skilled musician and his mother an omnivorous reader and their eldest child, the novelist and poet, inherited these traits.

A delicate child, Hardy received a slight and somewhat irregular education; he attended a village school, studied a

little Latin and French, and fiddled at country dances. At six-
teen he was apprenticed to an architect in Dorchester. Here
for the next five years he led a busy and varied life; he read
his Latin classics, taught himself Greek, worked all day on
architectural drawing and at night played the part of unpaid
musician at some country dance or village festival. In 1862
he went to London to pursue his studies and remained there
for five years, enjoying the pleasures of a country lad in town,
music, dancing, and the play. Before the close of this period
he was writing verses which were to find no publisher for
many years. His genius was one that ripened slowly. He said
of himself: ' I was a child till I was sixteen; a youth till I was
twenty-five; a young man till I was forty or fifty.'

In 1869 he returned to Dorchester, resumed work with his
old master and began the composition of his first novel, *The
Poor Man and the Lady,* a vigorous and sweeping social
satire. The manuscript came into the hands of George Mere-
dith, then reader for Chapman and Hall, who strongly ad-
vised against publication but suggested his trying a more
carefully planned and less radical novel. Hardy took his ad-
vice, threw away his first book, and set himself to work again.
In 1871 his *Desperate Remedies* was published anonymously
and at his own expense — he is said to have lost £15 by the
venture. His fourth novel, *Far From the Madding Crowd,*
which appeared serially in the *Cornhill Magazine* (1874), was
Hardy's first popular success. It was written in the country, in
part out of doors, on whatever material came to the author's
hand, a scrap of paper, a chip of wood, or a broken piece of
slate.

From this time on for the next twenty years Hardy's life
was that of the popular and successful novelist. His tragic
tale of *Tess* (1891), however, was rejected by two magazines
and he was forced to bowdlerize it before it saw print in a
third. His last novel, *Jude the Obscure* (1895), like *Tess,* was
heavily cut for periodical publication; its appearance in book
form was greeted with a howl of vituperation such as had not
been heard since the appearance of *Poems and Ballads.*
Hardy was flooded with abusive letters; a bishop wrote to the
papers to say that he had burned the book and attempted to
stop its circulation in lending libraries. The result was curi-
ous but by no means inexplicable; Hardy stopped writing

novels altogether and for the rest of his life said what he had to say in verse.

The common notion that Hardy suddenly switched from fiction to poetry is of course erroneous. He had been writing verse at intervals from early youth, had laid it aside during his long years as a novelist, and now returned to it when he felt that self-respect would no longer permit him to endure the slings and arrows of public abuse. And there was another reason: ' Perhaps,' he said, ' I can express more fully in verse ideas and emotions which run counter to the inert crystallized opinion — hard as a rock — which the vast body of men have vested interests in supporting. To cry out in a passionate poem that the Supreme Mover . . . must be either limited in power, unknowing or cruel . . . will cause them merely a shake of the head, but to put it in argumentative prose will make them sneer or foam and set all the literary contortionists jumping upon me, a harmless agnostic, as if I were a clamorous atheist.' And so for the next thirty years Hardy returned to his first love. His volumes of verse reach from *Wessex Poems* in 1898 to *Winter Words* in the year of his death and include his epic drama of the Napoleonic wars, *The Dynasts* (1903–8), the most ambitious and magnificent achievement in modern English poetry. There is a certain irony, which Hardy must have appreciated to the full, in the fact that the much abused novelist was in his last years honoured as no English man of letters but Tennyson had ever been. He was recognized by all good judges as the Dean of living English writers; King George invested him with the Order of Merit in 1910; he received the Gold Medal of the Royal Society of Literature in 1912; he was made LL.D. and D.C.L. by various English and Scottish universities. When he died in 1928 his heart was buried where it belonged in a country churchyard of his own Wessex; his ashes were interred in the Poet's Corner of Westminster Abbey.

There has been a tendency in the criticism of Hardy's work to consider him as a philosopher rather than as a poet and to stigmatize him as a gloomy pessimist. This is quite wrong. The philosophy that underlies Hardy's poetry is in the main that of the scientifically dominated nineteenth century. What he himself considered his one original contribution, the conception that the unconscious Will behind all natural phe-

413

nomena and all human life may at long last grow conscious and take on the human attributes of sympathy and pity, is a poet's dream rather than a philosopher's dogma. Hardy at times admitted his pessimism; occasionally he denied it and called himself an evolutionary meliorist. Certainly he tended to look at the darker side of life; his was a nature that, to use his own words, became ' vocal at tragedy rather than at comedy.' But even so there were compensations: memories grave and gay, the gentler aspects of nature, the ' higher loyalties ' that lift the race of man above the animal world; best of all, perhaps, the consciousness of honesty in facing life and the poet's just pride in the mastery of his art. Certainly it is not as a pessimist or a philosopher that Hardy will be remembered in the years to come, but as a poet.

Of Hardy's poetry it is perhaps too soon to pronounce the final judgment. It is in a very real sense ' new poetry ' and marks the furthest departure from the decorated, didactic, and idealistic standard of Victorian verse — a fact the more remarkable since Hardy began to write poetry at a time when the influence of Tennyson was all-powerful. Certain affinities with earlier poets, Wordsworth, for example, and Browning, can be easily traced, but Hardy is an original as he is a revolutionary poet. His influence upon later poetry has been very marked and the time may come when Hardy will be considered a liberator and inspirer as Wordsworth was. He has left a great mass of poetry that ranges from the gigantic *Dynasts* to the simplest and briefest lyric. It might be roughly divided into three classes: tales, philosophic poems, and pure lyrics. The tales, comic, satiric, tragic, represent to some extent Hardy the novelist writing in verse. Of many of them one might ask what, if anything, has been gained by their verse form. The best of them are those that deal, like the best of Hardy's prose, with the life of his Wessex peasants — *The Dead Choir,* for example, or *A Tramp-Woman's Tragedy*. Hardy was an Antaeus who drew strength in verse as in prose from contact with his native soil. The philosophic poems are characterized not only by Hardy's sincerity and frankness, but by an extraordinary power and sweep of imagination as in *God-Forgotten, New Year's Eve, The Convergence of Twain.* They form, so to speak, a lyric chorus to the epic-dramatic presentation of his thought in *The Dynasts*.

414

✤ THOMAS HARDY ✤

Of the lyrics, which compose the main body of Hardy's verse, it is difficult to speak generally and impartially. Some of them are breath-taking in their simple loveliness. On the other hand Hardy is not at all times the clear-voiced singer; his 'muted music' sometimes falters and jars. His dislike of 'poetic diction,' his desire to use the simplest speech of men, often breaks in upon his verse with a flat prosaic word or phrase. No English poet, not even Browning, has taken quite such liberties with the language, and at times this liberty seems to degenerate into licence. Yet his best lyrics, such as *The Voice of the Thorn, Seasons of Her Year, Rain on a Grave,* seem to sing themselves with a simplicity, directness, and poignancy unmatched in English poetry since Words-worth. And Hardy has, what Wordsworth lacked, an immense technical control of metre and rhythm. The old country music of his youth lies behind much of his verse; its sweet and simple tunes, its turns and trills, pauses, refrains, and repetitions. Here as everywhere Hardy is at his best when he is nearest home in Wessex. Realism, sincerity, breadth of view, and homeliness, these are the chief and abiding characteristics of Hardy's verse. Not one of the greatest of English poets, perhaps, but one who has his own peculiar charm, a certain wistful appeal for sympathy and for pity in the tangled skein of human life. He is not an easy poet to come in close touch with: in the words of a greater poet:

> You must love him, ere to you
> He will seem worthy of your love.

THE OXEN

Christmas Eve, and twelve of the clock.
   'Now they are all on their knees,'
An elder said as we sat in a flock
   By the embers in hearthside ease.

We pictured the meek mild creatures where
   They dwelt in their strawy pen,
Nor did it occur to one of us there
   To doubt they were kneeling then.

415

So fair a fancy few would weave
    In these years! Yet, I feel,
If someone said on Christmas Eve,
    ' Come; see the oxen kneel,

' In the lonely barton by yonder coomb
    Our childhood used to know,'
I should go with him in the gloom,
    Hoping it might be so.

THE DEAD QUIRE

I

Beside the Mead of Memories,
    Where Church-way mounts to Moaning Hill,
The sad man sighed his phantasies:
    He seems to sigh them still.

II

' 'Twas the Birth-tide Eve, and the hamleteers
Made merry with ancient Mellstock zest,
But the Mellstock quire of former years
    Had entered into rest.

III

' Old Dewy lay by the gaunt yew tree,
And Reuben and Michael a pace behind,
And Bowman with his family
    By the wall that the ivies bind.

IV

' The singers had followed one by one,
Treble, and tenor, and thorough-bass;
And the worm that wasteth had begun
    To mine their mouldering place.

416

V

'For two-score years, ere Christ-day light,
Mellstock had throbbed to strains from these;
But now there echoed on the night
    No Christmas harmonies.

VI

'Three meadows off, at a dormered inn,
The youth had gathered in high carouse,
And, ranged on settles, some therein
    Had drunk them to a drowse.

VII

'Loud, lively, reckless, some had grown,
Each dandling on his jigging knee
Eliza, Dolly, Nance, or Joan —
    Livers in levity.

VIII

'The taper flames and hearthfire shine
Grew smoke-hazed to a lurid light,
And songs on subjects not divine
    Were warbled forth that night.

IX

'Yet many were sons and grandsons here
Of those who, on such eves gone by,
At that still hour had throated clear ·
    Their anthems to the sky.

X

'The clock belled midnight; and ere long
One shouted, " Now 'tis Christmas morn;
Here's to our women old and young,
    And to John Barleycorn! "

XI

' They drink the toast and shout again:
The pewter-ware rings back the boom,
And for a breath-while follows then
    A silence in the room.

XII

' When nigh without, as in old days,
The ancient quire of voice and string
Seemed singing words of prayer and praise
    As they had used to sing:

XIII

' *While shepherds watch'd their flocks by night,* —
Thus swells the long familiar sound
In many a quaint symphonic flight —
    To, *Glory shone around.*

XIV

' The sons defined their fathers' tones,
The widow his whom she had wed,
And others in the minor moans
    The viols of the dead.

XV

' Something supernal has the sound,
As verse by verse the strain proceeds,
And stilly staring on the ground
    Each roysterer holds and heeds.

XVI

' Towards its chorded closing bar
Plaintively, thinly, waned the hymn,
Yet lingered, like the notes afar
    Of banded seraphim.

XVII

' With brows abashed, and reverent tread,
The hearkeners sought the tavern door:
But nothing, save wan moonlight, spread
    The empty highway o'er.

XVIII

' While on their hearing fixed and tense
The aerial music seemed to sink,
As it were gently moving thence
    Along the river brink.

XIX

' Then did the Quick pursue the Dead
By crystal Froom that crinkles there;
And still the viewless quire ahead
    Voiced the old holy air.

XX

' By Bank-wall wicket, brightly bleached,
It passed, and 'twixt the hedges twain,
Dogged by the living; till it reached
    The bottom of Church Lane.

XXI

' There, at the turning, it was heard
Drawing to where the churchyard lay:
But when they followed thitherward
    It smalled, and died away.

XXII

' Each headstone of the quire, each mound,
Confronted them beneath the moon;
But no more floated therearound
    That ancient Birth-night tune.

XXIII

' There Dewy lay by the gaunt yew tree,
There Reuben and Michael, a pace behind,
And Bowman with his family
  By the wall that the ivies bind. . . .

XXIV

' As from a dream each sobered son
Awoke, and musing reached his door:
'Twas said that of them all, not one
  Sat in a tavern more.'

XXV

— The sad man ceased; and ceased to heed
His listener, and crossed the leaze
From Moaning Hill towards the mead —
  The Mead of Memories.

FRIENDS BEYOND

William Dewy, Tranter Reuben, Farmer Ledlow late at
      plough,
  Robert's kin, and John's, and Ned's,
And the Squire, and Lady Susan, lie in Mellstock churchyard
  now!

' Gone,' I call them, gone for good, that group of local hearts
  and heads;
  Yet at mothy curfew-tide,
And at midnight when the noon-heat breathes it back from
  walls and leads,

They've a way of whispering to me — fellow-wight who yet
  abide —
  In the muted, measured note
Of a ripple under archways, or a lone cave's stillicide:

❖ THOMAS HARDY ❖

' We have triumphed: this achievement turns the bane to
   antidote,
   Uusuccesses to success,
Many thought-worn eves and morrows to a morrow free of
   thought.

' No more need we corn and clothing, feel of old terrestrial
   stress;
   Chill detraction stirs no sigh;
Fear of death has even bygone us: death gave all that we pos-
   sess.'

W. D. — ' Ye mid burn the old bass-viol that I set such value
   by.'
   Squire. — ' You may hold the manse in fee,
You may wed my spouse, may let my children's memory of me
   die.'

Lady S. — ' You may have my rich brocades, my laces; take
   each household key;
   Ransack coffer, desk, bureau;
Quiz the few poor treasures hid there, con the letters kept by
   me.'

Far. — ' Ye mid zell my favourite heifer, ye mid let the char-
   lock grow,
   Foul the grinterns, give up thrift.'
Far. Wife. — ' If ye break my best blue china, children, I shan't
   care or ho.'

All. — ' We've no wish to hear the tidings, how the people's
   fortunes shift;
   What your daily doings are;
Who are wedded, born, divided; if your lives beat slow or
   swift.

' Curious not the least are we if our intents you make or mar,
   If you quire to our old tune,
If the City stage still passes, if the weirs still roar afar.'

421

— Thus, with very gods' composure, freed those crosses late
    and soon
  Which in life, the Trine allow
(Why, none witteth) , and ignoring all that haps beneath the
    moon,

William Dewy, Tranter Reuben, Farmer Ledlow late at
    plough,
  Robert's kin, and John's, and Ned's,
And the Squire, and Lady Susan, murmur mildly to me now.

A SINGER ASLEEP

(Algernon Charles Swinburne, 1837–1909)

I

In this fair niche above the unslumbering sea,
  That sentrys up and down all night, all day,
From cove to promontory, from ness to bay,
The Fates have fitly bidden that he should be
  Pillowed eternally.

II

— It was as though a garland of red roses
Had fallen about the hood of some smug nun
When irresponsibly dropped as from the sun,
In fulth of numbers freaked with musical closes,
Upon Victoria's formal middle time
  His leaves of rhythm and rhyme.

III

O that far morning of a summer day
When, down a terraced street whose pavements lay
Glassing the sunshine into my bent eyes,
I walked and read with a quick glad surprise
  New words, in classic guise, —

IV

The passionate pages of his earlier years,
Fraught with hot sighs, sad laughters, kisses, tears;
Fresh-fluted notes, yet from a minstrel who
Blew them not naïvely, but as one who knew
     Full well why thus he blew.

V

I still can hear the brabble and the roar
At those thy tunes, O still one, now passed through
That fitful fire of tongues then entered new!
Their power is spent like spindrift on this shore;
     Thine swells yet more and more.

VI

— His singing-mistress verily was no other
Than she the Lesbian, she the music-mother
Of all the tribe that feel in melodies;
Who leapt, love-anguished, from the Leucadian steep
Into the rambling world-encircling deep
     Which hides her where none sees.

VII

And one can hold in thought that nightly here
His phantom may draw down to the water's brim,
And hers come up to meet it, as a dim
Lone shine upon the heaving hydrosphere,
And mariners wonder as they traverse near,
     Unknowing of her and him.

VIII

One dreams him sighing to her spectral form:
' O teacher, where lies hid thy burning line;
Where are those songs, O poetess divine
Whose very orts are love incarnadine? '
And her smile back: ' Disciple true and warm,
     Sufficient now are thine.' . . .

IX

So here, beneath the waking constellations,
Where the waves peal their everlasting strains,
And their dull subterrene reverbations
Shake him when storms make mountains of their plains —
Him once their peer in sad improvisations,
And deft as wind to cleave their frothy manes —
I leave him, while the daylight gleam declines
    Upon the capes and chines.

IN A WOOD

From ' *The Woodlanders* '

Pale beech and pine so blue,
    Set in one clay,
Bough to bough cannot you
    Live out your day?
When the rains skim and skip,
Why mar sweet comradeship,
Blighting with poison-drip
    Neighbourly spray?

Heart-halt and spirit-lame,
    City-opprest,
Unto this wood I came
    As to a nest;
Dreaming that sylvan peace
Offered the harrowed ease —
Nature a soft release
    From men's unrest.

But, having entered in,
    Great growths and small
Show them to men akin —
    Combatants all!
Sycamore shoulders oak,
Bines the slim sapling yoke,
Ivy-spun halters choke
    Elms stout and tall.

Touches from ash, O wych,
   Sting you like scorn!
You, too, brave hollies, twitch
   Sidelong from thorn.
Even the rank poplars bear
Lothly a rival's air,
Cankering in black despair
   If overborne.

Since, then, no grace I find
   Taught me of trees,
Turn I back to my kind,
   Worthy as these.
There at least smiles abound,
There discourse trills around,
There, now and then, are found
   Life-loyalties.

THE DARKLING THRUSH

I leant upon a coppice gate
   When Frost was spectre-gray,
And Winter's dregs made desolate
   The weakening eye of day.
The tangled bine-stems scored the sky
   Like strings of broken lyres,
And all mankind that haunted night
   Had sought their household fires.

The land's sharp features seemed to be
   The Century's corpse outleant,
His crypt the cloudy canopy,
   The wind his death-lament.
The ancient pulse of germ and birth
   Was shrunken hard and dry,
And every spirit upon earth
   Seemed fervourless as I.

At once a voice arose among
   The bleak twigs overhead
In a full-hearted evensong
   Of joy illimited;

An aged thrush, frail, gaunt, and small,
    In blast-beruffled plume,
Had chosen thus to fling his soul
    Upon the growing gloom.

So little cause for carolings
    Of such ecstatic sound
Was written on terrestrial things
    Afar or nigh around,
That I could think there trembled through
    His happy good-night air
Some blessed Hope, whereof he knew
    And I was unaware.

THE IMPERCIPIENT

(*At a Cathedral Service*)

That with this bright believing band
    I have no claim to be,
That faiths by which my comrades stand
    Seem fantasies to me,
And mirage-mists their Shining Land,
    Is a strange destiny.

Why thus my soul should be consigned
    To infelicity,
Why always I must feel as blind
    To sights my brethren see,
Why joys they've found I cannot find,
    Abides a mystery.

Since heart of mine knows not that ease
    Which they know; since it be
That He who breathes All's Well to these
    Breathes no All's-Well to me,
My lack might move their sympathies
    And Christian charity!

426

I am like a gazer who should mark
    An inland company
Standing upfingered, with, ' Hark! hark!
    The glorious distant sea! '
And feel, ' Alas, 'tis but yon dark
    And wind-swept pine to me! '

Yet I would bear my shortcomings
    With meet tranquillity,
But for the charge that blessed things
    I'd liefer not have be.
O, doth a bird deprived of wings
    Go earth-bound wilfully!

.   .   .   .   .   .

Enough. As yet disquiet clings
    About us. Rest shall we.

NEW YEAR'S EVE

I have finished another year,' said God,
    ' In grey, green, white, and brown;
I have strewn the leaf upon the sod,
Sealed up the worm within the clod,
    And let the last sun down.'

' And what's the good of it? ' I said,
    ' What reasons made you call
From formless void this earth we tread,
When nine-and-ninety can be read
    Why nought should be at all?

' Yea, Sire; why shaped you us, " who in
    This tabernacle groan " —
If ever a joy be found herein,
Such joy no man had wished to win
    If he had never known! '

Then he: ' My labours — logicless —
    You may explain; not I:
Sense-sealed I have wrought, without a guess
That I evolved a Consciousness
    To ask for reasons why.

427

' Strange that ephemeral creatures who
   By my own ordering are,
Should see the shortness of my view,
Use ethic tests I never knew,
   Or made provision for! '

He sank to raptness as of yore,
   And opening New Year's Day
Wove it by rote as theretofore,
And went on working evermore
   In his unweeting way.

A. E. HOUSMAN
1859–   *

The little that is known of Mr. Housman's life does little enough to explain his poetry; and this, apparently, is as he would have it. He is, of all living writers, the least communicative; it seems impossible to discover even where he was born. Yet some few facts are known and they are not without significance.

He received the usual public school education of an English boy, went to Oxford, failed, we are told, in his final examinations in classics and philosophy, and went to London where he became for ten years a clerk in the Patent Office. Long and diligent study of the classics he had neglected in college made him one of the most able, accurate, and, as the phrase goes, scientific scholars living. He was appointed Professor of Latin at University College, London, a post which he held for ten years, and then removed to Cambridge where he still lives Professor of Latin, Fellow of Trinity, editor of the obscurest of Latin poets, contributor to classical journals, and devastating critic of other less accurate and scientific scholars. He has published two small volumes of verse, *A Shropshire Lad* (1896) and *Last Poems* (1922). Is it possible to trace a connexion between such an uneventful life and the tone, the temper, the exquisite finish of his matchless and peculiarly individual lyric verse? Hardly, it would seem; but possibly the poet himself furnishes a clue.

Mr. Housman tells us in the preface to *Last Poems* that the greater part of his first book was written under a ' continuous excitement in the early months of 1895.' That would be shortly after he had emerged from the ten years of drudgery as a clerk in London, ten years in which, apparently, the iron had entered deep into his soul. He did not succumb, he fought his way through and gained a post of some reputation and fixed security. Then, we may imagine, came a shock of some sort which unsealed the hidden spring and allowed the poems of the *Shropshire Lad* to gush forth, a clear, sparkling, but shortlived stream. The preface to *Last Poems* goes on to say that most of the lyrics of that volume — shorter by half than the *Shropshire Lad* — date between '95 and 1910 — these the last running of the first inspiration — and about a quarter of them belong to April of 1922, a belated afterglow — to change the figure — of his lyric gift. Since 1910 Mr. Housman has written only a little handful of lyrics; he has renounced poetry for scholarship, the laurel for the critic's rule and measure.

It is possible, perhaps, with the exercise of some imagination to paint a picture, suggestive if not altogether accurate. Here is a country boy in London, affected by deadly nostalgia for the country sights and sounds, ' the happy highways where he went and cannot come again.' There are no such sights and sounds in London, ' only men,' and men ' too unhappy to be kind.' There are no *London Voluntaries* in Mr. Housman's work, no record of friends or lovers in the great city. His one helper seems to have been a Grecian statue whose ' earnest and grave regard ' bade him endure, be strong. Is this perhaps an allegory of the studies which helped the poet through those early years? This at least we may say: those studies gave the poet a perfection and refinement of form, a gift for saying or implying much in a few brief lines, for which in English poetry we must go back to Landor and behind Landor to the poets of the Greek *Anthology*.

The greater part of Housman's poetry is set in a very definite framework. He has revealed, perhaps created would be the better word, a Shropshire that is a poetic parallel to Hardy's Wessex. And he has peopled this country with lads and lasses who are, it must be said, a singularly unhappy lot. They kill each other and themselves, lie long in jail, die on the gallows. The most notable trait of the girls seems to be their inconstancy; they are quick to forget dead lovers and lie beside another lad. And the poet assumes, for the most part, the rustic mask of one of these lads. It is not always a satisfactory disguise. Even if one knew nothing of Housman the scholar it would be difficult to identify Housman the poet with the Terence who eats his victuals fast enough. One does not expect a Shropshire lad to break out with such a tragic indictment of the universe as rings through the lines of ' Be

still, my soul,' or to trace the truceless battle in his heart to
the age-long warfare of races on the Welsh Marches. But in
one way at least this mask has justified the wearing; it has
prompted the poet to speak with a homely vigour that was
rare enough among the poets of the '90's. There is hardly a
word or phrase in the two volumes that might not have been
spoken by a Shropshire lad who had read his Bible in youth
and listened to the liturgy in an English church.

Behind the mask one catches glimpses of an unhappy and
disillusioned poet; Nature to him is no kindly mother, but
prompt to send a storm to make an end of May. Man delights
him not; youth passes, age brings degeneration, and death
ends all. There is no grimmer poem in English than that in
which the bones that make man's skeleton complain of their
servitude and long for the time when they may lie in peace,
and these bones the poet calls the *Immortal Part* destined to
last for ages after ' the fire of sense, the smoke of thought '
are blown clean away. Bitter pessimism all this, and it would
be as useless as impossible for the critic to deny or evade it.
But even to the bitterest pessimist there are certain compensa-
tions and these appear from time to time in Housman's work.
There is still the beauty of nature; man may pass but still
the loveliest of trees is ' hung with bloom along the bough,'
and the memory lingers of ' the quietest places under the sun,'
a wistful memory that finds its perfect expression in the last
of the *Last Poems, Fancy's Knell*. And there is the trained and
hardened stoicism with which the poet faces the heavy burden
of life — ' bear it we can, and if we can we must.' He has laid
to heart the story of the Spartans who sat down and combed
their hair before the battle that was to end them. ' Trouble's
sure ' in this ill-made world but he bids us

> face it as a wise man would,
> And train for ill and not for good.

The very bitterness of his verse may be, he thinks, a tonic and
an antidote to weaker men.

And finally there is the supreme compensation of art. To
praise the art of Housman would be a waste of words. The
subtle variation of flow and pause in his apparently simple
metres, the haunting melody of certain songs, these — to speak
of nothing else — are eloquent of the craftsman's mastery of

431

and delight in his art. Life in the world is not wholly worthless to the singer who can set youth dancing to his music, who can lift

> the light delaying,
> And flute the sun to sleep.

From *A SHROPSHIRE LAD*

II

LOVELIEST OF TREES

Loveliest of trees, the cherry now
  Is hung with bloom along the bough,
And stands about the woodland ride
Wearing white for Eastertide.

Now, of my threescore years and ten,
Twenty will not come again,
And take from seventy springs a score,
It only leaves me fifty more.

And since to look at things in bloom
Fifty springs are little room,
About the woodlands I will go
To see the cherry hung with snow.

IV

REVEILLE

Wake: the silver dusk returning
    Up the beach of darkness brims,
And the ship of sunrise burning
    Strands upon the eastern rims.

Wake: the vaulted shadow shatters,
    Trampled to the floor it spanned,
And the tent of night in tatters
    Straws the sky-pavilioned land.

Up, lad, up, 'tis late for lying:
　　Hear the drums of morning play;
Hark, the empty highways crying,
　　' Who'll beyond the hills away? '

Towns and countries woo together,
　　Forelands beacon, belfries call;
Never lad that trod on leather
　　Lived to feast his heart with all.

Up, lad: thews that lie and cumber
　　Sunlit pallets never thrive;
Morns abed and daylight slumber
　　Were not meant for man alive.

Clay lies still, but blood's a rover;
　　Breath's a ware that will not keep.
Up, lad; when the journey's over
　　There'll be time enough to sleep.

VII

WHEN SMOKE STOOD UP FROM LUDLOW

When smoke stood up from Ludlow,
　　And mist blew off from Teme,
And blithe afield to ploughing
　　Against the morning beam
　　I strode beside my team,

The blackbird in the coppice
　　Looked out to see me stride,
And hearkened as I whistled
　　The trampling team beside,
　　And fluted and replied:

' Lie down, lie down, young yeoman;
　　What use to rise and rise?
Rise man a thousand mornings'
　　Yet down at last he lies,
　　And then the man is wise.'

I heard the tune he sang me,
   And spied his yellow bill;
I picked a stone and aimed it
   And threw it with a will:
   Then the bird was still.

Then my soul within me
   Took up the blackbird's strain,
And still beside the horses
   Along the dewy lane
   It sang the song again:

' Lie down, lie down, young yeoman;
   The sun moves always west;
The road one treads to labour
   Will lead one home to rest,
   And that will be the best.'

IX

ON MOONLIT HEATH

On moonlit heath and lonesome bank
   The sheep beside me graze;
And yon the gallows used to clank
   Fast by the four cross ways.

A careless shepherd once would keep
   The flocks by moonlight there,
And high amongst the glimmering sheep
   The dead man stood on air.

They hang us now in Shrewsbury jail:
   The whistles blow forlorn,
And trains all night groan on the rail
   To men that die at morn.

There sleeps in Shrewsbury jail tonight,
   Or wakes, as may betide,
A better lad, if things went right,
   Than most that sleep outside.

And naked to the hangman's noose
  The morning clocks will ring
A neck God made for other use
  Than strangling in a string.

And sharp the link of life will snap,
  And dead on air will stand
Heels that held up as straight a chap
  As treads upon the land.

So here I'll watch the night and wait
  To see the morning shine,
When he will hear the stroke of eight
  And not the stroke of nine;

And wish my friend as sound a sleep
  As lads' I did not know,
That shepherded the moonlit sheep
  A hundred years ago.

XIX

TO AN ATHLETE DYING YOUNG

The time you won your town the race
  We chaired you through the market-place;
Man and boy stood cheering by,
And home we brought you shoulder-high.

Today, the road all runners come,
Shoulder-high we bring you home,
And set you at your threshold down,
Townsman of a stiller town.

Smart lad, to slip betimes away
From fields where glory does not stay
And early though the laurel grows
It withers quicker than the rose.

Eyes the shady night has shut
Cannot see the record cut,
And silence sounds no worse than cheers
After earth has stopped the ears:

Now you will not swell the rout
Of lads that wore their honours out,
Runners whom renown outran
And the name died before the man.

So set, before its echoes fade,
The fleet foot on the sill of shade,
And hold to the low lintel up
The still-defended challenge-cup.

And round that early-laureled head
Will flock to gaze the strengthless dead,
And find unwithered on its curls
The garland briefer than a girl's.

XXI

BREDON HILL

In summertime on Bredon
  The bells they sound so clear;
Round both the shires they ring them
  In steeples far and near,
  A happy noise to hear.

Here of a Sunday morning
  My love and I would lie,
And see the coloured counties,
  And hear the larks so high
  About us in the sky.

The bells would ring to call her
  In valleys miles away:
'Come all to church, good people;
  Good people, come and pray.'
  But here my love would stay.

And I would turn and answer
  Among the springing thyme,
'Oh, peal upon our wedding,
  And we will hear the chime,
  And come to church in time.'

But when the snows at Christmas
   On Bredon top were strown,
My love rose up so early
   And stole out unbeknown
   And went to church alone.

They tolled the one bell only,
   Groom there was none to see,
The mourners followed after,
   And so to church went she,
   And would not wait for me.

The bells they sound on Bredon,
   And still the steeples hum.
'Come all to church, good people,' —
   Oh, noisy bells, be dumb;
   I hear you, I will come.

XXVI

ALONG THE FIELD

Along the field as we came by
   A year ago, my love and I,
The aspen over stile and stone
Was talking to itself alone.
'Oh who are these that kiss and pass?
A country lover and his lass;
Two lovers looking to be wed;
And time shall put them both to bed,
But she shall lie with earth above,
And he beside another love.'

And sure enough beneath the tree
There walks another love with me,
And overhead the aspen heaves
Its rainy-sounding silver leaves;
And I spell nothing in their stir,
But now perhaps they speak to her,

And plain for her to understand
They talk about a time at hand
When I shall sleep with clover clad,
And she beside another lad.

XXVIII

THE WELSH MARCHES

High the vanes of Shrewsbury gleam
Islanded in Severn stream;
The bridges from the steepled crest
Cross the water east and west.

The flag of morn in conqueror's state
Enters at the English gate:
The vanquished eve, as night prevails,
Bleeds upon the road to Wales.

Ages since the vanquished bled
Round my mother's marriage-bed;
There the ravens feasted far
About the open house of war.

When Severn down to Buildwas ran,
Coloured with the death of man,
Couched upon her brother's grave
The Saxon got me on the slave.

The sound of fight is silent long
That began the ancient wrong;
Long the voice of tears is still
That wept of old the endless ill.

In my heart it has not died,
The war that sleeps on Severn side;
They cease not fighting, east and west,
On the marches of my breast.

Here the truceless armies yet
Trample, rolled in blood and sweat,
They kill and kill and never die;
And I think that each is I.

None will part us, none undo
The knot that makes one flesh of two,
Sick with hatred, sick with pain,
Strangling — When shall we be slain?

When shall I be dead and rid
Of the wrong my father did?
How long, how long, till spade and hearse
Put to sleep my mother's curse?

XXXI

ON WENLOCK EDGE

On Wenlock Edge the wood's in trouble,
   His forest fleece the Wrekin heaves;
The gale, it plies the saplings double,
And thick on Severn snow the leaves.

'Twould blow like this through holt and hanger
When Uricon the city stood:
'Tis the old wind in the old anger,
But then it threshed another wood.

Then, 'twas before my time, the Roman
At yonder heaving hill would stare:
The blood that warms an English yeoman,
The thoughts that hurt him, they were there.

There, like the wind through woods in riot,
Through him the gale of life blew high;
The tree of man was never quiet:
Then 'twas the Roman, now 'tis I.

The gale, it plies the saplings double,
It blows so hard, 'twill soon be gone:
To-day the Roman and his trouble
Are ashes under Uricon.

XL

INTO MY HEART

Into my heart an air that kills
　From yon far country blows:
What are those blue remembered hills,
　What spires, what farms are those?

That is the land of lost content,
　I see it shining plain,
The happy highways where I went
　And cannot come again.

XLIII

THE IMMORTAL PART

When I meet the morning beam,
　Or lay me down at night to dream,
I hear my bones within me say,
'Another night, another day.

'When shall this slough of sense be cast,
This dust of thoughts be laid at last,
The man of flesh and soul be slain
And the man of bone remain?

'This tongue that talks, these lungs that shout,
These thews that hustle us about,
This brain that fills the skull with schemes,
And its humming hive of dreams, —

'These to-day are proud in power
And lord it in their little hour:
The immortal bones obey control
Of dying flesh and dying soul.

' 'Tis long till eve and morn are gone:
Slow the endless night comes on,
And late to fulness grows the birth
That shall last as long as earth.

'Wanderers eastward, wanderers west,
Know you why you cannot rest?
'Tis that every mother's son
Travails with a skeleton.

'Lie down in the bed of dust;
Bear the fruit that bear you must;
Bring the eternal seed to light,
And morn is all the same as night.

'Rest you so from trouble sore,
Fear the heat o' the sun no more,
Nor the snowing winter wild,
Now you labour not with child.

'Empty vessel, garment cast,
We that wore you long shall last.
— Another night, another day.'
So my bones within me say.

Therefore they shall do my will
To-day while I am master still,
And flesh and soul, now both are strong,
Shall hale the sullen slaves along,

Before this fire of sense decay,
This smoke of thought blow clean away,
And leave with ancient night alone
The steadfast and enduring bone.

XLVIII

BE STILL, MY SOUL, BE STILL

Be still, my soul, be still; the arms you bear are brittle,
    Earth and high heaven are fixt of old and founded
        strong.
Think rather, — call to thought, if now you grieve a little,
    The days when we had rest, O soul, for they were long.

Men loved unkindness then, but lightless in the quarry
   I slept and saw not; tears fell down, I did not mourn;
Sweat ran and blood sprang out and I was never sorry:
   Then it was well with me, in days ere I was born.

Now, and I muse for why and never find the reason,
   I pace the earth, and drink the air, and feel the sun.
Be still, be still, my soul; it is but for a season:
   Let us endure an hour and see injustice done.

Ay, look: high heaven and earth ail from the prime foundation;
   All thoughts to rive the heart are here, and all are vain:
Horror and scorn and hate and fear and indignation —
   Oh, why did I awake? when shall I sleep again?

LII

FAR IN A WESTERN BROOKLAND

Far in a western brookland
   That bred me long ago
The poplars stand and tremble
   By pools I used to know.

There, in the windless night-time,
   The wanderer, marvelling why,
Halts on the bridge to hearken
   How soft the poplars sigh.

He hears: no more remembered
   In fields where I was known,
Here I lie down in London
   And turn to rest alone.

There, by the starlit fences,
   The wanderer halts and hears
My soul that lingers sighing
   About the glimmering weirs.

LIV

WITH RUE MY HEART IS LADEN

With rue my heart is laden
    For golden friends I had,
For many a rose-lipt maiden
    And many a lightfoot lad.

By brooks too broad for leaping
    The lightfoot boys are laid;
The rose-lipt girls are sleeping
    In fields where roses fade.

From LAST POEMS

I

THE WEST

Beyond the moor and mountain crest
    — Comrade, look not on the west —
The sun is down and drinks away
From air and land the lees of day.

The long cloud and the single pine
Sentinel the ending line,
And out beyond it, clear and wan,
Reach the gulfs of evening on.

The son of woman turns his brow
West from forty counties now,
And, as the edge of heaven he eyes,
Thinks eternal thoughts, and sighs.

Oh wide's the world, to rest or roam,
With change abroad and cheer at home,
Fights and furloughs, talk and tale,
Company and beef and ale.

But if I front the evening sky
Silent on the west look I,
And my comrade, stride for stride,
Passes silent at my side.

Comrade, look not on the west:
'Twill have the heart out of your breast;
'Twill take your thoughts and sink them far,
Leagues beyond the sunset bar.

Oh lad, I fear that yon's the sea
Where they fished for you and me,
And there, from whence we both were ta'en,
You and I shall drown again.

Send not on your soul before
To dive from that beguiling shore,
And let not yet the swimmer leave
His clothes upon the sands of eve.

Too fast to yonder strand forlorn
We journey, to the sunken bourn,
To flush the fading tinges eyed
By other lads at eventide.

Wide is the world, to rest or roam,
And early 'tis for turning home:
Plant your heel on earth and stand,
And let's forget our native land.

When you and I are spilt on air
Long we shall be strangers there;
Friends of flesh and bone are best:
Comrade, look not on the west.

IX

THE CHESTNUT CASTS HIS FLAMBEAUX

The chestnut casts his flambeaux, and the flowers
   Stream from the hawthorn on the wind away,
The doors clap to, the pane is blind with showers.
   Pass me the can, lad; there's an end of May.

There's one spoilt spring to scant our mortal lot,
   One season ruined of our little store.
May will be fine next year as like as not:
   Oh ay, but then we shall be twenty-four.

444

We for a certainty are not the first
   Have sat in taverns while the tempest hurled
Their hopeful plans to emptiness, and cursed
   Whatever brute and blackguard made the world.

It is in truth iniquity on high
   To cheat our sentenced souls of aught they crave,
And mar the merriment as you and I
   Fare on our long fool's-errand to the grave.

Iniquity it is; but pass the can.
   My lad, no pair of kings our mothers bore;
Our only portion is the estate of man:
   We want the moon, but we shall get no more.

If here to-day the cloud of thunder lours
   To-morrow it will hie on far behests;
The flesh will grieve on other bones than ours
   Soon, and the soul will mourn in other breasts.

The troubles of our proud and angry dust
   Are from eternity, and shall not fail.
Bear them we can, and if we can we must.
   Shoulder the sky, my lad, and drink your ale.

XIII

THE DESERTER

What sound awakened me, I wonder,
   For now 'tis dumb.'
'Wheels on the road most like, or thunder:
   Lie down: 'twas not the drum.'

Toil at sea and two in haven
   And trouble far:
Fly, crow, away, and follow, raven,
   And all that croaks for war.

'Hark, I heard the bugle crying,
   And where am I?
My friends are up and dressed and dying,
   And I will dress and die.'

445

' Oh love is rare and trouble plenty
   And carrion cheap,
And daylight dear at four-and-twenty:
   Lie down again and sleep.'

' Reach me my belt and leave your prattle:
   Your hour is gone:
But my day is the day of battle,
   And that comes dawning on.

' They mow the field of man in season:
   Farewell, my fair,
And, call it truth or call it treason,
   Farewell the vows that were.'

' Ay, false heart, forsake me lightly:
   'Tis like the brave.
They find no bed to joy in rightly
   Before they find the grave.

' Their love is for their own undoing,
   And east and west
They scour about the world a-wooing
   The bullet to their breast.

' Sail away the ocean over,
   Oh sail away,
And lie there with your leaden lover
   For ever and a day.'

XXV

THE ORACLES

Tis mute, the word they went to hear on high Dodona
    mountain
  When winds were in the oakenshaws and all the cauldrons
  tolled,
And mute's the midland navel-stone beside the singing
    fountain,
  And echoes list to silence now where gods told lies of old.

✣ A. E. HOUSMAN ✣

I took my question to the shrine that has not ceased from
    speaking,
  The heart within, that tells the truth and tells it twice as
    plain;
And from the cave of oracles I heard the priestess shrieking
  That she and I should surely die and never live again.

Oh priestess, what you cry is clear, and sound good sense
    I think it;
  But let the screaming echoes rest, and froth your mouth
    no more.
'Tis true there's better boose than brine, but he that drowns
    must drink it;
  And oh, my lass, the news is news that men have
    heard before.

*The King with half the East at heel is marched from lands
    of morning;*
  *Their fighters drink the rivers up, their shafts benight
    the air.*
*And he that stands will die for nought, and home there's
    no returning.*
  The Spartans on the sea-wet rock sat down and combed
    their hair.

XXVII

THE SIGH THAT HEAVES THE GRASSES

The sigh that heaves the grasses
    Whence thou wilt never rise
Is of the air that passes
    And knows not if it sighs.

The diamond tears adorning
    Thy low mound on the lea,
Those are the tears of morning,
    That weeps, but not for thee.

FANCY'S KNELL

When lads were home from labour
   At Abdon under Clee,
A man would call his neighbour
   And both would send for me.
And where the light in lances
   Across the mead was laid,
There to the dances
   I fetched my flute and played.

Ours were idle pleasures,
   Yet oh, content we were,
The young to wind the measures,
   The old to heed the air;
And I to lift with playing
   From tree and tower and steep
The light delaying,
   And flute the sun to sleep.

The youth toward his fancy
   Would turn his brow of tan,
And Tom would pair with Nancy
   And Dick step off with Fan;
The girl would lift her glances
   To his, and both be mute:
Well went the dances
   At evening to the flute.

Wenlock Edge was umbered,
   And bright was Abdon Burf,
And warm between them slumbered
   The smooth green miles of turf;
Until from grass and clover
   The upshot beam would fade
And England over
   Advanced the lofty shade.

The lofty shade advances,
   I fetch my flute and play:
Come, lads, and learn the dances
   And praise the tune to-day.
To-morrow, more's pity,
   Away we both must hie,
To air the ditty,
   And to earth I.

ROBERT BRIDGES
1844–1930

When in 1913 Mr. Asquith appointed Robert Bridges to the Laureateship, there were a few who recognized that he had done the right thing in preserving an honourable office, then fallen into disesteem, and had restored its prestige by this appointment. Bridges, for his part, was as great a poet as had ever held the post, with the exception of Wordsworth and Tennyson, and did not covet the honour, but the notoriety which it brought him did him no harm. Save for it he might have been written down with Spenser and Gray as a poet's poet. He deserved and gained a wider public. The poets and critics had, as early as 1890, acknowledged his powers, and he will be perpetually secure with them.

The events of his life are so much of the conventional sort that one is surprised to discover what an amazing man in many ways Bridges was. He had followed the usual path through Eton and Oxford into the practice of medicine. In 1882 after years of success in his profession — he was a Fellow of the Royal College of Physicians and a member of the staff in two London hospitals — he deliberately put aside all he had gained and turned himself to poetry. The mighty Muse, 'wooer of virgin thought,' makes him whom she loves reckless for her sake. He was setting about his new vocation at thirty-eight, though he had written considerable verse previously. His call he knew to be genuine and he could disregard the superstition that good poets, like good men, are supposed to die young.

> I will be what God made me, nor protest
> Against the bent of genius in my time,
> That science of my friends robs all the best,
> While I love beauty, and was born to rhyme.

If his poetic vitality was unusually late in arriving, its longevity was equally remarkable. No poet can match his feat of

450

publishing in his eighty-fifth year a great philosophic poem (*The Testament of Beauty*) into the writing of which went all his store of wisdom, a perfected technique, and a love of the beauty he was celebrating as passionate as that which Keats evinced at twenty.

Much of his early work issued almost tentatively from the private press of his friend Mr. Henry Daniel, Provost of Worcester College. There first were published the expanded collection of his sonnet-sequence *The Growth of Love* and the *Shorter Poems* in five 'books,' modest little volumes which are already prized by bibliophiles. Gradually the circle of his renown spread wider until his Alma Mater, to whom he had been a devoted son, gave him in 1912 his first public recognition with an honourary doctorate in letters and the publication of his poetry in the Oxford Poets, and thus ' ranked him living, with the dead immortals.'

In spite of his learning, which was extensive, Bridges remained a poet. A constant battler for the preservation of the best of the older order, he could be an iconoclast when it suited his wisdom. His quixotism, which often proved after the event to be inviolable good sense, was the delight and despair of his friends. In the midst of a searching essay on prosody he halts for a moment to say: ' I think I have liked some verses better because they do not scan and thus displease pedants. I should have put Blake into the " Golden Treasury " in 1861.' He preferred to have children for his patients, first because they couldn't tell him untruths about their symptoms and secondly, because they were obliged to take the remedies which he prescribed for them. When he was organizing the Society for Pure English, which during his lifetime was referred to as ' Bridges's private Academy,' he came near suffering the resignation of the association's secretary because he objected to a proposed list of members on the grounds of the impurity of their politics as well as their English. He was overruled, but later vindicated when the new members neglected to pay their dues.

His friends, most of whom he outlived, bear witness to the virtue in the man. For three of them, Canon Dixon, Digby Dolben, and Father Hopkins he performed the great service of discovering and fostering their latent poetic abilities. When the reticence which has thus far kept from us the more per-

sonal facts of his life is broken down by time, we shall have
from them more pictures like this from a letter of Sir Walter
Raleigh's to confirm with circumstance what we know of him
already.

Robert Bridges has just been in on the way down the hill.
He is delightfully grumpy. He mentions thing after thing
which is commonly believed and says that of course it's not so.
He's always right. His intellect has been so completely self-
indulged that it now can't understand rubbish. He has never
obeyed anyone or adapted himself to anyone, so he's as clear
as crystal, and can't do with fogs.

Bridges's poetry will always delight the bookish man whose
peculiar pleasure it is to become at will a citizen of any cen-
tury. To such a man often comes an undefined but very dis-
tinct longing to escape from the immediate hurly-burly and
be for the moment, not an Elizabethan or a Georgian, but
simply to live in an older, happier, quieter time. Bridges is
the poet for this man for he seems to have listened to the
purest speech and the most moving cadences of each genera-
tion's poet. He is a scholar gypsy who has watched time's in-
cidental changes but has not been shaken by them. His lyric
verse is full and rich and perfected, not archaic or imitative
but redolent of lavender and rose, a sunnier time and a more
musical day. Suggestions of the excellencies of all great Eng-
lish verse seems to have crowded into his lines, something of
the lightness of Chaucer, the lingering sweetness of Spenser,
the gravity of Milton, the liquidity of Shelley. As our life
grows more hurried and noisy and the pursuit of machine-
made pleasures edge out of our existence the more austere
raptures, Bridges will be increasingly valued. He knew how
to live in a sick world without falling ill of the contagion.

> O that the earth, or only this fair isle wer' ours
>   Amid the ocean's blue billows,
> With flowing woodland, stately mountain and valley,
>   Cascaded and lilied river;
> Nor ever a mortal envious, laborious,
>   By anguish or dull care opprest,
> Should come polluting with remorseful countenance
>   Our haunt of easy gaiety.

❖ ROBERT BRIDGES ❖

Bridges was fortunate in his endowments and in the hour of his birth. His lyric gift was as great as that of any English poet; his critical sense could match it. He could judge his own poetry as sharply as he could mark the faults and beauties of Milton and Keats. He wrote, for that reason, nearly always at his best. He refused, indeed, to belabour his muse, for when the fit was not on him, he put aside his versifying and puzzled over metrical experiments or badgered the academies with his tracts on pure English and phonetic script. He was privileged to be the last of the Victorians and may soon be called the first of the 'moderns.' He lived through the perplexities of the '70's, the hedonism of the '90's, the innocent ingenuousness of the 1900's, the disillusionments of the '20's, but from the welter of baffled faiths and scepticisms of all these years he emerged with the only philosophy which can in the modern world bring a man to a ripe old age.

Like Hardy and Meredith, with whom his name is most naturally linked, he accepted calmly all the findings of science which were most destructive of the old order. But he did not content himself with the ironic consolations of Meredith's comic spirit, nor could he conceivably have followed Hardy to a reluctant evolutionary meliorism. There was no necessity. Obviously at those auspicious times when the world brimmed with poetic interest for him such that ' the sight of a tree, a picture on the wall of his bed room would suggest subjects in such abundance that he was almost embarrassed by them,' life and joy were one. The remembrance of those moments suffused the days which followed and coloured his whole life. He was a poet of joy not, as some literal-minded critics seem to think, from a humanitarian sense of duty, but because he wrote only when he had been seized by a full delight and his blood had ' tasted of the breath of God again.'

The final and completely formed expression of his philosophy (what an inadequate word for the vital spirit of a man!) is set down in the *Testament of Beauty*. Baldly stated its import is that the urge of nature, no matter what its aberrations may be, working through the perfectable instincts of Selfhood and of Breed, moves towards the creation of a more spiritual life, towards beauty, that is to say. The best we have experienced of nature, of friendship, of love, is to be called beauty and through beauty is joy given. One can point to many of his poems before the *Testament* where this idea is adumbrated. It occurs with surprising succinctness in a sonnet published in 1876:

> For beauty being the best of all we know
> Sums up all the unsearchable and secret aims
> Of nature, and on joys whose earthly names
> Were never told, can form and sense bestow.

I LOVE ALL BEAUTEOUS THINGS

> I love all beauteous things,
>   I seek and adore them;
> God hath no better praise,
> And man in his hasty days
>   Is honoured for them.
>
> I too will something make
>   And joy in the making;
> Altho' tomorrow it seem
> Like the empty words of a dream
>   Remembered on waking.

THERE IS A HILL BESIDE THE SILVER THAMES

> There is a hill beside the silver Thames,
>   Shady with birch and beech and odorous pine:
> And brilliant underfoot with thousand gems
> Steeply the thickets to his floods decline.
>   Straight trees in every place
>   Their thick tops interlace,
> And pendant branches trail their foliage fine
>   Upon his watery face.
>
> Swift from the sweltering pasturage he flows:
> His stream, alert to seek the pleasant shade,
> Pictures his gentle purpose, as he goes
> Straight to the caverned pool his toil has made.

His winter floods lay bare
　　The stout roots in the air:
His summer streams are cool, when they have played
　　Among their fibrous hair.

A rushy island guards the sacred bower,
And hides it from the meadow, where in peace
The lazy cows wrench many a scented flower,
Robbing the golden market of the bees:
　　And laden barges float
　　By banks of myosote;
And scented flag and golden flower-de-lys
　　Delay the loitering boat.

And on this side the island, where the pool
Eddies away, are tangled mass on mass
The water-weeds, that net the fishes cool,
And scarce allow a narrow stream to pass;
　　Where spreading crowfoot mars
　　The drowning nenuphars,
Waving the tassels of her silken grass
　　Below her silver stars.

But in the purple pool there nothing grows,
Not the white water-lily spoked with gold;
Though best she loves the hollows, and well knows
On quiet streams her broad shields to unfold:
　　Yet should her roots but try
　　Within these deeps to lie,
Not her long reaching stalk could ever hold
　　Her waxen head so high.

Sometimes an angler comes, and drops his hook
Within its hidden depths, and 'gainst a tree
Leaning his rod, reads in some pleasant book,
Forgetting soon his pride of fishery;
　　And dreams, or falls asleep,
　　While curious fishes peep
About his nibbled bait, or scornfully
　　Dart off and rise and leap.

455

And sometimes a slow figure 'neath the trees,
In ancient-fashioned smock, with tottering care
Upon a staff propping his weary knees,
May by the pathway of the forest fare:
    As from a buried day
    Across the mind will stray
Some perishing mute shadow, — and unaware
    He passeth on his way.

Else, he that wishes solitude is safe,
Whether he bathe at morning in the stream:
Or lead his love there when the hot hours chafe
The meadows, busy with a blurring stream;
    Or watch, as fades the light,
    The gibbous moon grow bright,
Until her magic rays dance in a dream,
    And glorify the night.

Where is this bower beside the silver Thames?
O pool and flowery thickets, hear my vow!
O trees of freshest foliage and straight stems,
No sharer of my secret I allow:
    Lest ere I come the while
    Strange feet your shades defile;
Or lest the burly oarsman turn his prow
    Within your guardian isle.

A PASSER–BY

Whither, O splendid ship, thy white sails crowding,
    Leaning across the bosom of the urgent West,
That fearest nor sea rising, nor sky clouding,
    Whither away, fair rover, and what thy quest?
    Ah! soon, when Winter has all our vales opprest,
When skies are cold and misty, and hail is hurling,
    Wilt thou glide on the blue Pacific, or rest
In a summer haven asleep, thy white sails furling.

I there before thee, in the country that well thou knowest,
    Already arrived am inhaling the odorous air:
I watch thee enter unerringly where thou goest,
    And anchor queen of the strange shipping there,

Thy sails for awnings spread, thy masts bare;
Nor is aught from the foaming reef to the snow-
    capped, grandest
  Peak, that is over the feathery palms more fair
Than thou, so upright, so stately, and still thou standest.

And yet, O splendid ship, unhailed and nameless,
  I know not if, aiming a fancy, I rightly divine
That thou hast a purpose joyful, a courage blameless,
  Thy port assured in a happier land than mine.
  But for all I have given thee, beauty enough is thine,
As thou, aslant with trim tackle and shrouding,
  From the proud nostril curve of a prow's line
In the offing scatterest foam, thy white sails crowding.

ELEGY

ON A LADY, WHOM GRIEF FOR THE DEATH OF HER BETROTHED KILLED

Assemble, all ye maidens, at the door,
  And all ye loves, assemble; far and wide
Proclaim the bridal, that proclaimed before
Has been deferred to this last eventide:
    For on this night the bride,
    The days of her betrothal over,
  Leaves the parental hearth for evermore;
To-night the bride goes forth to meet her lover.

Reach down the wedding vesture, that has lain
  Yet all unvisited, the silken gown:
Bring out the bracelets, and the golden chain
  Her dearer friends provided: sere and brown
    Bring out the festal crown,
  And set it on her forehead lightly:
Though it be withered, twine no wreath again;
This only is the crown she can wear rightly.

Cloak her in ermine, for the night is cold,
And wrap her warmly, for the night is long,
In pious hands the flaming torches hold,
While her attendants, chosen from among

Her faithful virgin throng,
May lay her in her cedar litter,
Decking her coverlet with sprigs of gold,
Roses, and lilies white that best befit her.

Sound flute and tabor, that the bridal be
Not without music, nor with these alone;
But let the viol lead the melody,
With lesser intervals, and plaintive moan
　　　Of sinking semitone;
　　And, all in choir, the virgin voices
　Rest not from singing in skilled harmony
The song that aye the bridegroom's ear rejoices.

Let the priests go before, arrayed in white,
And let the dark-stoled minstrels follow slow,
Next they that bear her, honoured on this night,
And then the maidens, in a double row,
　　　Each singing soft and low,
　　And each on high a torch upstaying:
　Unto her lover lead her forth with light,
With music, and with singing, and with praying.

'Twas at this sheltering hour he nightly came,
And found her trusty window open wide,
And knew the signal of the timorous flame,
That long the restless curtain would not hide
　　　Her form that stood beside;
　　As scarce she dared to be delighted,
　Listening to that sweet tale, that is no shame
To faithful lovers, that their hearts have plighted.

But now for many days the dewy grass
Has shown no markings of his feet at morn:
And watching she has seen no shadow pass
The moonlit walk, and heard no music borne
　　　Upon her ear forlorn.
　　In vain has she looked out to greet him;
　He has not come, he will not come, alas!
So let us bear her out where she must meet him.

Now to the river bank the priests are come:
The bark is ready to receive its freight:
Let some prepare her place therein, and some
Embark the litter with its slender weight:
    The rest stand by in state,
      And sing her a safe passage over
   While she is oared across to her new home,
Into the arms of her expectant lover.

And thou, O lover, that art on the watch,
Where, on the banks of the forgetful streams,
The pale indifferent ghosts wander, and snatch
The sweeter moments of their broken dreams, —
    Thou, when the torchlight gleams,
      When thou shalt see the slow procession,
   And when thine ears the fitful music catch,
Rejoice, for thou art near to thy possession.

LAST WEEK OF FEBRUARY, 1890

Hark to the merry birds, hark how they sing!
   Although 'tis not yet spring
     And keen the air;
Hale Winter, half resigning ere he go,
   Doth to his heiress shew
     His kingdom fair.

In patient russet is his forest spread,
   All bright with bramble red,
     With beechen moss
And holly sheen: the oak silver and stark
   Sunneth his aged bark
     And wrinkled boss.

But neath the ruin of the withered brake
   Primroses now awake
     From nursing shades:
The crumpled carpet of the dry leaves brown
   Avails not to keep down
     The hyacinth blades.

The hazel hath put forth his tassels ruffed;
   The willow's flossy tuft
     Hath slipped him free:
The rose amid her ransacked orange hips
   Braggeth the tender tips
     Of bowers to be.

A black rook stirs the branches here and there,
   Foraging to repair
     His broken home:
And hark, on the ash-boughs! Never thrush did sing
   Louder in praise of spring,
     When spring is come.

THE EVENING DARKENS OVER

The evening darkens over.
   After a day so bright
The windcapt waves discover
That wild will be the night.
There's a sound of distant thunder.

The latest sea-birds hover
Along the cliff's sheer height;
As in the memory wander
Last flutterings of delight,
White wings lost on the white.

There's not a ship in sight;
And as the sun goes under
Thick clouds conspire to cover
The moon that should rise yonder.
Thou art alone, fond lover.

I NEVER SHALL LOVE THE SNOW AGAIN

I never shall love the snow again
   Since Maurice died:
With corniced drift it blocked the lane
And sheeted in a desolate plain
   The country side.

❖ ROBERT BRIDGES ❖

The trees with silvery rime bedight
    Their branches bare.
By day no sun appeared; by night
The hidden moon shed thievish light
    In the misty air.

We fed the birds that flew around
    In flocks to be fed:
No shelter in holly or brake they found.
The speckled thrush on the frozen ground
    Lay frozen and dead.

We skated on stream and pond; we cut
    The crinching snow
To Doric temple or Arctic hut;
We laughed and sang at nightfall, shut
    By the fireside glow.

Yet grudged we our keen delights before
    Maurice should come.
We said, In-door or out-of-door
We shall love life for a month or more,
    When he is home.

They brought him home; 'twas two days late
    For Christmas day:
Wrapped in white, in solemn state,
A flower in his hand, all still and straight
    Our Maurice lay.

And two days ere the year outgave
    We laid him low,
The best of us truly were not brave,
When we laid Maurice down in his grave
    Under the snow.

THE PHILOSOPHER TO HIS MISTRESS

Because thou canst not see,
   Because thou canst not know
The black and hopeless woe
That hath encompassed me:
Because, should I confess
The thought of my despair,
My words would wound thee less
Than swords can hurt the air:

Because with thee I seem
As one invited near
To taste the faery cheer
Of spirits in a dream;
Of whom he knoweth nought
Save that they vie to make
All motion, voice and thought
A pleasure for his sake:

Therefore more sweet and strange
Has been the mystery
Of thy long love to me
That doth not quit, nor change,
Nor tax my solemn heart,
That kisseth in a gloom,
Knowing not who thou art
That givest, nor to whom.

Therefore the tender touch
Is more; more dear the smile:
And thy light words beguile
My wisdom overmuch:
And O with swiftness fly
The fancies of my song
To happy worlds, where I
Still in thy love belong.

MY DELIGHT AND THY DELIGHT

My delight and thy delight
    Walking, like two angels white,
In the gardens of the night:

  My desire and thy desire
Twining to a tongue of fire,
Leaping live, and laughing higher;

Through the everlasting strife
In the mystery of life.

  Love, from whom the world begun,
Hath the secret of the sun.

  Love can tell, and love alone,
Whence the million stars were strewn,
Why each atom knows its own,
How, in spite of woe and death,
Gay is life, and sweet is breath:

  This he taught us, this we knew,
Happy in his science true,
Hand in hand as we stood
'Neath the shadows of the wood,
Heart to heart as we lay
In the dawning of the day.

PATER FILIO

Sense with keenest edge unusèd,
   Yet unsteel'd by scathing fire;
Lovely feet as yet unbruisèd
  On the ways of dark desire;
Sweetest hope that lookest smiling
O'er the wilderness defiling!

Why such beauty, to be blighted
  By the swarm of foul destruction?
Why such innocence delighted,
  When sin stalks to thy seduction?
All the litanies e'er chaunted
Shall not keep thy faith undaunted.

463

I have pray'd the sainted Morning
　To unclasp her hands to hold thee;
From resignful Eve's adorning
　Stol'n a robe of peace to enfold thee;
With all charms of man's contriving
Arm'd thee for thy lonely striving.

Me too once unthinking Nature
　— Whence Love's timeless mockery took me, —
Fashioned so divine a creature,
　Yea, and like a beast forsook me.
I forgave, but tell the measure
Of her crime in thee, my treasure.

THE WINNOWERS

Betwixt two billows of the downs
　　The little hamlet lies,
And nothing sees but the bald crowns
　Of the hills, and the blue skies.

Clustering beneath the long descent
　And grey slopes of the wold,
The red roofs nestle, oversprent
　With lichen yellow as gold.

We found it in the mid-day sun
　Basking, what time of year
The thrush his singing has begun,
　Ere the first leaves appear.

High from his load a woodman pitched
　His faggots on the stack:
Knee-deep in straw the cattle twitched
　Sweet hay from crib and rack:

And from the barn hard by was borne
　A steady muffled din;
By which we knew that threshèd corn
　Was winnowing, and went in.

The sunbeams on the motey air
  Streamed through the open door,
And on the brown arms moving bare,
  And the grain upon the floor.

One turns the crank, one stoops to feed
  The hopper, lest it lack,
One in the bushel scoops the seed,
  One stands to hold the sack.

We watched the good grain rattle down,
  And the awns fly in the draught;
To see us both so pensive grown
  The honest labourers laughed:

Merry they were, because the wheat
  Was clean and plump and good,
Pleasant to hand and eye, and meet
  For market and for food.

It chanced we from the city were,
  And had not gat us free
In spirit from the store and stir
  Of its immensity:

But here we found ourselves again.
  Where humble harvests bring
After much toil but little grain,
  'Tis merry winnowing.

THE HILL PINES WERE SIGHING

The hill pines were sighing,
  O'ercast and chill was the day:
A mist in the valley lying
Blotted the pleasant May.

But deep in the glen's bosom
Summer slept in the fire
Of the odorous gorse-blossom
And the hot scent of the brier.

465

A ribald cuckoo clamoured,
And out of the copse the stroke
Of the iron axe that hammered
The iron heart of the oak.

Anon a sound appalling,
As a hundred years of pride
Crashed, in the silence falling:
And the shadowy pine-trees sighed.

ELEGY

The wood is bare: a river-mist is steeping
    The trees that winter's chill of life bereaves:
Only their stiffened boughs break silence, weeping
    Over their fallen leaves;

That lie upon the dank earth brown and rotten,
    Miry and matted in the soaking wet:
Forgotten with the spring, that is forgotten
    By them that can forget.

Yet it was here we walked when ferns were springing,
    And through the mossy bank shot bud and blade: —
Here found in summer, when the birds were singing,
    A green and pleasant shade.

'Twas here we loved in sunnier days and greener;
    And now, in this disconsolate decay,
I come to see her where I most have seen her,
    And touch the happier day.

For on this path, at every turn and corner,
    The fancy of her figure on me falls:
Yet walks she with the slow step of a mourner,
    Nor hears my voice that calls.

So through my heart there winds a track of feeling,
    A path of memory, that is all her own:
Whereto her phantom beauty ever stealing
    Haunts the sad spot alone.

About her steps the trunks are bare, the branches
　　Drip heavy tears upon her downcast head,
And bleed from unseen wounds that no sun stanches,
　　　　For the year's sun is dead.

And dead leaves wrap the fruits that summer planted:
　　And birds that love the South have taken wing.
The wanderer, loitering o'er the scene enchanted,
　　　　Weeps, and despairs of spring.

LONG ARE THE HOURS THE SUN IS ABOVE

Long are the hours the sun is above,
　　But when evening comes I go home to my love.

I'm away the daylight hours and more,
Yet she comes not down to open the door.

She does not meet me upon the stair, —
She sits in my chamber and waits for me there.

As I enter the room she does not move:
I always walk straight up to my love;

And she lets me take my wonted place
At her side, and gaze in her dear dear face.

There as I sit, from her head thrown back
Her hair falls straight in a shadow black.

Aching and hot as my tired eyes be,
She is all that I wish to see.

And in my wearied and toil-dinned ear,
She says all things that I wish to hear.

Dusky and duskier grows the room,
Yet I see her best in the darker gloom.

When the winter eves are early and cold,
The firelight hours are a dream of gold.

And so I sit here night by night,
In rest and enjoyment of love's delight.

But a knock at the door, a step on the stair
Will startle, alas, my love from her chair.

If a stranger comes she will not stay:
At the first alarm she is off and away.

And he wonders, my guest, usurping her throne,
That I sit so much by myself alone.

I WILL NOT LET THEE GO

I will not let thee go.
Ends all our month-long love in this?
Can it be summed up so,
Quit in a single kiss?
I will not let thee go.

I will not let thee go.
If thy words' breath could scare thy deeds,
As the soft south can blow
And toss the feathered seeds,
Then might I let thee go.

I will not let thee go.
Had not the great sun seen, I might;
Or were he reck'oned slow
To bring the false to light,
Then might I let thee go.

I will not let thee go.
The stars that crowd the summer skies
Have watched us so below
With all their million eyes,
I dare not let thee go.

I will not let thee go.
Have we not chid the changeful moon,
Now rising late, and now
Because she set too soon,
And shall I let thee go?

I will not let thee go.
Have not the young flowers been content,
   Plucked ere their buds could blow,
   To seal our sacrament?
   I cannot let thee go.

I will not let thee go.
I hold thee by too many bands:
   Thou sayest farewell, and lo!
   I have thee by the hands,
   And will not let thee go.

I HAVE LOVED FLOWERS THAT FADE

I have loved flowers that fade,
   Within those magic tents
Rich hues have marriage made
With sweet unmemoried scents:
A honeymoon delight, —
A joy of love at sight,
That ages in an hour: —
My song be like a flower!

I have loved airs, that die
Before their charm is writ
Along a liquid sky
Trembling to welcome it.
Notes, that with pulse of fire
Proclaim the spirit's desire,
Then die, and are nowhere: —
My song be like an air!

Die, song, die like a breath,
And wither as a bloom:
Fear not a flowery death,
Dread not an airy tomb!
Fly with delight, fly hence!
'Twas thine love's tender sense
To feast; now on thy bier
Beauty shall shed a tear.

469

RUDYARD KIPLING
1865–   *

udyard Kipling, ' the uncrowned laureate of the British
Empire,' broke in upon the literary world of London
like a fresh north wind upon a sultry summer after-
noon. The world that he found in London was steeped in the
atmosphere of Wilde, of Beardsley, of the *Yellow Book*, an at-
mosphere of sophistication and aesthetic decadence. His com-
ing was greeted with sneers and cheers — sneers from the fash-
ionable critics of the day, cheers from the man in the street
once more listening to a writer who would tell him tales
and sing him songs of common men in language that a com-
mon man could understand. By sheer energy, by prolific and
varied production, by creative work in prose and verse that
bore the unmistakable stamp of genius, he forced himself up-
ward, and in 1907 the award of the Nobel Prize for Litera-
ture to him, first of all English writers to be so honoured,
proclaimed his recognition as a master.

A brief summary of the facts of Kipling's life will serve to
explain, though it cannot wholly account for, the nature of
his work and the characteristics of his genius. His father,
J. Lockwood Kipling, artist and writer, married one of four
lovely sisters — two of the others married Burne-Jones and
Edward Poynter, later President of the Royal Academy — and
took her at once to India where he had obtained a post in the
art school at Bombay. There, in December 1865, their first
child, Rudyard, was born. For six years he lived in India,
drinking in with the unsated appetite of a precocious child
the sights and sounds and smells, the manners, customs, and
traditions of the East that he was to recreate in later years.

In 1871, after the manner of Anglo-Indian children, he was
sent back to England where he boarded for six years in
a harsh and puritanical household, unhappy memories of
which appear in *Ba Ba Black Sheep* and *The Light that
Failed*. He was rescued by his father in 1877 and sent to the

470   * Died 1936.

Limited Service College at Westward Ho. This is the school of *Stalky and Co.*, and all readers of that book have long since recognized in the gig-lamped Beetles, Kipling himself. Scattered references throughout *Stalky* show Beetles-Kipling as an omnivorous reader, as well as a budding poet and printer-editor of the school paper. School over, Kipling was given the choice of a university or a return to India and like a wise youth he chose India. Seven years or so he spent as a reporter and sub-editor of English papers in India; he came to know Anglo-Indian life, society, officialdom, army, as no one had ever known it before, and the eyes behind the heavy glasses were keen enough to pierce the veil that hangs between the Anglo-Indian and the native. He not only saw but he took notes and printed. Before he left India after his apprenticeship in journalism his name was known from Cape Comorin to Simla for the sketches, stories, and verses that he had contributed to his papers, over and above his regular work as reporter and editor. In 1889 he left India as special correspondent for his paper and came, via China, Japan, and America, to London. Like Dick in *The Light that Failed* he came to conquer, and after a brief period of struggle and obscurity burst into dazzling fame with *Plain Tales from the Hills, Life's Handicap,* and *Barrack-Room Ballads.*

To continue would be little more than to set down the names and dates of his many books. He married an American wife, lived for some few years in Vermont, travelled widely about the world, and finally settled in his own England where he has struck deep roots in the sacred soil, an English Ulysses at home after much wandering and many experiences on land and sea with all sorts and conditions of men.

Kipling's fame rests and will always rest, no doubt, on his prose rather than on his verse. In fact there are certain critics of the more sophisticated sort who flatly deny him the title of a poet. This is a modern verdict certain to be set aside in posterity's court of appeal. Kipling has written much, perhaps too much verse; some of it certainly is true poetry. In the mean time, while waiting for the final judgment, there is something that can be said.

In the first place Kipling is the first of the new poets who find in the everyday life and work of the world the stuff of poetry. His early verse brought back poetry to the common man at a time when it was tending to wither in the hothouse of aestheticism. And this was because, to paraphrase his own words, ' through God's grace he saw nought common upon earth.' He saw Romance where others were blind to it, in the ordered functioning of the engine as in the toil of the working man or the life of Tommy Atkins. In a sense rather different from Wordsworth, Kipling is the poet of the unpoetical. *Mandalay, Danny Deever, Gunga Din* have become the common property of the English speaking peoples. It is no small thing to write the songs of an imperial race and this Kipling has done. There is, moreover, one strong strain running through the greater part of his work — the note of energy, of the strenuous life. Kipling has put Carlyle's Gospel of Work to music, and the music is not one of careless effort or misdirected energy but is set to the tune of McAndrews's engines when they ' lift their lesson ':

' Law, Orrder, Duty an' Restraint, Obedience, Discipline! '

It was a lesson much needed in the 1890's and one that was not unheeded in the bitter years that were to follow.

It might seem as if another of the notes in Kipling's song clashed with this praise of ordered energy. For Kipling is in a very special way the poet of the eternal *Wanderlust* in man. He himself has ranged about the world ' for to admire an' for to see,' and he has heard ' the call of the off-shore wind ' that troubles the hearts and starts the feet of the young men on the long trail. But the clash is only apparent. The Seven Seas over which he has wandered are the seas on which Englishmen sailed before him carrying the flag of England to build up the Empire. The wildest of the wanderers, explorer, vortrekker, man of the Lost Legion, has played his part in this work, and on the farthest shores of the Empire the native-born have ' learned from their wistful mothers to call old England "home." ' The *Wanderlust* itself is but one phase of that untiring energy which has built up the Empire. And it is of the Empire that Kipling is the true poet laureate. Casting behind him the doctrinaire ideas of mid-Victorian days with their ignorance of and indifference to the so-called Colonies, Kipling has caught up the note of Tennyson and sung — even preached at times in rather uninspired verse — the glories, the responsibilities, the duties of the island race. It is theirs to bear the white man's burden, to fight famine and pestilence, to extend the rule of order over ' lesser breeds without the Law,' and the reward is the consciousness of work well done and, if Fate allows, a return to the homeland where the race was born, where the Abbey stands, where

> Memory, Use, and Love make live
> Us and our fields alike.

All the later poetry of Kipling is full to overflowing with the sights and sounds, the stories and legends of the England where the wanderer has come to rest, in a fair ground, in ' Sussex by the sea.'

Change of theme, the shift from *Departmental Ditties* and *Barrack-Room Ballads* to songs of England, has coincided with a remarkable and, one may say, a lovely change of tune in Kipling's verse. From the beginning a master of the technique of verse, his early poems were often frank imitations in the metre of Poe, of Browning, of Swinburne. Many of them — too many — went to jazz tunes before the word ' jazz ' was invented. His early critics called him a banjo poet; and the unmistakable ' tinka-tinka-tink ' of the banjo was sometimes varied with the blare of the trombone as in the clangorous lines of *The English Flag*. But all this has altered; the noisier instruments have been exchanged for harp and flute. In the latest poems we seem to hear another Kipling than the poet of the machine, the Seven Seas, and the Empire; the same Kipling, no doubt, who turned in prose from *Soldiers Three* to write the *Brushwood Boy, A Habitation Enforced,* and that most wistful of all ghost stories, *They*. And these songs are set to old and simple English melodies, folk-song, chanty, ballad, and carol. Little dashes of dialect give a homely sweetness to the verse and the passing gleam of some folk-lore fancy seems to show that the poet has listened to the call of Puck and entered into ' Merlin's Isle of Gramarye.'

THE BELL BUOY

They christened my brother of old —
　　And a saintly name he bears —
They gave him his place to hold
　　At the head of the belfry-stairs,
　　Where the minster-towers stand
And the breeding kestrels cry.
　　Would I change with my brother a league inland?
　　(*Shoal! 'Ware shoal!*) Not I!

In the flush of the hot June prime,
　　O'er sleek flood-tides afire,
I hear him hurry the chime
　　To the bidding of checked Desire;
　　Till the sweated ringers tire
And the wild bob-majors die.
　　Could I wait for my turn in the godly choir?
　　(*Shoal! 'Ware shoal!*) Not I!

When the smoking scud is blown,
　　When the greasy wind-rack lowers,
Apart and at peace and alone,
　　He counts the changeless hours.
　　He wars with darkling Powers
　　(I war with a darkling sea) ;
　　Would he stoop to my work in the gusty mirk?
　　(*Shoal! 'Ware shoal!*) Not he!

There was never a priest to pray,
　　There was never a hand to toll,
When they made me guard of the bay,
　　And moored me over the shoal.
　　I rock, I reel, and I roll —
My four great hammers ply —
　　Could I speak or be still at the Church's will?
　　(*Shoal! 'Ware shoal!*) Not I!

The landward marks have failed,
　　The fog-bank glides unguessed,
The seaward lights are veiled,
　　The spent deep feigns her rest:

But my ear is laid to her breast,
I lift to the swell — I cry!
   Could I wait in sloth on the Church's oath?
(Shoal! 'Ware shoal!) Not I!

At the careless end of night
   I thrill to the nearing screw;
I turn in the clearing light
   And I call to the drowsy crew;
   And the mud boils foul and blue
As the blind bow backs away.
   Will they give me their thanks if they clear the banks?
(Shoal! 'Ware shoal!) Not they!

The beach-pools cake and skim,
   The bursting spray-heads freeze,
I gather on crown and rim
   The grey, grained ice of the seas,
   Where, sheathed from bitt to trees,
The plunging colliers lie.
   Would I barter my place for the Church's grace?
(Shoal! 'Ware shoal!) Not I!

Through the blur of the whirling snow,
   Or the black of the inky sleet,
The lanterns gather and grow,
   And I look for the homeward fleet.
   Rattle of block and sheet —
' Ready about — stand by! '
   Shall I ask them a fee ere they fetch the quay?
(Shoal! 'Ware shoal!) Not I!

I dip and I surge and I swing
   In the rip of the racing tide,
By the gates of doom I sing,
   On the horns of death I ride.
   A ship-length overside,
Between the course and the sand,
   Fretted and bound I bide
      Peril whereof I cry.
   Would I change with my brother a league inland?
(Shoal! 'Ware shoal!) Not I!

FORD O' KABUL RIVER

Kabul town's by Kabul river —
 Blow the bugle, draw the sword —
There I lef' my mate for ever,
 Wet an' drippin' by the ford.
 Ford, ford, ford o' Kabul river,
 Ford o' Kabul river in the dark!
 There's the river up and brimmin', an' there's 'arf a
 squadron swimmin'
 'Cross the ford o' Kabul river in the dark.

Kabul town's a blasted place —
 Blow the bugle, draw the sword —
'Strewth I sha'n't forget 'is face
 Wet an' drippin' by the ford!
 Ford, ford, ford o' Kabul river,
 Ford o' Kabul river in the dark!
 Keep the crossing-stakes beside you, an' they will surely
 guide you
 'Cross the ford o' Kabul river in the dark.

Kabul town is sun and dust —
 Blow the bugle, draw the sword —
I'd ha' sooner drownded fust
 'Stead of 'im beside the ford.
 Ford, ford, ford o' Kabul river,
 Ford o' Kabul river in the dark!
 You can 'ear the 'orses threshin', you can 'ear the men
 a-splashin',
 'Cross the ford o' Kabul river in the dark.

Kabul town was ours to take —
 Blow the bugle, draw the sword —
I'd ha' left it for 'is sake —
 'Im that left me by the ford.
 Ford, ford, ford o' Kabul river,
 Ford o' Kabul river in the dark!
 It's none so bloomin' dry there; ain't you never comin'
 nigh there,
 'Cross the ford o' Kabul river in the dark?

Kabul town'll go to hell —
  Blow the bugle, draw the sword —
'Fore I see him 'live an' well —
  'Im the best beside the ford.
    Ford, ford, ford o' Kabul river,
      Ford o' Kabul river in the dark!
    Gawd 'elp 'em if they blunder, for their boots'll pull 'em
      under,
      By the ford o' Kabul river in the dark.

Turn your 'orse from Kabul town —
  Blow the bugle, draw the sword —
'Im an' 'arf my troop is down,
  Down an' drownded by the ford.
    Ford, ford, ford o' Kabul river,
      Ford o' Kabul river in the dark!
    There's the river low an' fallin', but it ain't no use o'
      callin'
      'Cross the ford o' Kabul river in the dark.

THE LAST CHANTEY

' And there was no more sea.'

Thus said the Lord in the Vault above the Cherubim,
  Calling to the Angels and the Souls in their degree:
    ' Lo! Earth has passed away
  On the smoke of Judgment Day.
That Our word may be established shall We gather up the
  sea? '

Loud sang the souls of the jolly, jolly mariners:
  ' Plague upon the hurricane that made us furl and flee!
    But the war is done between us,
    In the deep the Lord hath seen us —
Our bones we'll leave the barracout', and God may sink the
  sea! '

Then said the soul of Judas that betrayèd Him:
  ' Lord, hast Thou forgotten Thy covenant with me?
    How once a year I go
    To cool me on the floe?
And Ye take my day of mercy if Ye take away the sea! '

Then said the soul of the Angel of the Off-shore Wind:
  (He that bits the thunder when the bull-mouthed breakers
      flee) :
    ' I have watch and ward to keep
    O'er Thy wonders on the deep,
And Ye take mine honour from me if Ye take away the sea! '

Loud sang the souls of the jolly, jolly mariners:
  ' Nay, but we were angry, and a hasty folk are we!
    If we worked the ship together
    Till she foundered in foul weather,
Are we babes that we should clamour for a vengeance on the
    sea? '

Then said the souls of the slaves that men threw overboard:
  ' Kennelled in the picaroon a weary band were we;
    But Thy arm was strong to save,
    And it touched us on the wave,
And we drowsed the long tides idle till Thy Trumpets tore
    the sea.'

Then cried the soul of the stout Apostle Paul to God:
  ' Once we frapped a ship, and she laboured woundily.
    There were fourteen score of these,
    And they blessed Thee on their knees,
When they learned Thy Grace and Glory under Malta by the
    sea! '

Loud sang the souls of the jolly, jolly mariners,
  Plucking at their harps, and they plucked unhandily:
    ' Our thumbs are rough and tarred,
    And the tune is something hard —
May we lift a Deepsea Chantey such as seamen use at sea? '

Then said the souls of the gentlemen-adventurers —
  Fettered wrist to bar all for red iniquity:
    ' Ho, we revel in our chains
    O'er the sorrow that was Spain's;
Heave or sink it, leave or drink it, we were masters of the sea! '

Up spake the soul of a grey Gothavn 'speckshioner —
  (He that led the flinching in the fleets of fair Dundee) :
    ' Oh, the ice-blink white and near,
    And the bowhead breaching clear!
Will Ye whelm them all for wantonness that wallow in the
    sea? '

Loud sang the souls of the jolly, jolly mariners,
  Crying: ' Under Heaven, here is neither lead nor lee!
    Must we sing for evermore
    On the windless, glassy floor?
Take back your golden fiddles and we'll beat to open sea! '

Then stooped the Lord, and He called the good sea up to
    Him,
  And 'stablished its borders unto all eternity,
    That such as have no pleasure
    For to praise the Lord by measure,
They may enter into galleons and serve Him on the sea.

Sun, wind, and cloud shall fail not from the face of it,
  Stinging, ringing spindrift, nor the fulmar flying free;
    And the ships shall go abroad
    To the Glory of the Lord
Who heard the silly sailor-folk and gave them back their sea!

JOBSON'S AMEN

Blessed be the English and all their ways and works.
  Cursed be the Infidels, Hereticks, and Turks! '
' Amen,' quo' Jobson, ' but where I used to lie
Was neither Candle, Bell nor Book to curse my brethren by:

' But a palm-tree in full bearing, bowing down, bowing down,
To a surf that drove unsparing at the brown-walled town —
Conches in a temple, oil-lamps in a dome —
And a low moon out of Africa said: " This way home! " '

' Blessed be the English and all that they profess.
Cursed be the Savages that prance in nakedness! '
' Amen,' quo' Jobson, ' but where I used to lie
Was neither shirt nor pantaloons to catch my brethren by:

' But a well-wheel slowly creaking, going round, going round,
By a water-channel leaking over drowned, warm ground —
Parrots very busy in the trellised pepper-vine —
And a high sun over Asia shouting: " Rise and shine! " '

' Blessed be the English and everything they own.
Cursed be the Infidels that bow to wood and stone! '
' Amen,' quo' Jobson, ' but where I used to lie
Was neither pew nor Gospelleer to save my brethren by:

' But a desert stretched and stricken, left and right, left and
    right,
Where the piled mirages thicken under white-hot light —
A skull beneath a sand-hill and a viper coiled inside —
And a red wind out of Libya roaring: " Run and hide! " '

' Blessed be the English and all they make or do.
Cursed be the Hereticks who doubt that this is true! '
' Amen,' quo' Jobson, ' but where I mean to die
Is neither rule nor calliper to judge the matter by:

' But Himalaya heavenward-heading, sheer and vast, sheer and
    vast,
In a million summits bedding on the last world's past;
A certain sacred mountain where the scented cedars climb,
And — the feet of my Belovèd hurrying back through Time! '

THE LONG TRAIL

There's a whisper down the field where the year has shot her
    yield,
  And the ricks stand grey to the sun,
Singing: ' Over then, come over, for the bee has quit the clover,
  And your English summer's done.'
      You have heard the beat of the off-shore wind,
      And the thresh of the deep-sea rain;
      You have heard the song — how long? how long?
      Pull out on the trail again!

Ha' done with the Tents of Shem, dear lass,
We've seen the seasons through,
And it's time to turn on the old trail, our own trail, the out
   trail,
Pull out, pull out, on the Long Trail — the trail that is al-
   ways new!

It's North you may run to the rime-ringed sun
   Or South to the blind Horn's hate;
Or East all the way into Mississippi Bay,
   Or West to the Golden Gate;
      Where the blindest bluffs hold good, dear lass,
      And the wildest tales are true,
      And the men bulk big on the old trail, our own trail,
         the out trail,
      And life runs large on the Long Trail — the trail that is
      always new.

The days are sick and cold, and the skies are grey and old,
   And the twice-breathed airs blow damp;
And I'd sell my tired soul for the bucking beam-sea roll
   Of a black Bilbao tramp;
      With her load-line over her hatch, dear lass,
      And a drunken Dago crew,
      And her nose held down on the old trail, our own trail,
         the out trail
      From Cadiz south on the Long Trail — the trail that is
      always new.

There be triple ways to take, of the eagle or the snake,
   Or the way of a man with a maid;
But the sweetest way to me is a ship's upon the sea
   In the heel of the North-East Trade.
      Can you hear the crash on her bows, dear lass,
      And the drum of the racing screw,
      As she ships it green on the old trail, our own trail, the
         out trail,
      As she lifts and 'scends on the Long Trail — the trail
      that is always new?

See the shaking funnels roar, with the Peter at the fore,
  And the fenders grind and heave,
And the derricks clack and grate, as the tackle hooks the crate,
  And the fall-rope whines through the sheave;
        It's ' Gang-plank up and in,' dear lass,
        It's ' Hawsers warp her through! '
        And it's ' All clear aft ' on the old trail, our own trail,
          the out trail,
        We're backing down on the Long Trail — the trail that
          is always new.

O the mutter overside, when the port-fog holds us tied,
  And the sirens hoot their dread,
When foot by foot we creep o'er the hueless viewless deep
  To the sob of the questing lead!
        It's down by the Lower Hope, dear lass,
        With the Gunfleet Sands in view,
        Till the Mouse swings green on the old trail, our own
          trail, the out trail,
        And the Gull Light lifts on the Long Trail — the trail
          that is always new.

O the blazing tropic night, when the wake's a welt of light
  That holds the hot sky tame,
And the steady fore-foot snores through the planet-powdered
      floors
  Where the scared whale flukes in flame!
        Her plates are flaked by the sun, dear lass,
        And her ropes are taut with the dew,
        For we're booming down on the old trail, our own trail,
          the out trail,
        We're sagging south on the Long Trail — the trail that
          is always new.

Then home, get her home, where the drunken rollers comb,
  And the shouting seas drive by,
And the engines stamp and ring, and the wet bows reel and
      swing,
  And the Southern Cross rides high!
        Yes, the old lost stars wheel back, dear lass,
        That blaze in the velvet blue.

They're all old friends on the old trail, our own trail,
   the out trail,
They're God's own guides on the Long Trail — the trail
   that is always new.

Fly forward, O my·heart, from the Foreland to the Start —
   We're steaming all too slow,
And it's twenty thousand mile to our little lazy isle
   Where the trumpet-orchids blow!
      You have heard the call of the off-shore wind
      And the voice of the deep-sea rain;
      You have heard the song. How long — how long?
      Pull out on the trail again!

The Lord knows what we may find, dear lass,
And The Deuce knows what we may do —
But we're back once more on the old trail, our own trail, the
   out trail,
We're down, hull down, on the Long Trail — the trail that is
   always new!

MY NEW–CUT ASHLAR

My new-cut ashlar takes the light
   Where crimson-blank the windows flare;
By my own work, before the night,
   Great Overseer, I make my prayer.

If there be good in that I wrought,
   Thy hand compelled it, Master, Thine —
Where I have failed to meet Thy thought
   I know, through Thee, the blame is mine.

One instant's toil to Thee denied
   Stands all Eternity's offence.
Of that I did with Thee to guide,
   To Thee, through Thee, be excellence.

Who, lest all thought of Eden fade,
   Bring'st Eden to the craftsman's brain —
Godlike to muse o'er his own Trade
   And manlike stand with God again!

The depth and dream of my desire,
 The bitter paths wherein I stray —
Thou knowest Who hast made the Fire,
 Thou knowest Who hast made the Clay.

One stone the more swings to her place
 In that dread Temple of Thy worth.
It is enough that through Thy Grace
 I saw naught common on Thy Earth.

Take not that vision from my ken —
 Oh whatso'er may spoil or speed,
Help me to need no aid from men
 That I may help such men as need!

PUCK'S SONG

See you the ferny ride that steals
 Into the oak-woods far?
O that was whence they hewed the keels
 That rolled to Trafalgar.

And mark you where the ivy clings
 To Bayham's mouldering walls?
O there we cast the stout railings
 That stand around St. Paul's.

See you the dimpled track that runs
 All hollow through the wheat?
O that was where they hauled the guns
 That smote King Philip's fleet.

Out of the Weald, the secret Weald,
 Men sent in ancient years,
The horse-shoes red at Flodden Field,
 The arrows at Poitiers!

See you our little mill that clacks,
 So busy by the brook?
She has ground her corn and paid her tax
 Ever since Domesday Book.

See you our stilly woods of oak,
And the dread ditch beside?
O that was where the Saxons broke
On the day that Harold died.

See you the windy levels spread
About the gates of Rye?
O that was where the Northmen fled,
When Alfred's ships came by.

See you our pastures wide and lone,
Where the red oxen browse?
O there was a City thronged and known,
Ere London boasted a house.

And see you, after rain, the trace
Of mound and ditch and wall?
O that was a Legion's camping-place,
When Caesar sailed from Gaul.

And see you marks that show and fade,
Like shadows on the Downs?
O they are the lines the Flint Men made,
To guard their wondrous towns.

Trackway and Camp and City lost,
Salt Marsh where now is corn;
Old Wars, old Peace, old Arts that cease,
And so was England born!

She is not any common Earth,
Water or wood or air,
But Merlin's Isle of Gramarye,
Where you and I will fare!

SUSSEX

God gave all men all earth to love,
But since our hearts are small,
Ordained for each one spot should prove
Belovèd over all;
That, as He watched Creation's birth,
So we, in godlike mood,
May of our love create our earth
And see that it is good.

So one shall Baltic pines content,
   As one some Surrey glade,
Or one the palm-grove's droned lament
   Before Levuka's trade.
Each to his choice, and I rejoice
   The lot has fallen to me
In a fair ground — in a fair ground —
   Yea, Sussex by the sea!

No tender-hearted garden crowns,
   No bosom'ed woods adorn
Our blunt, bow-headed, whale-backed Downs,
   But gnarled and writhen thorn —
Bare slopes where chasing shadows skim,
   And through the gaps revealed
Belt upon belt, the wooded, dim
   Blue goodness of the Weald.

Clean of officious fence or hedge,
   Half-wild and wholly tame,
The wise turf cloaks the white cliff edge
   As when the Romans came.
What sign of those that fought and died
   At shift of sword and sword?
The barrow and the camp abide,
   The sunlight and the sward.

Here leaps ashore the full Sou'west
   All heavy-winged with brine,
Here lies above the folded crest
   The Channel's leaden line;
And here the sea-fogs lap and cling,
   And here, each warning each,
The sheep-bells and the ship-bells ring
   Along the hidden beach.

We have no waters to delight
   Our broad and brookless vales —
Only the dewpond on the height
   Unfed, that never fails,

Whereby no tattered herbage tells
  Which way the season flies —
Only our close-bit thyme that smells
  Like dawn in Paradise.

Here through the strong unhampered days
  The tinkling silence thrills;
Or little, lost, Down churches praise
  The Lord who made the hills:
But here the Old Gods guard their round,
  And, in her secret heart,
The heathen kingdom Wilfred found
  Dreams, as she dwells, apart.

Though all the rest were all my share,
  With equal soul I'd see
Her nine-and-thirty sisters fair,
  Yet none more fair than she.
Choose ye your need from Thames to Tweed,
  And I will choose instead
Such lands as lie 'twixt Rake and Rye
  Black Down and Beachy Head.

I will go out against the sun
  Where the rolled scarp retires,
And the Long Man of Wilmington
  Looks naked toward the shires;
And east till doubling Rother crawls
  To find the fickle tide,
By dry and sea-forgotten walls,
  Our ports of stranded pride.

I will go north about the shaws
  And the deep ghylls that breed
Huge oaks and old, the which we hold
  No more than Sussex weed;
Or south where windy Piddinghoe's
  Begilded dolphin veers,
And black beside wide-bankèd Ouse
  Lie down our Sussex steers.

So to the land our hearts we give
   Till the sure magic strike,
And Memory, Use, and Love make live
   Us and our fields alike —
That deeper than our speech and thought,
   Beyond our reason's sway,
Clay of the pit whence we were wrought
   Yearns to its fellow-clay.

God gives all men all earth to love,
   But since man's heart is small,
Ordains for each one spot shall prove
   Belovèd over all.
Each to his choice, and I rejoice
   The lot has fallen to me
In a fair ground — in a fair ground —
   Yea, Sussex by the sea!

CITIES AND THRONES AND POWERS

Cities and Thrones and Powers,
   Stand in Time's eye,
Almost as long as flowers,
   Which daily die:
But, as new buds put forth
   To glad new men,
Out of the spent and unconsidered Earth,
   The Cities rise again.

This season's Daffodil,
   She never hears,
What change, what chance, what chill,
   Cut down last year's;
But with bold countenance,
   And knowledge small,
Esteems her seven days' continuance,
   To be perpetual.

So Time that is o'er-kind,
   To all that be,
Ordains us e'en as blind,
   As bold as she:

That in our very death,
  And burial sure,
Shadow to shadow, well persuaded, saith,
  ' See how our works endure! '

JOHN MASEFIELD
1878–

No fitter choice for the post of Poet Laureate could have been made by the first Labour Prime Minister than that of John Masefield. It was the formal official recognition of a writer who had long since endeared himself to the hearts of thousands as the poet, ' not of the princes and prelates,' rather of the scorned, the rejected, the slave, the sailor, the stoker, the tired lookout. Masefield himself had known heartbreaking toil, poverty, rejection. He had felt, like Thomson, a sense ' of fellowship in all disastrous fight,' but without a trace of Thomson's pessimism. He had established himself as a man of letters, essayist, novelist, and poet; he had served in the War as a Red Cross helper and had glorified the splendid, tragic failure of England at Gallipoli in prose that almost reached the height of immortal poetry. All in all a fit, if widely different successor to his neighbour and friend, the poet-artist Bridges, who had left the throne vacant.

So reticent has Masefield been about his life (his own confession of what his life has been is embodied in his poem *Biography*), so many legends have gathered about him, that a brief statement of such facts as are known may serve to give some idea of his career and character. He was born in Herefordshire, one of the western counties of England, on June 1, 1878. His parents, respectable middle-class people, died while he was still a child. He received a good school education, but early showed a greater love for wandering than for books. Accordingly he was apprenticed on the *Conway,* the English training-ship for the merchant service, and for three years sailed all about the world. He knew the fury of a Cape Horn gale, the splendour of a tropic night at sea, the serene beauty of the Cordilleras seen at sunrise from the vessel's deck. Before his apprenticeship was over, he resigned from the service. The ostensible reason was a touch of sun; he says himself that he found it gave him too little time for study, and that he wanted to write. He landed in New York with five dollars in his pocket and started in search of a job. For a few months he tried his hand at various occupations, ending as a waiter in a West Side saloon. He has left a vivid sketch of this place in *Tarpaulin' Muster*. Here he was discovered by a fellow Englishman, appropriately enough a Shropshire lad, who got him a decent job in a carpet factory at Yonkers. For two years the young man earned his daily bread by daily toil and fed his mind by 'passionate reading' of the great English poets. He discovered Chaucer, who was to be his master in narrative verse, drank deep of Keats and Shelley, read Shakespeare through and through, and naturally enough began to write verse. He sailed for England in 1897 to take up his career.

It was a slow business. He lived for a time in a London lodging house, worked for six months on the staff of the *Manchester Guardian*, and wrote incessantly. In 1902 his first volume, *Salt Water Ballads*, achieved a certain success and introduced him to the acquaintance of various writers, notably Synge and Yeats whose influence is unmistakable in his early work. He wrote a vigorous novel, of the old buccaneering days, *Captain Margaret*, a play or two — *Nan*, a grimly pathetic tragedy has been repeatedly performed — to say nothing of miscellaneous hackwork. It was not until 1911 that the publication in the *English Review* of his first long narrative poem, *The Everlasting Mercy*, won for him instant recognition as a new, a true, and really great poet and brought him the Polignac prize of £500. He followed this by a series of long narratives in verse, *The Widow in the Bye Street* (1912), *Dauber* (1912), *The Daffodil Fields* (1913).

To continue would be only to catalogue his voluminous production, prose and verse, lyric, dramatic, and narrative. He lives at Boar's Hill, a few miles out of Oxford; he has built a little theatre in his garden where the Boar's Hill Players produce poetic plays, his own and others. He presides over the Oxford recitations, contests in the oral delivery of verse, for Masefield, like Kipling, believes in bringing poetry back to the people not as lines printed in a book, but as music ringing in the ears. He is as representative a Laureate of the twentieth century, perhaps, as Tennyson was of the Victorian age.

It is impossible to form any just appreciation of Masefield

from a handful of his lyrics in an anthology. In fact many of
the best known of his songs belong to his first, least original,
and least important period. Following the example of Kip-
ling he sang, in rhythms reminiscent of the older poet, the
toils and sorrows and strange deaths of the common man, espe-
cially of the sailor. But even in these early songs a note is
heard that is rare enough in Kipling, the note of pity, a wist-
ful desire that Kipling seldom expressed for peace and beauty.
But the true Masefield comes first to light in his longer narra-
tives as the poet in love with action, physical, swift, and fear-
less. Saul Kane's wild run in *The Everlasting Mercy* is perhaps
the simplest, lowest form of this joy in action:

> The men who don't know to the root
> The joy of being swift of foot,
> Have never known divine and fresh
> The glory of the gift of flesh
>
> . . . .
>
> Oh if you want to know delight,
> Run naked in an autumn night.

Something finer is expressed in the united rush of hounds,
horses, and men in the pursuit of the fox. Highest of all comes
Dauber's struggle with his own shrinking flesh as well as with
the angry elements in the storm at sea. It is characteristic of
Masefield that he loves the action regardless of the event, suc-
cess or failure. Kipling's riotous sailors brought the *Bolivar*
safe across the bay; Dauber falls from the yard and dies. It is
not too much to say that as a rule Masefield's sympathy goes
with the loser rather than the winner in life's game. He wrests
his story to let Reynard escape when every chance was against
him. In his play *Pompey* his heart goes out to the beaten man
rather than to the victorious Caesar, and in one of his most
striking poems he calls the ghost of Pompey from the grave to
warn his conqueror of impending death, for

> the house is falling,
> The beaten men come into their own.

But there is another side to Masefield, one often forgotten
or overlooked by admirers of his poems of action. Exquisitely
sensitive to beauty, he has become more and more the wor-

shipper of an immanent divine idea which finds its embodiment in the sights and sounds of nature, in the work of men's hands, in ships for example, most of all in the forms, the faces, and characters of men and women. Saul Kane's conversion is not so much from sin to righteousness as from the filth of riot to the beauty of clean living. Dauber, who endures all things that he may come to realize and to re-create the beauty of the sea and of all that moves upon or above it, is a true type of Masefield himself. No poet since Chaucer has shown such joy in the portrayal of English characters as Masefield in the first part of *Reynard the Fox*. And his love of beauty becomes in the end the religion of the poet. Man's sense of beauty, man's power to create beauty, to live and love beautifully, is that which lifts him above the material frame of things and holds out to him a dim intimation of immortality.

It is easy to find faults in Masefield's work. Quite apart from the coarse language and profanity which shocked some readers of his early poems, there is a careless, at times almost slovenly, ease about his verse, a tendency to drop into prosaic rhythm, a trick of wresting or coining words to fit the metre and the rhyme. But all this may be excused, as one excuses the lapses of Byron and Sir Walter. Masefield offers us a splendid body of poetry, quick with life and suffused with beauty. No fitter description of his work can be given than his own words which tell of the song of his mythical King Cole:

> He breathed a piping of this life of ours,
> The half-seen prize, the difficult pursuit.

> .   .   .   .

> And man the marvellous thing that in the dark
> Works with his little strength to make a light,
> His wit that strikes, his hope that tends, a spark,
> His sorrow of soul in toil, that brings delight,
> His friends who make salt sweet and blackness bright,
> His birth and growth and change; and death the wise,
> His peace, that puts a hand upon his eyes.

A CONSECRATION

Not of the princes and prelates with periwigged charioteers
Riding triumphantly laurelled to lap the fat of the
years, —
Rather the scorned — the rejected — the men hemmed in with
the spears;

The men of the tattered battalion which fights till it dies,
Dazed with the dust of the battle, the din and the cries,
The men with the broken heads and the blood running into
their eyes.

Not the be-medalled Commander, beloved of the throne,
Riding cock-horse to parade when the bugles are blown,
But the lads who carried the koppie and cannot be known.

Not the ruler for me, but the ranker, the tramp of the road,
The slave with the sack on his shoulders pricked on with the
goad,
The man with too weighty a burden, too weary a load.

The sailor, the stoker of steamers, the man with the clout,
The chantyman bent at the halliards putting a tune to the
shout,
The drowsy man at the wheel and the tired lookout.

Others may sing of the wine and the wealth and the mirth,
The portly presence of potentates goodly in girth; —
Mine be the dirt and the dross, the dust and scum of the earth!

Theirs be the music, the colour, the glory, the gold;
Mine be a handful of ashes, a mouthful of mould.
Of the maimed, of the halt and the blind in the rain and the
cold —
Of these shall my songs be fashioned, my tales be told.   Amen.

✤ JOHN MASEFIELD ✤

SEA–FEVER

I must go down to the seas again, to the lonely sea and the sky,
And all I ask is a tall ship and a star to steer her by,
And the wheel's kick and the wind's song and the white sail's
    shaking,
And a grey mist on the sea's face and a grey dawn breaking.

I must go down to the seas again, for the call of the running
    tide
Is a wild call and a clear call that may not be denied;
And all I ask is a windy day with the white clouds flying,
And the flung spray and the blown spume, and the sea-gulls
    crying.

I must go down to the seas again to the vagrant gypsy life,
To the gull's way and the whale's way where the wind's like
    a whetted knife;
And all I ask is a merry yarn from a laughing fellow-rover,
And a quiet sleep and a sweet dream when the long trick's
    over.

D'AVALOS' PRAYER

When the last sea is sailed and the last shallow charted,
    When the last field is reaped and the last harvest
    stored,
When the last fire is out and the last guest departed,
    Grant the last prayer that I shall pray, Be good to me, O
    Lord!

And let me pass in a night at sea, a night of storm and thunder,
    In the loud crying of the wind through sail and rope and
    spar;
Send me a ninth great peaceful wave to drown and roll me
    under
    To the cold tunny-fishes' home where the drowned galleons
    are.

And in the dim green quiet place far out of sight and hearing,
   Grant I may hear at whiles the wash and thresh of the sea-
      foam
About the fine keen bows of the stately clippers steering
   Towards the lone northern star and the fair ports of home.

THE RIDER AT THE GATE

A windy night was blowing on Rome,
  The cressets guttered on Caesar's home,
The fish-boats, moored at the bridge were breaking
The rush of the river to yellow foam.

The hinges whined to the shutters shaking,
When clip-clop-clep came a horse-hoofs raking
The stones of the road at Caesar's gate;
The spear-butts jarred at the guard's awaking.

'Who goes there?' said the guard at the gate.
'What is the news, that you ride so late?'
'News most pressing, that must be spoken
To Caesar alone, and that cannot wait.'

'The Caesar sleeps; you must show a token
That the news suffice that he be awoken.
What is the news, and whence do you come?
For no light cause may his sleep be broken.'

'Out of the dark of the sands I come,
From the dark of death, with news for Rome,
A word so fell that it must be uttered
Though it strike the soul of the Caesar dumb.'

Caesar turned in his bed and muttered,
With a struggle for breath the lamp-flame guttered;
Calpurnia heard her husband moan:
                    'The house is falling,
The beaten men come into their own.'

'Speak your word,' said the guard at the gate;
'Yes, but bear it to Caesar straight,
Say " Your murderer's knives are honing,
Your killer's gang is lying in wait."

496

' Out of the wind that is blowing and moaning,
Through the city palace and the country loaning,
I cry, " For the world's sake, Caesar, beware,
And take this warning as my atoning.

' " Beware of the Court, of the palace stair,
Of the downcast friend, who speaks so fair,
Keep from the Senate, for Death is going
On many men's feet to meet you there."

' I, who am dead, have ways of knowing
Of the crop of death that the quick are sowing.
I, who was Pompey, cry it aloud
From the dark of death, from the wind blowing.

  I, who was Pompey, once was proud,
Now I lie in the sand without a shroud;
I cry to Caesar out of my pain,
" Caesar, beware, your death is vowed." '

The light grew grey on the window-pane,
The windcocks swung in a burst of rain,
The window of Caesar flung unshuttered,
The horse-hoofs died into wind again.

Caesar turned in his bed and muttered,
With a struggle for breath the lamp-flame guttered;
Calpurnia heard her husband moan:
                    ' The house is falling,
The beaten men come into their own.'

C. L. M.

In the dark womb where I began
My mother's life made me a man.
Through all the months of human birth
Her beauty fed my common earth.
I cannot see, nor breathe, nor stir,
But through the death of some of her.

497

Down in the darkness of the grave
She cannot see the life she gave.
For all her love, she cannot tell
Whether I use it ill or well,
Nor knock at dusty doors to find
Her beauty dusty in the mind.

If the grave's gates could be undone,
She would not know her little son,
I am so grown. If we should meet
She would pass by me in the street,
Unless my soul's face let her see
My sense of what she did for me.

What have I done to keep in mind
My debt to her and womankind?
What woman's happier life repays
Her for those months of wretched days?
For all my mouthless body leeched
Ere Birth's releasing hell was reached?

What have I done, or tried, or said
In thanks to that dear woman dead?
Men triumph over women still,
Men trample women's rights at will,
And man's lust roves the world untamed.
.   .   .   .
O grave, keep shut lest I be shamed.

ALFRED NOYES

1880–

Few living English poets are better known or more endeared to American lovers of poetry than Alfred Noyes. And with good reason; for this poet is linked to the American land, life, and thought by closer ties than any of his British contemporaries. He married an American wife; he has travelled America from North to South and from East to West, has gazed into the abyss of the Grand Canyon and heard the thunder of the river of stars as it sweeps to the cataract of Niagara. Other Englishmen have travelled in our country, but Noyes has lived with us. He has lectured on poetry and read his own poems in hundreds of our cities; he has held a chair of literature in one of our colleges and fostered the first faint spark of poetic talent in some imaginative undergraduate, while in a leisure hour he refereed a boat-race on Lake Carnegie. And it is not only with the outer and visible life of America that this poet is in touch, but with something deeper. He embodies certain English characteristics, love of liberty, hatred of war, moral earnestness, and the vision of high ideals, which are our best inheritance from England.

There is not much material for a biography of Alfred Noyes; outwardly, at least, his life has been uneventful. Born in Staffordshire in central England, he spent a good part of his boyhood near the sea and came to Oxford a vigorous athlete. He entered Exeter College, where his name now appears along with that of William Morris in a storied window in the Hall. He rowed in his college boat, contributed to a college periodical, and, apparently, spent many hours in writing verse. It is not surprising that he gained little distinction as a scholar. But he was soon to gain it in a better way, for his first volume of verse, *The Loom of Years,* appeared in 1902 and at once attracted the attention of discerning critics. From this time, any account of his life would be little more than a chronological list of his various works. By 1910 he had published enough poems to collect them in two volumes. He had written the epic of England's heroic age — *Drake,* 1908 — he followed it with one of his best known and most delightful books — *Tales of the Mermaid Tavern.* In 1913 he was invited to America to deliver the Lowell lectures. He charmed audiences wherever he went by his readings — " noble stuff to read aloud " Gosse had called his verse — and Alice Meynell, a keen critic, called Noyes the best reader she had ever heard. He came to Princeton as professor of English Literature in 1914 just before the World War. Debarred by defective eyesight from service at the front, he served his country effectively by voice and pen. He resigned his post at Princeton some years after the war and since 1922 has lived in England the life of a poet and man of letters. He has written a novel, numerous stories, a volume of literary criticism, and a play or two, but his crowning work is the great trilogy — *The Torch-Bearers,* composed of *The Watchers of the Sky, The Book of Earth,* and *The Last Voyage.*

No anthology, however carefully compiled, can do full justice to the work of Alfred Noyes. He is a master of the verse-tale, and any verse-tale longer than a ballad is by its very length excluded from the ordinary anthology. But there are certain other characteristics of his work which may be mentioned. First of all one may note his extraordinary sense of rhythm. Poe defined poetry as the rhythmic creation of beauty. It is not, perhaps, a full and final definition, but so far as it goes it amply justifies the claim of Mr. Noyes from the very beginning of his work to the title of poet, for he has always been a lover of beauty who told his love in singing rhythm. Indeed a harsh critic might urge that in his earlier work the rhythm was rather redundant than restrained, that a too frequent employment of the repetend, for example, tended toward monotony. Yet it must be said that the strongly marked rhythm of his early work lends itself with special ease to recitation and from the beginning Mr. Noyes has written for the ear rather than for the eye.

There has been a very marked evolution in the poetic progress of Mr. Noyes. Beginning as a popular poet re-acting and protesting against the exotic school of the '90s with poems that he himself called " almost nonsense verse," he pushed on into the field of narrative poetry, ballad, verse-tale, and epic, a texture all shot through with lyric refrains. Gifted to a high degree with what may be called historic imagination, he was able to re-create the past, legend or history, situations, events, and characters, as in the *Tales of the Mermaid Tavern* where Shakespeare and his fellows come alive again. For such work he has evolved an easy unadorned blank verse that serves admirably the purpose of narrative, but would be, perhaps, too bald except for the lyric interludes.

Finally Mr. Noyes in his latest work has become the philosophic poet, re-creating the past to interpret the present. His Kepler in *The Torch-Bearers* distinguishes between two kinds of poets, the egoistic subjective who " lives in a silly world of his own making " and the other sort

> Whose mind still moves
> In vital concord with the soul of things;
> So that it thinks in music.

It is to this class that Mr. Noyes belongs. Conservative by temper and tradition, his mind is none the less saturated with the latest scientific thought. He protests alike against the religious bigotry of the past and the scientific materialism of so much of the present. To him science and the Faith are separated indeed by gulfs, " but only gulfs, not clashing contraries," and over these a bridge may be thrown which will unite them in a " great golden symphony of thought." It is to the proud title of such a pontifex that Mr. Noyes aspires. It may be that the bridge which he has thrown across the gulf is too insubstantial to bear the tread of most mortal feet, but the aim is noble and the vision, culminating in the Mass at sea in *The Last Voyage,* is in the truest sense sublime. Certain it is that future historians of English literature must cease to regard Alfred Noyes as the singer of *The Barrel-Organ* and *The Highwayman,* and deal with him as a poet who, in his own time and his own fashion, attempts like Milton to justify the ways of God to men.

From *TALES OF THE MERMAID TAVERN*

WILL SHAKESPEARE'S OUT

I

Will Shakespeare's out like Robin Hood
  With his merry men all in green,
To steal a deer in Charlecote wood
  Where never a deer was seen.

II

He's hunted all a night of June,
  He's followed a phantom horn,
He's killed a buck by the light of the moon,
  Under a fairy thorn.

III

He's carried it home with his merry, merry band,
  There never was haunch so fine;
For this buck was born in Elfin-land
  And fed upon sops-in-wine.

IV

This buck had browsed on elfin boughs
  Of rose-marie and bay,
And he's carried it home to the little white house
  Of sweet Anne Hathaway.

V

' The dawn above your thatch is red!
  Slip out of your bed, sweet Anne!
I have stolen a fairy buck,' he said,
  ' The first since the world began.

VI

'Roast it on a golden spit,
  And see that it do not burn;
For we never shall feather the like of it
  Out of the fairy fern.'

VII

She scarce had donned her long white gown
  And given him kisses four,
When the surly Sheriff of Stratford-town
  Knocked at the little green door.

VIII

They have gaoled sweet Will for a poacher;
  But squarely he fronts the squire,
With ' When did you hear in your woods of a deer?
  Was it under a fairy briar? '

IX

Sir Thomas he puffs, — ' If God thought good
  My water-butt ran with wine,
Or He dropt me a buck in Charlecote wood,
  I wot it is mine, not thine! '

X

' If you would eat of elfin meat,'
  Says Will, ' you must blow up your horn!
Take your bow, and feather the doe
  That's under the fairy thorn!

XI

' If you would feast on elfin food,
  You've only the way to learn!
Take your bow and feather the doe
  That's under the fairy fern! '

XII

They're hunting high, they're hunting low,
  They're all away, away,
With horse and hound to feather the doe
  That's under the fairy spray!

XIII

Sir Thomas he raged! Sir Thomas he swore!
  But all and all in vain;
For there never was deer in his woods before,
  And there never would be again!

MOUNTAIN LAUREL

Dedicated to my friends Carl and E. B. Stoeckel, in memory of one of their music festivals at Norfolk, Connecticut.

(A Connecticut Poet Returns to his Hills Singing)

I have been wandering in the lonely valleys,
  Where mountain laurel grows
And, in among the rocks, and the tall dark pine-trees
  The foam of the young bloom flows,
In a riot of rose-white stars, all drenched with the dew-fall,
  And musical with the bee,
Let the fog-bound cities over their dead wreaths quarrel.
  Wild laurel for me!

Wild laurel — mountain laurel —
  Bright as the breast of a cloud at break of day,
White-flowering laurel, wild mountain laurel,
  Rose-dappled snowdrifts, warm with the honey of May!
On the happy hill-sides, in the green valleys of Connecticut.
  Where the trout-streams go carolling to the sea, ...
I have laughed with the lovers of song and heard them singing
  ' Wild laurel for me! '

Far, far away is the throng that has never known beauty,
  Or looked upon unstained skies.
Did they think that my songs would scramble for withered
    bay-leaves
  In the streets where the brown fog lies?
They never have seen their wings, then, beating westward,
  To the heights where song is free,
To the hills where the laurel is drenched with the dawn's own
    colours,
  Wild laurel for me!

Wild laurel — mountain laurel —
  Where Robert o' Lincoln sings in the dawn and the dew,
White-flowering laurel, — wild mountain laurel
  Where song springs fresh from the heart, and the heart is
    true!
They have gathered the sheep to their fold, but where is the
    eagle?
  They have bridled their steeds, but when have they tamed
    the sea,
They have caged the wings, but never the heart of the singer,
  ' Wild laurel for me!'

If I never should find you again, O, lost companions,
  When the rose-red month begins,
With the wood-smoke curling blue by the Indian river,
  And the sound of the violins,
In dreams the breath of your green glens would still haunt me,
  Where night and her stars, drawing down on blossom and
    tree,
Turn earth to heaven, and whisper their love till daybreak.
  Wild laurel for me!

Wild laurel — mountain laurel —
  O, mount again, wild wings, to the stainless blue,
White-flowering laurel, wild mountain laurel,
  And all the glory of song that the young heart knew.
I have lived. I have loved. I have sung in the happy valleys
  Where the trout-streams go carolling to the sea,
I have met the lovers of song in the sunset bringing
  ' Wild laurel for me!'

PRINCETON
(1917)

The first four lines of this poem were written for inscription on the first joint memorial to the American and British soldiers who fell in the Revolutionary War. This memorial was recently dedicated at Princeton.

I

Here Freedom stood, by slaughtered friend and foe,
  And, ere the wrath paled or that sunset died,
Looked through the ages: then, with eyes aglow,
  Laid them, to wait that future, side by side.

II

Now lamp-lit gardens in the blue dusk shine
  Through dog-wood red and white,
And round the grey quadrangles, line by line,
  The windows fill with light,
Where Princeton calls to Magdalen, tower to tower,
  Twin lanthorns of the law,
And those cream-white magnolia boughs embower
  The halls of old Nassau.

III

The dark bronze tigers crouch on either side
  Where red-coats used to pass,
And round the bird-loved house where Mercer died
  And violets dusk the grass,
By Stony Brook that ran so red of old,
  But sings of friendship now,
To feed the old enemy's harvest fifty-fold
  The green earth takes the plough.

IV

Through this May night if one great ghost should stray
  With deep remembering eyes,
Where that old meadow of battle smiles away
  Its blood-stained memories,

If Washington should walk, where friend and foe
  Sleep and forget the past,
Be sure his unquenched heart would leap to know
  Their hosts are joined at last.

V

Be sure he walks, in shadowy buff and blue,
  Where those dim lilacs wave,
He bends his head to bless, as dreams come true,
  The promise of that grave,
Then with a vaster hope than thought can scan,
  Touching his ancient sword,
Prays for that mightier realm of God in man,
  ' Hasten Thy Kingdom, Lord.

VI

' Land of new hope, land of the singing stars,
  Type of the world to be,
The vision of a world set free from wars
  Takes life, takes form, from thee,
Where all the jarring nations of this earth.
  Beneath the all-blessing sun,
Bring the new music of mankind to birth
  And make the whole world one.'

VII

And those old comrades rise around him there,
  Old foemen, side by side,
With eyes like stars upon the brave night-air,
  And young as when they died,
To hear your bells, O beautiful Princeton towers,
  Ring for the world's release.
They see you, piercing like gray swords through flowers,
  And smile from hearts at peace.

From THE LAST VOYAGE

TELL ME YOU THAT SING

Tell me you
    That sing in the black-thorn
Out of what Mind
    Your melody springs.
Is it the World-soul
    Throbs like a fountain
Up thro' the throat
    Of an elf with wings?

Five sweet notes
    In a golden order,
Out of that deep realm
    Quivering through,
Flashed like a phrase
    Of light through darkness.
But *Who* entangled them?
    Tell me, *Who?*

You whose throats
    In the rain-drenched orchard
Peal your joys
    In a cadenced throng;
You whose wild notes,
    Fettered by Beauty,
Move like the stars
    In a rounded song;

Yours is the breath
    But *Whose* is the measure,
Shaped in an ecstasy
    Past all art?
Yours is the spending;
    Whose is the treasure?
Yours is the blood-beat;
    Whose is the heart?

Minstrels all
    That have woven your housen
Of withies and twigs
    With a Mind in-wrought,
Ye are the shuttles;
    But, out of what Darkness
Gather your thoughtless
    Patterns of thought?

Bright eyes glance
    Through your elfin doorways,
Roofed with rushes,
    And lined with moss.
Whose are the voiceless
    Pangs of creation?
Yours is the wild bough:
    Whose is the Cross?

Carols of light
    From a lovelier kingdom,
Gleams of a music
    On earth unheard,
Scattered like dew
    By the careless wayside,
Pour through the lifted
    Throat of a bird.

WIZARDS

There's many a proud wizard in Araby and Egypt
    Can read the silver writing of the stars as they run;
And many a dark gypsy, with a pheasant in his knapsack,
    Has gathered more by moonshine than wiser men have won;
But *I* know a Wizardry
    Can take a buried acorn
And whisper forests out of it, to tower against the sun.

There's many a magician in Bagdad and Benares
    Can read you — for a penny — what your future is to be;
And a flock of crazy prophets that by staring at a crystal
    Can fill it with more fancies than there's herring in the sea;

But *I* know a Wizardry
    Can break a freckled egg-shell
And shake a throstle out of it, in every hawthorn-tree.

There's many a crafty alchemist in Mecca and Jerusalem;
    And Michael Scott and Merlin were reckoned very wise;
But *I* know a Wizardry
    Can take a wisp of sun-fire
And round it to a planet, and roll it through the skies,
    With cities, and sea-ports, and little shining windows,
And hedgerows and gardens, and loving human eyes. . . .

WILFRID WILSON GIBSON
1878–

Gibson was the first of the 'new' poets of this century to gain a general recognition, chiefly through the excitement which was aroused by the publication of *Daily Bread* (1910). In this volume, his eighth, he relinquished decisively his earlier enthusiasm for medieval themes and atmosphere and announced himself the deliberate champion of the labouring man and the recorder of the tragedies of his existence. It was inevitable that Gibson should be drawn to the group of younger poets who were bent on revolution. With Drinkwater, Monro, Marsh, and Brooke he helped to inaugurate the annual collection of *Georgian Poetry* which for a dozen years acquainted the world with the best work of the newer generation. In 1914, with Abercrombie and Drinkwater, he edited the quarterly *New Numbers* during the single year of its life. Save for this brief period before the war, Gibson has associated very little with the literary world, preferring to live secluded in Hertfordshire.

In 1917 he came to America to lecture. The poems which he wrote during those six months and called by such deceptive names as *In Indiana, On Broadway* and *By Lake Michigan* are full of nostalgia for English friends and English countryside. He was eager to be at the Front, though the authorities had rejected him three times. Finally in October he was allowed to join the Service Corps as a private. The scenes of which he was a part moved him to write some of the very little absolute poetry which the war induced. Since then he has published little which can stand beside this war verse and his earlier work in *Stonefolds, Daily Bread, Fires,* and *Thoroughfares.*

Mr. Gibson would probably not like to be reminded that when he was young and foolish he wrote poetry like this:

> From cups of crystal and amethyst
> And golden bowls of summer, sapphire-lipped
> We drank deep draughts of life, O love, together.

With great diligence he has excised from collections of his verse all evidence of his having once sown Swinburnean wild oats. This has demanded the discarding of most of his first three volumes, since they are devoted to hymning the Virgin and disclosing the private sorrow of pale queens with cloudy hair. Yet even in this early verse signs pointed ahead to his later preoccupation with the lives of simple working folk. In *Urlyn the Harper* we come on sketches of the Stone-Breaker, the Shepherd, the Ploughman, in which, before he has followed them inside their cottages, he dreams about their life as he imagines it may be. The voice of hungry generations cries in the *Weary Singers:*

> Why have the singers left us here to die
> Who sang so merrily through the morn?
> Why have they left us, songless and forlorn,
>   To perish darkling, with no flaming word
> Nor song for pilot star?

It was the Prelude to *Daily Bread,* a confession of his own waking from oblivion, which marked the point when poetry once more, after its long subservience to art for art's sake, acknowledged its concern with a wide humanity.

> I caught the stormy summons of the sea
> Through whose unresting conflict day and night
> Surges the dauntless human harmony.

The idylls of labour in this volume advance remarkably beyond the earlier work of a similar kind in *Stonefolds* simply because Gibson makes a deeper plunge into the lives he tries to understand. The stories formed from the casualties in the submerged existence of fisherfolk, sailors, riveters, furnacemen, deal with the inescapable realities of poverty and death and childbirth, desertion and loneliness. The victims do not attempt to understand the social wrongs from which their class suffers. They do not even complain, but they humbly realize one fact and utter it haltingly; sometimes, providentially, before it is too late:

> Yet when all the babes are fed,
>   Love, are there not crumbs to treasure?

The annals of the poor have continued to be the predominant inspiration of Gibson's narrative poetry. Since 1910 there has been, indeed, little change in his art save when he has made trial of new ways of presenting a story. For the most part he has used a narrative formula which permits the subject to muse — always in completely formed sentences — about the situation in which he finds himself. A typical line will show the simplicity of this formula:

> 'Twas well
> He'd work to stop him thinking. He was glad
> His mate to-night was not a talky lad.

The stream of consciousness, as one can readily see, is not analyzed after the fashion of Joyce and his followers, and must strike those who are accustomed to a more subtle method as indirect and often cumbersome.

In his first idylls Gibson cared mainly to tell a good story. One traces subsequently a feeling for the surroundings and conditions which evoke the tragic conclusions. Since 1917 some impulse driving him to a closer scrutiny of the mental processes of his characters has made him allow them more liberty in their musings. Eddies of past experience, fragments of forgotten living and subterranean longings swirl over the tension of the present moment in such stories as *The Rocklight* and *The Platelayer*. Gibson avows this change of method by calling the poems in this volume (*Livelihood*) dramatic reveries. One may conjecture that this desire to explore motives determined his use of the definitely dramatic form for *Krindlesyke* (1922) and *Kestrel Edge* (1924).

Gibson undoubtedly owes his reputation to his early stories of working people. Yet it is within the range of possibility that later critics, not impressed by the mere content of these stories as we are for whom they possess the charm of novelty, will be more taken with other achievements. There has been little said of the distinctive qualities of his war lyrics, in particular the sharp and almost exultant irony which he attains in them by the use, for picturing the ghastliest scenes of war, of verse-forms long associated with exalted emotion. Nor has it been noticed that he has come closer to the springs of folk poetry than any of his contemporaries except Mr. Housman. His versatility, alone, warrants the belief that he will be longest read of the group of young poets whose numbers were so wasted by the war.

THE BLIND ROWER

And since he rowed his father home,
His hand has never touched an oar.
All day he wanders by the shore,
And hearkens to the swish of foam.
Though blind from birth, he still could row
As well as any lad with sight;
And knew strange things that none may know
Save those who live without the light.

When they put out that Summer eve
To sink the lobster-pots at sea,
The sun was crimson in the sky;
And not a breath was in the sky,
The brooding thunder-laden sky
That, heavily and wearily,
Weighed down upon the waveless sea
That scarcely seemed to heave.

The pots were safely sunk; and then
The father gave the word for home:
He took the tiller in his hand,
And, in his heart already home,
He brought her nose round towards the land,
To steer her straight for home.

He never spoke,
Nor stirred again:
A sudden stroke,
And he lay dead,
With staring eyes, and lips of lead.

The son rowed on, and nothing feared:
And sometimes, merrily,
He lifted up his voice and sang,
Both high and low,
And loud and sweet:
For he was ever gay at sea,
And ever glad to row,
And rowed as only blind men row:

And little did the blind lad know
That death was at his feet:
For still he thought his father steered;
Nor knew that he was all alone
With death upon the open sea.
And strangely on the silence rang
That lonely melody,
As, through the livid, brooding gloom
By rock and reef, he rowed for home —
The blind man rowed the dead man home.

But, as they neared the shore,
He rested on his oar:
And, wondering that his father kept
So very quiet in the stern,
He laughed and asked him if he slept;
And vowed he heard him snore just now.
Though, when his father spoke no word
A sudden fear upon him came:
And, crying on his father's name,
With flinching heart, he heard
The water lapping on the shore;
And all his blood ran cold to feel
The shingle grate beneath the keel:
And stretching over towards the stern,
His knuckle touched the dead man's brow.

But help was near at hand;
And he came safe to land:
Though none has ever known
How he rowed in alone,
And never touched a reef.
Some say they saw the dead man steer —
The dead man steer the blind man home,
Though, when they found him dead,
His hand was cold as lead.

So, ever restless to and fro,
In every sort of weather,
The blind lad wanders on the shore,
And hearkens to the foam.

His hand has never touched an oar,
Since they came home together —
The blind, who rowed his father home —
The dead, who steered his blind son home.

GERANIUMS

Stuck in a bottle on the window-sill,
  In the cold gaslight burning gaily red
Against the luminous blue of London night,
These flowers are mine: while somewhere out of sight
In some black-throated alley's stench and heat,
Oblivious of the racket of the street,
A poor old weary woman lies in bed.

Broken with lust and drink, blear-eyed and ill,
Her battered bonnet nodding on her head,
From a dark door she clutched my sleeve and said:
' I've sold no bunch to-day, nor touched a bite . . .
Son, buy sixpenn'orth, and 'twill mean a bed.'

So, blazing gaily red
Against the luminous deeps
Of starless London night
They burn for my delight,
While somewhere, snug in bed,
A worn old woman sleeps.

And yet to-morrow will these blooms be dead
With all their lively beauty; and to-morrow
May end the light lusts and the heavy sorrow
Of that old body with the nodding head.
The last oath muttered, the last pint drained deep,
She'll sink, as Cleopatra sank, to sleep,
Nor need to barter blossoms for a bed.

THE VINDICTIVE STAIRCASE
OR
THE REWARD OF INDUSTRY

In a doomed and empty house in Houndsditch
All night long I lie awake and listen,
While all night the ghost of Mrs. Murphy
Tiptoes up and down the wheezy staircase,
Sweeling ghostly grease of quaking candles.

Mrs. Murphy, timidest of spectres,
You who were the cheeriest of charers,
With the heart of innocence and only
Torn between a zest for priests and porter,
Mrs. Murphy of the ample bosom —
Suckler of a score or so of children
(' Children? Bless you! Why, I've buried six, sir.')
Who in forty years wore out three husbands,
And one everlasting, shameless bonnet,
Which I've little doubt was coffined with you —
Mrs. Murphy, wherefor do you wander,
Sweeling ghostly grease of quaking candles,
Up and down the stairs you scrubbed so sorely,
Scrubbed till they were naked, dank, and aching?

Now that you are dead, is this their vengeance?
Recollecting all you made them suffer
With your bristled brush and soapy water
When you scrubbed them naked, dank, and aching,
Have they power to hold your ghostly footsteps
Chained as to an everlasting treadmill?

Mrs. Murphy, think you 'twould appease them
If I rose now in my shivering nightshirt,
Rose and told them how you, too, had suffered —
You, their seeming tyrant, but their bondslave —
Toiling uncomplaining in their service
Till your knuckles and your knees were knotted
Into writhing fires of red rheumatics,
And how, in the end, 'twas they who killed you?

517

Even should their knots still harden to you,
Bow your one and all-enduring bonnet
Till your ear is level with my keyhole,
While I whisper ghostly consolation:
Know this house is marked out for the spoiler,
Doomed to fall to Hobnails with his pickaxe;
And its crazy staircase chopped to firewood,
Splintered, bundled, burned to smoke and ashes,
Soon shall perish, scattered to the four winds.
Then, God rest your spirit, Mrs. Murphy!

Yet, who knows! A staircase . . . Mrs. Murphy,
God forbid that you be doomed to tiptoe
Through eternity, a timid spectre,
Sweeling ghostly grease of quaking candles,
Up and down the spectre of a staircase,
While all night I lie awake and listen
In a damned and ghostly house in Houndsditch!

ON THE EMBANKMENT

Down on the sunlit ebb, with the wind in her sails, and free
Of cable and anchor, she swept rejoicing to seek the sea.

And my.eyes and my heart swept out with her,
When at my elbow I felt a stir;
And, glancing down, I saw a lad —
A shambling lad with shifty air,
Weak-chested, stunted and ill-clad,
Who watched her with unseeing stare.

Dull watery grey eyes he had,
Blinking beneath the slouching cap
That hid the low-browed, close-cropped head:
And as I turned to him he said
With hopeless hang-dog air:
' Just out of gaol three days ago,
And I'll be back before I know:
For nothing else is left a chap
When once he's been inside . . . and so . . .'

Then dumb he stood with sightless stare
Set on the sunlit, windy sail of the far-off boat that free
Of cable and anchor, still swept on rejoicing to seek the sea.

My heart is a sunlit, windy sail:
My heart is a hopeless lad in gaol.

THE PLATELAYER

Tapping the rails as he went by
    And driving the slack wedges tight,
He walked towards the morning sky
Between two golden lines of light
That dwindled slowly into one
Sheer golden rail that ran right on
Over the fells into the sun.

And dazzling in his eyes it shone,
That golden track, as left and right
He swung his clinking hammer — ay,
'Twas dazzling after that long night
In Hindfell tunnel, working by
A smoky flare, and making good
The track the rains had torn . . .
                              Clink, clink,
On the sound metal — on the wood
A duller thwack!
                    It made him blink,
That running gold. . . .
                              'Twas sixteen hours
Since he'd left home — his garden smelt
So fragrant with the heavy showers
When he left home — and now he felt
That it would smell more fresh and sweet
After the tunnel's reek and fume
Of damp warm cinders. 'Twas a treat
To come upon the scent and bloom
That topped the cutting by the wood
After the cinders of the track,
The cinders and tarred sleepers — good
To lift your eyes from gritty black

Upon that blaze of green and red. . . .
And she'd be waiting by the fence,
And with the baby . . .
                              Straight to bed
He'd make, if he had any sense,
And sleep the day; but like as not,
When he'd had breakfast, he'd turn to
And hoe the back potato-plot:
'Twould be one mass of weeds he knew.
You'd think each single drop of rain
Turned as it fell into a weed.
You seemed to hoe and hoe in vain.
Chickweed and groundsel didn't heed
The likes of him — and bindweed, well,
You hoed and hoed — still its white roots
Ran deeper. . . .
                      'Twould be good to smell
The fresh-turned earth, and feel his boots
Sink deep into the brown wet mould,
After hard cinders. . . .
                              And, maybe
The baby, sleeping good as gold
In its new carriage under a tree,
Would keep him company, while his wife
Washed up the breakfast-things.
                                    'Twas strange,
The difference that she made to life,
That tiny baby girl.
                          The change
Of work would make him sleep more sound.
'Twas sleep he needed. That long night
Shovelling wet cinders underground,
With breaking back, the smoky light
Stinging his eyes till they were sore. . . .

He'd worked the night that she was born,
Standing from noon the day before
All through the winter's night till morn,
Laying fog-signals on the line
Where it ran over Devil's Ghyll. . . .

And she was born at half-past nine,
Just as he'd stood aside until
The Scots Express ran safely by. . . .
He'd but to shut his eyes to see
Those windows flashing blindingly
A moment through the blizzard — he
Could feel again that slashing snow
That seemed to cut his face.
                    But they,
The passengers, they couldn't know
What it cost him to keep the way
Open for them. So snug and warm
They slept or chattered, while he stood
And faced all night that raking storm —
The little house beside the wood
For ever in his thoughts: and he
Not knowing what was happening . . .

But all went well as well could be
With Sally and the little thing.
And it had been worth while to wait
Through that long night with work to do,
To meet his mother at the gate
With such good news, and find it true,
Ay, truer than the truth.
                  He still
Could see his wife's eyes as he bent
Over the bairn. . . .
             The Devil's Ghyll
Had done its worst, and he was spent;
But he'd have faced a thousand such
Wild nights as thon, to see that smile
Again, and feel that tender touch
Upon his cheek.
            'Twas well worth while
With such reward. And it was strange,
The difference such a little thing
Could make to them — how it could change
Their whole life for them, and could bring
Such happiness to them, though they

Had seemed as happy as could be
Before it came to them.
                    The day
Was shaping well: and there was she,
The lassie sleeping quietly
Within her arms, beside the gate.

The storm had split that lilac tree.
But he was tired, and it must wait.

THE CONSCRIPT

Indifferent, flippant, earnest, but all bored,
  The doctors sit in the glare of electric light
Watching the endless stream of naked white
Bodies of men for whom their hasty award
Means life or death maybe or the living death
Of mangled limbs, blind eyes or a darkened brain:
And the chairman, as his monocle falls again
Pronounces each doom with easy indifferent breath.

Then suddenly I shudder as I see
A young man stand before them wearily,
Cadaverous as one already dead:
But still they stare untroubled as he stands
With arms outstretched and drooping thorn-crowned head,
The nail-marks glowing in his feet and hands.

RAGTIME

A minx in khaki struts the limelit boards:
  With false moustache, set smirk and ogling eyes
And straddling legs and swinging hips she tries
To swagger it like a soldier, while the chords
Of rampant ragtime jangle, clash and clatter,
And over the brassy blare and drumming din
She strains to squirt her squeaky notes and thin
Spirtle of sniggering lascivious patter.

Then out into the jostling Strand I turn,
And down a dark lane to the quiet river,
One stream of silver under the full moon,
And think of how cold searchlights flare and burn
Over dank trenches where men crouch and shiver,
Humming, to keep their hearts up, that same tune.

RUPERT BROOKE

I

Your face was lifted to the golden sky
    Ablaze beyond the black roofs of the square
As flame on flame leapt, flourishing in air
Its tumult of red stars exultantly
To the cold constellations dim and high;
And, as we neared, the roaring ruddy flare
Kindled to gold your throat and brow and hair
Until you burned, a flame of ecstasy.

The golden head goes down into the night
Quenched in cold gloom — and yet again you stand
Beside me now with lifted face alight
As, flame to flame and fire to fire, you burn . . .
Then, recollecting, laughingly you turn
And look into my eyes and take my hand.

II

Once in my garret — you being far away
Tramping the hills and breathing upland air,
Or so I fancied — brooding in my chair,
I watched the London sunlight feeble and grey
Dapple my desk, too tired to labour more,
When, looking up, I saw you standing there,
Although I'd caught no footstep on the stair,
Like sudden April at my open door.

Though now beyond earth's farthest hills you fare,
Song-crowned, immortal, sometimes it seems to me
That, if I listen very quietly,

523

Perhaps I'll hear a light foot on the stair
And see you, standing with your angel air,
Fresh from the uplands of eternity.

III

Your eyes rejoiced in colour's ecstasy,
Fulfilling even their uttermost desire,
When, over a great sunlit field afire
With windy poppies streaming like a sea
Of scarlet flame that flaunted riotously
Among green orchards of that western shire,
You gazed as though your heart could never tire
Of life's red flood in summer revelry.

And as I watched you, little thought had I
How soon beneath the dim, low-drifting sky
Your soul should wander down the darkling way
With eyes that peer a little wistfully,
Half-glad, half-sad, remembering, as they see
Lethean poppies, shrivelling ashen grey.

IV

October chestnuts showered their perishing gold
Over us as beside the stream we lay
In the Old Vicarage garden that blue day,
Talking of verse and all the manifold
Delights a little net of words may hold,
While in the sunlight water-voles at play
Dived under a trailing crimson bramble-spray,
And walnuts thudded on the soft black mould.

Your soul goes down unto a darker stream
Alone, O friend, yet even in death's deep night
Your eyes may grow accustomed to the dark,
And Styx for you may have the ripple and gleam
Of your familiar river, and Charon's bark
Tarry by that old garden of your delight.

WILLIAM HENRY DAVIES
1871–

The biography of nearly every English poet runs according to a formula which includes his public school, his university, his struggle for a publisher, and finally a favourable review in the *Times*. If his biographer has anything more exciting to record than a conversion to the Church of Rome or a literary quarrel of some magnitude, he is lucky. Mr. Davies's story provides a grateful diversion. In the first place he was born in a Welsh public-house and apprenticed to a trade — an unorthodox beginning certainly. This might conceivably have led to a respectable poetical career (one remembers Jonson and Gay and Keats) had he not abandoned England entirely to adopt in America the profession of a tramp. For six years he rode the rods, begged at back doors, slept in country jails, worked when he was compelled to, and loafed when he could do so without fear of starvation. He all but died of malaria in a Mississippi swamp and he buried a leg in Canada after an unsuccessful attempt at boarding a moving freight train.

During these aimless years he read the English classics in such tattered editions as he could afford and cherished a half-formed idea of becoming a poet himself. To this end he settled finally in a London lodging-house where he contrived to live on a legacy which gave him eight shillings a week, while preparing a book of verses for publication. He had no very clear idea of how a book gets itself into circulation and his account of the various schemes he formulated to accomplish his end would be amusing if they were not such a pathetic revelation of the vicissitudes which genius, so inauspiciously born, has to undergo. At last he hit on the idea of publishing his poems at his own expense and sending copies to various prominent men, requesting them to purchase, if they 'required a half-crown book of verses.' It was a fortunate plan, for among others who were impressed with the value of his poetry was Bernard Shaw, whose subsequent championing of the poetry of the ' super-tramp ' has certainly been no hindrance to its popularity. Davies became, in fact, something of a fad with the artists, who enjoyed his oddity, and with the fashionable folk who cultivate the newly great. He seems to have wandered through their studios and drawing-rooms as a kind of astonished Christopher Sly, proud of his sudden fame, but cautiously on the outlook for snubs and wary of flattering patrons.

Davies's best work is contained in his early volumes, *The Soul's Destroyer* (1906), *New Poems* (1907), *Nature Poems* (1908), *Farewell to Poesy* (1910), *Songs of Joy* (1911), *Foliage* (1913). A collective edition was published in 1928. It is fortunate that Davies began in 1903 to issue an account of his years of vagabondage. *The Autobiography of a Super-tramp, Beggars,* and *The True Traveller* are unique in the literature of roguery. Strangely enough they give one more of an idea of their author's ingenuousness than does his poetry. It seems a marvel that one so little aware of the usual literary qualities of form and climax as the teller of these rambling though delightful picaresque tales, can be the author of poetry which impresses one as the work of a craftsman bred in the tradition of a highly sophisticated art.

The most remarkable trait of Davies's poetry is its joyousness, a fortunate coincidence since at the time he emerged from the obscurity of a Kennington doss-house the Georgian poets were making simplicity and innocence the order of the day. Certainly no literary man among his contemporaries knows as much about the possible depths of human degradation or has looked on at so many scenes of violence and bestiality and suffering. How can it be that such a man can write like a happy child of a world full of sunshine? His naïveté is not the affected innocence of the weary worldling. Those who compare his poetry to that of the Elizabethans are undiscerning. It has none of the richness of mood, no suggestion of what ' in the ways of a thousand years men have come to desire.' Nor does it really resemble the *Songs of Innocence* to which it has been compared. The external world is clear and objective to Davies, not symbolical.

> I pass through life a laughing man,
> Untouched by any sin.

He confesses in *Sadness and Joy* that Joy can make ten songs for him while Sadness is making four. This may be the answer. The evil in the world will not change into song for him and he is a lyric poet and must sing.

He has not grown into a fatuous middle age however. His later poetry, although it is inferior in melody and rapture to the earlier, shows a maturing vision. In fact a passage in *Later Days* seems to intimate that he chafes under the designations which the critics compel him to adhere to as a poet. He prints there an excellent poem in the Hardy manner and comments:

Now if I sent this poem to an editor it would probably be returned, and another, whose subject was a butterfly or bird, a daisy or a tree, would be accepted. The reason for this is that I have been labelled as a Nature poet, whom the deeper problems of life do not concern. For that reason I am not allowed to give my critics the lie, but must stick to my butterflies, my bees and my birds.

Davies's nature — and in spite of this plaint it is his poetry in her praise which will secure him immortality — is not the nature of the romantic poets. He feels no sense of any divinity deeply interfused; the skylark is decidedly not a symbol of his own intricate emotions. He talks to the birds and the cows like a companion of the road and preaches to them like a modern St. Francis. He bids the sparrows stop fighting and behave as the lady-like linnets do. Though a worshipper of her beauty, he is on intimate terms with the moon. In his vagabonding he was forced to rely on nature as a friend to save him from perishing of cold or heat or boredom. His nature poetry is a grateful record of their friendship.

THE KINGFISHER

It was the Rainbow gave thee birth,
    And left thee all her lovely hues;
And, as her mother's name was Tears,
    So runs it in thy blood to choose
For haunts the lonely pools, and keep
In company with trees that weep.

Go you and, with such glorious hues,
　　Live with proud Peacocks in green parks;
On lawns as smooth as shining glass,
　　Let every feather show its mark;
Get thee on boughs and clap thy wings
Before the windows of proud kings.

Nay, lovely Bird, thou art not vain;
　　Thou hast no proud ambitious mind;
I also love a quiet place
　　That's green, away from all mankind;
A lonely pool, and let a tree
Sigh with her bosom over me.

THE ELEMENTS

No house of stone
　　Was built for me;
When the Sun shines —
　　I am a bee.

No sooner comes
　　The Rain so warm,
I come to light —
　　I am a worm.

When the Winds blow,
　　I do not strip,
But set my sails —
　　I am a ship.

When Lightning comes,
　　It plays with me
And I with it —
　　I am a tree.

When drowned men rise
　　At Thunder's word,
Sings Nightingale —
　　I am a bird.

NO MASTER

Indeed this is sweet life! my hand
Is under no proud man's command;
There is no voice to break my rest
Before a bird has left its nest;
There is no man to change my mood,
Would I go nutting in the wood;
No man to pluck my sleeve and say —
I want thy labour for this day;
No man to keep me out of sight,
When that dear Sun is shining bright.
None but my friends shall have command
Upon my time, my heart and hand;
I'll rise from sleep to help a friend,
But let no stranger orders send,
Or hear my curses fast and thick,
Which in his purse-proud throat will stick
Like burs. If I cannot be free
To do such work as pleases me,
Near woodland pools and under trees,
You'll get no work at all; for I
Would rather live this life and die
A beggar on a thief, than be
A working slave with no days free.

THE SLEEPERS

As I walked down the waterside
This silent morning, wet and dark;
Before the cocks in farmyards crowed,
Before the dogs began to bark;
Before the hour of five was struck
By old Westminster's mighty clock:

As I walked down the waterside
This morning, in the cold damp air,
I saw a hundred women and men
Huddled in rags and sleeping there:
These people have no work, thought I,
And long before their time they die.

That moment, on the waterside,
   A lighted car came at a bound;
I looked inside, and saw a score
   Of pale and weary men that frowned;
Each man sat in a huddled heap,
Carried to work while fast asleep.

Ten cars rushed down the waterside,
   Like lighted coffins in the dark;
With twenty dead men in each car,
   That must be brought alive by work:
These people work too hard, thought I,
And long before their time they die.

THE EXAMPLE

Here's an example from
   A Butterfly;
That on a rough, hard rock
   Happy can lie;
Friendless and all alone
On this unsweetened stone.

Now let my bed be hard,
   No care take I;
I'll make my joy like this
   Small Butterfly;
Whose happy heart has power
To make a stone a flower.

FANCY'S HOME

Tell me, Fancy, sweetest child,
   Of thy parents and thy birth;
Had they silk, and had they gold,
   And a park to wander forth,
With a castle green and old?

In a cottage I was born,
    My kind father was Content,
My dear mother Innocence;
    On wild fruits of wonderment
I have nourished ever since.

TRULY GREAT

My walls outside must have some flowers,
    My walls within must have some books;
A house that's small; a garden large,
    And in it leafy nooks.

A little gold that's sure each week;
    That comes not from my living kind,
But from a dead man in his grave,
    Who cannot change his mind.

A lovely wife, and gentle too;
    Contented that no eyes but mine
Can see her many charms, nor voice
    To call her beauty fine.

Where she would in that stone cage live,
    A self-made prisoner, with me;
While many a wild bird sang around,
    On gate, on bush, on tree.

And she sometimes to answer them,
    In her far sweeter voice than all;
Till birds, that loved to look on leaves,
    Will doat on a stone wall.

With this small house, this garden large,
    This little gold, this lovely mate,
With health in body, peace at heart —
    Show me a man more great.

531

JOY

Poor souls, who think that joy is bought
    With pelf;
The bait that captures joy is joy
    Itself.
My joy it came mysteriously
    At birth;
I give it to, not take it from
    The earth.
Have pity on my enemy:
    Again,
And yet again, my triumph gives
    Him pain.
Come, Death, give me life's perfect end;
    Take me
In my sleep, Oh Death, and do not
    Wake me.

THE CHILD AND THE MARINER

A dear old couple my grandparents were,
  And kind to all dumb things; they saw in Heaven
The lamb that Jesus petted when a child;
Their faith was never draped by Doubt: to them
Death was a rainbow in Eternity,
That promised everlasting brightness soon.
An old seafaring man was he; a rough
Old man, but kind; and hairy, like the nut
Full of sweet milk. All day on shore he watched
The winds for sailors' wives, and told what ships
Enjoyed fair weather, and what ships had storms;
He watched the sky, and he could tell for sure
What afternoons would follow stormy morns,
If quiet nights would end wild afternoons.
He leapt away from scandal with a roar,
And if a whisper still possessed his mind,
He walked about and cursed it for a plague.
He took offence at Heaven when beggars passed,
And sternly called them back to give them help.

In this old captain's house I lived, and things
That house contained were in ships' cabins once:
Sea-shells and charts and pebbles, model ships;
Green weeds, dried fishes stuffed, and coral stalks;
Old wooden trunks with handles of spliced rope,
With copper saucers full of monies strange,
That seemed the savings of dead men, not touched
To keep them warm since their real owners died;
Strings of red beads, methought were dipped in blood,
And swinging lamps, as though the house might move;
An ivory lighthouse built on ivory rocks,
The bones of fishes and three bottled ships.
And many a thing was there which sailors make
In idle hours, when on long voyages,
Of marvellous patience, to no lovely end.
And on those charts I saw the small black dots
That were called islands, and I knew they had
Turtles and palms, and pirates' buried gold.

There came a stranger to my grandad's house,
The old man's nephew, a seafarer too;
A big, strong able man who could have walked
Tom Barlum's hill all clad in iron mail;
So strong he could have made one man his club
To knock down others — Henry was his name,
No other name was uttered by his kin.
And here he was, insooth ill-clad, but oh,
Thought I, what secrets of the sea are his!
This man knows coral islands in the sea,
And dusky girls heart-broken for white men;
This sailor knows of wondrous lands afar,
More rich than Spain, when the Phoenicians shipped
Silver for common ballast, and they saw
Horses at silver mangers eating grain;
This man has seen the wind blow up a mermaid's hair
Which, like a golden serpent, reared and stretched
To feel the air away beyond her head.
He begged my pennies, which I gave with joy —
He will most certainly return some time
A self-made king of some new land, and rich.
Alas that he, the hero of my dreams,

Should be his people's scorn; for they had grown
To proud command of ships, whilst he had toiled
Before the mast for years, and well content;
Him they despised, and only Death could bring
A likeness in his face to show like them.
For he drank all his pay, nor went to sea
As long as ale was easy got on shore.

Now, in his last long voyage he had sailed
From Plymouth Sound to where sweet odours fan
The Cingalese at work, and then back home —
But came not near his kin till pay was spent.
He was not old, yet seemed so; for his face
Looked like the drowned man's in the morgue, when it
Has struck the wooden wharves and keels of ships.
And all his flesh was pricked with Indian ink,
His body marked as rare and delicate
As dead men struck by lightning under trees,
And pictured with fine twigs and curlèd ferns;
Chains on his neck and anchors on his arms;
Rings on his fingers, bracelets on his wrist;
And on his breast the *Jane* of Appledore
Was schooner rigged, and in full sail at sea.
He could not whisper with his strong hoarse voice
No more than could a horse creep quietly;
He laughed to scorn the men that muffled close
For fear of wind, till all their neck was hid,
Like Indian corn wrapped up in long green leaves.
He knew no flowers but seaweeds brown and green,
He knew no birds but those that followed ships.
Full well he knew the water-world; he heard
A grander music there than we on land,
When organ shakes a church; swore he would make
The sea his home, though it was always roused
By such wild storms as never leave Cape Horn;
Happy to hear the tempest grunt and squeal
Like pigs heard dying in a slaughterhouse.
A true-born mariner, and this his hope —
His coffin would be what his cradle was,
A boat to drown in and be sunk at sea;
To drown at sea and lie a dainty corpse

534

Salted and iced in Neptune's larder deep.
This man despised small coasters, fishing smacks;
He scorned those sailors who at night and morn
Can see the coast, when in their little boats
They go a six days' voyage and are back
Home with their wives for every Sabbath day.
Much did he talk of tankards of old beer,
And bottled stuff he drank in other lands,
Which was a liquid fire like Hell to gulp.
But Paradise to sip.

          And so he talked;
Nor did those people listen with more awe
To Lazarus — whom they had seen stone dead —
Than did we urchins to that seaman's voice.
He many a tale of wonder told: of where,
At Argostoli, Cephalonia's sea
Ran over the earth's lip in heavy floods;
And then again of how the strange Chinese
Conversed much as our homely Blackbirds sing.
He told us how he sailed in one old ship
Near that volcano Martinique, whose power
Shook like dry leaves the whole Caribbean seas;
And made the Sun set in a sea of fire
Which only half was his; and dust was thick
On deck, and stones were pelted at the mast.
So, as we walked along, that seaman dropped
Into my greedy ears such words that sleep
Stood at my pillow half the night perplexed.
He told how isles sprang up and sank again,
Between short voyages, to his amaze;
How they did come and go, and cheated charts;
Told how a crew was cursed when one man killed
A bird that perched upon a moving barque;
And how the sea's sharp needles, firm and strong,
Ripped open the bellies of big, iron ships;
Of mighty icebergs in the Northern seas,
That haunt the far horizon like white ghosts.
He told of waves that lift a ship so high
That birds could pass from starboard unto port
Under her dripping keel.

Oh, it was sweet
To hear that seaman tell such wondrous tales:
How deep the sea in parts, that drownèd men
Must go a long way to their graves and sink
Day after day, and wander with the tides.
He spake of his own deeds;.of how he sailed
One summer's night along the Bosphorus,
And he, — who knew no music like the wash
Of waves against a ship, or wind in shrouds —
Heard then the music on that woody shore
Of nightingales, and feared to leave the deck,
He thought 'twas sailing into Paradise.

To hear these stories all we urchins placed
Our pennies in that seaman's ready hand;
Until one morn he signed for a long cruise,
And sailed away — we never saw him more.
Could such a man sink in the sea unknown?
Nay, he had found a land with something rich,
That kept his eyes turned inland for his life.
' A damn bad sailor and a landshark too,
No good in port or out ' — my grandad said.

LEISURE

What is this life if, full of care,
    We have no time to stand and stare.

No time to stand beneath the boughs
And stare as long as sheep or cows.

No time to see, when woods we pass,
Where squirrels hide their nuts in grass.

No time to see, in broad daylight,
Streams full of stars, like skies at night.

No time to turn at Beauty's glance,
And watch her feet, how they can dance.

No time to wait till her mouth can
Enrich that smile her eyes began.

A poor life this if, full of care,
We have no time to stand and stare.

✤ WILLIAM HENRY DAVIES ✤

SWEET STAY–AT–HOME

Sweet Stay-at-Home, sweet Well-content,
Thou knowest of no strange continent:
Thou hast not felt thy bosom keep
A gentle motion with the deep;
Thou hast not sailed in Indian seas,
Where scent comes forth in every breeze.
Thou hast not seen the rich grape grow
For miles, as far as eyes can go;
Thou hast not seen a summer's night
When maids could sew by a worm's light;
Nor the North Sea in spring send out
Bright hues that like birds flit about
In solid cages of white ice —
Sweet Stay-at-Home, all these long hours
Thou hast not seen black fingers pick
White cotton when the bloom is thick,
Nor heard black throats in harmony;
Nor hast thou sat on stones that lie
Flat on the earth, that once did rise
To hide proud kings from common eyes,
Thou hast not seen plains full of bloom
Where green things had such little room
They pleased the eye like fairer flowers —
Sweet Stay-at-Home, all these long hours,
Sweet Well-content, sweet Love-one-place,
Sweet, simple maid, bless thy dear face;
For thou hast made more homely stuff
Nurture thy gentle self enough;
I love thee for a heart that's kind —
Not for the knowledge in thy mind.

WALTER DE LA MARE
1873–

Many young poets contributed to the five volumes of Georgian Poetry that appeared between 1911 and 1922. Two of the greatest, Brooke and Flecker, are dead; a third is the present Poet Laureate. Of all the rest, Walter de la Mare seems most certain of a place in the noble army of English poets. Since the death of Robert Bridges there is no one left, it is fair to say, who can match his delicate artistry, his atmosphere of otherwhere, and his singing grace.

Little is known of De la Mare's life and what we know is not in the least exciting. He has not wandered in search of adventure, served abroad, or starved in London. He was born in a village in Kent in 1873; on the father's side the descendant of an old Huguenot family, on the mother's of a good Scotch family, the Brownings. He attended St. Paul's Cathedral School, founded a school-boy paper there, and left at seventeen years of age to enter the office of the Anglo-American Oil Company. Here he served for eighteen years until in 1908 a government grant and a pension of one hundred pounds set him free to devote himself to letters.

He had already begun to distinguish himself; various stories had appeared in English magazines under the pen-name of Walter Ramal. His first volume of poems *Songs of Childhood,* 1901, was accepted by Andrew Lang for publication and generously praised by him in Longman's Magazine. A first novel, *Henry Brocken,* a fantastic story of a boy's encounters with the characters he had loved best in English literature, came out in 1904. The *Poems* of 1906 showed a distinct development in power and grasp; *The Three Mulla-Muggers,* a delightful child's story, written for his own children, of the adventures of three semi-human royal monkeys, dates from 1910. The *Listeners,* 1912, very definitely established him as a poet and a group of poems from this book was included in the first volume of *Georgian Poetry.* Since then he has published *Peacock Pie,* 1913, *Motley,* 1918,

the *Veil,* 1921; last of all up to the present, *The Captive
and Other Poems,* 1928. He has written a number of stories
in some of which the influence of Poe, in others, strangely con-
trasting, that of Henry James, is plainly visible, and also a
pair of novels, of which the *Memoirs of a Midget,* 1921, is
by far the best known, although the earlier, *The Return,*
1910, had won for him the Polignac Prize.

Of all English poets living or dead, De la Mare is pecu-
liarly the poet of childhood; the poet of the child's open play
and secret laughter, the child's fancies, fears, and visions. And
this is because he has realized as no other poet has ever
done " the astonishingly full and vivid life it (the child)
is leading — and being led by. The life, that is, of what, so to
speak is outside of itself and what is inside of itself: its body
life, its mind life, and its spirit life." His earliest poems were
The Songs of Childhood; his latest book *Poems for Chil-
dren* adds a score or so of hitherto unpublished poems that
belong to this class. There is no " writing down " to the infant
mind in any of these; he writes songs of and for children be-
cause the child's mind and life is of ever fresh and entrancing
interest to him. The songs range from the simplest jingles such
as children might sing at play, through stories and ballads
such as they love to hear, to poems whose deeper significance
only the child-like mind of later years can fully apprehend.

There is, it would seem, a close relation between *The
Songs of Childhood* and the poet's later maturer work. He
has progressed like Blake from " songs of innocence " to
" songs of experience "; but his latest and loveliest poems are
poems of dreamland and of dreams. If we may accept George
Moore's definition of " pure poetry " as " something that the
poet creates outside of himself," that is, poetry free from sub-
jectivity, from the poet's personal opinions, beliefs, and dog-
mas, De la Mare stands out as the truest, clearest singer of
" pure poetry " alive today in England. He has no message to
deliver, no doctrine to enforce — such purposes he believes are
fatal to pure poetry. The intention " to teach, to instruct, to
edify, or solely to pass the time away," he tells us, " is no more
likely than the mere intention to write a poem to result in a
poem." In an age of growing, if not dominant realism in verse,
De la Mare has remained true to his vision; there are barely a
dozen poems in his work that deal with what is called " real

life." It is not without significance that of all the English poets who lived through the World War De la Mare alone has written no " war poems." Poetry has been for him always a way of escape from the " real world " into a world of higher realities.

It is not likely that De la Mare will ever become a " popular poet "; but it is quite safe to prophesy that his exquisite mastery of his art, his grotesque and whimsical fancy, his " innocency of vision," will always endear him to the elect who love poetry for its own lovely sake. Like his own old shepherd Nod,

> His are the quiet steeps of dreamland,
>   The waters of no-more-pain,
> His ram's bell rings 'neath an arch of stars,
>   ' Rest, rest, and rest again.'

ALL THAT'S PAST

Very old are the woods;
    And the buds that break
Out of the brier's boughs,
    When March winds wake,
So old with their beauty are —
    Oh, no man knows
Through what wild centuries
    Roves back the rose.

Very old are the brooks;
    And the rills that rise
Where snow sleeps cold beneath
    The azure skies
Sing such a history
    Of come and gone,
Their every drop is as wise
    As Solomon.

Very old are we men;
    Our dreams are tales
Told in dim Eden
    By Eve's nightingales;

We wake and whisper awhile,
But, the day gone by,
Silence and sleep like fields
Of amaranth lie.

THE DARK CHÂTEAU

In dreams a dark château
Stands ever open to me,
In far ravines dream-waters flow,
Descending soundlessly;
Above its peaks the eagle floats,
Lone in a sunless sky;
Mute are the golden woodland throats
Of the birds flitting by.

No voice is audible. The wind
Sleeps in its peace.
No flower of the light can find
Refuge beneath its trees;
Only the darkening ivy climbs
Mingled with wilding rose,
And cypress, morn and evening, time's
Black shadow throws.

All vacant, and unknown;
Only the dreamer steps
From stone to hollow stone,
Where the green moss sleeps,
Peers at the rivers in its deeps,
The eagle lone in the sky,
While the dew of evening drips,
Coldly and silently.

Would that I could steal in! —
Into each secret room;
Would that my sleep-bright eyes could win
To the inner gloom;
Gaze from its high windows,
Far down its mouldering walls,
Where amber-clear still Lethe flows,
And foaming falls.

541

But ever as I gaze,
    From slumber soft doth come
Some touch my stagnant sense to raise
    To its old earthly home;
Fades then that sky serene;
    And peak of ageless snow;
Fades to a paling dawn-lit green,
    My dark château.

THE GHOST

Who knocks?' ' I, who was beautiful,
    Beyond all dreams to restore,
I, from the roots of the dark thorn am hither,
    And knock on the door.'

' Who speaks?' ' I — once was my speech
    Sweet as the bird's on the air,
When echo lurks by the waters to heed;
    'Tis I speak thee fair.'

' Dark is the hour! ' ' Ay, and cold.'
    ' Lone is my house.' ' Ah, but mine? '
' Sight, touch, lips, eyes yearned in vain.'
    ' Long dead these to thine . . .'

Silence. Still faint on the porch
    Brake the flames of the stars.
In gloom groped a hope-wearied hand
    Over keys, bolts, and bars.

A face peered. All the grey night
    In chaos of vacancy shone;
Nought but vast sorrow was there —
    The sweet cheat gone.

THE SONG OF THE MAD PRINCE

Who said, 'Peacock Pie'?
    The old King to the sparrow:
Who said, 'Crops are ripe'?
    Rust to the harrow:
Who said, 'Where sleeps she now?
    Where rests she now her head,
Bathed in eve's loveliness'? —
    That's what I said.

Who said, 'Ay, mum's the word';
    Sexton to willow:
Who said, 'Green dusk for dreams,
    Moss for a pillow'?
Who said, 'All Time's delight
    Hath she for narrow bed;
Life's troubled bubble broken'? —
    That's what I said.

THE LITTLE GREEN ORCHARD

Some one is always sitting there,
            In the little green orchard;
    Even when the sun is high
    In noon's unclouded sky,
    And faintly droning goes
    The bee from rose to rose,
Some one in shadow is sitting there,
            In the little green orchard.

Yes, and when twilight is falling softly
            In the little green orchard;
    When the grey dew distils
    And every flower-cup fills;
    When the last blackbird says,
    'What — what!' and goes·her way — s-sh!
I have heard voices calling softly
            In the little green orchard.

Not that I am afraid of being there,
   In the little green orchard;
 Why, when the moon's been bright,
 Shedding her lonesome light,
 And moths like ghosties come,
 And the horned snail leaves home:
I've sat there, whispering and listening there,
   In the little green orchard.

Only it's strange to be feeling there,
   In the little green orchard;
 Whether you paint or draw,
 Dig, hammer, chop, or saw;
 When you are most alone,
 All but the silence gone . . .
Some one is waiting and watching there,
   In the little green orchard.

THE OLD ANGLER

Twilight leaned mirrored in a pool
 Where willow boughs swept green and hoar,
Silk-clear the water, calm and cool,
 Silent the weedy shore:

There in abstracted, brooding mood
 One fishing sate. His painted float
Motionless as a planet stood;
 Motionless his boat.

A melancholy soul was this,
 With lantern jaw, gnarled hand, vague eye;
Huddled in pensive solitariness
 He had fished existence by.

Empty his creel; stolen his bait —
 Impassively he angled on,
Though mist now showed the evening late
 And daylight well-nigh gone.

Suddenly, like a tongueless bell,
  Downward his gaudy cork did glide;
A deep, low-gathering, gentle swell
  Spread slowly far and wide.

Wheeped out his tackle from noiseless winch,
  And furtive as a thief, his thumb,
With nerve intense, wound inch by inch
  A line no longer numb.

What fabulous spoil could thus unplayed
  Gape upward to a mortal air? —
He stoops engrossed; his tanned cheek greyed;
  His heart stood still: for there,

Wondrously fairing, beneath the skin
  Of secretly bubbling water seen,
Swims — not the silver of scale and fin —
  But gold immixt with green.

Deeply astir in oozy bed,
  The darkening mirror ripples and rocks:
And lo — a wan-pale, lovely head,
  Hook tangled in its locks!

Cold from her haunt — a Naiad slim.
  Shoulder and cheek gleamed ivory white;
Though now faint stars stood over him,
  The hour hard on night.

Her green eyes gazed like one half-blind
  In sudden radiance; her breast
Breathed the sweet air, while gently twined,
  'Gainst the cold water pressed,

Her lean webbed hands. She floated there,
  Light as a scentless petalled flower,
Water-drops dewing from her hair
  In tinkling beadlike shower.

So circling sidelong, her tender throat
　　Uttered a grieving, desolate wail;
Shrill o'er the dark pool lapsed its note,
　　Piteous as nightingale.

Ceased Echo. And he? — a life's remorse
　　Welled to a tongue unapt to charm,
But never a word broke harsh and hoarse
　　To quiet her alarm.

With infinite stealth his twitching thumb
　　Tugged softly at the tautened gut,
Bubble-light, fair, her lips now dumb,
　　She moved, and struggled not;

But with set, wild, unearthly eyes
　　Pale-gleaming, fixed as if in fear,
She couched in the water, with quickening sighs,
　　And floated near.

In hollow heaven the stars were at play;
　　Wan glow-worms greened the pool-side grass;
Dipped the wide-bellied boat. His prey
　　Gazed on; nor breathed. Alas! —

Long sterile years had come and gone;
　　Youth, like a distant dream, was sped;
Heart, hope, and eyes had hungered on. . . .
　　He turned a shaking head,

And clumsily groped amid the gold,
　　Sleek with night dews, of that tangling hair,
Till pricked his finger keen and cold
　　The barb imbedded there.

Teeth clenched, he drew his knife — ' Snip, snip,' —
　　Groaned, and sate shivering back; and she,
Treading the water with birdlike dip,
　　Shook her sweet shoulders free:

Drew backward, smiling, infatuate fair,
   His life's disasters in her eyes,
All longing and folly, grief, despair,
   Daydreams and mysteries.

She stooped her brow; laid low her cheek,
   And, steering on that silk-tressed craft,
Out from the listening, leaf-hung creek,
   Tossed up her chin, and laughed —

A mocking, icy, inhuman note.
   One instant flashed that crystal breast,
Leaned, and was gone. Dead-still the boat:
   And the deep dark at rest.

Flits moth to flower. A water-rat
   Noses the placid ripple.   And lo!
Streams a lost meteor. Night is late,
   And daybreak zephyrs flow. . . .

And he — the cheated? Dusk till morn,
   Insensate, even of hope forsook,
He muttering squats, aloof, forlorn,
   Dangling a baitless hook.

RUPERT BROOKE
1887–1915

Henry James said of him, with a finality which would satisfy all who knew him casually or intimately: 'One liked absolutely everything about him, without the smallest exception; so that he appeared to convert before one's eyes all that happened to him, or that ever might, not only to his advantage as a source of life and experience, but to the enjoyment on its own side of a sort of illustrational virtue or glory.' This is, in a way even now at a distance of years, the most important fact about Rupert Brooke. He was loved as few have been loved by their fellowmen, and his death in the springtime of his greatness stirred the pity of Englishmen and Americans at the moment when the thought of death had little power to shock since it was more constantly in men's minds than the hope of living. His life instantly assumed symbolical meaning. Whatever of youth, ambition, talent, personal grace and beauty was being prodigally sacrificed, he represented. It is safe to say that his death first fully roused our consciousness to the terrifying waste of things most valuable that the war would demand. Because of the meaning which the twenty-eight brief years of his life have fortuitously been given, to judge soberly his accomplishment as a poet will be for a long time next to impossible.

The matrix of his life was the public school and university, Rugby and King's College, Cambridge. With extraordinary gusto he played the games, exulted in the enthusiasms, defied the past and planned the future in the common life of those schools. No boy, it seems, has been more typical of the typical best which such nurturing can produce, or more successful at its conventional preoccupations. At Cambridge he was a Fabian Socialist and for a time a vegetarian. He revived the drooping dramatic club, punted and argued, versified and swam at Grantchester, made his holiday in Switzerland and plunged into literature and music. The habit of sociability was fixed in him at Cambridge and the records of the Olympian sessions of which he made the centre are so numerous that the miracle is how he ever found time for poetry. He rushed from one felicity to the next with a speed which we may interpret as the insistence of his fate that he should taste the sum of earthly joys before they were snatched away from him.

His letters — there are few to match them in the rare distillation of their author's self — force the admission that in the midst of the wonder and delight he had little idea of what he wanted or what he might do. His months in Germany and Italy after going down from the university, the winning of the Cambridge fellowship in 1913, even his journey across America to the South Seas and his sojourn there under palm trees and brilliant skies, did little more than fortify his insularity and make him love more tenaciously what he already loved at home.

The war literally came to his rescue. The adventure which he had always thought to find just around the corner was gloriously arrived — ' Well, if Armageddon's *on*, I suppose one should be there.' That he was deceived, in part, like the other thousands who with such impetuous bravery died in those first days, does not change the fact for him or those for whom he spoke, that there was at last something important to live for now that there was a cause to die for. He had prepared himself for death in front of the foe, but Fate stubbornly preferred that his friends should carry his Apollonian body, slain by blood-poisoning on the anniversary of Shakespeare's death, to its rest on the marble heights of the island of Scyros.

Fewer than a hundred poems remain and nearly a score of them, juvenilia and experiments in metre, Brooke might not have reprinted had he lived to the respectable age when a poet issues a collective edition of his work. Yet from the poems on which it is fair to him to pass judgment, how clearly do the dominant urges of his life appear, the contradictions and the ardent affirmations. The beguiling intimacy of his poetry must put the critic on his guard lest he be carried away by those personal traits, revealed there, which took the hearts of all who knew the poet. To a degree he is, of course, what is invariably said of him, the poet of those who are young in body and heart, if to be young is to hate the thought of dying, to

549

love to desperation, to know that each dawn will bring new pleasure, and to loathe worse than death the thought of growing old and fat and stodgy.

But if this were all, not even the legend of his life would illude us into believing that he might have been a great poet. We can admire, because it is most characteristic and most appealing, his searching, never satisfied curiosity about his own emotional response to life. He has no sooner sworn by all the gods to love to infinity than his intelligence calls him fool and he abruptly takes back his oath.

> I said I splendidly loved you; it's not true.

After each ecstasy follows resentment at his having allowed himself to be swept off his feet. Exhilarated by the thought of human nobility, he watches a ' dirty middle-aged tradesman in a railway-carriage for hours, and loves every dirty greasy sulky wrinkle in his weak chin,' but in another mood two snoring, sweating Germans are — just what they are.

He was, self-confessed, the great lover of common earthly joys, an enraptured materialist, yet in the Examination Room a heavenly visitation of archangels eddied and swayed around him. It is quite as if Keats had visited Shelley's grotto in the Pisan woods and allowed himself to imagine that he heard the Pythian priestess uttering her oracles from below. Can we wonder that a boy who stood bewildered between the splendours of the physical world and metaphysical wonders beyond, scarcely aware that he was a metaphysical poet in reality, should find his surest ground in the mockery and sheer fun of *The Funeral of Youth* and *Grantchester*? The touch of theatricality in such a poem as *Ante Aram* one might suspect to be the result of his fear of the impermanence of his mood. Not until the war sonnets are these sudden contradictions resolved in ringing affirmation.

One is reluctant to speak of Brooke's growth as an artist. He had so short a time in which to learn his craft that it seems ungenerous to dwell on his immaturity. He was, it must be admitted, a somewhat careless versifier, carrying licence to the point where his rhythms become either sluggish or staccato. He used too many words and was often content with less than the inevitable phrase. Mr. Marsh in his most satisfying *Memoir* prints some of the fragments on which Brooke was at work when he died. They prove there were better things still to come, and with that promise our fruitless queries get the only answer they can have.

THE GREAT LOVER

I have been so great a lover: filled my days
  So proudly with the splendour of Love's praise,
The pain, the calm, and the astonishment,
Desire illimitable, and still content,
And all dear names men use, to cheat despair,
For the perplexed and viewless streams that bear
Our hearts at random down the dark of life.
Now, ere the unthinking silence on that strife
Steals down, I would cheat drowsy Death so far,
My night shall be remembered for a star
That outshone all the suns of all men's days.
Shall I not crown them with immortal praise
Whom I have loved, who have given me, dared with me
High secrets, and in darkness knelt to see
The inenarrable godhead of delight?
Love is a flame; — we have beaconed the world's night.
A city: — and we have built it, these and I.
An emperor: — we have taught the world to die.
So, for their sakes I loved, ere I go hence,
And the high cause of Love's magnificence,
And to keep loyalties young, I'll write those names
Golden for ever, eagles, crying flames,
And set them as a banner, that men may know,
To dare the generations, burn, and blow
Out on the wind of Time, shining and streaming. . . .

These I have loved:
                White plates and cups, clean-gleaming,
Ringed with blue lines; and feathery, faery dust;
Wet roofs, beneath the lamp-light; the strong crust
Of friendly bread; and many-tasting food;
Rainbows; and the blue bitter smoke of wood;
And radiant raindrops couching in cool flowers;
And flowers themselves, that sway through sunny hours,
Dreaming of moths that drink them under the moon;
Then, the cool kindliness of sheets, that soon

551

Smooth away trouble; and the rough male kiss
Of blankets; grainy wood; live hair that is
Shining and free; blue-massing clouds; the keen
Unpassioned beauty of a great machine;
The benison of hot water; furs to touch;
The good smell of old clothes; and other such —
The comfortable smell of friendly fingers,
Hair's fragrance, and the musty reek that lingers
About dead leaves and last year's ferns. . . .

                                        Dear names,
And thousand other throng to me! Royal flames;
Sweet water's dimpling laugh from tap or spring;
Holes in the ground; and voices that do sing;
Voices in laughter, too; and body's pain,
Soon turned to peace; and the deep-panting train;
Firm sands; the little dulling edge of foam
That browns and dwindles as the wave goes home;
And washen stones, gay for an hour; the cold
Graveness of iron; moist black earthen mould;
Sleep; and high places; footprints in the dew;
And oaks; and brown horse-chestnuts, glossy-new;
And new-peeled sticks; and shining pools on grass; —
All these have been my loves. And these shall pass,
Whatever passes not, in the great hour,
Nor all my passion, all my prayers, have power
To hold them with me through the gate of Death.
They'll play deserter, turn with the traitor breath,
Break the high bond we made, and sell Love's trust
And sacramented covenant to the dust.
— Oh, never a doubt but, somewhere, I shall wake,
And give what's left of love again, and make
New friends, now strangers. . . .

                              But the best I've known,
Stays here, and changes, breaks, grows old, is blown
About the winds of the world, and fades from brains
Of living men, and dies.

                        Nothing remains.
O dear my loves, O faithless, once again
This one last gift I give: that after men
Shall know, and later lovers, far-removed,
Praise you, ' All these were lovely '; say, ' He loved.'

THE HILL

Breathless, we flung us on the windy hill,
  Laughed in the sun, and kissed the lovely grass.
 You said, ' Through glory and ecstasy we pass;
Wind, sun, and earth remain, the birds sing still,
When we are old, are old. . . .' ' And when we die
  All's over that is ours; and life burns on
Through other lovers, other lips,' said I,
' Heart of my heart, our heaven is now, is won! '

' We are Earth's best, that learnt her lesson here.
  Life is our cry. We have kept the faith! ' we said:
  ' We shall go down with unreluctant tread
Rose-crowned into the darkness! ' . . . Proud we were,
And laughed, that had such brave true things to say.
— And then you suddenly cried, and turned away.

THE CHILTERNS

Your hands, my dear, adorable,
  Your lips of tenderness
— Oh, I've loved you faithfully and well,
  Three years, or a bit less.
  It wasn't a success.

Thank God, that's done! and I'll take the road,
  Quit of my youth and you,
The Roman road to Wendover
  By Tring and Lilley Hoo,
  As a free man may do.

For youth goes over, the joys that fly,
  The tears that follow fast;
And the dirtiest things we do must lie
  Forgotten at the last;
  Even Love goes past.

What's left behind I shall not find,
    The splendour and the pain;
The splash of sun, the shouting wind,
    And the brave sting of rain,
    I may not meet again.

But the years, that take the best away,
    Give something in the end;
And a better friend than love have they,
    For none to mar or mend,
    That have themselves to friend.

I shall desire and I shall find
    The best of my desires;
The autumn road, the mellow wind
    That soothes the darkening shires.
    And laughter, and inn-fires.

White mist about the black hedgerows,
    The slumbering Midland plain,
The silence where the clover grows,
    And the dead leaves in the lane,
    Certainly, these remain.

And I shall find some girl perhaps,
    And a better one than you,
With eyes as wise, but kindlier,
    And lips as soft, but true.
    And I daresay she will do.

SONNET

I said I splendidly loved you; it's not true.
    Such long swift tides stir not a land-locked sea.
On gods or fools the high risk falls — on you —
    The clean clear bitter-sweet that's not for me.
Love soars from earth to ecstasies unwist.
    Love is flung Lucifer-like from Heaven to Hell.
But — there are wanderers in the middle mist,
    Who cry for shadows, clutch, and cannot tell

Whether they love at all, or, loving, whom:
   An old song's lady, a fool in fancy dress,
Or phantoms, or their own face on the gloom;
   For love of Love, or from heart's loneliness.
Pleasure's not theirs, nor pain. They doubt, and sigh,
   And do not love at all. Of these am I.

THE OLD VICARAGE, GRANTCHESTER

(Café des Westens, Berlin, May 1912)

Just now the lilac is in bloom,
   All before my little room;
   And in my flower-beds, I think,
Smile the carnation and the pink;
And down the borders, well I know,
The poppy and the pansy blow . . .
Oh! there the chestnuts, summer through,
Beside the river make for you
A tunnel of green gloom, and sleep
Deeply above; and green and deep
The stream mysterious glides beneath,
Green as a dream and deep as death.
— Oh, damn! I know it! and I know
How the May fields all golden show,
And when the day is young and sweet,
Gild gloriously the bare feet
That run to bathe . . .
              Du lieber Gott!

Here am I, sweating, sick, and hot,
And there the shadowed waters fresh
Lean up to embrace the naked flesh.
Temperamentvoll German Jews
Drink beer around; — and *there* the dews
Are soft beneath a morn of gold.
Here tulips bloom as they are told;
Unkempt about those hedges blows
An English unofficial rose;
And there the unregulated sun
Slopes down to rest when day is done,

And wakes a vague unpunctual star,
A slippered Hesper; and there are
Meads towards Haslingfield and Coton
Where *das Betreten's* not *verboten*.

εἴθε γενοίμην . . . would I were
In Grantchester, in Grantchester! —
Some, it may be, can get in touch
With Nature there, or Earth, or such.
And clever modern men have seen
A Faun a-peeping through the green,
And felt the Classics were not dead,
To glimpse a Naiad's reedy head,
Or hear the Goat-foot piping low: . . .
But these are things I do not know.
I only know that you may lie
Day long and watch the Cambridge sky,
And, flower-lulled in sleepy grass,
Hear the cool lapse of hours pass,
Until the centuries blend and blur
In Grantchester, in Grantchester. . . .
Still in the dawnlit waters cool
His ghostly Lordship swims his pool,
And tries the strokes, essays the tricks,
Long learnt on Hellespont, or Styx.
Dan Chaucer hears his river still
Chatter beneath a phantom mill.
Tennyson notes, with studious eye,
How Cambridge waters hurry by . . .
And in that garden, black and white,
Creep whispers through the grass all night;
And spectral dance, before the dawn,
A hundred Vicars down the lawn;
Curates, long dust, will come and go
On lissom, clerical, printless toe;
And oft between the boughs is seen
The sly shade of a Rural Dean . . .
Till, at a shiver in the skies,
Vanishing with Satanic cries,
The prim ecclesiastic rout
Leaves but a startled sleeper-out,

❖ RUPERT BROOKE ❖

Grey heavens, the first bird's drowsy calls,
The falling house that never falls.

God! I will pack, and take a train,
And get me to England once again!
For England's the one land, I know,
Where men with Splendid Hearts may go;
And Cambridgeshire, of all England,
The shire for Men who Understand;
And of *that* district I prefer
The lovely hamlet Grantchester.
For Cambridge people rarely smile,
Being urban, squat, and packed with guile;
And Royston men in the far South
Are black and fierce and strange of mouth;
At Over they fling oaths at one,
And worse than oaths at Trumpington,
And Ditton girls are mean and dirty,
And there's none in Harston under thirty,
And folks in Shelford and those parts
Have twisted lips and twisted hearts,
And Barton men make Cockney rhymes,
And Coton's full of nameless crimes,
And things are done you'd not believe
At Madingley, on Christmas Eve.
Strong men have run for miles and miles,
When one from Cherry Hinton smiles;
Strong men have blanched, and shot their wives,
Rather than send them to St. Ives;
Strong men have cried like babes, bydam,
To hear what happened at Babraham.
But Grantchester! ah, Grantchester!
There's peace and holy quiet there,
Great clouds along pacific skies,
And men and women with straight eyes,
Lithe children lovelier than a dream,
A bosky wood, a slumbrous stream,
And little kindly winds that creep
Round twilight corners, half asleep.
In Grantchester their skins are white;
They bathe by day, they bathe by night;

The women there do all they ought;
The men observe the Rules of Thought.
They love the Good; they worship Truth;
They laugh uproariously in youth;
(And when they get to feeling old,
They up and shoot themselves, I'm told) . . .

Ah God! to see the branches stir
Across the moon at Grantchester!
To smell the thrilling-sweet and rotten
Unforgettable, unforgotten
River-smell, and hear the breeze
Sobbing in the little trees.
Say, do the elm-clumps greatly stand
Still guardians of that holy land?
The chestnuts shade, in reverend dream,
The yet unacademic stream?
Is dawn a secret shy and cold
Anadyomene, silver-gold?
And sunset still a golden sea
From Haslingfield to Madingley?
And after, ere the night is born,
Do hares come out about the corn?
Oh, is the water sweet and cool,
Gentle and brown, above the pool?
And laughs the immortal river still
Under the mill, under the mill?
Say, is there Beauty yet to find?
And Certainty? and Quiet kind?
Deep meadows yet, for to forget
The lies, and truths, and pain? . . . oh! yet
Stands the Church clock at ten to three?
And is there honey still for tea?

TIARE TAHITI

Mamua, when our laughter ends,
And hearts and bodies, brown as white,
Are dust about the doors of friends,
Or scent ablowing down the night,

Then, oh! then, the wise agree,
Comes our immortality.
Mamua, there waits a land
Hard for us to understand.
Out of time, beyond the sun,
All are one in Paradise,
You and Pupure are one,
And Taü, and the ungainly wise.
There, the Eternals are, and there
The Good, the Lovely, and the True,
And Types, whose earthly copies were
The foolish broken things we knew;
There is the Face, whose ghosts we are;
The real, the never-setting Star;
And the Flower, of which we love
Faint and fading shadows here;
Never a tear, but only Grief;
Dance, but not the limbs that move;
Songs in Song shall disappear;
Instead of lovers, Love shall be;
For hearts, Immutability;
And there, on the Ideal Reef,
Thunders the Everlasting Sea!

And my laughter, and my pain,
Shall home to the Eternal Brain.
And all lovely things, they say,
Meet in Loveliness again;
Miri's laugh, Teïpo's feet,
And the hands of Matua,
Stars and sunlight there shall meet,
Coral's hues and rainbows there,
And Teüra's braided hair;
And with the starred *tiare's* white,
And white birds in the dark ravine,
And *flamboyants* ablaze at night,
And jewels, and evening's after-green,
And dawns of pearl and gold and red,
Mamua, your lovelier head!
And there'll no more be one who dreams
Under the ferns, of crumbling stuff,

Eyes of illusion, mouth that seems,
All time-entangled human love.
And you'll no longer swing and sway
Divinely down the scented shade,
Where feet to Ambulation fade,
And moons are lost in endless Day.
How shall we wind these wreaths of ours,
Where there are neither heads nor flowers?
Oh, Heaven's Heaven! — but we'll be missing
The palms, and sunlight, and the south;
And there's an end, I think, of kissing,
When our mouths are one with Mouth. . . .

    Taü here, Mamua,
Crown the hair, and come away!
Hear the calling of the moon,
And the whispering scents that stray
About the idle warm lagoon.
Hasten, hand in human hand,
Down the dark, the flowered way,
Along the whiteness of the sand,
And in the water's soft caress,
Wash the mind of foolishness,
Mamua, until the day.
Spend the glittering moonlight there
Pursuing down the soundless deep
Limbs that gleam and shadowy hair,
Or floating lazy, half-asleep.
Dive and double and follow after,
Snare in flowers, and kiss, and call,
With lips that fade, and human laughter
And faces individual,
Well this side of Paradise! . . .
There's little comfort in the wise.

MUTABILITY

They say there's a high windless world and strange,
  Out of the wash of days and temporal tide,
  Where Faith and Good, Wisdom and Truth abide,
Æterna corpora, subject to no change.

There the sure suns of these pale shadows move;
   There stand the immortal ensigns of our war;
   Our melting flesh fixed Beauty there, a star,
And perishing hearts, imperishable Love. . . .

Dear, we know only that we sigh, kiss, smile;
   Each kiss lasts but the kissing; and grief goes over;
   Love has no habitation but the heart.
Poor straws! on the dark flood we catch awhile,
   Cling, and are borne into the night apart.
   The laugh dies with the lips, ' Love ' with the lover.

PEACE

Now, God be thanked Who has matched us with His hour,
   And caught our youth, and wakened us from sleeping,
With hand made sure, clear eye, and sharpened power,
   To turn, as swimmers into cleanness leaping,
Glad from a world grown old and cold and weary,
   Leave the sick hearts that honour could not move,
And half-men, and their dirty songs and dreary,
   And all the little emptiness of love!

Oh! we, who have known shame, we have found release there,
   Where there's no ill, no grief, but sleep has mending,
   Naught broken save this body, lost but breath;
Nothing to shake the laughing heart's long peace there
   But only agony, and that has ending;
   And the worst friend and enemy is but Death.

THE SOLDIER

If I should die, think only this of me:
   That there's some corner of a foreign field
That is for ever England. There shall be
   In that rich earth a richer dust concealed;
A dust whom England bore, shaped, made aware,
   Gave, once, her flowers to love, her ways to roam,
A body of England's, breathing English air,
   Washed by the rivers, blest by suns of home.

And think, this heart, all evil shed away,
   A pulse in the eternal mind, no less
      Gives somewhere back the thoughts by England given;
Her sights and sounds; dreams happy as her day;
   And laughter, learnt of friends; and gentleness,
      In hearts at peace, under an English heaven.

JAMES ELROY FLECKER
1884–1915

James Elroy Flecker followed the usual path of an English public school and university education. He showed no remarkable prowess at the customary tasks but developed a great enthusiasm for modern languages and learned to make a poet's use of the classics. After a season of schoolmastering, he fixed on the Consular Service as a career and in 1908 entered Caius College, Cambridge for two years' training in Oriental languages. His service in the East (Constantinople, Smyrna, Beirut) was interrupted by an attack of tuberculosis the danger of which he refused at first to appreciate. The last year and a half of his life he spent in Switzerland fighting the disease. In spite of the tragic brevity of his working years, Flecker was established at his death as a lyric poet of distinction. His novel, *The King of Alsander,* is a delightful romance touched with, and saved from prettiness, by his peculiar, slightly sardonic humour. He had begun to demonstrate power as a critic; *Hassan,* his finest venture, showed on production, after his death, an extraordinary understanding of dramatic values. Had he lived, he might have offered to the English stage such a combination of wit and splendour and poetry as it has never of late years enjoyed.

Flecker's friends and biographers have sought repeatedly to explain the unexpected paradoxes in his temperament and the inconsistencies in his poetry. The explanation, if one is needed, should be simple. Flecker was above all an individualist. He was in fact stubborn. In every decision of his personal life he depended on his own intelligence and nothing else. He worked out his poetic salvation in the same way, slowly but vigorously. He might have become the conventional English minor poet, remembered a generation or two after his death for a few delicate lyrics and some easy translations from Catullus and the pastoral poets; he might have thrown in his lot with his contemporaries of the Georgian school who were bent on bringing English poetry back to polite subjects and simple diction after its alien captivity under Symbolism and Decadence in the '90's. But he preferred to seek those subjects and styles which suited his taste and accorded with his firm convictions about his own abilities. In consequence, he cannot be labelled this or that sort of poet or branded with the sign of any school.

It is often said that no modern English poet makes us see and smell the Orient as Flecker does. We might suppose, if this were true, that he had lost his heart to the mystery and splendour of Lebanon and Bagdad. Yet how are we to account for this passage in one of his letters: 'I consider this (*The Gates of Damascus*) to be my greatest poem — and I am glad you seem to agree. It was inspired by Damascus itself by the way. I loathe the East and the Eastern and spent all my time there dreaming of Oxford. Yet it seems — even to hardened Orientalists that I understand.' The answer is that Flecker knew, no matter how much he might long for England at Brumana, that he had found in the East the substance on which his poetry might feed. Here was intense colour everywhere, blue and silver, red and gold; and he had delighted in brilliant colour since the time when, as a little boy, his father used to take him to watch the signal lights on the railway flash green and yellow in the black night. He had found what suited his desire, legend and romance mixed with cruelty and sordidness, a blending of qualities which his wit and imagination were especially able to cope with. And so it is that we see with Flecker's eyes

The dragon-green, the luminous, the dark, the serpent-haunted
    sea,
The snow-besprinkled wine of earth, the white-and-blue flower
    foaming sea,

and we are certain that it is no Eastern poet who says:

O spiritual pilgrim rise: the night has grown her single horn;
The voices of the souls unborn are half adream with Paradise.

Flecker had little need to go outside his own well-formed ideas about poetry for a theory of art. In the preface to *The Golden Journey to Samarkand* he did, however, swear allegiance to the Parnassians, that company of French poets who endeavoured in the third quarter of the last century to correct the extravagances of the romanticists. Yet here again he shows his individualism. His verse was already 'Parnassian' before he heard the word. The title he adopted because it served as a convenient catchword to explain to a conservative public what he was trying to do. He had obviously striven to free himself from the web of the senses and to remove from his poetry all traces of sentimentalism. He discovered in Gautier's *L'Art* the model he had unconsciously been using:

> Oui, l'oeuvre sort plus belle
> D'une forme au travail
> Rebelle
> Vers, marbre, onyx, émail.

He found in the type of the Parnassian poet — so sharply defined in the preface — a description of himself: 'The French Parnassian has a tendency to use traditional forms and even to employ classical subjects. His desire in writing poetry is to create beauty; his inclination is toward a beauty somewhat statuesque. He is apt to be dramatic and objective rather than intimate.'

TO A POET A THOUSAND YEARS HENCE

I who am dead a thousand years,
    And wrote this sweet archaic song,
Send you my words for messengers
    The way I shall not pass along.

I care not if you bridge the seas,
    Or ride secure the cruel sky,
Or build consummate palaces
    Of metal or of masonry.

But have you wine and music still,
    And statues and a bright-eyed love,
And foolish thoughts of good and ill,
    And prayers to them who sit above?

How shall we conquer? Like a wind
   That falls at eve our fancies blow,
And old Mæonides the blind
   Said it three thousand years ago.

O friend unseen, unborn, unknown,
   Student of our sweet English tongue,
Read out my words at night, alone:
   I was a poet, I was young.

Since I can never see your face,
   And never shake you by the hand,
I send my soul through time and space
   To greet you. You will understand.

TENEBRIS INTERLUCENTEM

A linnet who had lost her way
   Sang on a blackened bough in Hell,
Till all the ghosts remembered well
The trees, the wind, the golden day.

At last they knew that they had died
When they heard music in that land,
And some one there stole forth a hand
To draw a brother to his side.

STILLNESS

When the words rustle no more
   And the last work's done,
When the bolt lies deep in the door,
   And Fire, our Sun,
Falls on the dark-laned meadows of the floor;

When from the clock's last chime to the next chime
   Silence beats his drum,
And Space with gaunt grey eyes and her brother Time
   Wheeling and whispering come,
She with the mould of form and he with the loom of rhyme:

Then twittering out in the night my thought-birds flee,
  I am emptied of all my dreams:
I only hear Earth turning, only see
  Ether's long bankless streams,
And only know I should drown if you laid not your hand on
    me.

THE OLD SHIPS

I have seen old ships sail like swans asleep
  Beyond the village which men still call Tyre,
With leaden age o'ercargoed, dipping deep
For Famagusta and the hidden sun
That rings black Cyprus with a lake of fire;
And all those ships were certainly so old
Who knows how oft with squat and noisy gun,
Questing brown slaves or Syrian oranges,
The pirate Genoese
Hell-raked them till they rolled
Blood, water, fruit and corpses up the hold.
But now through friendly seas they softly run,
Painted the mid-sea blue or shore-sea green,
Still patterned with the vine and grapes in gold.

But I have seen,
Pointing her shapely shadows from the dawn
And image tumbled on a rose-swept bay,
A drowsy ship of some yet older day;
And, wonder's breath indrawn,
Thought I — who knows — who knows — but in that same
(Fished up beyond Ææa, patched up new
— Stern painted brighter blue —)
That talkative, bald-headed seaman came
(Twelve patient comrades sweating at the oar)
From Troy's doom-crimson shore,
And with great lies about his wooden horse
Set the crew laughing, and forgot his course.

It was so old a ship — who knows, who knows?
— And yet so beautiful, I watched in vain
To see the mast burst open with a rose,
And the whole deck put on its leaves again.

THE QUEEN'S SONG

Had I the power
    To Midas given of old
To touch a flower
    And leave the petals gold
I then might touch thy face,
    Delightful boy,
And leave a metal grace,
    A graven joy.

Thus would I slay, —
    Ah, desperate device!
The vital day
    That trembles in thine eyes,
And let the red lips close
    Which sang so well,
And drive away the rose
    To leave a shell.

Then I myself,
    Rising austere and dumb
On the high shelf
    Of my half-lighted room,
Would place the shining bust
    And wait alone,
Until I was but dust,
    Buried unknown.

Thus in my love
    For nations yet unborn,
I would remove
    From our two lives the morn,
And muse on loveliness
    In mine arm-chair,
Content should Time confess
    How sweet you were.

OAK AND OLIVE

I

Though I was born a Londoner,
　And bred in Gloucestershire,
I walked in Hellas years ago
　With friends in white attire:
And I remember how my soul
　Drank wine as pure as fire.

And when I stand by Charing Cross
　I can forget to hear
The crash of all those smoking wheels,
　When those cold flutes and clear
Pipe with such fury down the street,
　My hands grow moist with fear.

And there's a hall in Bloomsbury
　No more I dare to tread,
For all the stone men shout at me
　And swear they are not dead;
And once I touched a broken girl
　And knew that marble bled.

II

But when I walk in Athens town
　That swims in dust and sun
Perverse, I think of London then
　Where massive work is done,
And with what sweep at Westminster
　The rayless waters run.

I ponder how from Attic seed
　There grew an English tree,
How Byron like his heroes fell,
　Fighting a country free,
And Swinburne took from Shelley's lips
　The kiss of Poetry.

And while our poets chanted Pan
   Back to his pipes and power,
Great Verrall, bending at his desk,
   ⁻And searching hour on hour
Found out old gardens, where the wise
   May pluck a Spartan flower.

III

When I go down the Gloucester lanes
   My friends are deaf and blind:
Fast as they turn their foolish eyes
   The Mænads leap behind,
And when I hear the fire-winged feet,
   They only hear the wind.

Have I not chased the fluting Pan
   Through Cranham's sober trees?
Have I not sat on Painswick Hill
   With a nymph upon my knees,
And she as rosy as the dawn,
   And naked as the breeze?

IV

But when I lie in Grecian fields,
   Smothered in asphodel,
Or climb the blue and barren hills,
   Or sing in woods that smell
With such hot spices of the South
   As mariners might sell —

Then my heart turns where no sun burns,
   To lands of glittering rain,
To fields beneath low-clouded skies
   New-widowed of their grain,
And Autumn leaves like blood and gold
   That strew a Gloucester lane.

V

Oh well I know sweet Hellas now,
  And well I knew it then,
When I with starry lads walked out —
  But ah, for home again!
Was I not bred in Gloucestershire,
  One of the Englishmen!

EPITHALAMION

Smile then, children, hand in hand
  Bright and white as the summer snow,
Or that young King of the Grecian land,
Who smiled on Thetis, long ago, —
So long ago when, heart aflame,
The grave and gentle Peleus came
To the shore where the halcyon flies
To wed the maiden of his devotion,
The dancing lady with sky-blue eyes,
Thetis, the darling of Paradise,
The daughter of old Ocean.
Seas before her rise and break,
Dolphins tumble in her wake
Along the sapphire courses:
With Tritons ablow on their pearly shells
With a plash of waves and a clash of bells
From the glimmering house where her Father dwells
She drives his white-tail horses!
And the boys of heaven gowned and crowned,
Have Aphrodite to lead them round,
Aphrodite with hair unbound
Her silver breasts adorning.
Her long, her soft, her streaming hair,
Falls on a silver breast laid bare
By the stir and swing of the sealit air
And the movement of the morning.

THE GOLDEN JOURNEY TO SAMARKAND
PROLOGUE

We who with songs beguile your pilgrimage
    And swear that Beauty lives though lilies die,
We Poets of the proud old lineage
    Who sing to find your hearts, we know not why, —

What shall we tell you? Tales, marvellous tales
    Of ships and stars and isles where good men rest,
Where nevermore the rose of sunset pales,
    And winds and shadows fall toward the West:

And there the world's first huge white-bearded kings
    In dim glades sleeping, murmur in their sleep,
And closer round their breasts the ivy clings,
    Cutting its pathway slow and red and deep.

II

And how beguile you? Death has no repose
    Warmer and deeper than that Orient sand
Which hides the beauty and bright faith of those
    Who made the Golden Journey to Samarkand.

And now they wait and whiten peaceably,
    Those conquerors, those poets, those so fair:
They know time comes, not only you and I,
    But the whole world shall whiten, here or there;

When those long caravans that cross the plain
    With dauntless feet and sound of silver bells
Put forth no more for glory or for gain,
    Take no more solace from the palm-girt wells.

When the great markets by the sea shut fast
    All that calm Sunday that goes on and on:
When even lovers find their peace at last,
    And Earth is but a star, that once had shone.

EPILOGUE

At the Gate of the Sun, Bagdad, in olden time

The Merchants (*together*)

Away, for we are ready to a man!
  Our camels sniff the evening and are glad.
Lead on, O Master of the Caravan:
  Lead on the Merchant-Princes of Bagdad.

The Chief Draper

Have we not Indian carpets dark as wine,
  Turbans and sashes, gowns and bows and veils,
And broideries of intricate design,
  And printed hangings in enormous bales?

The Chief Grocer

We have rose-candy, we have spikenard,
  Mastic and terebinth and oil and spice,
And such sweet jams meticulously jarred
  As God's own Prophet eats in Paradise.

The Principal Jews

And we have manuscripts in peacock styles
  By Ali of Damascus; we have swords
Engraved with storks and apes and crocodiles,
  And heavy beaten necklaces, for Lords.

The Master of the Caravan

But you are nothing but a lot of Jews.

The Principal Jews

Sir, even dogs have daylight, and we pay.

The Master of the Caravan

But who are ye in rags and rotten shoes,
  You dirty-bearded, blocking up the way?

The Pilgrims

We are the Pilgrims, master; we shall go
  Always a little further: it may be
Beyond that last blue mountain barred with snow,
  Across that angry or that glimmering sea,

White on a throne or guarded in a cave
  There lives a prophet who can understand
Why men were born: but surely we are brave,
  Who make the Golden Journey to Samarkand.

The Chief Merchant

We gnaw the nail of hurry. Master, away!

One of the Women

  O turn your eyes to where your children stand.
Is not Bagdad the beautiful? O stay!

The Merchants (*in chorus*)

We take the Golden Road to Samarkand.

An Old Man

Have you not girls and garlands in your homes,
  Eunuchs and Syrian boys at your command?
Seek not excess: God hateth him who roams!

The Merchants (*in chorus*)

We make the Golden Journey to Samarkand.

A Pilgrim with a Beautiful Voice

Sweet to ride forth at evening from the wells
  When shadows pass gigantic on the sand,
And softly through the silence beat the bells
  Along the Golden Road to Samarkand.

574

A Merchant

We travel not for trafficking alone:
  By hotter winds our fiery hearts are fanned:
For lust of knowing what should not be known
  We make the Golden Journey to Samarkand,

The Master of the Caravan

Open the gate, O watchman of the night!

The Watchman

Ho, travellers, I open. For what land
Leave you the dim-moon city of delight?

The Merchants (*with a shout*)

We make the Golden Journey to Samarkand

[*The Caravan passes through the gate*]

The Watchman (*consoling the women*)

What would ye, ladies? It was ever thus.
  Men are unwise and curiously planned.

A Woman

They have their dreams, and do not think of us.

Voices of the Caravan (*in the distance, singing*)

We make the Golden Journey to Samarkand

GATES OF DAMASCUS

Four great gates has the city of Damascus,
  And four Grand Wardens, on their spears reclining,
All day long stand like tall stone men
  And sleep on the towers when the moon is shining.

This is the song of the East Gate Warden
When he locks the great gate and smokes in his garden.

575

Postern of Fate, the Desert Gate, Disaster's Cavern, Fort of Fear,
The Portal of Bagdad am I, the Doorway of Diarbekir.

The Persian Dawn with new desires may net the flushing mountain spires:
But my gaunt buttress still rejects the suppliance of those mellow fires.

Pass not beneath, O Caravan, or pass not singing. Have you heard
That silence where the birds are dead yet something pipeth like a bird?

Pass not beneath! Men say there blows in stony deserts still a rose
But with no scarlet to her leaf — and from whose heart no perfume flows.

Wilt thou bloom red where she buds pale, thy sister rose? Wilt thou not fail
When noonday flashes like a flail? Leave nightingale the caravan!

Pass then, pass all! ' Bagdad! ' ye cry, and down the billows of blue sky
Ye beat the bell that beats to hell, and who shall thrust ye back? Not I.

The Sun who flashes through the head and paints the shadows green and red, —
The Sun shall eat thy fleshless dead, O Caravan, O Caravan!

And one who licks his lips for thirst with fevered eyes shall face in fear
The palms that wave, the streams that burst, his last mirage, O Caravan!

And one — the bird-voiced Singing-man — shall fall behind thee, Caravan!
And God shall meet him in the night, and he shall sing as best he can.

And one the Bedouin shall slay, and one, sand-stricken on the way
Go dark and blind; and one shall say — ' How lonely is the Caravan! '

Pass out beneath, O Caravan, Doom's Caravan, Death's
    Caravan!
I had not told ye, fools, so much, save that I heard your
    Singing-man.

        This was sung by the West Gate's keeper
        When heaven's hollow dome grew deeper.

I am the gate toward the sea: O sailor men, pass out from me!
I hear you high on Lebanon, singing the marvels of the sea.

The dragon-green, the luminous, the dark, the serpent-haunted
    sea,
The snow-besprinkled wine of earth, the white-and-blue-flower
    foaming sea.

Beyond the sea are towns with towers, carved with lions and
    lily flowers,
And not a soul in all those lonely streets to while away the
    hours.

Beyond the towns, an isle where, bound, a naked giant bites
    the ground:
The shadow of a monstrous wing looms on his back: and still
    no sound.

Beyond the isle a rock that screams like madmen shouting
    in their dreams,
From whose dark issues night and day blood crashes in a
    thousand streams.

Beyond the rock is Restful Bay, where no wind breathes or
    ripple stirs,
And there on Roman ships, they say, stand rows of metal
    mariners.

Beyond the bay in utmost West old Solomon the Jewish King
Sits with his beard upon his breast, and grips and guards his
    magic ring:

And when that ring is stolen, he will rise in outraged majesty,
And take the World upon his back, and fling the World be-
    yond the sea.

This is the song of the North Gate's master,
Who singeth fast, but drinketh faster.

I am the gay Aleppo Gate: a dawn, a dawn and thou art there:
Eat not thy heart with fear and care, O brother of the beast we
hate!

Thou hast not many miles to tread, nor other foes than fleas
to dread;
Homs shall behold thy morning meal and Hama see thee safe
in bed.

Take to Aleppo filigrane, and take them paste of apricots,
And coffee tables botched with pearl, and little beaten
brassware pots:

And thou shalt sell thy wares for thrice the Damascene
retailers' price,
And buy a fat Armenian slave who smelleth odorous and nice.

Some men of noble stock were made: some glory in the
murder-blade:
Some praise a Science or an Art, but I like honourable Trade!

Sell them the rotten, buy the ripe! Their heads are weak; their
pockets burn.
Aleppo men are mighty fools. Salaam Aleikum! Safe return!

This is the song of the South Gate Holder,
A silver man, but his song is older.

I am the Gate that fears no fall: the Mihrab of Damascus wall,
The bridge of booming Sinai: the Arch of Allah all in all.

O spiritual pilgrim rise: the night has grown her single horn:
The voices of the souls unborn are half adream with Paradise.

To Meccah thou hast turned in prayer with aching heart and
eyes that burn:
Ah Hajji, whither wilt thou turn when thou art there, when
thou art there?

God be thy guide from camp to camp: God be thy shade from
well to well;
God grant beneath the desert stars thou hear the Prophet's
camel bell.

And God shall make thy body pure, and give thee knowledge
    to endure
This ghost-life's piercing phantom-pain, and bring thee out to
    Life again.

And God shall make thy soul a Glass where eighteen thousand
    Æons pass,
And thou shalt see the gleaming Worlds as men see dew upon
    the grass.

And son of Islam, it may be that thou shalt learn at journey's
    end
Who walks thy garden eve on eve, and bows his head, and
    calls thee Friend.

WAR SONG OF THE SARACENS

We are they who come faster than fate: we are they who
    ride early or late:
We storm at your ivory gate: Pale Kings of the Sunset, beware!
Not on silk nor in samet we lie, not in curtained solemnity die
Among women who chatter and cry, and children who mum-
    ble a prayer.
But we sleep by the ropes of the camp, and we rise with a
    shout, and we tramp
With the sun or the moon for a lamp, and the spray of the
    wind in our hair.

From the lands, where the elephants are, to the forts of Merou
    and Balghar,
Our steel we have brought and our star to shine on the ruins
    of Rum.
We have marched from the Indus to Spain, and by God we
    will go there again;
We have stood on the shore of the plain where the Waters of
    Destiny boom.
A mart of destruction we made at Jalula where men were
    afraid,
For death was a difficult trade, and the sword was a broker of
    doom;

And the Spear was a Desert Physician who cured not a few of
    ambition,
And drave not a few to perdition with medicine bitter and
    strong:
And the shield was a grief to the fool and as bright as a deso-
    late pool,
And as straight as the rock of Stamboul when their cavalry
    thundered along:
For the coward was drowned with the brave when our battle
    sheered up like a wave,
And the dead to the desert we gave, and the glory to God in
    our song.

BRUMANA

Oh shall I never never be home again?
    Meadows of England shining in the rain
Spread wide your daisied lawns: your ramparts green
With briar fortify, with blossom screen
Till my far morning — and O streams that slow
And pure and deep through plains and playlands go,
For me your love and all your kingcups store,
And — dark militia of the southern shore,
Old fragrant friends — preserve me the last lines
Of that long saga which you sung me, pines,
When, lonely boy, beneath the chosen tree
I listened, with my eyes upon the sea.

O traitor pines, you sang what life has found
The falsest of fair tales.
Earth blew a far-horn prelude all around,
That native music of her forest home,
While from the sea's blue fields and syren dales
Shadows and light noon-spectres of the foam
Riding the summer gales
On aery viols plucked an idle sound.
Hearing you sing, O trees,
Hearing you murmur, ' There are older seas,
That beat on vaster sands,
Where the wise snailfish move their pearly towers
To carven rocks and sculptured promont'ries,' ·

Hearing you whisper, ' Lands
Where blaze the unimaginable flowers.'

Beneath me in the valley waves the palm,
Beneath, beyond the valley, breaks the sea;
Beneath me sleep in mist and light and calm
Cities of Lebanon, dream-shadow-dim,
Where Kings of Tyre and Kings of Tyre did rule
In ancient days in endless dynasty,
And all around the snowy mountains swim
Like mighty swans afloat in heaven's pool.

But I will walk upon the wooded hill
Where stands a grove, O pines, of sister pines,
And when the downy twilight droops her wing
And no sea glimmers and no mountain shines
My heart shall listen still.
For pines are gossip pines the wide world through
And full of runic tales to sigh or sing.
'Tis ever sweet through pines to see the sky
Mantling a deeper gold or darker blue.
'Tis ever sweet to lie
On the dry carpet of the needles brown,
And though the fanciful green lizard stir
And windy odours light as thistledown
Breathe from the lavdanon and lavender,
Half to forget the wandering and pain,
Half to remember days that have gone by,
And dream and dream that I am home again!

THE DYING PATRIOT

Day breaks on England down the Kentish hills,
    Singing in the silence of the meadow-footing rills,
Day of my dreams, O day!
  I saw them march from Dover, long ago,
  With a silver cross before them, singing low,
Monks of Rome from their home where the blue seas break
    in foam,
  Augustine with his feet of snow.

Noon strikes on England, noon on Oxford town,
— Beauty she was statue cold — there's blood upon her gown:
Noon of my dreams, O noon!
   Proud and godly kings had built her, long ago,
   With her towers and tombs and statues all arow,
With her fair and floral air and the love that lingers there,
   And the streets where the great men go.

Evening on the olden, the golden sea of Wales,
When the first star shivers and the last wave pales:
O evening dreams!
   There's a house that Britons walked in, long ago,
   Where now the springs of ocean fall and flow,
And the dead robed in red and sea-lilies overhead
   Sway when the long winds blow.

Sleep not, my country: though night is here, afar
Your children of the morning are clamorous for war:
Fire in the night, O dreams!
   Though she send you as she sent you, long ago,
   South to desert, east to ocean, west to snow,
West of these out of seas colder than the Hebrides
     I must go
Where the fleet of stars is anchored and the young
     Star-captains glow.

NOTES

DANTE GABRIEL ROSSETTI

THE BLESSED DAMOZEL — Rossetti has also treated this subject in painting.
American 'corn' is not known in England where the word means wheat or other grain.

MY SISTER'S SLEEP — This poem does not refer to Rossetti's own sister.

AVE
Michael's coming is a church legend of the Blessed Virgin's death.

THE STAFF AND SCRIP is based upon a tale (No. 25) in the *Gesta Romanorum*, a collection of Latin stories popular in the Middle Ages.

JENNY
Mrs. Quickly — *Merry Wives of Windsor*, IV, i, 64
Priapus is the god of generative powers.
Danaë was confined by her father in a tower and wooed by Zeus as a shower of gold.

SISTER HELEN — According to a medieval superstition melting and torturing a waxen image of a person would bring suffering and death upon him.

THE WHITE SHIP
Berold speaks of the sacrament carried in procession as 'the Body of Christ.'

THE BALLAD OF DEAD LADIES is translated from François Villon's *Ballade des Dames du Temps Jadis*.

MARY MAGDALENE — In Rossetti's drawing Mary has left a procession of revellers and is ascending by a sudden impulse the steps of the house where she sees Christ. Her lover has followed her and is trying to turn her back.

THE HOUSE OF LIFE — In astrology the heavens are divided into houses, most important of which is the house of human life.

18. Genius in Beauty
Michael is Michelangelo

77. Soul's Beauty was written for Rossetti's painting, *Sibylla Palmifera*, the palm-bearing Sibyl.

78. Body's Beauty was written for Rossetti's painting, *Lady Lilith*.

COVENTRY PATMORE

THE POET'S CONFIDENCE
After the death of Moses, Joshua led the Israelites into Canaan, the Promised Land. *Joshua*, I.

'And it came to pass, as the ark of the covenant of the Lord came to the city of David, that Michal the daughter of Saul looking out at a window saw king David dancing and playing: and she despised him in her heart.' *I Chronicles*, XV, 29.

WINTER

Those who consulted, at Lebadea in Bœotia, the oracle of Trophonius, builder of the temple of Apollo at Delphi, always returned looking melancholy and dejected.

TO THE BODY

His Spouse — the soul

'As for the Jebusites the inhabitants of Jerusalem, the children of Judah could not drive them out: but the Jebusites dwell with the children of Judah at Jerusalem unto this day.' *Joshua*, XV, 63.

'By faith Enoch was translated that he should not see death.' *Hebrews*, XI, 5.

'There appeared a chariot of fire, and horses of fire . . . and Elijah went up by a whirlwind into heaven.' *II Kings*, II, 11.

The Lady is the Virgin who, after her death, was carried to heaven by angels and left in her tomb roses and lilies.

CHRISTINA ROSSETTI

IN AN ARTIST'S STUDIO — that of her brother, Dante Gabriel Rossetti

A BIRTHDAY

vair — a kind of squirrel fur used in the fourteenth century on costly dresses

WILLIAM MORRIS

THE EVE OF CRECY

basnets — helmets

banneret — a knight who could lead vassals into the field under his own banner

THE GILLIFLOWER OF GOLD

giroflée — gilliflower

'Honneur . . . preux!' — Honour to the sons of the valiant!

tabard — mantle worn by knights

THE LITTLE TOWER

hauberk — coat of mail

glaive — sword

His severed head shall be set on a spike and crowned in derision with a paper crown.

THE HAYSTACK IN THE FLOODS

The six men are the Judges who, while Jehane is confined in the Chatelet prison in Paris, will try her as a witch.

❖ NOTES ❖

THE EARTHLY PARADISE is a collection of stories in verse, two for each month; one drawn from a classical, one from a medieval, source. Each pair is preceded by a poem embodying the spirit of the month.

The palace of Morpheus, god of sleep, has a gate of ivory.

ALGERNON CHARLES SWINBURNE

HYMN TO PROSERPINE — Proserpine is the goddess of the underworld.

The Roman Emperor Julian, who had renounced Christianity, is purported to have said on his deathbed, 'Thou hast conquered, Galilean.'

Venus rose from the foam at Cythera.

A little soul for a little bears up this corpse which is man — ψυχάριον εἶ βαστάζον νεκρόν. — Epictetus.

ITYLUS

Philomela and Procne were daughters of Pandion, king of Athens. Procne was wife of Tereus, king of Thrace. He raped Philomela and cut out her tongue that she might not betray him but she wove the story into a piece of tapestry which she sent to her sister. They then killed Procne's son, Itylus, and served him at a feast to his father. Fleeing from the wrath of Tereus, they were changed into birds, Philomela to a nightingale and Procne to a swallow.

THE TRIUMPH OF TIME was written after Swinburne had been rejected in love.

DOLORES

The Thalassian is Venus born of the sea.

'The implacable beautiful tyrant' is the Emperor Nero who persecuted the Christians, 'the children of change,' and played upon his harp while Rome burned.

Cybele, mother of the gods, was worshiped at Mt. Ida and at Dindymus in Phrygia. She rode in a chariot drawn by lions.

SAPPHICS

The Sapphic stanza is:

$$— \cup \mid — — \mid — \mid \mid \cup \cup \mid — \cup \mid — \breve{}$$
$$— \cup \mid — — \mid — \mid \mid \cup \cup \mid — \cup \mid — \breve{}$$
$$— \cup \mid — — \mid — \mid \mid \cup \cup \mid — \cup \mid — \breve{}$$
$$— \cup \cup \mid — \breve{}$$

AVE ATQUE VALE — Swinburne wrote this 'Hail and Farewell' in 1867 under the shock of what proved to be a false report of the death of the author of *The Flowers of Evil*.

Baudelaire in his *Lesbos* describes the island as mourning for the death of Sappho who cast herself into the sea from the heights of Leucas.

The Titan-woman is a reference to Baudelaire's poem, *La Géante*.

In the opening scene of Æschylus' *Choephori* Orestes and his sister, Electra, meet at the tomb of their father, Agamemnon, who was slain by his wife,

Clytaemnestra, and her paramour. Orestes offers as a sacrifice to the dead a lock of his hair, symbol of mourning and of votive dedication.

The Venus of the hollow hill is the Venus of the Venusberg. Behind these verses lies the Tannhäuser legend.

Niobe's children were slain by Apollo and Diana because she had expressed pride in having more offspring than their mother, Latona.

TRISTRAM OF LYONESSE — Sir Tristram of Lyonesse loved Iseult, wife of Mark, king of Cornwall, and she loved him better than her life. Their story has been told and retold by poets ever since the Middle Ages.

Christopher Marlowe's *Hero and Leander*, published in 1598, is perhaps the best poetic version of the story of the swimming of the Hellespont.

When Alcyone, daughter of Æolus, god of winds, learned that her husband was drowned she threw herself into the sea and was changed into a halcyon, a kingfisher.

Rosamond, mistress of Henry II of England, was murdered by his jealous queen, Eleanor.

Cleopatra, going to meet Antony for the first time, dressed herself as Venus.

Phaeton, attempting to drive the chariot of the sun, fell into the river Eridanus. His sisters, lamenting his fate, were turned into poplar trees and their tears became amber as they dropped into the stream.

Dante in the Fifth Canto of the *Inferno* gives the loveliest version of the story of Paolo and Francesca. Married to Gianciotto da Rimini, Francesca fell in love with his younger brother Paolo. Gianciotto slew them both.

Angelica, a beautiful and faithless Oriental princess, drove mad her lover Orlando.

A SONG IN TIME OF ORDER — In 1852 'order' was restored in Europe by the suppression of all revolutionary republicanism. Louis Napoleon Buonaparte, who had been elected President of the second French Republic, overthrew the government by a *coup d'état* and proclaimed himself Emperor. France reinstated Pope Pius IX who, a few years earlier, had been forced to flee from Rome because of his lack of sympathy with Italy in her struggle to throw off the Austrian yoke.

Cayenne was made a French penal colony in 1852.

HERTHA is the Germanic goddess of the earth. Swinburne uses her to personify the life force.

A JACOBITE'S FAREWELL

1716 marked the end of the unsuccessful attempt to secure the throne of England for James II's son, known as the Old Pretender. Swinburne liked to imagine that his ancestors had made great sacrifices for the Stuart cause.

THE SISTERS, ACT V

lift — the sky

whin — gorse

muirside — moorside

JAMES THOMSON

SUNDAY UP THE RIVER

Cockaigne — the land of cockneys. Thomson perhaps refers as well to its other meaning, an imaginary country of idleness and luxury.

THE CITY OF DREADFUL NIGHT

Through me is the way into the woeful city. — Dante, *Divina Commedia*, *Inferno*, Canto III, l. 1.

> Then of the mazy toil, the mazy motions,
> Of all celestial, all terrestial things,
> Circling in ceaseless rings,
> Ever returning where they took their start:
> Of these can I divine
> No use, no fruit.
>
> Leopardi, *Canto Notturno.*

> Alone eternal one, with whom the being
> Of every creature closes,
> In thee, O Death, reposes
> Our nature, naked waif;
> Not happy, no, but safe
> From the old pain. . . .
> And therefore to be blessed
> Fate has denied to mortals
> And likewise to the dead.
>
> Leopardi, *Dialogo di Federico Ruysch e delle
> Sue Mummie,* 'Coro di Morti nello Studio
> di Federico Ruysch.'

Thomson thought this poem 'one of the marvels of literature.'

1. They leave all hope behind who enter there — Leave all hope, ye who enter! — Dante saw these words written above the gate to hell. *Inferno*, Canto III, l. 9.

'Though the Garden of thy Life be wholly waste, the sweet flowers withered, the fruit-trees barren, over the wall hang ever the rich dark clusters of the Vine of Death, within easy reach of thy hand which may pluck them when it will.' — Thomson's note on the last stanza.

4. Sabbath of the Serpents — a midnight meeting supposed to be held annually by daemons and witches under the leadership of Satan.

21. the pure sad artist — Albrecht Dürer
teen — sorrow
threne — lamentation

THOMAS EDWARD BROWN

CLIFTON — For nearly thirty years Brown was a master at Clifton College, a modern foundation but one of the most important English public schools.

I was thy neighbour once, thou rugged Pile!
Four summer weeks I dwelt in sight of thee:
I saw thee every day: and all the while
Thy Form was sleeping on a glassy sea.

> William Wordsworth, *Elegiac Stanzas*
> *Suggested by a Picture of Peele Castle, in a*
> *Storm, Painted by Sir George Beaumont.*

IN THE COACH. 5. The Pazons — The Parsons
   glebe — portion of land going with a clergyman's benefice

'Blow ye the trumpet in Zion, and sound an alarm in my holy mountain:
   let all the inhabitants of the land tremble: for the day of the Lord cometh,
   for it is nigh at hand.' *Joel*, II, 1.

collec' — collect, a short prayer in the Church of England service

pestlin' — reading the epistle

farlin' rush — farthing candle

thallure — enough

CHALSE A KILLEY
   sallies — willows

> the poet's pen
> . . . . gives to airy nothing
> A local habitation and a name.
> *A Midsummer-Night's Dream*, V, i, 15–17.

Parson Drury succeeded Brown's father as vicar at Braddon in the Isle of
   Man. The persons and places in this poem are actual.

Romans — Roman Catholics

sthrooghed — stroked

the Dhoor — 'a well of "black water" on the Andreas Road.' — Brown's
   note

THE ORGANIST IN HEAVEN — Samuel S. Wesley, 1810-76, composer of ecclesi-
astical music and organist in many English cathedrals.

ANDREW LANG

ALMAE MATRES
   scarlet gown — the daily academic dress of the St. Andrews student is
   scarlet in memory of the Cardinal who founded that university.

   Isis — the Thames at Oxford

   Magdalen — an Oxford college

OF HIS LADY'S OLD AGE — translated from Pierre de Ronsard, *Sonnets pour
Helène*, Livre II, Sonnet 42, 'Quand vous serez bien vieille, au soir, à la chandelle.'

MARTIAL IN TOWN — Martial, ?40-?102, Latin epigrammatist born in Spain
   Brother had we . . . loveth best. — Martial, Bk. V, Epigram 20

❖ NOTES ❖

MELEAGER — a Greek poet who flourished c. 95 B.C. The poem translated here is found in the *Greek Anthology*, Section V, Epigram 136.

BALLADE OF HIS CHOICE OF A SEPULCHRE
   the Windburg — a mountain south of Selkirk, Lang's birthplace

AUSTIN DOBSON

THE LADIES OF ST. JAMES'S
   St. James's — a fashionable district in London
   ombre — a card game popular in eighteenth-century society

A DEAD LETTER

> At church in silks and satins new,
> With hoops of monstrous size,
> She never slumbered in her pew —
> But when she shut her eyes.
>> Oliver Goldsmith, *An Elegy on
>> that Glory of her Sex, Mrs. Mary
>> Blaize*

Dutch William — Prince William of Orange became King William III of England. He reigned 1688-1702.

Tithonus was the son of Laomedon, king of Troy. Aurora persuaded the gods to grant him immortality.

Vapours were fits of hypocondria or hysteria affected by eighteenth-century ladies.

Bonzes — statuettes of Buddhist monks

Hector's horse-plume which frightened his baby son is described in the *Iliad*, Bk. VI, l. 469.

A POSTSCRIPT TO 'RETALIATION'
   Goldsmith's *Retaliation* was a series of mock epitaphs on his friends.
   Johnson's Dictionary defines anfractuosity as 'fulness of windings and turnings.'

POT-POURRI — a jar of dried rose leaves for perfuming a room
   Si jeunesse savait — See '*Good-Night, Babette!*' for the rest of the proverb.
   Charlotte Corday stabbed Marat, the French Revolutionary terrorist.

A GENTLEMAN OF THE OLD SCHOOL
   Ranelagh — a pleasure garden near London
   Mall — a fashionable walking place
   To pink your man is to wound your opponent in a duel.

A FANCY FROM FONTENELLE
   De mémoires des Roses on n'a point vu mourir le Jardinier — Within the memory of the roses none has ever seen the Gardener die.

589

❖ NOTES ❖

TO A MISSAL OF THE THIRTEENTH CENTURY
Missal — an illuminated service book for the Mass

A GARDEN SONG
Alcinoüs, king of the Phaecians was celebrated for his gardens.
The Pierides are the nine Muses.

IN AFTER DAYS is a rondeau in form.

ARS VICTRIX — adapted from Gautier's 'L'Art,' *Émaux et Camées*
Erycine — Venus

ERNEST DOWSON

NON SUM QUALIS ERAM BONAE SUB REGNO CYNARAE — Dowson takes his title from Horace's *Odes* (Bk. IV, Ode 1, ll. 3-4) but his exposition of why he is not what he was under the reign of Cynara is quite different from Horace's.

VITAE SUMMA BREVIS SPEM NOS VETAT INCOHARE LONGAM — Again Dowson takes his title from Horace (*Odes*, Bk. I, Ode 4, l. 15) but the treatment of the theme is again his own.

O MORS! QUAM AMARA EST MEMORIA TUA HOMINI PACEM HABENTI IN SUBSTANTIIS SUIS
in substantiis suis — in his worldly goods

LIONEL JOHNSON

THE DAY OF COMING DAYS
Inisfail — Island of Rest, a poetical name of Ireland

PARNELL — Charles Stewart Parnell, 1840-91. An Irish patriot who converted Gladstone and the Liberal Party to the cause of home-rule for Ireland. His political career was ruined by his appearance as co-respondent in a divorce case and he died shortly afterwards.

BY THE STATUE OF KING CHARLES AT CHARING CROSS
Speak after sentence — After he had been sentenced to death Charles asked permission to speak; it was refused because he had not recognized the right of the court to try him.

THE DARK ANGEL
Paraclete — the Holy Ghost

ARTHUR SYMONS

IN FOUNTAIN COURT — in the Temple, London, where Symons lived for a time with Yeats

LA MÉLINITE: MOULIN-ROUGE — In May, 1892, Symons saw La Mélinite for the first time in Le Jardin de Paris. She danced in a quadrille, he wrote, 'young and girlish, the more provocative because she played as a prude, with an assumed modesty; *décolletée* nearly to the waist, in the Oriental fashion. She had long black curls around her face; and had about her a depraved virginity. And she caused in me, even then, a curious sense of depravity that perhaps comes into the verses I wrote on her. There, certainly, on the night of May 22nd, danced in her feverish, her perverse, her enigmatical beauty, La Mélinite, to her own image in the mirror.'

IN IRELAND 2. By the Pool at the Third Rosses
  Rosses — marsh

WILLIAM BUTLER YEATS

DOWN BY THE SALLEY GARDENS
  salley — willow

THE LAKE ISLE OF INNISFREE — Yeats as a boy was vastly influenced by Thoreau's *Walden*. He says in his *Autobiographies:* 'I planned to live someday in a cottage on a little island called Innisfree.'

THE BALLAD OF FATHER GILLIGAN
  Mavrone — my grief

GERARD MANLEY HOPKINS

THE BUGLER'S FIRST COMMUNION
  squander — disperse
  brandle — shake

INVERSNAID — one of the finest points on Loch Lomond
  comb — small valley or hollow
  degged — sprinkled or damp

CARRION COMFORT — 'Date must be 1885, and this is probably the sonnet "written in blood," of which he wrote in May of that year.' — Bridges's note.

FRANCIS THOMPSON

THE POPPY
  Monica — daughter of the Meynells
  'And when the day of Pentecost was fully come, they were all with one accord in one place. . . . And there appeared unto them cloven tongues like as of fire, and it sat upon each of them. And they were all filled with the Holy Ghost, and began to speak with other tongues, as the Spirit gave them utterance.' — *Acts*, II, 1.

THE MAKING OF VIOLA
  Viola — daughter of the Meynells

❖ NOTES ❖

ARAB LOVE-SONG

    hunchèd camels — 'cloud shapes observed by travellers in the East.' — Thompson's note

TO THE DEAD CARDINAL OF WESTMINSTER — Henry Edward Manning, 1808-92, Roman Catholic Cardinal of Westminster

    Uranian — heavenly

    spring of Dis — river Styx

THE HOUND OF HEAVEN

    I slept, methinks, and woke . . . pulled my life upon me — the reference is to Samson

THE KINGDOM OF GOD

    'How shall we sing the Lord's song in a strange land?' *Psalms*, CXXXVII, 4.

    'And Jacob . . . dreamed, and behold a ladder set upon the earth, and the top of it reached to heaven: and behold the angels of God ascending and descending on it.' *Genesis*, XXVIII, 12.

    Gennesareth — Sea of Galilee

ALICE MEYNELL

SAN LORENZO'S MOTHER — Born to a noble family, Lorenzo at nineteen obeyed a vision and entered the Church against the earnest desire of his family who wished him to marry.

THE LADY POVERTY — Members of Saint Francis' order must renounce absolutely all their property. This renunciation is symbolized as a marriage between Saint Francis and Lady Poverty.

AT NIGHT

    To W. M. — Wilfrid Meynell, her husband

WILLIAM ERNEST HENLEY

IN HOSPITAL

    XIV. Ave, Caesar! morituri salutamus! — the gladiators' cry

    XXV. Apparition — a portrait of Stevenson

    Shorter-Catechist — a teacher of the Presbyterean shorter catechism; i.e., somewhat sanctimonious

BALLADE OF DEAD ACTORS

    Sir Peter Teazle in Sheridan's *School for Scandal*

    Shakespeare's *Timon of Athens*

    Millimant — heroine of Congreve's *The Way of the World*

    The Thunder huddles with the Snow — stage machines for producing thunder and snow

RHYMES AND RHYTHMS
    XXIII. hierophantic — priestlike

LONDON VOLUNTARIES
    III. Scherzando — a musical term meaning playfully
    Clement's, Bride's, Paul's — London churches
    Our Sailor — statue of Nelson on a column with lions at its base
    picture-place — the National Gallery

ROBERT LOUIS STEVENSON

THE VAGABOND
    lave — rest

A SONG OF THE ROAD
    gauger — a revenue officer who measures the contents of casks

TO ANDREW LANG
    Stevenson uses 'sanhedrin,' the supreme council in ancient Jerusalem, to refer to dry-as-dust scholars and pedantic critics
    Helicon is a mountain in Boeotia, held sacred by the Greeks as the residence of Apollo and the Muses

THE BLAST — 1875
    gangrels — vagabonds
    sneckdraw — latch lifter, sly fellow
    forjaskit — tired out
    clamjamfried — 'junked'
    but and ben — outer and inner rooms of a typical two-room Scotch cottage
    spate — sudden storm

THE SPAEWIFE — The Fortuneteller
    brander — broil
    spierin' — asking
    kye — cattle
    pree — to try by tasting

GEORGE MEREDITH

MODERN LOVE
    I. the sword between — In the days of chivalry chastity between lovers was considered insured by the presence of a naked sword.
    VIII. The God — Apollo

THOMAS HARDY

THE OXEN — It is a folk belief that at the hour of Christ's birth the oxen kneel as they did in the stable at Bethlehem.
    barton — farmyard

THE DEAD QUIRE

 wicket — a small gate

 leaze — pasture

FRIENDS BEYOND

 A tranter is a carrier

 leads — lead roofs

 stillicide — the flowing of a liquid drop by drop

 hold the manse in fee — hold as one's absolute and rightful possession

 charlock — wild mustard

 grinterns — compartments in a granary

A SINGER ASLEEP

 Swinburne is buried in Bonchurch in the Isle of Wight.

 ness — headland

 fulth — fulness

 spindrift — spray

 hydrosphere — the aqueous envelope of the earth

 orts — fragments left from a meal. Only fragments of Sappho's poems remain.

 chines — ridges

IN A WOOD

 The Woodlanders is a novel by Hardy.

THE DARKLING THRUSH

 coppice — wood

NEW YEAR'S EVE

 'For we know that if our earthly house of this tabernacle were dissolved, we have a building of God, an house not made with hands, eternal in the heavens. For in this we groan, earnestly desiring to be clothed upon with our house which is from heaven.' *II Corinthians*, V, 1-2.

 unweeting — unknowing

A. E. HOUSMAN

A Shropshire Lad

IX. 'Hanging in chains was called keeping sheep by moonlight.' — Housman's note

Bredon Hill — pronounced Breedon

XXXI. At Wroxeter near Shrewsbury there are remains of the Roman city of Uriconium burned by the Saxons in the sixth century.

Last Poems

THE ORACLES

 Dodona was the seat of the oldest Greek oracle dedicated to Zeus.

594

The source of the last stanza is the seventh book of Herodotus which describes the invasion of Greece by Xerxes, king of Persia, and the defence at Thermopylae.

RUDYARD KIPLING

THE BELL BUOY

bob-majors — a technical term for a particular peal of bells

bitt — a post on the deck of a ship to which ropes are made fast

trees — cross trees, horizontal timbers at the head of the lower mast to support the topmast

FORD O' KABUL RIVER is founded on an experience of a squadron of British cavalry during the Afghan War of 1879.

THE LAST CHANTEY

'And I saw a new heaven and a new earth: for the first heaven and the first earth were passed away; and there was no more sea.' *Revelation,* XXI, 1.

barracout' — the barracuda, a carnivorous West Indian fish

picaroon — a pirate ship, here a slave ship

To frap a ship is to wrap it about the hull with cable to keep it from breaking apart.

Gothavn — Godthaab, a port in Greenland

A 'speckshioner is the chief harpooner on a whaling vessel who directs the flinching; i.e., the slicing of blubber from the whale's bones.

bowhead — the Arctic right whale

neither lead (pronounced leed) nor lea — neither open channel (in an ice field) nor sheltered anchorage

fulmar — an Arctic sea bird

THE LONG TRAIL

'God shall enlarge Japheth, and he shall dwell in the tents of Shem; and Canaan shall be his servant.' *Genesis,* IX, 27.

rime — hoarfrost

Bilbao — a port in Spain

A flag known as the blue Peter is hoisted as a signal of immediate sailing.

MY NEW-CUT ASHLAR

ashlar — a square-hewn building stone

PUCK'S SONG

ride — a road or avenue for riding, usually through woods

Guns used against the Spanish Armada were forged in Sussex.

Isle of Gramarye — Magic Island

❖ NOTES ❖

Sᴜssᴇx

Levuka — one of the Fiji Islands

Weald — open country

barrow — an ancient burial mound

The Saxons in Surrey, the last of the Germanic groups to be brought to Christianity, were converted by St. Wilfred, Archbishop of York, who lived from c. 634-709.

shaws — thickets

ghylls — wooded ravines

JOHN MASEFIELD

A Cᴏɴsᴇᴄʀᴀᴛɪᴏɴ

koppie — small hill in South Africa. The reference is to the Boer War

D'Aᴠᴀʟᴏs' Pʀᴀʏᴇʀ — D'Avalos was a sixteenth-century Spanish soldier and adventurer who fought, founded and governed cities in Ecuador and Peru.

Tʜᴇ Rɪᴅᴇʀ ᴀᴛ ᴛʜᴇ Gᴀᴛᴇ

cressets — metal vessels, on poles, holding oil lights

loaning — uncultivated ground near a farmhouse

WILFRID WILSON GIBSON

Tʜᴇ Vɪɴᴅɪᴄᴛɪᴠᴇ Sᴛᴀɪʀᴄᴀsᴇ

Houndsditch — a squalid district in London, in the old city

Oɴ ᴛʜᴇ Eᴍʙᴀɴᴋᴍᴇɴᴛ — the terrace and road along the Thames in London

RUPERT BROOKE

Tʜᴇ Cʜɪʟᴛᴇʀɴs — hills between Oxford and London

Tʜᴇ Oʟᴅ Vɪᴄᴀʀᴀɢᴇ, Gʀᴀɴᴛᴄʜᴇsᴛᴇʀ

Das Betreten verboten — Trespassing forbidden

εἴθε γενοίμην — would I were

ghostly Lordship — Grantchester, about three miles from Cambridge, possesses a great store of literary associations. Chaucer's Miller ground corn by the bridge there; Byron's Pool was once the bathing place of his Lordship before he was a ghost; Tennyson was often seen in the village when an undergraduate at Cambridge. Brooke himself lived in Grantchester for a time.

JAMES ELROY FLECKER

Tᴏ ᴀ Pᴏᴇᴛ ᴀ Tʜᴏᴜsᴀɴᴅ Yᴇᴀʀs Hᴇɴᴄᴇ

Maeonides — Homer

❖ NOTES ❖

The Old Ships
  bald-headed seaman — Ulysses

Oak and Olive
  hall in Bloomsbury — the British Museum
  Arthur Woolgar Verrall, 1851-1912, was a classical scholar and Professor of
    English Literature, Cambridge University.
  Mænads — bacchantes

Epithalamion — a nuptial song
  Thetis — chief of the sea nymphs and mother of Achilles
  Peleus — king of the Myrmidons in Thessaly and father of Achilles

Gates of Damascus
  Salaam Aleikum! — Peace be upon you!

Brumana is in Lebanon. Flecker went there from Beirut for the mountain air
when his condition became serious.

BIBLIOGRAPHY

The following brief bibliography makes no pretence to even approximate completeness. It is meant to be a first-aid to the teacher and to the student who is lured by the selections into a wider reading in or about this poet or that. It offers first of all a list of the Collected Poems of the writers included in this anthology, followed where necessary by the names and dates of volumes of poetry that have appeared since the publication of the Collected Poems. This in turn is followed by such biographies as are available and by a few representative critical essays and studies. Except for one or two exceptions, no reference has been made to matter appearing only in journals and magazines.

GENERAL

G. K. CHESTERTON — The Victorian Age in Literature (Holt, 1913)

J. W. CUNLIFFE — English Literature during the Last Half-Century (Macmillan, 1923)

O. ELTON — Survey of English Literature, vol. 4 (Macmillan, 1920)

H. WALKER — Literature of the Victorian Age (Cambridge University Press, 1920)

HOLMAN HUNT — Pre-Raphaelitism and the Pre-Raphaelite Brotherhood (Macmillan, 1905)

H. J. C. GRIERSON — Lyrical Poetry — Blake to Hardy (Harcourt, 1929)

T. E. WELBY — The Victorian Romantics (Howe, 1929)

The Eighteen Eighties — ed. by De la Mare (Cambridge University Press, 1930)

ANDREWS and PERCIVAL — Poetry of the Nineties (Harcourt, 1926)

O. BURDETT — The Beardsley Period (Lane 1925)

H. JACKSON — The Eighteen Nineties (Kennerley, 1914)

W. B. YEATS — Autobiographies (Macmillan, 1927)

CHARLES WILLIAMS — Poetry at Present, containing studies of Hardy, Bridges, Housman, Kipling, Yeats, Davies, De la Mare, Masefield, and Gibson (Oxford University Press, 1930)

DANTE GABRIEL ROSSETTI

    Collected Works — ed. by W. M. Rossetti (Ellis, 1890)

    Poems and Translations — includes Poems of 1870, Early Italian Poets, The New Life (Oxford University Press)

The House of Life — ed. with introduction and notes by P. F. Baum (Harvard University Press, 1928)

R. L. Mégroz — Dante Gabriel Rossetti (Faber and Gwyer, 1928)

Evelyn Waugh — Rossetti, His Life and Work (Duckworth, 1928)

COVENTRY PATMORE

Poems — with introduction by Basil Champneys (Bell, 1906)

Selected Poems of Coventry Patmore — ed. with introduction by Derek Patmore (Chatto and Windus, 1931)

Edmund Gosse — Coventry Patmore (Scribners, 1905)

CHRISTINA ROSSETTI

Poetical Works — ed. with memoir by W. M. Rossetti (Macmillan, 1904)

Dorothy Margaret Stuart — Life of Christina Rossetti (Macmillan, 1930)

WILLIAM MORRIS

Collected Works — introductions by May Morris, 24 vols. (Longmans, 1910-1915)

Poetical Works — 11 vols. (Longmans, 1896-1898)

J. W. Mackail — Life of William Morris (Longmans, 1922)

A. Clutton-Brock — William Morris (Holt, 1914)

A. Compton-Rickett — William Morris, a study in personality (Jenkins, 1913)

SWINBURNE

Complete Works — ed. by Gosse and Wise, 20 vols. (Heinemann, 1925-1927)

Poems — 6 vols. (Harper)

Selections — ed. with introduction by W. O. Raymond (Harcourt, 1925)

Edmund Gosse — Life of Algernon Charles Swinburne (Macmillan, 1917)

S. Chew — Swinburne (Little, 1929)

W. B. D. Henderson — Swinburne and Landor (Macmillan, 1918)

T. E. Welby — A Study of Swinburne (Doran, 1926)

JAMES THOMSON

Poetical Works — ed. with memoir by Bertram Dobell (Reeves, 1895)

Poems — selected by G. H. Gerould (Holt, 1927)

J. E. Meeker — The Life and Poetry of James Thomson (Yale University Press, 1917)

T. E. BROWN

Collected Poems — with introduction by Henley (Macmillan, 1927)

S. G. Simpson — Thomas Edward Brown (Scott, 1907)

A Memorial Volume, 1830-1930 (Cambridge University Press, 1930)

ANDREW LANG

Poetical Works — 4 vols. (Longmans, 1923)

❖ BIBLIOGRAPHY ❖

Andrew Lang; a Symposium — in Quarterly Review, April, 1913
G. S. Gordon — Andrew Lang, a lecture (Oxford University Press, 1928)

AUSTIN DOBSON
 Complete Poetical Works (Oxford University Press, 1923)
 Alban Dobson — Austin Dobson, Some Notes (Oxford University Press, 1928)

ERNEST DOWSON
 Complete Poems (The Medusa Head, New York, 1928)
 Poems — with memoir by A. Symons (Lane, 1915)
 V. G. Plarr — Ernest Dowson (Gomme, 1914)

LIONEL JOHNSON
 Poetical Works (Matthews, 1915)
 Some Winchester Letters (Macmillan, 1919)
 C. K. Shorter — Lionel Johnson (Matthews, 1908)

ARTHUR SYMONS
 Poems — 2 vols. (Heinemann, 1921)
 T. E. Welby — Arthur Symons (Philpot, 1925)

WILLIAM BUTLER YEATS
 Poetical Works — 2 vols. (Macmillan, 1912-1916)
 The Wild Swans at Coolei, 1919 (Macmillan, 1919)
 Selected Poems, Lyrical and Narrative (Macmillan, 1930)
 E. A. Boyd — Ireland's Literary Renaissance (Knopf, 1922)
 Edmund Wilson — Axel's Castle (Scribners, 1931)
 F. Reid — W. B. Yeats (Secker, 1915)
 A. Symons — in " Studies in Prose and Verse " (Dent, 1904)
 J. Middleton Murry — in " Aspects of Literature " (Collins, 1920)

GERARD MANLEY HOPKINS
 Poems with notes by Robert Bridges, author's preface, and critical intro-
  duction by Charles Williams (Milford, 1918)
 G. F. Lahey — Life of G. M. Hopkins (Oxford University Press, 1930)
 J. Middleton Murry — in " Aspects of Literature."

FRANCIS THOMPSON
 The Works, Poems, vols. I and II (Scribners, 1913)
 E. Meynell — Life of Francis Thompson (Scribners, 1926)
 J. Freeman — in "Moderns" — an essay on Patmore and F. Thompson
  (Oxford University Press, 1929)
 R. L. Mégroz — Francis Thompson (Faber, 1927)

ALICE MEYNELL
 Poems — Complete edition (Burns, Oates & Washburn, 1923)

Viola Meynell — Alice Meynell (Cape, 1929)
A. Noyes — in "Some Aspects of Modern Poetry" (Hodder, 1924)
J. C. Squire in London Mercury Jan. 1923

W. E. HENLEY
    Poems (Scribners, 1928)
    Kennedy Williamson — W. E. Henley (Shaylor, 1930)
    A. Noyes — in "Some Aspects of Modern Poetry"

R. L. STEVENSON
    Complete Poems (Scribners, 1923)
    G. Balfour — Life of R. L. Stevenson (Scribners, 1915)
    J. A. Stuart — R. L. Stevenson, a critical biography (Little, Brown, 1924)
    Sidney Dark — R. L. Stevenson (Hodder and Stoughton, 1931)
    Walter Raleigh — R. L. Stevenson, a lecture (Arnold, 1908)
    N. W. Garrod — The Poetry of Robert Louis Stevenson in "The Profession of Poetry" (Clarendon Press 1929)

GEORGE MEREDITH
    Poetical Works — edited with notes by G. M. Trevelyan (Scribners, 1912)
    R. E. Sencourt — The Life of George Meredith (Scribners, 1929)
    G. M. Trevelyan — Poetry and Philosophy of George Meredith (Constable, 1912)

THOMAS HARDY
    Collected Poems (Macmillan, 1926)
    Winter Words (Macmillan, 1928)
    The Dynasts (Macmillan, 1927)
    Florence E. Hardy — The Early Life of Thomas Hardy (Macmillan, 1928)
                      — The Later Years of Thomas Hardy (Macmillan, 1930)
    S. Chew — Thomas Hardy, Poet and Novelist (Knopf, 1928)
    G. R. Elliott — in "The Cycle of Modern Poetry" (Princeton University Press, 1929)
    J. Middleton Murry — in "Some Aspects of Literature"

A. E. HOUSMAN
    A Shropshire Lad, authorized edition (Holt, 1924)
    Last Poems (Holt, 1922)
    J. de L. Ferguson — "The Belligerent Don" in Saturday Review of Literature, March 27, 1926
    H. W. Garrod — in "The Profession of Poetry" (Oxford University Press, 1929)
    G. M. Harper — in "The Spirit of Delight" (Holt, 1928)

ROBERT BRIDGES
    Poetical Works — 6 vols. (Oxford University Press, 1929)
    The Testament of Beauty (Clarendon Press, 1929)

F. E. B. Young — Robert Bridges (Secker, 1914)
Darrell Figgis — in "Studies and Appreciations" (Dent, 1912)
Arthur Symons — in "Studies in Prose and Verse" (Dent, 1904)

RUDYARD KIPLING
　　Collected Verse (Doubleday, 1919)
　　Songs from Books (Doubleday, 1912)
　　The Years Between (Doubleday, 1919)
　　R. A. Durand — Handbook to the Poetry of Rudyard Kipling (Hodder
　　　　and Stoughton, 1914)
　　Cyril Falls — Rudyard Kipling, a critical study (Secker, 1915)
　　R. Thurston Hopkins — Rudyard Kipling, a character study (Simpkin, 1915)
　　　　　　　　— Kipling's Sussex (Appleton, 1921)
　　R. Le Gallienne — Rudyard Kipling, a criticism (Lane, 1900)

JOHN MASEFIELD
　　Poems — collected edition, 4 vols. (Macmillan, 1925)
　　Midsummer Night (Macmillan, 1928)
　　Minnie Maylow's Story (Macmillan, 1931)
　　W. H. Hamilton — John Masefield, a critical study (Macmillan, 1922)
　　Amy Lowell — in "Poetry and Poets" (Houghton Mifflin, 1930)
　　Charles Williams — in "Poetry at Present" (Oxford University Press, 1930)
　　L. T. Nicholl — "John Masefield in Yonkers" in The Bookman, January,
　　　　1919

ALFRED NOYES
　　Collected Poems — Vols. I and II (Stokes, 1913)
　　　　　　　　— Vol. III (Stokes, 1914)
　　　　　　　　— Vol. IV (Stokes, 1927)
　　The Torch-Bearers — I, Watchers of the Sky (Stokes, 1923)
　　　　　　　　— II, The Book of Earth (Stokes, 1925)
　　　　　　　　— III, The Last Voyage (Stokes, 1930)
　　Walter Jerrold — Alfred Noyes, with bibliographical list (Shaylor, 1930)
　　Edward Davison — in "Some Modern Poets" (Harpers, 1928)
　　Rica Brenner — in "Ten Modern Poets" (Harcourt, Brace, 1930)

WILFRID WILSON GIBSON
　　Collected Poems (Macmillan, 1926)
　　The Golden Room (Macmillan, 1928)
　　Hazards (Macmillan, 1930)
　　Charles Williams in "Poetry at Present"

W. H. DAVIES
　　The Autobiography of a Super-Tramp (Knopf, 1925)

Later Days (Doran, 1926)

Collected Poems (Cape, 1929)

Ambition and Other Poems (Cape, 1929)

D. Figgis — in "Studies and Appreciations" (Dent, 1912)

Charles Williams — in "Poetry at Present"

WALTER DE LA MARE

Collected Poems (Holt, 1920)

The Veil (Holt, 1922)

Selected Poems (Holt, 1927)

Poems for Children (Constable, 1930)

R. L. Mégroz — Walter de la Mare (Hodder and Stoughton, 1924)

F. Reid — Walter de la Mare, including a list of books by De la Mare (Faber, 1929)

Edward Davison — in "Some Modern Poets"

RUPERT BROOKE

Collected Poems — with introduction by G. E. Woodberry and a biographical note by Margaret Lovington (Lane, 1915)

Collected Poems with a Memoir (Sidgwick and Jackson, 1918)

Letters from America — with preface by H. James (Scribners, 1916)

Edward Marsh — Rupert Brooke (Lane, 1918)

JAMES ELROY FLECKER

Collected Poems — with an introduction by J. C. Squire (Secker, 1916)

Hassan (Knopf, 1924)

Don Juan (Knopf, 1925)

Some Letters from Abroad — with reminiscences by Hellè Flecker and an introduction by J. C. Squire (Heinemann, 1930)

Douglas Goldring — James Elroy Flecker (Chapman and Hall, 1922)

Geraldine Hodgson — The Life of James Elroy Flecker (Houghton Mifflin, 1925)

INDEX OF AUTHORS

INDEX OF TITLES AND FIRST LINES

607

❖ INDEX OF TITLES AND FIRST LINES ❖

❖ INDEX OF TITLES AND FIRST LINES ❖

❖ INDEX OF TITLES AND FIRST LINES ❖

❖ INDEX OF TITLES AND FIRST LINES ❖

❖ INDEX OF TITLES AND FIRST LINES ❖